This is just the volume that sociolegal scholars have been waiting for! *The Asian Law and Society Reader* is an elegantly organized, comprehensive, and accessible text, analyzing contemporary substantive topics within enduring legacies of colonialism and rapid legal and social transformation. The text illuminates the significance of this innovative and rich body of research for all law and society scholars today – wherever one works in the world.
—Eve Darian-Smith, Professor and Chair of Global and International Studies, University of California, Irvine, and coeditor of the *Routledge Handbook of Law and Society* (2021)

This book is a treasure trove of law and society research, spanning a massive diversity of societies and an equally broad array of issues. There is no scholar of the region who will fail to learn from it, and it will be of great use for teaching and research.
—Tom Ginsburg, Leo Spitz Professor of International Law, Ludwig and Hilde Wolf Research Scholar, and Professor of Political Science, University of Chicago

This intelligently curated collection brings together a new generation of Asian law and society research. It is exactly the right starting point for getting up to speed on the diversity of the field, or for anyone who wants to learn more about Asian politics and society through the lens of law.
—Rachel Stern, Professor of Law and Political Science and Pamela P. Fong and Family Distinguished Chair in China Studies, School of Law, University of California, Berkeley

In the twenty-first century, Asia will surely become another center for law and society scholarship. The inherent diversity of Asia will be further developed and conducive to future-oriented institutional experiments and knowledge innovation. From this point of view, the publication of *The Asian Law and Society Reader* is of great significance. I believe that it is the best introductory guide for Asian law and society research at this stage, and is also an indispensable reference for carrying out law and society education in Asian countries.
—Weidong Ji, University Professor of Humanities and Social Sciences, Shanghai Jiao Tong University, and President, China Institute for Socio-Legal Studies

This book examines the meaning and action of law in diverse Asian societies through a detailed examination of a wide range of issues. Readers will gain in-depth knowledge of various topics and will be able to read the universal significance of law and society studies in Asia.
—Yoshitaka Wada, Professor of Law, Faculty of Law, Waseda University, Tokyo

Grounded in rich empirical research, this volume extends the epistemological and methodological imagination of law and society. Intellectual conversations between empirical essays and insightful commentary reveal intellectual journeys of scholars and the field itself, achieving both a bird's-eye view of the field and insights into the lives of ordinary people as they negotiate socio-legal realities on the ground.
—Yukiko Koga, Associate Professor of Anthropology, Yale University

# THE ASIAN LAW AND SOCIETY READER

The first reader on Asian law and society scholarship, this book features reading selections from a wide range of Asian countries – East, South, Southeast, and Central Asia – along with original commentaries by the three editors on the theoretical debates and research methods pertinent to the discipline. Organized by themes and topical areas, the reader enables scholars and students to break out of country-specific silos to make theoretical connections across national borders. It meets a growing demand for law and society materials in institutions and universities in Asia and around the world. It is written at a level accessible to advanced undergraduate students and graduate students as well as experienced researchers, and serves as a valuable teaching tool for courses focused on Asian law and society in law schools, area studies, history, religion, and social science fields such as sociology, anthropology, politics, government, and criminal justice.

Lynette J. Chua is the author of *Mobilizing Gay Singapore: Rights and Resistance in an Authoritarian State* (2014); *The Politics of Love in Myanmar: LGBT Mobilization and Human Rights as a Way of Life* (2019); and *The Politics of Rights and Southeast Asia* (2022). She is also President of the Asian Law & Society Association (2022–23).

David M. Engel was a former President of the Law & Society Association, and has received its Kalven Award, Book Prize, and Article Prize. He is author or coauthor of *Injury and Injustice* (2018); *The Myth of the Litigious Society* (2016); and *Tort, Custom, and Karma: Globalization and Legal Consciousness in Thailand* (2010).

Sida Liu is a sociologist of law specializing in Chinese law, the legal profession, and sociolegal theory. He is coauthor of *Criminal Defense in China: The Politics of Lawyers at Work* (with Terence C. Halliday, 2016).

# The Asian Law and Society Reader

**LYNETTE J. CHUA**
National University of Singapore

**DAVID M. ENGEL**
State University of New York at Buffalo

**SIDA LIU**
University of Hong Kong

Shaftesbury Road, Cambridge CB2 8EA, United Kingdom

One Liberty Plaza, 20th Floor, New York, NY 10006, USA

477 Williamstown Road, Port Melbourne, VIC 3207, Australia

314–321, 3rd Floor, Plot 3, Splendor Forum, Jasola District Centre, New Delhi – 110025, India

103 Penang Road, #05–06/07, Visioncrest Commercial, Singapore 238467

Cambridge University Press is part of Cambridge University Press & Assessment, a department of the University of Cambridge.

We share the University's mission to contribute to society through the pursuit of education, learning and research at the highest international levels of excellence.

www.cambridge.org
Information on this title: www.cambridge.org/9781108836418

DOI: 10.1017/9781108864824

© Lynette J. Chua, David M. Engel, and Sida Liu 2023

This publication is in copyright. Subject to statutory exception and to the provisions of relevant collective licensing agreements, no reproduction of any part may take place without the written permission of Cambridge University Press & Assessment.

First published 2023

*A catalogue record for this publication is available from the British Library*

*A Cataloging-in-Publication data record for this book is available from the Library of Congress*

ISBN 978-1-108-83641-8 Hardback
ISBN 978-1-108-81899-5 Paperback

Cambridge University Press & Assessment has no responsibility for the persistence or accuracy of URLs for external or third-party internet websites referred to in this publication and does not guarantee that any content on such websites is, or will remain, accurate or appropriate.

*To my students at the National University of Singapore and Yale-NUS College*
Lynette J. Chua

*To my granddaughters, Sylvie and Scarlett*
David M. Engel

*To my mother, Han Lingqiao*
Sida Liu

---

*In memory of Keebet von Benda-Beckmann,
dear friend and distinguished scholar*

---

# Contents

| | | |
|---|---|---|
| Acknowledgments | | *page* xvii |
| Publisher's Acknowledgments | | xviii |
| **Introduction** | | 1 |
| 1 | Religion | 19 |
| 2 | Legal Pluralism | 74 |
| 3 | Disputing | 114 |
| 4 | Legal Consciousness | 139 |
| 5 | Legal Mobilization | 183 |
| 6 | Legal Professions | 227 |
| 7 | Courts | 273 |
| 8 | Crime and Justice | 309 |
| 9 | Practicing Law and Society Scholarship in Asia | 348 |
| Index | | 385 |

# Detailed Table of Contents

| | |
|---|---|
| Acknowledgments | *page* xvii |
| Publisher's Acknowledgments | xviii |
| **Introduction** . . . . . . . . . . . . . . . . . . . . | 1 |
|   I.1 What Is Law and Society? | 2 |
|   I.2 The Evolution of Law and Society in Asia | 6 |
|   I.3 The Plan of This Book: Chapters and Crosscutting Themes | 9 |
|   References | 17 |
| 1  **Religion** . . . . . . . . . . . . . . . . . . . . . . | 19 |
|   I Legal Dimensions of the Classical Asian Religious Traditions | 20 |
|     1.1 Hinduism as a Legal Tradition, *Donald R. Davis Jr.* | 20 |
|     1.2 Introducing Buddhism and Law, *Rebecca Redwood French and Mark A. Nathan* | 23 |
|     1.3 Taoism: The Enduring Tradition, *Russell Kirkland* | 28 |
|     1.4 The Notion of Shari'a, *Arskal Salim* | 31 |
|   II Law in the Landscape of Sacred Practices | 34 |
|     1.5 State Law and the Law of Sacred Centers, *David M. Engel and Jaruwan Engel* | 35 |
|   III The Arrival of "Modern" Law and the Concept of Secularism | 43 |
|     1.6 The Aborted Restoration of "Indigenous" Law in India, *Marc Galanter* | 44 |
|     1.7 Smash Temples, Burn Books: Comparing Secularist Projects in India and China, *Peter van der Veer* | 47 |

  1.8 Judging in God's Name: State Power, Secularism, and the Politics of Islamic Law in Malaysia, *Tamir Moustafa*   51
 IV Law, Religion, and Conflict in Contemporary Asia   59
  1.9 Theorising Talk about "Religious Pluralism" and "Religious Harmony" in Singapore, *Vineeta Sinha*   60
  1.10 Securing the Sasana through Law: Buddhist Constitutionalism and Buddhist-Interest Litigation in Sri Lanka, *Benjamin Schonthal*   64
  1.11 "Conventional Wisdom" and the Politics of Shinto in Postwar Japan, *John Breen*   69
 References   72

## 2   Legal Pluralism . . . . . . . . . . . . . . . . . . . . 74
 I Evolution of the Concept of Legal Pluralism   77
  2.1 Legal Pluralism, Social Theory, and the State, *Keebet von Benda-Beckmann and Bertram Turner*   78
 II Legal Pluralism as State Policy   82
  2.2 Global Doctrine and Local Knowledge: Law in South East Asia, *Andrew Harding*   83
  2.3 Beyond Democratic Tolerance: Witch Killings in Timor-Leste, *Rebecca Strating and Beth Edmondson*   87
  2.4 Muslim Mandarins in Chinese Courts: Dispute Resolution, Islamic Law, and the Secular State in Northwest China, *Matthew S. Erie*   92
 III Legal Pluralism from the Ground Up   101
  2.5 Gender, Power, and Legal Pluralism: Rajasthan, India, *Erin P. Moore*   102
 References   111

## 3   Disputing . . . . . . . . . . . . . . . . . . . . . . . 114
 I Dispute-Based Fieldwork   116
  3.1 Conflict in the Village, *Fernanda Pirie*   116
 II Dispute Processing and Litigation   120
  3.2 "What He Did Was Lawful": Divorce Litigation and Gender Inequality in China, *Ke Li*   121
 III Alternative Dispute Resolution   129
  3.3 Community Mediation as a Hybrid Practice: The Case of Mediation Boards in Sri Lanka, *Sepalika Welikala*   130
 References   136

*Detailed Table of Contents* xiii

## 4 Legal Consciousness . . . . . . . . . . . . . . . . . . . 139
I National, Local, and Global Dimensions 141
 4.1 Kawashima and the Changing Focus on Japanese Legal Consciousness: A Selective History of the Sociology of Law in Japan, *Masayuki Murayama* 142
 4.2 Globalization and the Decline of Legal Consciousness: Torts, Ghosts, and Karma in Thailand, *David M. Engel* 147

II The Role of Traditional Practices 153
 4.3 Legal Consciousness of the Leftover Woman: Law and *Qing* in Chinese Family Relations, *Qian Liu* 153

III Rights Consciousness 161
 4.4 (Un)Becoming a Man: Legal Consciousness of the Third Gender Category in Pakistan, *Muhammad Azfar Nisar* 162
 4.5 Islamic Law, Women's Rights, and Popular Legal Consciousness in Malaysia, *Tamir Moustafa* 169

IV Relational Legal Consciousness 176
 4.6 Justice, Emotion, and Belonging: Legal Consciousness in a Taiwanese Family Conflict, *Hsiao-Tan Wang* 177
References 181

## 5 Legal Mobilization . . . . . . . . . . . . . . . . . . . 183
I Scope of Legal Mobilization 185
 5.1 Constructing SSLM: Insights from Struggles over Women's Rights in Nepal, *Margaret Becker* 186

II Legal Mobilization Tactics 192
 5.2 The Politics of Love in Myanmar: LGBT Mobilization and Human Rights as a Way of Life, *Lynette J. Chua* 192
 5.3 Labour Law and (In)justice in Workers' Letters in Vietnam, *Tu Phuong Nguyen* 196
 5.4 Pragmatic Resistance, Law, and Social Movements in Authoritarian States: The Case of Gay Collective Action in Singapore, *Lynette J. Chua* 199
 5.5 Performing Artivism: Feminists, Lawyers, and Online Legal Mobilization in China, *Di Wang and Sida Liu* 201
 5.6 Litigation Dilemmas: Lessons from the Marcos Human Rights Class Action, *Nate Ela* 205

## III Legal Mobilization Effects — 208

- 5.7 Indigeneity and Legal Pluralism in India: Claims, Histories, Meanings, *Pooja Parmar* — 210
- 5.8 The Paradox of Vernacularization: Women's Human Rights and the Gendering of Nationhood, *Sealing Cheng* — 212
- 5.9 Mobilizing the Law in China: "Informed Disenchantment" and the Development of Legal Consciousness, *Mary E. Gallagher* — 216
- 5.10 A People's Constitution: The Everyday Life of Law in the Indian Republic, *Rohit De* — 220

References — 224

# 6 Legal Professions . . . . . . . . . . . . . . . . . 227

## I The Plurality of Law Practitioners — 228

- 6.1 Origins of the Indonesian Advocacy, *Daniel S. Lev* — 228
- 6.2 India's Grand Advocates: A Legal Elite Flourishing in the Era of Globalization, *Marc Galanter and Nick Robinson* — 232
- 6.3 Setting the Limits: Who Controls the Size of the Legal Profession in Japan?, *Kay-Wah Chan* — 237
- 6.4 Practising on the Moon: Globalization and the Legal Consciousness of Foreign Corporate Lawyers in Myanmar, *Arm Tungnirun* — 242

## II Lawyers in the Market — 245

- 6.5 Lawyers, State Officials, and Significant Others: Symbiotic Exchange in the Chinese Legal Services Market, *Sida Liu* — 246
- 6.6 Just Like Global Firms: Unintended Gender Parity and Speculative Isomorphism in India's Elite Professions, *Swethaa Ballakrishnen* — 249
- 6.7 The Juridification of Cause Advocacy in Socialist Asia: Vietnam as a Case Study, *John Gillespie* — 253

## III Lawyers and State Transformations — 257

- 6.8 The Political Origins of Professional Identity: Lawyers, Judges, and Prosecutors in Taiwan's State Transformation, *Ching-fang Hsu* — 258
- 6.9 Civil Society and the Lawyers' Movement of Pakistan, *Sahar Shafqat* — 262
- 6.10 The Political Origins of Cause Lawyering in Hong Kong, *Waikeung Tam* — 267

References — 271

*Detailed Table of Contents*

7    Courts . . . . . . . . . . . . . . . . . . . . . . 273
     I  Courts as Cultural Symbols                          274
         7.1  Legal Consciousness as Viewed through the Judicial Iconography of the Madras High Court, *Rahela Khorakiwala*    274
         7.2  Judging in the Buddha's Court: A Buddhist Judicial System in Contemporary Asia, *Benjamin Schonthal*    277
         7.3  Are Women Getting (More) Justice? Malaysia's *Sharia* Courts in Ethnographic and Historical Perspective, *Michael G. Peletz*    281
     II  Courts as Social Organizations    282
         7.4  Punitive Processes? Judging in Thai Lower Criminal Courts, *Duncan McCargo*    283
         7.5  Chinese Courts as Embedded Institutions, *Kwai Hang Ng and Xin He*    288
         7.6  The Elastic Ceiling: Gender and Professional Career in Chinese Courts, *Chunyan Zheng, Jiahui Ai, and Sida Liu*    293
     III  Courts as Political Battlegrounds    296
         7.7  The Judicialization of Politics in Taiwan, *Chien-Chih Lin*    297
         7.8  The Judicial System and Democratization in Post-Conflict Cambodia, *Kheang Un*    304
     References    306

8    Crime and Justice . . . . . . . . . . . . . . . . . . . 309
     I  Punishment    310
         8.1  The Benevolent Paternalism of Japanese Criminal Justice, *Daniel H. Foote*    310
         8.2  Governing through Killing: The War on Drugs in the Philippines, *David T. Johnson and Jon Fernquest*    315
         8.3  Body Count Politics: Quantification, Secrecy, and Capital Punishment in China, *Tobias Smith*    319
     II  Justice    323
         8.4  The Expression of Justice in China, *Flora Sapio, Susan Trevaskes, Sarah Biddulph, and Elisa Nesossi*    323
         8.5  Old Wine in New Wineskins? A Trial of Restorative Justice in a Korean Criminal Court, *Won Kyung Chang*    329

|   |   |   |
|---|---|---:|
| | III  The Criminal Process | 334 |
| | 8.6  In Search of Judicial Legitimacy: Criminal Sentencing in Vietnamese Courts, *Trang (Mae) Nguyen* | 334 |
| | 8.7  Performing Order, Making Money, *Nick Cheesman* | 337 |
| | 8.8  Justice Is a Secret: *Compromise* in Rape Trials, *Pratiksha Baxi* | 343 |
| | References | 346 |
| 9 | **Practicing Law and Society Scholarship in Asia** . . . . . . . .348 | |
| | I  Gaining Access and Getting Data | 350 |
| | 9.1  Tort, Custom, and Karma: Globalization and Legal Consciousness in Thailand, *David M. Engel and Jaruwan Engel* | 350 |
| | 9.2  Constituting Religion: Islam, Liberal Rights, and the Malaysian State, *Tamir Moustafa* | 354 |
| | 9.3  China and Islam: The Prophet, the Party, and Law, *Matthew S. Erie* | 356 |
| | 9.4  A People's Constitution: The Everyday Life of Law in the Indian Republic, *Rohit De* | 361 |
| | 9.5  Labour Law and (In)justice in Workers' Letters in Vietnam, *Tu Phuong Nguyen* | 364 |
| | II  Navigating Identities | 367 |
| | 9.6  Indigeneity and Legal Pluralism in India: Claims, Histories, Meanings, *Pooja Parmar* | 367 |
| | 9.7  Public Secrets of Law: Rape Trials in India, *Pratiksha Baxi* | 371 |
| | III  Practicing Law and Society Research in the Digital Age | 376 |
| | 9.8  Doing Ethnography on Social Media: A Methodological Reflection on the Study of Online Groups in China, *Di Wang and Sida Liu* | 376 |
| | References | 383 |
| Index | | 385 |

# Acknowledgments

The *Asian Law and Society Reader* is inspired by our experiences of conducting law and society research in Asia and teaching it in undergraduate and graduate classrooms for decades. Throughout our professional lives, the three of us have been fortunate to have been involved in the Law & Society Association (LSA) and, from its inception in 2016, the Asian Law & Society Association (ALSA). Both the LSA and ALSA have provided invaluable settings in which to present our research, learn about the scholarship of our counterparts around the world, and share our teaching experiences. This book crystallizes many of the lessons and fruitful discussions that we have had with students, friends, and colleagues, who have enriched our intellectual lives.

We are grateful to the research assistants who contributed to this project at various stages: Wen Weiyang, Jeanette Yeo, and Umika Sharma at the National University of Singapore (NUS); Xie Yihui at Yale-NUS College; Yang Keyi at the State University of New York at Buffalo; and Gihad Nasr at the University of Toronto. We are indebted to NUS Law for housing the project, which is supported by the Ministry of Education, Singapore, under its Academic Research Fund – Tier 2 (MOE2018-T2–1-101) – and Wendy Wee for her tireless help with all things related to the research budget. In addition, we are thankful for the supplementary funding provided by the JY Pillay Global Asia Programme (WBS C-607-003-098-001) at Yale-NUS College and an ad hoc grant provided by the Centre for Asian Legal Studies at NUS Law.

Above all, we wish to thank our own mentors and teachers, who introduced us to the joys and wonders of conducting law and society research.

# Publisher's Acknowledgments

The Press has made every effort to contact the copyright holders of works reprinted in *The Asian Law and Society Reader*. It has not been possible in every case, however, and we would welcome correspondence from individuals or companies we have been unable to trace. We will undertake to rectify errors or omissions in future editions of the book. We would like to thank all the authors represented in this work, as well as the following publishers for the permission to reprint their material:

**1.1**: Republished with permission of Oxford University Press on behalf of the American Academy of Religion from Donald R. Davis, Jr. (2007), "Hinduism as a Legal Tradition," *Journal of the American Academy of Religion* 75 (2): 241–67, doi: 10.1093/jaarel/lfm004; permission conveyed through Copyright Clearance Center, Inc.

**1.2**: Republished with permission of Cambridge University Press from Rebecca Redwood French and Mark A. Nathan (2014), "Introducing Buddhism and Law," in *Buddhism and Law: An Introduction*, edited by Rebecca Redwood French and Mark A. Nathan (Cambridge University Press), 1–28, doi: 10.1017/CBO9781139044134; permission conveyed through Publishers' Licensing Services Ltd.

**1.3**: Republished with permission of Taylor & Francis Ltd. from Russell Kirkland (2004), *Taoism: The Enduring Tradition* (Routledge), 31–3, 144–9, doi: 10.4324/9780203646717; permission conveyed through Copyright Clearance Center, Inc.

**1.4**: Republished with permission of University of Hawai'i Press from Arskal Salim (2008), *Challenging the Secular State: The Islamization of Law in Modern Indonesia* (University of Hawai'i Press), chap. 1: "The Notion of Shari'a," 11–15, doi: 10.21313/hawaii/9780824832377.001.0001; permission conveyed through Copyright Clearance Center, Inc.

*Publisher's Acknowledgments* xix

1.5: Republished with permission of Stanford University Press from David and Jaruwan Engel (2010), *Tort, Custom, and Karma: Globalization and Legal Consciousness in Thailand* (Stanford University Press), chap. 3: "State Law and the Law of Sacred Centers," 47–76, www.sup.org/books/title/?id=10202; permission conveyed through Copyright Clearance Center, Inc.

1.6: Republished with permission of Cambridge University Press on behalf of the Society for the Comparative Study of Society and History from Marc Galanter (1972), "The Aborted Restoration of 'Indigenous' Law in India," *Comparative Studies in Society and History* 14 (1): 53–70, doi: 10.1017/S0010417500006502; permission conveyed through Copyright Clearance Center, Inc.

1.7: Republished with permission of Oxford University Press from Peter van der Veer (2011), "Smash Temples, Burn Books: Comparing Secularist Projects in India and China," in *Rethinking Secularism*, edited by Craig Calhoun, Mark Juergensmeyer, and Jonathon VanAntwerpen, 17–25 (Oxford University Press); permission conveyed through Publishers' Licensing Services Ltd.

1.8: Republished with permission of Oxford University Press from Tamir Moustafa (2014), "Judging in God's Name: State Power, Secularism, and the Politics of Islamic Law in Malaysia," *Oxford Journal of Law and Religion*, 3 (1): 152–67, doi: 10.1093/ojlr/rwt035; permission conveyed through Copyright Clearance Center, Inc.

1.9: Republished with permission of Taylor & Francis Ltd. from Vineeta Sinha (2005), "Theorising 'Talk' about 'Religious Pluralism' and 'Religious Harmony' in Singapore," *Journal of Contemporary Religion* 20 (1): 25–40, doi: 10.1080/13537900520003 13891.

1.10: Republished with permission of Cambridge University Press from Benjamin Schonthal (2016), "Securing the Sasana Through Law: Buddhist Constitutionalism and Buddhist-Interest Litigation in Sri Lanka," *Modern Asian Studies* 50 (6): 1966–2008, doi: 10.1017/S0026749X15000426; permission conveyed through Copyright Clearance Center, Inc.

1.11: Republished with permission of the copyright holder (John Breen) from John Breen (2010), "'Conventional Wisdom' and the Politics of Shinto in Postwar Japan," *Politics and Religion* 4 (1): 68–82, doi: 10.54561/prjo401068b; this Open Access article was published by the Center for Study of Religion and Religious Tolerance (Belgrade) under the CC-BY-NC-SA 4.0 license.

2.1: Republished with permission of Taylor & Francis Ltd. from Keebet von Benda-Beckmann and Bertram Turner (2018), "Legal Pluralism, Social Theory, and the State," *The Journal of Legal Pluralism and Unofficial Law*

50 (3): 255–74, doi: 10.1080/07329113.2018.1532674; this Open Access article was published under the CC-BY 4.0 license.

**2.2**: Republished with permission of Cambridge University Press on behalf of the British Institute of International and Comparative Law from Andrew Harding (2002), "Global Doctrine and Local Knowledge: Law in South East Asia," *International and Comparative Law Quarterly* 51 (1): 35–53, doi: 10.1093/iclq/51.1.35; permission conveyed through Copyright Clearance Center, Inc.

**2.3**: Republished with permission of SAGE Publications Ltd. on behalf of the German Institute for Global and Area Studies (GIGA) from Rebecca Strating and Beth Edmondson (2015), "Beyond Democratic Tolerance: Witch Killings in Timor-Leste," *Journal of Current Southeast Asian Affairs* 34 (3): 37–64, doi: 10.1177/186810341503400302; this Open Access article was published under the CC-BY-ND 3.0 license.

**2.4**: Republished with permission of Cambridge University Press on behalf of the American Bar Foundation from Matthew S. Erie (2015), "Muslim Mandarins in Chinese Courts: Dispute Resolution, Islamic Law, and the Secular State in Northwest China," *Law & Social Inquiry* 40 (4): 1001–30, doi: 10.1111/lsi.12137; permission conveyed through Copyright Clearance Center, Inc.

**2.5**: Republished with permission of American Ethnological Society from Erin P. Moore (1993), "Gender, Power, and Legal Pluralism: Rajasthan, India," *American Ethnologist* 20 (3): 522–42, doi: 10.1525/ae.1993.20.3.02a00040. Not for sale or further reproduction.

**3.1**: Republished with permission of Koninklijke Brill N.V. from Fernanda Pirie (2006), *Peace and Conflict in Ladakh: The Construction of a Fragile Web of Order* (Brill), chap. 4: "Conflict in the Village," 68–87, doi: 10.1163/ej.9789004155961.i-238.29; permission conveyed through Copyright Clearance Center, Inc.

**3.2**: Republished with permission of John Wiley & Sons, Inc., on behalf of The University of Denver/Colorado Seminary from Ke Li (2015), "'What He Did Was Lawful': Divorce Litigation and Gender Inequality in China," *Law & Policy* 37 (3): 153–79, doi: 10.1111/lapo.12034; permission conveyed through Copyright Clearance Center, Inc.

**3.3**: Republished with permission of Cambridge University Press on behalf of the China Institute for Socio-Legal Studies at Shanghai Jiao Tong University from Sepalika Welikala (2016), "Community Mediation as a Hybrid Practice: The Case of Mediation Boards in Sri Lanka," *Asian Journal of Law and Society* 3 (2): 399–422, doi: 10.1017/als.2016.32; permission conveyed through Copyright Clearance Center, Inc.

4.1: Republished with permission of Cambridge University Press from Masayuki Murayama (2013), "Kawashima and the Changing Focus on Japanese Legal Consciousness: A Selective History of the Sociology of Law in Japan," *International Journal of Law in Context* 9 (4): 565–89, doi: 10.1017/S174455231300030X; permission conveyed through Copyright Clearance Center, Inc.

4.2: Republished with permission of Cambridge University Press on behalf of the American Bar Foundation from David M. Engel (2005), "Globalization and the Decline of Legal Consciousness: Torts, Ghosts, and Karma in Thailand," *Law & Social Inquiry* 30 (3): 469–514, doi: 10.1111/j.1747-4469.2005.tb00351.x; permission conveyed through Copyright Clearance Center, Inc.

4.3: Republished with permission of Cambridge University Press on behalf of the China Institute for Socio-Legal Studies, Shanghai Jiao Tong University from Qian Liu (2018), "Legal Consciousness of the Leftover Woman: Law and *Qing* in Chinese Family Relations," *Asian Journal of Law and Society* 5 (1): 7–27, doi: 10.1017/als.2017.28; permission conveyed through Copyright Clearance Center, Inc.

4.4: Republished with permission of SAGE Publications Ltd. on behalf of Sociologists for Women in Society from Muhammad Azfar Nisar (2018), "(Un)Becoming a Man: Legal Consciousness of the Third Gender Category in Pakistan," *Gender & Society* 32 (1): 59–81, doi: 10.1177/0891243217740097; permission conveyed through Copyright Clearance Center, Inc.

4.5: Republished with permission of Cambridge University Press on behalf of the American Bar Foundation from Tamir Moustafa (2013), "Islamic Law, Women's Rights, and Popular Legal Consciousness in Malaysia," *Law & Social Inquiry* 38 (1), 168–88, doi: 10.1111/j.1747-4469.2012.01298.x; permission conveyed through Copyright Clearance Center, Inc.

4.6: Republished with permission of John Wiley & Sons, Ltd., on behalf of the Law and Society Association from Hsiao-Tan Wang (2019), "Justice, Emotion, and Belonging: Legal Consciousness in a Taiwanese Family Conflict," *Law & Society Review* 53 (3): 764–90, doi: 10.1111/lasr.12422; permission conveyed through Copyright Clearance Center, Inc.

5.1: Reprinted with permission of Taylor & Francis Ltd. from Margaret Becker (2015), "Constructing SSLM: Insights from Struggles over Women's Rights in Nepal," *Asian Studies Review* 39 (2): 247–65, doi: 10.1080/10357823.2015.1021754.

5.2: Republished with permission of Stanford University Press from Lynette J. Chua (2019), *The Politics of Love in Myanmar: LGBT Mobilization and Human Rights as a Way of Life* (Stanford University Press), doi: 10.1515/9781503607453; permission conveyed through Copyright Clearance Center, Inc.

5.3: Republished with permission of Cambridge University Press on behalf of the China Institute for Socio-Legal Studies, Shanghai Jiao Tong University from Tu Phuong Nguyen (2018), "Labour Law and (In)justice in Workers' Letters in Vietnam," *Asian Journal of Law & Society* 5 (1): 25–47, doi: 10.1017/als.2017.29; permission conveyed through Copyright Clearance Center, Inc.

5.4: Republished with permission of John Wiley & Sons, Inc., on behalf of the Law and Society Association from Lynette J. Chua (2012), "Pragmatic Resistance, Law, and Social Movements in Authoritarian States: The Case of Gay Collective Action in Singapore," *Law & Society Review* 46 (4): 713–48, doi: 10.1111/j.1540-5893.2012.00515.x; permission conveyed through Copyright Clearance Center, Inc.

5.5: Republished with permission of Cambridge University Press on behalf of the American Bar Foundation from Di Wang and Sida Liu (2020), "Performing Artivism: Feminists, Lawyers, and Online Legal Mobilization in China," *Law & Social Inquiry* 45 (3): 678–705, doi: 10.1017/lsi.2019.64; permission conveyed through Copyright Clearance Center, Inc.

5.6: Republished with permission of Cambridge University Press on behalf of the American Bar Foundation from Nate Ela (2017), "Litigation Dilemmas: Lessons from the Marcos Human Rights Class Action," *Law & Social Inquiry* 42 (2): 479–508, doi: 10.1111/lsi.12207; permission conveyed through Copyright Clearance Center, Inc.

5.7: Republished with permission of Cambridge University Press from Pooja Parmar (2015), *Indigeneity and Legal Pluralism in India: Claims, Histories, Meanings* (Cambridge University Press), doi: 10.1017/CBO9781139962896; permission conveyed through Publishers' Licensing Services Ltd.

5.8: Reproduced with permission of the George Washington University Institute for Ethnographic Research from Sealing Cheng (2011), "The Paradox of Vernacularization: Women's Human Rights and the Gendering of Nationhood," *Anthropological Quarterly* 84 (2): 475–505, doi: 10.1353/anq.2011.0021

5.9: Reproduced with permission of John Wiley & Sons on behalf of the Law and Society Association from Mary E. Gallagher (2006), "Mobilizing the Law in China: 'Informed Disenchantment' and the Development of Legal Consciousness," *Law & Society Review* 40 (4): 783–816, doi: 10.1111/j.1540-5893.2006.00281.x; permission conveyed through Copyright Clearance Center, Inc.

*Publisher's Acknowledgments*

5.10: Reproduced with permission of Princeton University Press from Rohit De (2018), *A People's Constitution: The Everyday Life of Law in the Indian Republic* (Princeton University Press), doi: 10.2307/j.ctv346n37; permission conveyed through Copyright Clearance Center, Inc.

6.1: Reproduced with permission of Cornell University Press on behalf of Cornell University's Southeast Asia Program from Daniel S. Lev (1976), "Origins of the Indonesian Advocacy," *Indonesia* 21: 135–69, doi: 10.2307/3350960.

6.2: Reprinted by permission of Taylor & Francis Ltd. from Marc Galanter and Nick Robinson (2013), "India's Grand Advocates: A Legal Elite Flourishing in the Era of Globalization," *International Journal of the Legal Profession* 20 (3): 241–65, doi: 10.1080/09695958.2014.912359.

6.3: Reprinted by permission of Taylor & Francis Ltd. from Kay-Wah Chan (2012), "Setting the Limits: Who Controls the Size of the Legal Profession in Japan?," *International Journal of the Legal Profession* 19 (2–3): 321–37, 10.1080/09695958.2012.783990.

6.4: Republished with permission of Cambridge University Press on behalf of the China Institute for Socio-Legal Studies, Shanghai Jiao Tong University from Arm Tungnirun (2018), "Practising on the Moon: Globalization and Legal Consciousness of Foreign Corporate Lawyers in Myanmar," *Asian Journal of Law and Society* 5 (1): 49–67, doi: 10.1017/als.2017.30; permission conveyed through Copyright Clearance Center, Inc.

6.5: Republished with permission of Cambridge University Press on behalf of SOAS University of London from Sida Liu (2011), "Lawyers, State Officials and Significant Others: Symbiotic Exchange in the Chinese Legal Services Market," *The China Quarterly* 206: 276–93, doi: 10.1017/S0305741011000269; permission conveyed through Copyright Clearance Center, Inc.

6.6: Republished with permission of John Wiley & Sons on behalf of the Law and Society Association from Swethaa S. Ballakrishnen (2019), "Just Like Global Firms: Unintended Gender Parity and Speculative Isomorphism in India's Elite Professions," *Law & Society Review* 53 (1): 108–40, doi: 10.1111/lasr.12381; permission conveyed through Copyright Clearance Center, Inc.

6.7: Reproduced with permission from the University of Wisconsin Law School from John Gillespie (2013), "The Juridification of Cause Advocacy in Socialist Asia: Vietnam as a Case Study," *Wisconsin International Law Journal* 31 (3): 672–701, URL: https://wilj.law.wisc.edu/wp-content/uploads/sites/1270/2019/10/Gillespie_Final.pdf.

6.8: Republished with permission of Cambridge University Press on behalf of the China Institute for Socio-Legal Studies, Shanghai Jiao Tong University from Ching-fang Hsu (2019), "The Political Origins of Professional Identity: Lawyers, Judges, and Prosecutors in Taiwan's State Transformation," *Asian Journal of Law and Society* 6 (2): 321–46, doi: 10.1017/als.2018.35; permission conveyed through Copyright Clearance Center, Inc.

6.9: Republished with permission of Cambridge University Press on behalf of the American Bar Foundation from Sahar Shafqat (2018), "Civil Society and the Lawyers' Movement of Pakistan," *Law & Social Inquiry* 43 (3): 889–914, doi: 10.1111/lsi.12283; permission conveyed through Copyright Clearance Center, Inc.

6.10: Republished with permission of Cambridge University Press from Waikeung Tam (2013), *Legal Mobilization under Authoritarianism: The Case of Post-Colonial Hong Kong* (Cambridge University Press), chap. 6, "The Political Origins of Cause Lawyering in Hong Kong," 115–34, doi: 10.1017/CBO9781139424394.009; permission conveyed through Publishers' Licensing Services Ltd.

7.1: Republished with permission of Cambridge University Press on behalf of the China Institute for Socio-Legal Studies, Shanghai Jiao Tong University from Rahela Khorakiwala (2018), "Legal Consciousness as Viewed through the Judicial Iconography of the Madras High Court," *Asian Journal of Law and Society* 5 (1): 111–33, doi: 10.1017/als.2017.33; permission conveyed through Copyright Clearance Center, Inc.

7.2: Republished with permission of Cambridge University Press on behalf of the China Institute for Socio-Legal Studies, Shanghai Jiao Tong University from Benjamin Schonthal (2020), "Judging in the Buddha's Court: A Buddhist Judicial System in Contemporary Asia," *Asian Journal of Law and Society* 8 (2): 1–22, doi: 10.1017/als.2020.13; permission conveyed through Copyright Clearance Center, Inc.

7.3: Republished with permission of John Wiley & Sons on behalf of the Law and Society Association from Michael G. Peletz (2018), "Are Women Getting (More) Justice? Malaysia's Sharia Courts in Ethnographic and Historical Perspective," *Law & Society Review* 52 (3): 652–84, doi: 10.1111/lasr.12346; permission conveyed through Copyright Clearance Center, Inc.

7.4: Republished with permission of Cambridge University Press on behalf of the China Institute for Socio-Legal Studies, Shanghai Jiao Tong University from Duncan McCargo (2020), "Punitive Processes? Judging in Thai Lower Criminal Courts," *Asian Journal of Law and Society* 8 (2): 324–47, doi:

10.1017/als.2020.22; permission conveyed through Copyright Clearance Center, Inc.

7.5: Republished with permission of Cambridge University Press from Kwai Hang Ng and Xin He (2017), *Embedded Courts: Judicial Decision-Making in China* (Cambridge University Press), chap. 1, "Chinese Courts as Embedded Institutions", doi: 10.1017/9781108339117.002; permission conveyed through Publishers' Licensing Services Ltd.

7.6: Republished with permission of John Wiley & Sons on behalf of the Law and Society Association from Chunyan Zheng, Jiahui Ai, and Sida Liu (2017), "The Elastic Ceiling: Gender and Professional Career in Chinese Courts," *Law & Society Review* 51 (1): 168–99, doi: 10.1111/lasr.12249; permission conveyed through Copyright Clearance Center, Inc.

7.7: Republished with permission of Cambridge University Press on behalf of the China Institute for Socio-Legal Studies, Shanghai Jiao Tong University from Chien-Chih Lin (2016), "The Judicialization of Politics in Taiwan," *Asian Journal of Law and Society* 3 (2): 299–326, doi: 10.1017/als.2016.10; permission conveyed through Copyright Clearance Center, Inc.

7.8: Reproduced with permission of the NIAS Press of the University of Copenhagen from Kheang Un (2009), "The Judicial System and Democratization in Post-Conflict Cambodia," in *Beyond Democracy in Cambodia: Political Reconstruction in a Post-Conflict Society*, edited by Joakim Öjendal and Mona Lilja, 70–100 (Nordic Institute of Asian Studies Press).

8.1: Republished with permission of the University of California, Berkeley, School of Law from Daniel H. Foote (1992), "The Benevolent Paternalism of Japanese Criminal Justice," *California Law Review* 80: 317–90, doi: 10.15779/Z38GQ7Q; permission conveyed through Copyright Clearance Center, Inc.

8.2: Republished with permission of Cambridge University Press on behalf of the China Institute for Socio-Legal Studies, Shanghai Jiao Tong University from David T. Johnson and Jon Fernquest (2018), "Governing through Killing: The War on Drugs in the Philippines," *Asian Journal of Law and Society* 5 (2): 359–90, doi: 10.1017/als.2018.12; permission conveyed through Copyright Clearance Center, Inc.

8.3: Republished with permission of Cambridge University Press on behalf of the American Bar Foundation from Tobias Smith (2020), "Body Count Politics: Quantification, Secrecy, and Capital Punishment in China," *Law & Social Inquiry* 45 (3): 706–27, doi: 10.1017/lsi.2020.10; permission conveyed through Copyright Clearance Center, Inc.

8.4: Republished with permission of Cambridge University Press from Flora Sapio, Susan Trevaskes, Sarah Biddulph, and Elisa Nesossi (2017) *Justice: The China Experience* (Cambridge University Press), chap. 1, "The Expression of Justice in China", doi: 10.1017/9781108115919.001; permission conveyed through Publishers' Licensing Services Ltd.

8.5: Republished with permission of Cambridge University Press on behalf of the China Institute for Socio-Legal Studies, Shanghai Jiao Tong University from Won Kyung Chang (2018), "Old Wine in New Wineskins? A Trial of Restorative Justice in a Korean Criminal Court," *Asian Journal of Law and Society* 5 (2): 391–411, doi: 10.1017/als.2017.34; permission conveyed through Copyright Clearance Center, Inc.

8.6: Republished with permission of Harvard Law School from Nguyen Trang (Mae) 2019, "In Search of Judicial Legitimacy: Criminal Sentencing in Vietnamese Courts," *Harvard Human Rights Journal* 32: 147–88, https://harvardhrj.com/wp-content/uploads/sites/14/2019/07/Nguyen_In-Search-of-Judicial-Legitimacy.pdf; permission conveyed through Copyright Clearance Center, Inc.

8.7: Republished with permission of Cambridge University Press from Nick Cheesman (2015), *Opposing the Rule of Law: How Myanmar's Courts Make Law and Order* (Cambridge University Press), chap. 6, doi: 10.1017/CBO9781316014936.008; permission conveyed through Publishers' Licensing Services Ltd.

8.8: Republished with permission of SAGE Publications Ltd. on behalf of the Institute of Economic Growth, Delhi from Pratiksha Baxi (2010), "Justice Is a Secret: *Compromise* in Rape Trials," *Contributions to Indian Sociology* 44 (3): 207–33, doi: 10.1177/006996671004400301; permission conveyed through Copyright Clearance Center, Inc.

9.1: Republished with permission of Stanford University Press from David M. Engel and Jaruwan Engel (2010), *Tort, Custom, and Karma: Globalization and Legal Consciousness in Thailand* (Stanford University Press), *www.sup.org/books/title/?id=10202*; permission conveyed through Copyright Clearance Center, Inc.

9.2: Republished with permission of Cambridge University Press from Tamir Moustafa (2018), *Constituting Religion: Islam, Liberal Rights, and the Malaysian State* (Cambridge University Press), doi: 10.1017/9781108539296; permission conveyed through Publishers' Licensing Services Ltd.

9.3: Republished with permission of Cambridge University Press from Mathew S. Erie (2016), *China and Islam: The Prophet, the Party, and Law*

*Publisher's Acknowledgments* xxvii

(Cambridge University Press), doi: 10.1017/9781107282063; permission conveyed through Publishers' Licensing Services Ltd.

9.4: Reproduced with permission of Princeton University Press from Rohit De (2018), *A People's Constitution: The Everyday Life of Law in the Indian Republic* (Princeton University Press), doi: 10.2307/j.ctv346n37; permission conveyed through Copyright Clearance Center, Inc.

9.5: Republished with permission of Cambridge University Press on behalf of the China Institute for Socio-Legal Studies, Shanghai Jiao Tong University from Tu Phuong Nguyen (2018), "Labour Law and (In)justice in Workers' Letters in Vietnam," *Asian Journal of Law & Society* 5 (1): 25–47, doi: 10.1017/als.2017.29; permission conveyed through Copyright Clearance Center, Inc.

9.6: Republished with permission of Cambridge University Press from Pooja Parmar (2015), *Indigeneity and Legal Pluralism in India: Claims, Histories, Meanings* (Cambridge University Press), doi: 10.1017/CBO9781139962896; permission conveyed through Publishers' Licensing Services Ltd.

9.7: Republished with permission of Oxford University Press, India from Pratiksha Baxi (2014), *Public Secrets of Law: Rape Trials in India* (Oxford University Press), doi: 10.1093/acprof:oso/9780198089568.001.0001.

9.8: Republished with permission of SAGE Publications Ltd. from Di Wang and Sida Liu (2021), "Doing Ethnography on Social Media: A Methodological Reflection on the Study of Online Groups in China," *Qualitative Inquiry* 27 (8/9): 977–87, doi: 10.1177/10778004211014610; this Open Access article was published under the CC-BY 4.0 license.

# Introduction

Is there any society in the world where the written laws accurately describe what people and institutions actually do, where people manage their affairs and resolve their conflicts precisely as the law codes prescribe, and where constitutional principles and regulatory requirements are scrupulously observed? The answer is certainly no. To achieve such a society would be impossible, and to live in it would at times be intolerable. Perhaps it is fortunate that there is always a difference between the dry abstractions and rigid mandates of black letter law and the messy complications of human existence – though we may sometimes wish the law had greater success in resolving those complications. The field of law and society chronicles this difference, this inevitable disparity between the promise of law and its delivery, between the rules and the reality. Law and society researchers expose the many ways in which law actually touches people's lives or remains dormant, in which law promotes justice or increases the potential for unfairness, inequality, and even violence.

In Asian countries, the difference between law on the books and law in everyday life presents itself with exceptional clarity. This is not surprising, since Asian legal systems are, for the most part, transplants from Europe or America, modified, to be sure, in their new surroundings, yet retaining key features that originated in distant and extremely dissimilar cultures. Colonial rulers or political elites imposed most Asian legal systems on populations who had little voice in their form or content. There was no assurance that laws and legal institutions established in this way would reflect the beliefs and behavior of ordinary people. Although most contemporary Asian legal systems have undergone considerable revision since they were first set up, observers have repeatedly noted the sharp contrast between the official laws of Asian states and the unofficial norms and practices familiar to most of the population. These gaps and disparities raise a number of very important questions, such as:

Why do Asian laws and legal institutions so often appear irrelevant to ordinary people? Why does law in Asian contexts fail so frequently to achieve its goals? What strategies for law reform are most likely to improve the situation? What role should law play – as opposed to unofficial customary practices – in resolving conflict in Asian societies? Under what circumstances have individuals and groups in Asia successfully mobilized the law and benefited from its application? What is the status of legal professionals in Asian societies, and what part might they play in advancing popular conceptions of justice?

Law and society researchers working in Asian settings have offered answers to these questions and others like them. It is not surprising that the field of Asian law and society has flourished in recent years and has attracted growing numbers of scholars, students, and policymakers who share a frustration with narrowly focused studies of legal rules or doctrinal exegeses. Although legal theory and the analysis of black letter law still predominate in many law schools, Asia has become a focal point for some of the most significant law and society research in recent years, and professional associations and centers for research and teaching in Asia have achieved greater prominence now than ever before. It is time, we believe, for a Reader that features the literature, theories, and methods of law and society research conducted in Asian settings.

This book presents studies that took place across the entire Asian region, from China, Japan, and Korea to Singapore and Indonesia, from Vietnam, Myanmar, and Thailand to Nepal, India, Sri Lanka, Pakistan, and elsewhere. It highlights the topics that have most interested law and society scholars who study Asia – we shall refer to them collectively as "Asian law and society scholars," though not all are themselves Asian by nationality or ethnicity – and it offers insights into the various ways in which the scholars conduct their research. It provides analyses of the classical legal and religious systems of Asia as well as the most recent law-related issues and developments. In short, this is a book designed not just for students but for scholars of Asia, for lawyers, judges, and policymakers, and for nonspecialists who wish to learn more about the region as seen through the lens of law and society research. It is intended to highlight some of the achievements and the most valuable insights of scholars working in Asia, and it is also meant to inspire further studies by pointing the way to new discoveries on the horizon. It is intended ultimately to contribute to better informed debates and decisions about laws, legal change, and justice in Asian societies.

## I.1 What Is Law and Society?

For readers unfamiliar with the field of law and society scholarship, it may be useful to begin with an explanation of the term. We proceed with caution, well aware that any definition will invite controversy. As law and society research has flourished in Asia and throughout the world, it has become vibrant, multicentered, creative, rapidly evolving, and highly diverse. As a result, law and society scholars nowadays tend to offer differing characterizations of their common field. Even the three editors of this Reader, who share longstanding involvements in the law and society field and are otherwise close colleagues and good friends, tend to define it in somewhat different terms.

This much we could probably agree on: In law and society scholarship, law and legal institutions are studied as social phenomena. Law is not presented as an autonomous system operating independent of its environment. As Lynn Mather (2008) puts it, "*Law is in society*, and most now agree with the argument Laura Nader made initially that the field should have been named 'Law *in* Society' rather than law *and* society." Because law is "embedded" in society, it cannot be studied exclusively on its own terms. The legal system's view of social phenomena, an internalized view that is necessarily constrained by law's own formal rules of relevance and textual interpretation, is like the shadowy vision of reality projected against the walls of the cave in Plato's famous allegory. But law and society researchers do not confine their view of society to the shadows projected inside the cave of the legal system itself. They study law directly, alongside other social and cultural phenomena. They stand in daylight outside the legal system, separate and apart from the legal actors and institutions whose behavior they wish to comprehend.

The tool kit of law and society scholars is ampler than that of traditional legal scholars and includes a number of quite different methodologies: historical or archival research, participant observation, qualitative interviews, broad-based surveys, other forms of quantitative data analysis, laboratory studies, and natural experiments, among others. Most law and society scholars use or at least draw upon empirical research, which Shari Diamond (2019) has defined as the "systematic organization of a series of observations with the method of data collection and analysis made available to the audience." Yet not all law and society scholarship fits within this definition of empirical research. What law and society researchers generally do *not* do is analyze law texts – judicial opinions, statutes, regulations, contracts, and the like – on their own terms rather than situating them in particular social and cultural contexts that must be brought into the discussion in one way or another.

It is almost easier to say what law and society is not than to say what it is. Law and society, as we have already observed, is not conventional legal scholarship of the kind familiar to law professors around the world. It is not merely the analysis of so-called black letter law, of legal doctrine, or of legal theory – though it sometimes takes black letter law as a starting point. Some law and society scholars may begin with a statute or a judicial opinion, but they rely on fieldwork to trace its impact, workings, or origins in society. Thus, law and society research can provide a useful real-world assessment of legal doctrine and can point to better rules and procedures and better legal institutions. Like conventional legal scholars, law and society researchers pursue theory, but law and society theories are grounded and derived from data and are not of the armchair variety. In short, there may be significant overlap, but the two fields – conventional legal analysis and law and society research – are by no means congruent.

Nor is law and society quite the same thing as law and development, though these two fields also share common roots and interrelate in many ways. Law and society scholars tend to be more skeptical about the capacity of law to achieve development goals and more critical of the unintended consequences that may accompany the instrumental use of liberal legalism to realize social change. At the same time, however, many law and development scholars view law and society research as an essential tool for their work, one that can help them achieve a better understanding of approaches that have worked or failed in the past and are likely to succeed or fail in the future. Moreover, despite law and society researchers' skepticism about law's actual effects, most of them – like their colleagues in the law and development field – aspire to promote progressive social change. Perhaps that is one of the reasons why membership in the two fields tends to overlap.

Lastly, law and society is not the same thing as critical legal studies, even though the two fields intersect in their distrust of liberal legalism's optimistic claims. Law and society researchers typically rely much more heavily on data and on empirical research methods, which critical legal scholars sometimes view as overly positivistic, a misleading characterization that is resisted by the many law and society scholars whose work is qualitative and/or interpretive. Put another way, law and society researchers are more inclined to take the assertions of critical legal scholars as research questions worthy of investigation rather than as self-verifying pronouncements. Indeed, despite the common influence of postmodern theory on both groups of scholars – the work of Foucault, de Certeau, Bourdieu, and others – law and society scholars are more inclined than "Crits" to assume that there is some version of truth (or "social facts," to use Durkheim's term) out there waiting to be discovered by thoughtful engagement with people or social institutions rather than viewing truth claims as hopelessly subjective and relativistic. Moreover, law and society scholars consider it important to allow the data to speak and surprise them. Unlike critical legal scholars, they distrust analyses that fail to develop unexpected insights or that arrive at conclusions identical to the starting point of the scholarly journey.

Even this short list of distinctions should suggest some of the rewards of doing law and society research. Law and society research reveals how law actually works – and how it fails. It listens closely and with some humility to the unheard voices of ordinary people, who are most significantly affected by laws and legal institutions – not just the words of elite actors. It persistently uncovers the gap between law's aims and its actual impact. It examines law's intended and unintended consequences, and it highlights the ways in which law may actually exacerbate problems of inequality in wealth and power. Law and society researchers do not merely theorize about inequality or oppression; they document them in the words and life experiences of real people in specific circumstances.

In selecting the readings for this book, we have attempted to illustrate the unique insights that can be gained from excellent law and society research conducted in Asian settings. Each selection is meant to exemplify law and society research designs and research methods at work. The readings are varied in their approach and in their subject matter; we do not insist on a single orthodoxy. But all the excerpts have one thing in common. They all display the rewards of open-minded, inquisitive, fieldwork-based, creatively designed research with the capacity to surprise the researcher as well as the reader about the role of law in the lives of Asian people. For us as editors of this book, shining a bright spotlight on Asian law and society as a way of thinking about and conducting one's research is even more important than the facts or findings reported in each excerpt. We hope that readers will share our appreciation for the distinctive and, indeed, indispensable contribution that law and society scholarship can make and the perspective it can bring to the study of Asian societies and their legal systems.

But readers may still be confused about the definition of law and society and the terminology used by different people to discuss this field of research. Is "law and society" the same as "law and social science"? Is something different meant by "sociolegal studies"? And how about the "sociology of law"? "Law and social science," it has been argued, is a narrower term than law and society, since it seems to exclude research that draws on disciplines outside the social sciences, such as literary theory, cultural studies, philosophy, the fine arts, and, some would say, history. If that is the case, then defining our field more broadly as "law and society" seems preferable to "law and social science." "Sociolegal studies," on the other hand, with or without a hyphen, is a reasonably inclusive term, and in this Reader we use it interchangeably with "law and society." The term "sociolegal" appears in the name of an important UK-based scholarly organization (the Socio-Legal Studies Association), but it is also employed adjectively by many law and society scholars worldwide.

Finally, there is the term "sociology of law," which may at first glance appear narrower than it actually is. Scholars who use this term, including members of the Japanese Association of Sociology of Law, the European-based Research Committee on Sociology of Law of the International Sociological Association, and the Sociology of Law section of the American Sociological Association, do not restrict their research to the theories and methods of the discipline of sociology – as opposed to political science, anthropology, psychology, history, geography, or the humanities. Rather, those who identify as sociology of law scholars are typically part of the mainstream of what is generally considered the law and society field, regardless of their disciplinary background.

## I.2 The Evolution of Law and Society in Asia

The field of law and society has expanded dramatically in Asia in the early twenty-first century, making the region a focal point for innovation in methods and theory. Along with the publication of hundreds of books and articles and the establishment of dozens of centers, institutes, and graduate programs dedicated to the study of Asian law and society, new Asia-focused scholarly journals have also been launched, and new professional associations have emerged alongside older associations of long standing. Hundreds of young, highly trained scholars have joined a prior generation of Asian law and society specialists to push the frontiers of research in new directions. Exciting findings based on fieldwork in Asia test old theories and generate new ones.

Admittedly, legal education in most Asian countries – like legal education elsewhere in the world – remains largely traditional, focusing narrowly on black letter law, legal theory, and rule memorization. Nevertheless, the social, economic, and political transformations underway throughout Asia have made it increasingly clear that conventional legal scholarship is no longer adequate to prepare lawyers, judges, and policymakers to succeed in this new social and economic environment. Changing times demand new approaches that are both wider and deeper than the old ones. The broad, interdisciplinary perspective of law and society has become more compelling than ever.

During this same period, the field of law and society has flourished worldwide, but it would be a mistake to regard Asian law and society strictly as a foreign import – yet another transplant from Europe or North America. Of course, global influences have been and remain important. But the field of law and society also has deep roots in Asia reaching back in some cases more than a century. Asian scholars and western scholars working in Asia have played an important part in the development of law and society as an international research field, both as researchers and as leaders in international scholarly associations. The history of Asian law and society should be mapped not as a wave of influence traveling from Global North to Global South but as a number of tributaries flowing from many Asian countries and from outside the region that have joined quite recently into a single broad river.

Consider, for example, the rather different law and society origin stories in four Asian countries: Japan, Indonesia, China, and India. *Japan* is home to the world's oldest law and society association, The Japanese Association of Sociology of Law (JASL), which was founded in 1947. Japanese law and society first took shape during the early years of the twentieth century, following the establishment of the "modern" Japanese legal regime based on European models. The contrast between traditional Japanese law ways and the new legal system attracted the interest of Japanese legal scholars, particularly Izutaro Suehiro, who drew on the work of Eugen Ehrlich (1936) and Roscoe Pound (1910) in his efforts to study the "living law" from a sociological perspective rather than simply analyzing the new written laws on their own terms. Suehiro and other Japanese scholars conducted fieldwork in China and Japan to ascertain the "effective social norms that people actually complied with as rules of conduct" (Murayama 2013:569). After World War II, a new generation of scholars, most notably Takeyoshi Kawashima and Masaji Chiba, continued these efforts. In this intellectual climate, law and society studies became institutionalized in Japan, not only by the formation of the JASL but also by the designation of sociology of law as "a major subject of law study even after the establishment of the new professional law schools" (Murayama 2013:581).

The emergence of law and society in *Indonesia* followed a very different path. Cornelis van Vollenhoven, an eminent Dutch anthropologist, contended that the Dutch colonial government needed a better understanding of Indonesian customary law, since "[m]isunderstanding its character led to illegal expropriation of land and other resources" (von Benda-Beckmann and Turner 2018:257). Accordingly, he inspired a generation of researchers to conduct fieldwork studies of "local laws" in Indonesia and their sometimes conflictual relationship to the colonial legal superstructure – similar to efforts by anthropologists in other societies that fell under the control of European imperialists. Thus, research by scholars of Indonesia in the so-called Adat School should be understood as a product of colonialism and also, at least to some extent, as a check on its transgressions. After the Netherlands relinquished control over Indonesia in 1949, a few Indonesian scholars – such as Tapi Omas Ihromi and Satjipto Rahardjo – continued to conduct research and train younger scholars in the law and society tradition, but the most important scholarship continued to be produced by non-Indonesians, such as Daniel S. Lev, Franz and Keebet von Benda-Beckmann, and Adriaan Bedner.

Law and society in *China* followed yet another trajectory, with little activity apparent in the earlier years of the twentieth century (except for the seminal work of Tung-Tsu Chu [1965]) but a dramatic efflorescence in the 1980s and 1990s. As the Chinese government began to support sociolegal research, two major conferences were held in Beijing in 1987 and 1988, and the translation into Chinese of classic and contemporary law and society studies, mostly from Europe and North America, made them available to a growing number of eager young Chinese students and scholars (Liu and Wang 2015). Fieldwork-based research began to appear in the 1990s, largely focused on rural Chinese settings; and major centers of teaching and research emerged afterward. Of considerable symbolic importance, one of the first sociolegal conferences that led to the founding of the Asian Law and Society Association took place at Shanghai Jiao Tong University, which also became the home of the *Asian Journal of Law and Society*, published by Cambridge University Press since 2014. The story of law and society in China is, therefore, one of dramatic and quite recent expansion, supported by the Chinese government and led by a few particularly influential figures, such as Suli Zhu and Weidong Ji.

Law and society in *India* developed in quite a different way. British colonial administrators, like the Dutch colonizers in Indonesia, did engage in research on customary law and traditional Indian religious traditions, particularly Hinduism. Nevertheless, Srinivas (1987) and others have noted that pre-independence research in the social sciences was hardly robust, and it was not until the post-independence period that social science research began to expand. In large part, this was because the new political leaders believed that a modern democratic state required good social science research in order to make sound policy decisions. Nevertheless, the Indian Council of Social Science Research showed little interest in law and society studies, although it did support some topics that we might consider sociolegal in nature, such as the study of social class, women, and rural poverty. Ironically, in light of the general neglect of law and society research in post-independence India, one of the world's leading law and society scholars at that time – Upendra Baxi – was Indian, and some of the most influential American and European law and society scholars of the late twentieth century were Indian specialists: Marc Galanter, Susanne Hoeber Rudolph and Lloyd Rudolph, Robert Kidder, and J. Duncan M. Derrett, among others. In recent years, however, Indian and other South Asian scholars, notably Pratiksha Baxi and her colleagues, have promoted law and society scholarship within India and South Asia by organizing a highly successful organization, known as LASSnet (Law and Social Sciences Research Network), based at the Centre for the Study of Law and

# Introduction

Governance, Jawaharlal Nehru University. LASSnet meets every two to three years and attracts hundreds of scholars from the region.

It is evident from these four illustrative examples that law and society has emerged in very different ways in different Asian countries – and in a few countries it has scarcely emerged at all. Western intellectual influences have been important, and colonialism played a key role in some instances, but scholars in Asia themselves deserve most of the credit for nurturing the study of law and society and applying it to the circumstances of Asian societies. Indeed, they were the ones who realized that law and society research was uniquely suited to grapple with the rapidly changing conditions in Asia, first to study the ripple effects of legal "modernization" and then to study the consequences of globalization and tumultuous political and economic change. Many have recognized that law and society research can provide a reliable foundation for policy decisions now facing Asian societies. Traditional legal education, with its narrow focus on doctrine, is clearly not up to the task.

## I.3 The Plan of This Book: Chapters and Crosscutting Themes

The literature on Asian law and society features a number of frequently recurring topics. To some extent, these topics are familiar to researchers in non-Asian settings as well, but those who study Asian societies tend to bring somewhat different emphases and perspectives. Moreover, because the settings in which they conduct research differ radically from those in which their colleagues labor elsewhere in the world, scholars of Asia have consistently contributed distinctive findings and theoretical conclusions. To provide an overview of the literature of Asian law and society, we have selected nine subject areas for inclusion in this Reader. They constitute the nine numbered chapters of our book:

1. Religion
2. Legal Pluralism
3. Disputing
4. Legal Consciousness
5. Legal Mobilization
6. Legal Professions
7. Courts
8. Crime and Justice
9. Practicing Law and Society Research in Asia

Before describing the content of these nine chapters, however, it is essential to highlight five meta-themes that crosscut all the chapters and all the readings.

These crosscutting themes can be thought of as the columns in a table in which the chapters are the rows.

The first crosscutting theme is *colonialism*. Though not a chapter of its own, colonialism is a conspicuous presence in virtually all the chapters of this book. The takeover of Asian societies by the imperial powers of England, France, the Netherlands, Portugal, Spain, Japan, Russia, Germany, and the United States profoundly disrupted the classical legal systems of Asia, established new and unfamiliar institutional arrangements, reshaped social hierarchies, and redefined the geopolitical spaces and boundaries of Asian states. Closely connected to the theme of colonialism is the concept of modernization. Beliefs about "modernity" and the elements contained in or implied by that term were typically imported by colonial governments and reinforced by the elite Asian actors they empowered. This led to an often-anomalous situation. In Europe, the idea of modernity was the product of protracted historical developments from the time of the Enlightenment to the twentieth century, but in Asia it was superimposed (or "transplanted") almost instantaneously on societies with quite different histories and cultures. As a result, phenomena that were thought to represent "modernity" – including the concept of modern law – were deployed by Asian actors in distinctive and often counterintuitive ways. The ideas and institutions of modernity could be experienced by Asian people both as culturally alien and – at the same time – as essential to achieving justice and protecting rights. As we shall see, these same ambiguities and paradoxes surrounding the concept of modernity can be found even in a country such as Thailand, which never experienced colonization by a European power.

As an extension of colonialism and modernity, a second theme runs through virtually every chapter of this Reader: *legal and political transformations*. Before the colonial era, and certainly after it came to an end, Asian states experienced tumultuous changes that had a profound importance for law. Whether triggered by war, by revolution, by economic change, or by globalization, these transformations altered the political and economic systems of Asian countries and the behavior and beliefs of their citizenry. Change is, of course, a constant in all human existence, but the transformations that have occurred in many Asian countries are radical, far-reaching, and frequent, and their relationship to law has been complex. For example, some Asian governments, both national and local, use law as an instrument to promote economic growth; and, in turn, economic booms and busts influence the progress and results of legal developments. Moreover, legal changes often have symbiotic yet conflictual relationships with changes in civil society. Social reforms and advances may, for example, trigger the rise of legal activity in the form of

# Introduction

public interest law, legal aid, and legal mobilization for social causes such as gender and marriage equality. Yet, even as social transformations foster the growth of progressive legal activism, Asian legal systems may also impose conservative structural and discursive constraints on social change, including limitations on civil society's ability to fight for social justice and political freedoms.

A third theme running through all the chapters of this Reader involves the twin concepts of hierarchy and power. *Inequality* is, of course, a mainstay of law and society research elsewhere in the world, but in Asia it takes on a distinctive and extremely important role. Most obvious, perhaps, is scholarship about the caste system in India, in which inequality was institutionalized as a central element in all legal arrangements (Dumont 1980; Derrett 1999) and was subsequently redressed by law (Galanter 1984). Even in Asian countries where the caste system did not exist, however, law became intertwined with officially recognized social hierarchies (e.g., Rabibhadana 1969) and with rigid distinctions in social class. Subsequently, when laws were enacted to oppose rather than to support inequality, the covert role of social hierarchy in the "living law" remained strong enough to attract the attention of law and society scholars in most Asian societies. The asymmetrical distributions of status imply as well an extreme inequality in power. Law and society scholars who study Asian countries almost invariably focus on inequities in status and wealth that work to the advantage of some social actors and the distinct disadvantage of others. We should add that status hierarchies in contemporary Asia can take many forms, even in societies that are self-identified as "democratic" or "socialist," where party affiliation or other social advantages can confer enormous power.

A fourth theme is that of *rights*. As a tool to resist injustice, to equalize power imbalances, and to assert individual autonomy, modern law – at least in theory – offers all citizens recourse to rights. Some of the most striking instances of legal mobilization in contemporary Asia involve individuals and groups invoking their rights to free themselves from oppressive circumstances and to transform society. Yet rights remain a controversial subject in Asian contexts. Some have claimed that the very idea of rights is alien to Asian cultures, where relationships and harmony are prized above individual self-realization. They find no analogues for the concept of rights in traditional Asian laws and cultures. In response, rights advocates have noted that anti-rights claims in Asia are typically voiced by entrenched elites or opponents of democracy, whose privileged positions are threatened by internationally sanctioned rights regimes. Others argue that local discourses share ideals and values similar to expressions of rights found in modern constitutional law or international human rights. Law and society scholars have explored rights, not necessarily by starting from a particular position in this normative debate, but by posing empirical questions about how people in Asian societies think about the individual, the family, the social group, and the state, and how they choose to use or avoid the law when confronted with situations they consider unjust. What does the concept of rights mean to ordinary people, and what variations or equivalent ideas do they express? How are their rights seen to be violated, in some instances, and vindicated in others? Some of the researchers' most striking findings reveal novel and creative strategies that transcend the simplistic rights/anti-rights binary.

A fifth set of crosscutting themes can be designated collectively as *identities*. Most law and society research assumes that the ways in which personhood is constructed – both in law and in culture – shape the conduct of legal actors in every possible situation. Law and society researchers have, for example, closely examined the construction of gender identities in Asia. Traditionally, the rights and interests of men have been favored within the official legal systems of Asia, but patriarchal views have not necessarily dominated in all contexts. Unofficial customary legal arrangements, for example, especially those involving animist belief systems, sometimes confer special powers on women, although the reverse is also very often the case. Recently, scholars have studied the legal experiences and consciousness of transgender persons, not only in the context of current policy debates but also in centuries-old customary practices. Identities based on sexuality have also received a great deal of attention from Asian law and society researchers. The influence of European colonial law appears to have brought greater intolerance of same-sex relationships, and scholars have studied growing resistance to this type of intolerance even as they attempt to reconstruct precolonial belief systems about human sexuality. Other forms of identity construction have also attracted the attention of law and society scholars. Researchers have, for example, explored ethnicity and race as factors that shape official and unofficial legal behavior and conflict. Urban versus rural identities have also proved extremely important in law and society scholarship on Asia. As we have seen, some of the pioneering Asian law and society studies took place in rural settings, based perhaps on the questionable assumption that there the researchers would find stronger evidence of tradition and cultural "authenticity." Whether true or not, this assumption is implicit in many of the readings this book presents.

Having described five sets of crosscutting themes that run through the entire book, we turn now to the nine substantive chapters that follow this introduction. They represent what we consider the predominant interests of law and society scholars working in Asia. In each chapter, we provide a representative selection of readings that clarify the nature and origins of the topic and the different approaches scholars have taken as they explore it. Our aim is not only to familiarize the reader with these different areas of research but also to highlight some of the best and most interesting work being done in the field – and to inspire additional research that might build on what has been accomplished thus far. Because our readers will probably have particular interests in certain countries or regions of Asia, we have made every attempt to offer selections addressing a number of different Asian countries in each chapter.

**Chapter 1: Religion.** This chapter contains readings on Hinduism, Buddhism, Islam, Confucianism, Taoism, and localized so-called "animist" religions based on spirits and nature. Although in premodern legal systems, law and religion were virtually indistinguishable, "modernity" required a separation of the two concepts. The readings address the arrival of European-style legal systems, often (but not always) imposed by colonial authorities, which carried with them some version of the principle of "secularism." In fact, secularism took on many different forms in Asian societies, each marking out a distinctive role for law, in some instances to police the separation of law and religion and, in other instances, to ensure that a particular religion retained a preferred place in society. The chapter concludes with readings about modern interactions between law and religion in three very different societies – Singapore, Sri Lanka, and Japan.

**Chapter 2: Legal Pluralism.** Although legal pluralism can be found in every society, it has been studied with particular intensity in Asia. Legal pluralism studies of Asian law and society are of three types. Some law and society scholars rely on the concept of legal pluralism to theorize official law in relation to various other legal orders operating in the same space. Legal pluralism provides them with a means to describe each of the multiple systems of law and to consider the ways in which they interact with one another. Other law and society scholars, adopting a more state-centric perspective, have studied how different Asian governments address the plurality of legal orders familiar to different population groups or different sectors of social life – such as the family, land and property, labor and employment, or religious affairs. They show how Asian states – colonial and postcolonial – use legal pluralism to legitimate and extend their power over Asia's diverse peoples. For a third group of law and society scholars, legal pluralism provides a framework for their "bottom up" research on law in everyday life. They show how individuals pick and choose among various legal orders as they deal with disputes, family matters, economic and social exchanges, claims to land and water, and other matters. The readings in this chapter illustrate all three of these approaches to the topic of legal pluralism in Asia.

**Chapter 3: Disputing.** The study of disputing and dispute resolution has been one of the central concerns of law and society scholars for the past fifty years. Rather than focusing narrowly on cases that have been litigated in state courts, law and society scholars broadened their perspective beyond state-sanctioned dispute resolution to include the handling of conflict in countless fora throughout society, ranging from neighborhood councils to consumer complaint boards to the interventions of shamans and village leaders. Law and society researchers working in Asian settings have been no exception. Some of the earlier studies were village-based, highlighting the largely conciliatory practices of dispute mediators who sought to maintain harmony within their community by promoting apology, restitution, and spiritual well-being. Recent studies in Asian societies examine the relationship between litigation and nonjudicial dispute resolution, highlighting the ways in which courts and judges are influenced by the handling of conflict outside the ambit of state law. A third type of law and society research illustrated by this chapter involves ADR – the attempt by the state to divert litigated cases to "alternative dispute resolution" procedures established as adjuncts to the formal system itself. Although ADR is sometimes touted as a restoration of traditional community mediation, law and society researchers have generally demonstrated that its close connection to the official legal system raises complex issues of justice and the protection of rights by persons who lack sufficient wealth or power to succeed within the formal judicial arenas.

**Chapter 4: Legal Consciousness.** Legal consciousness refers to the ways in which people think and act in relation to law, including situations in which they view law as relevant and useful and those in which they reject law or never consider it at all. Some of the earliest law and society research in Asia – in Japan, Korea, and Indonesia, for example – attempted to explore the phenomenon of legal consciousness at the national level. Typically, such research depicted Asians as law-averse and non-litigious, but subsequently those characterizations were challenged and revised by scholars who proposed more complex explanations for the infrequency of litigation in some Asian societies. The readings in this chapter follow the evolution in legal consciousness research, from efforts to identify national traits to studies that examine the interaction of globalization and customary practices to produce unique forms of consciousness within different social groupings. The readings also explore the ways in which official definitions of rights are refracted through the lens of legal consciousness. The chapter concludes with a look at recent law and society studies that take a less individualistic approach to rights and emphasize instead the relational dimensions of legal consciousness.

**Chapter 5: Legal Mobilization.** Legal mobilization refers to the use of law to express claims and desires in order to achieve change or protect interests. It can be carried out by individuals or by a group of people acting collectively. Importantly, legal mobilization encompasses more than going to court to litigate disputes, an action that may prove ineffective or even irrelevant in some Asian contexts. In addition to litigation, legal mobilization occurs in other ways, even when an individual or group merely articulates a problem to a confidante in terms of rights or other legal concepts. In Asia, this broader concept of legal mobilization is especially apropos, since so much "legal" activity – broadly construed – takes place far from the justice institutions the state has established. In this chapter, the readings illustrate the range of tactics used by those who mobilize the law to achieve their goals. They also illustrate both the risks and the rewards associated with the invocation of legal rights in Asian societies. As the authors make clear, rights can have paradoxical effects, and can simultaneously empower and disempower or stigmatize those who use them. In some instances, however, the results are hugely beneficial to those who felt hopeless in the absence of legal protection.

**Chapter 6: Legal Professions.** The legal professions in Asia are a plural concept. Many Asian countries are civil law jurisdictions in which lawyers, judges, and prosecutors are separately licensed. Even in common law jurisdictions, lawyers rarely are a homogeneous professional group. In addition, there are many paralegal or unauthorized occupational groups that parallel the profession of lawyers. The meaning of being a "lawyer" in Asia, therefore, is often more complex and controversial than in the North American or European contexts. The vastly different types of legal professions across Asia range from barristers and solicitors in Hong Kong and unified legal professions in India, Pakistan, Malaysia, Singapore, and other former British colonies, to Continental-style judges and prosecutors in Japan, Korea, and Taiwan, to Soviet-style "iron triangles" of police, procurators, and judges in China and Central Asia, and to the vast number of unlicensed "barefoot" lawyers across the continent. This chapter provides an overview of the plurality of legal professions in different Asian countries and their demographic and sociological characteristics. It goes on to highlight the market for legal services, demonstrating not only the connections between lawyers and different kinds of clients and practice areas, but also the interactions between the legal professions, the judicial system, and the state. The chapter concludes with a few readings on the role of lawyers in transforming the state – and the impact of state transformations on the lawyers themselves.

**Chapter 7: Courts.** This chapter examines courts in Asia as cultural symbols, social organizations, and political battlegrounds. As cultural symbols, courts are often embedded in religions, colonial legacies, and local norms. These cultural symbols are found in both informal tribunals and more institutionalized religious and secular courts. As social organizations, courts are intertwined with bureaucratic hierarchies, political influences, and the career trajectories of judges. This is particularly salient in civil law jurisdictions across Asia. As political battlegrounds, courts provide a space for the judicialization of politics as well as a soil for judicial corruption. The readings also examine the complexity of judicial decision-making in different national contexts. In addition, the readings highlight the nature and impact of judicial reforms, which take place amidst broader political and social changes in both democratic and authoritarian contexts and can lead to tensions as well as encourage new alliances.

**Chapter 8: Crime and Justice.** The criminal justice system constitutes a major component of the legal system in every country. Unlike criminology, law and society research does not seek to calculate crime rates or identify causes of crime but instead focuses on how criminal justice interacts with other elements of law and society, such as lawmaking, human rights, violence, and the rule of law. Furthermore, law and society scholars consider justice a culturally sensitive concept, something socially constructed and politically embedded. As lawyers have been discussed in detail in earlier chapters, this chapter highlights the role of the police, prosecutors, and judges in the criminal process and examines the domestic and transnational forces that shape criminal justice reforms across Asia. The chapter also emphasizes the administration of criminal justice in everyday policing, including violence, torture, and other forms of power abuse affecting marginalized groups such as women, the poor, indigenous peoples, and ethnic and religious minorities. It further interrogates the cultural meanings and everyday manifestations of justice in criminal trials and other coercive systems of social control in different Asian countries.

**Chapter 9: Practicing Law and Society Scholarship in Asia.** This final chapter contains readings that illustrate how law and society scholars have conducted or drawn on empirical research to pursue questions and build theory about law in Asian societies. It is, however, not a guide for pursuing various research methods or a manual for asking and answering research questions. Rather, the purpose of this chapter is to provide useful examples of how Asian law and society scholars go about their work, what challenges they encounter, and how they address them. It features both classic research methods and new and innovative approaches. One set of readings illustrates

# Introduction

how researchers have obtained access to their subjects and how they have collected data. A second set of readings shows how researchers have wrestled with aspects of their own identities in relation to the research site and the people whom they study. Do they position themselves as insiders, outsiders, or some other type of figure? A third set of readings illustrates law and society researchers practicing their craft in the digital age, using social media and other advancements in communication technologies to pursue their research questions. All three sets of readings are drawn from studies that appear in Chapters 1 through 8. In this way, readers will be able to peek behind the curtain, so to speak, and gain a better understanding of how the authors featured in this book struggled with the challenges faced by all researchers – and how they successfully overcame them.

## REFERENCES

von Benda-Beckmann, Keebet and Bertram Turner. 2018. "Legal Pluralism, Social Theory, and the State." *Journal of Legal Pluralism and Unofficial Law* 50 (3): 255–74. doi:10.1080/07329113.2018.1532674

Chu, Tung-Tsu. 1965. *Law and Society in Traditional China*, 2nd ed. Paris: Mouton. doi: 10.2307/2050688

Derrett, J. Duncan M. 1999. *Religion, Law, and the State in India*. New York: Oxford University Press. doi: 10.1093/iclqaj/13.1.371

Diamond, Shari Seidman. 2019. "Empirical Legal Scholarship: Observations on Moving Forward." *Northwestern University Law Review* 113: 1229–41.

Dumont, Louis. 1980. *Homo Hierarchicus: The Caste System and Its Implications*. Chicago: University of Chicago.

Ehrlich, Eugen. 1936. *Fundamental Principles of the Sociology of Law*. Cambridge, MA: Harvard University Press. doi: 10.4324/9780203791127

Galanter, Marc. 1984. *Competing Equalities: Law and the Backward Classes in India*. Berkeley: University of California Press. doi: 10.1093/iclqaj/34.3.658

Liu, Sida and Zhizhou Wang. 2015. "The Fall and Rise of Law and Social Science in China." *Annual Review of Law and Social Science* 11: 373–94. doi: 10.1146/annurev-lawsocsci-120814-121329

Mather, Lynn. 2008. "Law and Society." In *The Oxford Handbook of Law and Politics*, edited by Gregory Caldeira, Daniel Keleman, and Keith Whittington, chapter 39. New York: Oxford University Press. doi: 10.1093/oxfordhb/9780199208425.003.0039 [Reprinted in Robert E. Goodin, ed., *The Oxford Handbook of Political Science*. New York: Oxford University Press (2009). doi: 10.1093/oxfordhb/9780199208425.001.0001].

Murayama, Masayuki. 2013. "Kawashima and the Changing Focus on Japanese Legal Consciousness: A Selective History of the Sociology of Law in Japan." *International Journal of Law in Context* 9 (4): 565–89. doi: 10.1017/s174455231300030x

Pound, Roscoe. 1910. "Law in Books and Law in Action." *American Law Review* 44: 12–36.

Rabibhadana, Akin. 1969. *The Organization of Thai Society in the Early Bangkok Period, 1782–1873*. Ithaca, NY: Southeast Asia Program, Cornell University.

Srinivas, M. N. 1987. "Development of Sociology in India: An Overview." *Economic and Political Weekly* 22 (4): 135–8.

**Suggested Readings**

Calavita, Kitty. 2010. *Invitation to Law & Society: An Introduction to the Study of Real Law*. Chicago: University of Chicago Press. doi: 10.7208/chicago/9780226089980.001.0001

Chua, Lynette J. and David M. Engel. 2015. "State and Personhood in Southeast Asia: The Promise and Potential for Law and Society Research." *Asian Journal of Law and Society* 2 (2): 211–28. doi: 10.1017/als.2015.10

Friedman, Lawrence M., Rogelio Pérez-Perdomo, and Manuel A. Gómez, eds. 2011. *Law in Many Societies: A Reader*. Stanford, CA: Stanford University Press. doi: 10.1017/s0020589312000383

Munger, Frank. 1998. "Mapping Law and Society." In *Crossing Boundaries: Traditions and Transformations in Law and Society Research*, edited by Austin Sarat, Marianne Constable, David Engel, Valerie Hans, and Susan Lawrence, 21–80. Evanston, IL: Northwestern University Press.

Sarat, Austin and Thomas R. Kearns. 1993. "Beyond the Great Divide: Forms of Legal Scholarship and Everyday Life." In *Law in Everyday Life*, edited by Austin Sarat and Thomas R. Kearns, 21–61. Ann Arbor: The University of Michigan Press. doi: 10.3998/mpub.23345

Valverde, Mariana, Kamari Clarke, Eve Darian-Smith, and Prabha Kotiswaran, eds. 2021. *The Routledge Handbook of Law and Society*. London and New York: Routledge. doi:10.4324/9780429293306

# 1 Religion

## Contents

| | | |
|---|---|---|
| I | Legal Dimensions of the Classical Asian Religious Traditions | 20 |
| II | Law in the Landscape of Sacred Practices | 34 |
| III | The Arrival of "Modern" Law and the Concept of Secularism | 43 |
| IV | Law, Religion, and Conflict in Contemporary Asia | 59 |

Asia is home to four of the five great world religions – Hinduism, Buddhism, Islam, and Christianity[*] – along with other classical philosophical and belief systems such as Confucianism and Taoism, as well as countless smaller, localized, and largely unwritten religious traditions. To understand Asian law in its social and cultural context, it is essential to ask how religious and/ or philosophical practices and beliefs influence legal activities and institutions and shared concepts of justice. Indeed, it is impossible to consider any aspect of Asian societies without reference to the religious and philosophical substrata that extend back through the millennia and remain extraordinarily important today among the peoples and nations of Asia.

This chapter focuses primarily on law and religion in Asia. But to speak of law and religion is somewhat misleading, since it implies that they are distinct from one another and that the task of sociolegal scholars is to examine the ways in which they interact. If religion is positioned outside of law and legal institutions, then it would seem that the task confronting researchers is to determine when and how religion may affect legal practices or values or, conversely, how law may affect religious organizations, beliefs, or activities. As we shall see, however, the notion that law and religion are separable or even distinguishable from one another made little sense within the historical

---

[*] The prevalence in Asia of the fifth world religion, Judaism, is considerably smaller.

traditions we shall consider. It is only in recent years that the separability of law and religion in Asia has even been thinkable, and one might argue that the imagined separation has never been achieved in practice. In the classical religions themselves, partitioning the legal from the sacred was never a central concern. It would be more accurate to speak of law *in* religion or even religion *as* law. As Clifford Geertz (1983) famously observed, both law and religion are ways of "imagining the real," and for most of the history of Asia, the two imaginings were one and the same.

We begin with an overview of premodern Asian religious traditions in order to gain an understanding of their legal dimensions, particularly in the period before Western law arrived in Asia. The readings that follow address Hinduism, Buddhism, Confucianism, Taoism, and Islam. Christianity played an important role in some Asian societies much later than the other world religions, and its history is entangled in the story of European imperialism, a topic that will receive attention in the later chapters of this book. For that reason, we do not include a separate reading on Christianity in this chapter. We should also point out that some scholars would disagree with our decision to include Confucianism and Taoism alongside Hinduism, Buddhism, and Islam. They might argue that Confucianism should not be considered a "religion" and that Taoism has little importance for the study of law in society. Other scholars, however, question both of these assumptions, and we leave it to readers to decide this matter for themselves. Our position is that both Confucianism and Taoism played a historical role in establishing fundamental understandings of justice, social order, individual obligation, and political legitimacy in China and other Asian societies. In that sense, they were at least functionally analogous to Hinduism, Buddhism, and Islam.

## I LEGAL DIMENSIONS OF THE CLASSICAL ASIAN RELIGIOUS TRADITIONS

### 1.1 Hinduism as a Legal Tradition, *Donald R. Davis Jr.*

In this article, Donald R. Davis Jr. contends that law is central to a proper understanding of Hinduism. Classical Hindu texts, known as *dharmaśāstras*, are not narrowly concerned with matters of individual piety or salvation or with supernatural beings; they also provide fundamental statements of social obligations, offenses, penances, statuses, and procedures for addressing wrongdoing and resolving conflict. "Law" as it appears in the *dharmaśāstras* is inextricably connected with a broader cosmology – a theory of the origin and structure of the universe and of human existence. Law in this sense goes far beyond the narrow categories of statutes and case law, crimes and punishments, injuries and contracts that are assumed to be its primary concerns in the modern state. Moreover, law in the Hindu tradition is a core component of religious practice and belief, not a distinct aspect of the *dharma* (a central concept of Hinduism, which Davis explicates in his article). The relationship between law and dharma, according to Davis, is not that of a slice in relation to the entire pie but rather that of the layer of pastry that is present in every slice. Davis makes the broader claim that scholars of Hinduism, unlike scholars of Islam, have failed to recognize the centrality of law to the overall theological framework. In his words, "Dharma as law stands at the center of Hindu ethical discussions and, thus, becomes central to an understanding of Hindu religious life." A true understanding of Hinduism, according to Davis, is impossible without a full recognition of its legal component.

> Hindu theologies are pervaded by legal rules, legal categories, and legal reasoning. A gigantic textual corpus and scholastic tradition – the Dharmaśāstras – are devoted to Hindu religious and legal duties. An increasing number of studies have appeared that describe the aspects of practical law among Hindu communities in several periods of Indic history. And yet, the idea of law figures, if at all, only at the remotest margins of Hindu studies as a field. The question is: what would happen if law became a category through which to think about Hinduism? [...]
>
> An intractable terminological problem must be addressed at the outset before I can speak of law in Hinduism. On the one hand, in the most familiar sense of law today, law refers to courts, contracts, and crime and punishment, especially as administered by a state; "the law" means legislation in the form of codes. The problem with this sense of law is that it is hopelessly exceptional, limited historically to recent centuries and geographically by and large to European countries and their current or former colonies. Many have ignored or are unaware that thinking of law as a system of rules backed by the sanctions of a nation-state is neither a widespread nor a very old way of conceiving law. In particular, the last part of the common definition, the notion that law must be administered by a state, especially a nation-state, is the most problematic, and I will ask readers to hold in abeyance the expectation that law must be administered by a state. It seems useful, however, to work with the basic conventional understanding of law both as a heuristic and in order to avoid any accusation of playing word-games. For that reason, I initially understand law in this essay to mean: a socially determined set of rules enforced by authoritative sanctions. On the other hand, law has regularly been used as a suitable, if incomplete, translation for the category of dharma, especially in

Dharmaśāstra contexts. In this view, understanding dharma as law necessitates an expansion of the familiar sense of law to include a wider variety of binding rules that would reach into the realms of religion and, to a lesser extent, morality. Dharma in Dharmaśāstra encompasses the prescriptions for, the acts of, and the effects of ritual, purification, diet, statecraft, and penance in addition to rules for legal procedure, contracts, property, corporations and partnerships, inheritance, marriage, and crimes of various sorts. However, no distinctions are made between these rules and acts that would correspond to a distinction of law and religion – they are the same; they are *dharma*. [...]

A series of shared features between *dharma* and law in the popular sense of a socially determined set of rules enforced by authoritative sanctions shows the close affiliation, though certainly not complete overlap, of the two concepts. A relationship of connection and semantic concomitance exists between dharma and law, and not merely a relationship of encompassment, in which dharma equals law plus religion plus morality, each of the subcategories isolatable from the other. By way of analogy, if we imagine *dharma* as a pie, law is less like a piece of the pie, distinct and separable from the other parts, and more like a layer of the pie, say the crust, present in every piece, but not fully representative of the whole. In this way, law is not merely an isolatable subset of *dharma* in Dharmaśāstra, but rather an integral and essential part of all *dharma*, even when part of the point of invoking dharma is to remake it along new theological lines. [...]

[D]harma and law are both expressed in the form of empirically ascertainable rules (*vidhi*, *codanā*) that are the "cause of knowing" *dharma* (*jñāpakahetu*). [...] Neither *dharma* nor law is morally intuited, but rather discerned through an investigation of empirical sources. These rules are concerned in the first place with the means and manner of legal acts (*karaṇatva*, *itikartavyatā*) that is, with specifying what differentiates ordinary acts from legal ones – mere *karma* from *dharma*. Legal acts in this sense are the "means for effecting" *dharma* (*kārakahetu*). The concern for correct or proper procedure also takes into account the inevitability of mistakes, intentional or not, that might nullify a mortgage, unfairly distribute an inheritance, or make an ancestral rite ineffective. Dharma in Dharmaśāstra provides for both punishments (*daṇḍa*) and penances (*prāyaścitta*) that ameliorate or rectify legal mistakes or transgressions. Punishment and penance, although conceptually distinct, nevertheless overlap in, for example, descriptions of thieves begging rulers for punishment (as a form of penance) or judges declaring both a punishment and a penance for adultery.

Finally, *dharma* and law both share a concern to address and eliminate doubts and disputes about what rule governs a particular situation or how to adjudicate conflicts over differing claims to be right or just. This technically comes under the heading of legal procedure (*vyavahāra*) but is also called "the cause of making judgments in cases of doubt" about dharma (*saṃdehanirṇayahetu*). Doubts and disputes over dharma are expected and normal in Dharmaśāstra, even as techniques and rules are provided for almost any possible contingency or situation. [...]

Unfortunately, the legal side of Hindu *dharma* has been lost for two reasons. First, Dharmaśāstra was improperly understood by the British as the law of the land and administered to "Hindus" as such in colonial India. This move had disastrous consequences in that Dharmaśāstra came to be seen for a long time as black-letter law and little else. Here, the legal side of dharma has ironically been lost precisely because the artificial colonial focus on Dharmaśāstra as legal codes could not be sustained in the light of either further investigation of the texts themselves or in the practical context of British colonial courts, both of which demonstrated that Dharmaśāstra was not a promulgated legal code. Second, reactions against this misconception of Dharmaśāstra, although fully necessary and appropriate at the time, have inhibited and marginalized inquiry into the Dharmaśāstra, especially its legal side, now seen as merely a British concoction [...]. Here, the legal side of dharma has been lost due to a false perception that Dharmaśāstra has little or no connection to reality.

## 1.2 Introducing Buddhism and Law, *Rebecca Redwood French and Mark A. Nathan*

In the following reading about Buddhism and law by Rebecca Redwood French and Mark A. Nathan, the role of dharma is central, just as it was in Davis's account of Hinduism and law. In the case of Buddhism, however, the study of dharma is largely associated with the teachings of one historical figure, Siddhārtha Gautama, rather than the pantheon of sacred beings who feature prominently in Hinduism. Concepts of law and justice in Buddhism are embedded in the transformative insight the Buddha himself achieved concerning "causality and karma, impermanence and the absence of self, suffering and liberation." Law is also reflected in the distinctive Buddhist conception of the righteous ruler, the *cakravartin*, or "wheel-turning" king, who protects the dharma and derives his legitimacy from righteousness rather than supernatural power and authority. A further distinctive aspect of

Buddhism and law is the Vinaya tradition, a set of rules established by the Buddha for the monastic community, with significant implications for the practices and obligations of lay followers.

*The Life of the Buddha*
Siddhārtha Gautama was born the son of a ruler in an area that is now southern Nepal and, according to the tradition, was raised in a life of princely luxury. Although the dates of his life are uncertain, a majority of scholars place his birth in the sixth century BCE. As it was foretold that his son was destined to become either a great king or a great religious teacher, it is said that Siddhārtha's father shielded him from any painful elements of life that might lead him along the latter path. However, the sacred biographies say that the prince eventually became curious about the world outside the walls of the palace and, leaving behind his wife and newborn child, studied under a number of teachers and experimented with different forms of ascetic practice that were common in India at the time, including some extreme austerities. Finding none of these methods efficacious, he finally sat down beneath a *pīpal* tree and determined not to move from the spot until he had achieved his goal. In the course of one evening, the canonical texts say he progressed through successive stages of meditative insight before arriving at a perfect understanding of the way things truly are, rather than how they might appear to the unenlightened – that is, an understanding of causality and karma, impermanence and the absence of self, suffering and liberation. The Buddha's awakening that night and his subsequent teachings and discourses based on that experience are both referred to as dharma.

The Buddha's teaching career began a few weeks after that event, we are told, and lasted some forty-five years. Over the course of that time, many people gathered around Śākyamuni, an honorific title meaning "the sage of the Śākyas," and the teachings called "turning the wheel of law" have continued to attract followers for 2,500 years. His first disciples were his five fellow ascetic practitioners. Significantly for the development of Buddhism as a religion [...] among those who became followers of the Buddha during his lifetime and thereafter, some left home to join the *saṅgha* (or *saṃgha*), while others remained householders and provided support for those who had "gone forth" into the religious life. At times the word *saṅgha* is used more inclusively to encompass both groups, but most often it refers to a community or an assembly of monks or nuns who, upon full ordination, take a vow to uphold the precepts and rules contained in the Buddhist law codes, which are called Vinaya. The basic dynamic at the heart of the link between the *saṅgha* and lay society has long been recognized as a type of reciprocal relationship. Laypeople earn karmic "merit" for themselves or loved ones by donating food, land, or other necessities and gifts to the *saṅgha*, while the monks and nuns serve as teachers of dharma and "fields of merit," especially through their observance of the *Vinaya*. [...]

*Dharma as Law*
The word *dharma* has a broad range of meanings in the wider Indian social, religious, political, and legal discourses. It can signify the natural order of the universe and society as well as one's duty or ritual obligations within that order. The nineteenth-century founders of Buddhist studies in Europe, notably Eugène Burnouf and Brian Hodgson, recognized that the word dharma had multiple meanings and was difficult to translate, but they considered "law" an acceptable or even preferred translation. [...] [A]s Frank Reynolds points out, "'Law' when it was used as a translation for Dharma, was used with cosmic, philosophical, and/or ethical connotations that were never associated – in any really intrinsic or crucial way – with legal systems or codes." [...]

One attribute shared by dharma and law may be universality. The law of cause and effect and other central doctrines described as the Buddha's dharma can be applied to all people and all sentient beings, for that matter – at all times. The conditioned nature of all things holds true no matter what a person's station in life or what beliefs that person may hold. Moreover, dharma also possesses a prescriptive aspect in addition to its descriptive component. [...] In other words, the Buddha did not simply describe reality as seen from his enlightened vantage point; he also laid down a number of principles for correct moral and ethical conduct based on his perfect insight and profound wisdom. [...]

One final way in which dharma enters this discussion of Buddhist law is through Buddhist textual references to a *cakravartin*, a "wheel-turning" king, the Buddhist image of an ideal ruler. [...] Like so many other central concepts in Buddhism, this notion of a "wheel-turning" king was common to Brahmanism and Jainism too, but in Buddhist teachings, Gethin tells us, "where *cakravartin* kings are described as conquering and ruling the whole earth not by violence or by the sword, but by righteousness (*dharma*), the wheel has also the connotation of 'the wheel of truth' (*dharma-cakra*)."[1]

---

[1] Rupert Gethin (2014), "Keeping the Buddha's Rules: The View from the Sūtra Piṭaka," in *Buddhism and Law: An Introduction*, edited by Rebecca Redwood French and Mark A. Nathan, 63–77 at 71 (New York: Cambridge University Press). [Editors' note]

In numerous places throughout the Buddhist scriptures, the Buddha is depicted as interacting with contemporary kings, instructing them in dharma and sometimes giving them advice. Although the texts clearly contain scattered views on kingship grounded in Buddhist ethics and virtue, Gethin cautions against reading a Buddhist form of constitutional law into them, as some have done, and concludes that at a minimum, discussions of kingship and the ideal of a cakravartin "have been used by Buddhists to reflect on how a king should behave."

*Buddhist Monasticism*
The relationship between those who leave home to become ordained monks and nuns and those who remain lay householders is central to an understanding of Buddhism as it spread throughout much of Asia. The establishment of a functioning and viable monastic community, which inevitably involved the establishment of monasteries and eventually the adoption of a monastic code to regulate the community, was an indispensable part of the transmission of Buddhism into new regions of Asia. This basic distinction is also important for any consideration of Buddhism and Law for two closely connected reasons. The first relates to persistent presumptions about the degree of distance separating these two groups of Buddhist practitioners, while the second concerns the set of rules or precepts that function as a Buddhist law code for individual monks and nuns and for the *saṅgha* as a communal body or organization.

Although the monastic ideal within Buddhism, as portrayed in some canonical sources) was peripatetic, solitary, and austere, echoing perhaps the paradigmatic story of the Buddha leading up to his awakening, a more sedentary lifestyle clearly became the norm early in the history of the *saṅgha* involving tight-knit communities of settled religious practitioners. These monasteries in time grew to become quite large and complex institutions, as the example of the famous monastery and university at Nalanda located in the present-day Indian State of Bihar shows. [...]

One reason for the perceived disjuncture between *saṅgha* and society was the false assumption that Buddhist monasticism is marked by otherworldliness and the complete separation from society. The biases that Western observers and generations of Buddhist scholars brought to bear on their conception of Buddhist monasticism, which was almost invariably compared to Christian forms of monasticism, certainly played a role. This has begun to change, however, in the last few decades. Changes in our understanding of Buddhist monasticism were spurred by two important trends in Buddhist studies in recent decades. First, there was a turn away from the normative descriptions found in Buddhist scriptural texts and more focus on the lived tradition as it is practiced in Buddhist monasteries and temples throughout Asia. Many of the preconceptions concerning Buddhist monasticism have come under scrutiny from the 1970s as more anthropologists began to conduct field studies of Buddhist communities in Asia. There is now a greater awareness and sensitivity to the institutional realities of life in a Buddhist monastery, and less criticism of deviations or devolutions from the ideal religious life described in the *sūtras*.

The second trend that has begun to reshape our understanding of Buddhist monasticism is the increased scholarly attention being given to *Vinaya* materials. The *Vinaya* is a set of canonical law texts containing rules, descriptions, case studies, definitions and punishments, and some ancillary material that was used to regulate the *saṅgha*. The more scholars scrutinize the contents of the *Vinaya*, the more shibboleths previously held by Buddhist Studies scholars concerning the nature of Buddhist monasticism have faltered. [...]

Vinaya *as Law*
The *Vinaya* comprises one-third of the Buddhist canon and is the first of the three "baskets" (*pitika*) to appear, followed by the discourses of the Buddha (Sūtra Pitika) and scholastic treatises or commentarial literature – the "further dharma" (Abhidharma Pitika). The use of the word *Vinaya* in singular form is quite common, especially when referring to it as part of a singular Buddhist canon, but this usage is merely conventional because, just as there are multiple canons, nearly a dozen *Vinayas* existed at one time. Six of these *Vinayas* have been preserved in a more or less complete form to the present day, and several more have survived only in fragments. Of the six that are extant, three are still in use today by monastic communities in Asia, and for simplicity they can be identified by the language of the Buddhist canon in which they are found: Pāli, Chinese, and Tibetan.

The core of the *Vinaya* lays out rules for monks and nuns to uphold individually and for the order to follow collectively. The tradition credits the Buddha himself with the creation of these rules on a case-by-case basis, but we may never know which (if any) of the rules can actually be traced to the time of the Buddha. The extant *Vinayas* almost certainly went through a sustained period of development before arriving in the written form that we have them today. [...] [I]n every *Vinaya* scholars have examined, the Buddha is depicted as the lawgiver. After hearing accounts from others and thoroughly investigating the "causes and conditions" surrounding a suspected transgression or moral lapse on the part of monks and nuns, the Buddha decided on cases as the highest spiritual and legal authority concerning what is good and true.

On that basis, he is said to have created a substantial body of law for the community of monks and nuns, making Buddhist law in this sense quite unique among the major world religions. A process of accommodation or adaptation to the legal, political, and social environments is plainly evident in the development of *Vinayas*, yet the existence of a complex law code gave the *saṅgha* sophisticated legal tools necessary to engage with lay society, political systems, and secular law wherever it became established.

All versions of the *Vinaya* have a similar structure. The material is divided into two main parts: the *Sūtravibhaṅga*, which contains the core list of rules called the *Prātimokṣa* that individual monks and nuns vow to uphold on full ordination; and the *Skandhaka*, which lays out the organizational procedures to be followed by the monastic community as a whole. The number of rules in the *Prātimokṣa* range from 219 to 371 depending on the school and gender of the practitioner. Women were initially excluded from joining the *saṅgha*, we are told, but after several years the Buddha reluctantly agreed to admit them. He did so, however, only after handing down a set of eight rules that appears to establish the subordination of nuns individually and collectively to their brethren, and additional requirements.

### 1.3 Taoism: The Enduring Tradition, Russell Kirkland

The influence of Confucianism and Taoism in China and throughout East and Southeast Asia can be compared to the foundational influence of Hinduism and Buddhism just discussed. It has long been assumed, however, that Confucianism should be regarded as a philosophy rather than a religion and that Taoism was more concerned with achieving an understanding of the natural order of things and practicing "nonaction" or even rejection of the political system rather than pursuit of law and social justice. Recent scholarship, however, has challenged all of these assumptions. In the following reading, Russell Kirkland contends that Taoism and Confucianism were closely linked, that both had attributes of what we might consider "religion," and that they were indeed concerned with matters of governance, political legitimacy, and the obligations of rulers and subjects.

Setting aside common oversimplifications, we can say that "Confucianism" is a useful label for a series of loosely interrelated cultural systems, of which some, but not all, were eventually exported to neighboring lands. One of them – two millennia old and still living – is a *liturgical* tradition in which Confucius is venerated as a divine being. At temples at Ch'ü-fu, and throughout China and the Chinese diaspora, priests pray and sing hymns to that divine being, who "existed before the sun and the moon." Of course, the Confucian intellectuals of the nineteenth and twentieth centuries were aware that Western intellectuals of that period would have no truck with such practices, so they taught Westerners that "Confucianism" was really just a humanistic value-system based upon the teachings of K'ung Ch'iu (Kong Qiu, 551–479 BCE), later known by some in China as K'ung-tzu (Kongzi). Thus stripped of its religious elements – priests, temples, prayers, hymns, and all other revoltingly "Catholic" phenomena – the sanitized construct of "Confucianism" offered to post-Enlightenment Westerners (and back to all later twentieth-century Chinese) was, as Max Weber assured us, not "a religion" at all, but merely a set of ethical and political teachings.

It is quite valid to identify many elements of Confucianism as "humanistic." But Confucian ideals were originally grounded in a belief that a man can fulfill the role of "the gentleman" (*chün-tzu*) and aid in restoring society's proper order by fulfilling the designs of *T'ien*. Since Westerners – and the Confucians who sought their approval – were threatened by the fact that Confucius and his followers based their prime values upon a belief in "God" – clearly the optimal translation of the term – the orthodox translation of *T'ien* became "Heaven," and to translate it otherwise remains sinological heresy even today. It is also sinological heresy to refute the Confucian denial that, for many hundreds of years, Confucian self-cultivation also included meditational practices that were in no important way different from those of the Ch'an (Zen) Buddhists from whom they had been learned. [...]

Confucius taught his followers to follow the correct and noble *tao*. And he also advocated that rulers should practice *wu-wei*, just like the *Tao te ching* and such "Legalists" as Shen Pu-hai.[1]

What most distinguished "classical Taoists" from others in early China was their interest in non-personalized spiritual realities, and in the transformative power of the person who has properly cultivated them. The Confucians' primary goal was to transform society by cultivating moral virtues and persuading rulers to do likewise. "Classical Taoists" were more focused on biospiritual cultivation, and sometimes suggested that such cultivation would transform the world. [...]

---

[1] *Wu-wei* is a practice of "non-action" or "non-doing" that places the individual – or the emperor – in alignment with the natural forces of the world. [Editors' note]

For hundreds of years, Taoist leaders served China's rulers as legitimatory aides, in a variety of distinct roles. A generation of scholars has now demonstrated that Taoism's leading representatives often took a keen interest in the prestige and power of the Chinese emperors, and that the emperors took an equally keen interest in them. As Anna Seidel observed:

> Awe for the Heaven-appointed monarch was at the foundation of Taoism – a religion which might even be characterized as a projection into the unseen world of the old imperial mythology .... By exalting the God Emperor, the Taoist priests were nurturing a potent myth – and this was nothing less than the force which held the vast Chinese empire together.[2]

The facts of history thus show that emperors' interest in Taoists over the centuries was not, as Confucian falsehoods have always told us, simply idiosyncrasy on the part of certain befuddled or gullible rulers. Rather, Taoism served a profound and deeply functional role within the political order, by providing generations of rulers with appropriate ceremonial and religious paradigms. [...]

In Chinese tradition – within Taoism, Confucianism, and the ritual and ideological traditions of the state itself – earthly authority and spiritual authority were regarded as, in essence, wholly identical. Modern Confucians seldom acknowledged that fact, and modern sinologues sometimes forgot that, into late imperial times, China's rulers and their subjects all shared the belief that all legitimate authority derives directly from *heavenly sources*. For centuries, Taoists and dynasts alike considered it to be Taoist masters' responsibility to assist the sovereign in managing his heavenly mandate. In medieval times, the emperor, the Taoist master, and the divine realities of Heaven were all seen as co-participants in the same process: unifying the world – "all under Heaven" – in a state of "Great Tranquility" (*t'ai-p'ing*). [...]

[B]y the third century BCE the entire political discourse of China – even under the Legalist regime of the state, and later dynasty, called Ch'in – had become filled with ideas that resonated with those of "the classical Taoists." The fact that the earliest commentary on the *Tao te ching* is found in the writings of the "Legalist" Han Fei suffices to show that no one in that age considered "Taoist ideas" to be "escapist," much less politically "subversive." And by the following century, the composers of the *Huai-nan-tzu* had developed a sophisticated model of government based on the well-accepted

---

[2] Anna Seidel (1983), "Imperial Treasures and Taoist Sacraments – Taoist Roots in the Apocrypha," in *Tantric and Taoist Studies*, 2, edited by Michel Strickmann, 291–371 at 370, 368 (Brussels: Institut Belge des Hautes Études Chinoises). [Editors' note]

idea that the only good ruler is a ruler who integrates his government with the forces of the cosmos. [...]

As Taoist religious movements arose in the second and third centuries, they struggled with the principal problem that had occupied Tung Chung-shu and later generations of Han-dynasty thinkers: What happens when historical events seem to show that current rulers are not in accord with the unseen forces of the cosmos? That problem was at the very heart of the *T'ai-p'ing ching*, and of Chang Tao-ling's T'ien-shih movement, just as it had been at the heart of the *Confucian* theories of Tung Chung-shu. For a while, at least, the T'ien-shih leadership appears to have lost hope that the Han ruling house still possessed the spiritual authority to govern the land. Confucians since the time of Mencius had insisted that only a worthy ruler can hold on to "Heaven's mandate" (*T'ien-ming*), and that an unworthy ruler, having lost that mandate, may not only legitimately be toppled, but truly deserves to be replaced. Such ideas, which Tung Chung-shu elaborated in great detail, were certainly not the ideas of anarchists, any more than they were ideas that arose among revolting peasants. And it was precisely from within that well-established framework of Confucian political thought – that the government *must* operate in accord with life's deeper realities – that "the Celestial Masters" arose.

Like everyone else in those days, the leaders of that movement held firmly to the belief that the ideal world-order required a wise and able monarch. But if the monarchy should falter – as it seemed to be faltering in the second century CE – the Celestial Masters, following the same principles that Mencius and Tung Chung-shu had enunciated, should seek to bring about a new political order, which would, unlike the faltering regime, show itself to be in full possession of Heaven's spiritual mandate. [...] Though students of modern China often associate Taoism with popular revolts, history shows that connections between Taoism and popular rebellion generally developed only when the reigning regime was demonstrably oppressive or ineffective. Whenever there seemed to be a worthy ruler, or even a plausible candidate for worthy ruler, Taoists of virtually every description seemed quite content to acknowledge the legitimacy of his authority.

### 1.4 The Notion of Shari'a, *Arskal Salim*

The role of law in Islam is frequently discussed though often misunderstood. In the following reading, Arskal Salim explains the distinction between *shari'a* and *fiqh*. Although *shari'a* is sometimes viewed as Islamic law, Salim suggests that this is an oversimplification. *Shari'a* comes from God via portions of the Qur'an, some of which are clearly legal in character (from a European perspective) while others are more properly understood as addressing broader "principal values" of Islam. *Shari'a* is revealed, immutable, and universally applicable. *Fiqh*, on the other hand, should be understood as Islamic jurisprudence, an effort by fallible humans to interpret and apply legal principles – including but not limited to those found in the *shari'a* – in specific circumstances. It is more similar to law in the European sense of the word. As Salim explains, Islamic legal codes in modern states may partially overlap with both *shari'a* and *fiqh*.

### The Notion of Shari'a

Many proponents of the formal implementation of shari'a characterize Islam as essentially a legal phenomenon. This has much to do with the fact that many modern Muslim scholars emphasize only the legal subject matter in defining the shari'a. No wonder then that the term shari'a is used interchangeably with 'Islamic law.' Yet this is not really accurate.

There is a variety in the degree of emphasis as to how much, and what kinds of, shari'a is legal. Many Muslim scholars have, on the one hand, held that shari'a means 'law' in its Western conception, though they are aware that the respective sources of shari'a and Western laws are different. As they see shari'a as identical to the Western concept of law, the formal application of shari'a in a modern nation-state, for them, is reasonable. However, there are also those who hold that the application of shari'a requires a state that is distinctly structured to be a legitimate working operative of Islamic law.

On the other hand, there are other Western scholars and a few reformist Muslims who are of the view that only certain parts of shari'a can appropriately be classified as law because shari'a is mixed with non-legal elements. This point of view asserts that in shari'a there exists all of religion, morality, and law, and that early Muslim scholars never distinguished between these.

Legal subject matter actually constitutes only a moderate part of the Qur'an, the primary source of shari'a. Of the more than six thousand verses of the Qur'an, there are only about five hundred that are definitely legal subject matter. They can be classified into five areas: (1) worship and rituals; (2) family matters; (3) trade and commerce; (4) crimes and punishments; and (5) government and international relations. However, according to Tahir Mahmood, these verses do not necessarily correspond with what in modern times is termed law. They "were supplemented, explained, interpreted and used as the basis for induction and deduction of legal rules" along the course of Islamic history. The Prophet, his companions, and the early Muslim jurists, one after the other, gradually developed the original law of the Qur'an into a wider legal fabric.

### Between Shari'a and Fiqh

One has seen that there is a gap between God as lawgiver and human beings as lawmakers. [...] In my view, this gap is inevitable if one has the perception that religious law in Islam is a monolithic concept. One has to accurately distinguish between shari'a and fiqh (Islamic jurisprudence) since the latter is not equivalent to shari'a. In fact, not all of fiqh is shari'a. They are distinctly different concepts. [...]

[W]hile shari'a comes from God through those verses of the Qur'an which do not need further clarification, fiqh (which literally means understanding) on the other hand is the interpretations of human beings of those Qur'anic legal verses that have imprecise or multiple meanings. Likewise, because shari'a is revealed, it takes only one form, while fiqh varies according to different individuals' reasoning. In addition, while it is imperative that shari'a be implemented, one can choose any legal understanding (fiqh) available and suitable to one's situation. Finally, shari'a is unchangeable and applicable to any time and any place, while fiqh is subject to change according to its local circumstances. These distinctions help to clarify that there are two distinct concepts of religious law in Islam, the immutable, transcendent shari'a and the mutable, temporal fiqh. In this sense, although it is still a much broader concept since it also deals with ritual worship, it is fiqh that is more comparable to what is currently called 'law,' and hence, when the term 'Islamic law' is used in this study it will refer mainly to fiqh, except when it is quoted from the work of another author.

### Two Kinds of Shari'a

Despite the differences between shari'a and law and between shari'a and fiqh, exactly to what extent a rule or law can be identified as shari'a remains unresolved. However, it is important to emphasize here that shari'a in legal rules is not only seen in legal texts, but is being found more in the substantive content of the legal rules. Here we have at least two kinds of shari'a. First it is mostly a set of legal rules, and second it is substantially a collection of principal values. [...]

The two kinds of shari'a above are important in this study. Both help determine what kind of shari'a is relevant or irrelevant to the concept of the modern nation-state. Given that the main concern of what is called law, in the

> modern sense, as it pertains to religion, is merely the right to worship and perform rituals, I will argue that dissonance would be more likely to occur in response to the perception that sees shari'a mostly as legal rules, rather than the view that considers shari'a as a natural way of *life* or a collection of principal values. In present-day Indonesia, it appears that the notion of shari'a as legal subject matter has more support among the proponents of the formal application of shari'a.

## II LAW IN THE LANDSCAPE OF SACRED PRACTICES

Despite the pervasive influence of Hinduism, Buddhism, Islam, and Christianity in Asian societies, these classical religious traditions rarely, if ever, appear in "pure" form in ordinary social life. Law and society scholars make a distinction between "law on the books" and "law in action," and the same could be said of religion in Asia and elsewhere. Religion on the books differs greatly from religion as practiced in the villages and urban neighborhoods of Asian peoples. Although concepts and images drawn from the so-called world religions are ubiquitous, people are just as concerned – sometimes far more concerned – with spirits, ghosts, signs and portents, the stars, and countless other supernatural or magical phenomena that are not mentioned or approved in the literatures of Hinduism, Buddhism, Islam, and Christianity. This is what we might call religion in action, and it merges seamlessly with the classical religious traditions. As Fernanda Pirie (2006:177) has observed of the landscape of sacred practices in Ladakh:

> In most villagers' eyes there is no real divide between Buddhism and other forms of ritual practice. Their cosmological concerns are dominated by the practical need to ensure physical fortune, fertility, and the biological continuity of the community. Local monks perform many exorcist rituals, and the *onpos* consider these practices to be part of their religious activities. The villagers regard the Buddhist deities as supreme cosmological beings with the greatest power to deal effectively with their troublesome evil spirits.

Religion in action has enormous significance for legal behavior and institutions, since it guides the everyday practices of ordinary people as they navigate their way through agreements and disputes, family relationships, issues of birth and death, political authority and legitimacy, and the like.

It constitutes a form of customary law that is deeply familiar to ordinary people and influences their engagement – if any – with the more distant and unfamiliar institutions of state law. The following selection illustrates some of the interconnections between law and the broader landscape of sacred practices in Asia.

## 1.5 State Law and the Law of Sacred Centers, *David M. Engel and Jaruwan Engel*

In this reading, David and Jaruwan Engel discuss Buddhism in northern Thailand and its relationship to the law of injuries. The injury practices discussed by their interviewees deviate radically from Buddhist doctrine enshrined in classical religious texts and draw extensively on animism, astrology, and spirit worship. Yet it would be a mistake to conclude that Buddhism at the village level was unimportant for these villagers. On the contrary, all considered themselves Buddhist and identified Buddhism as the foundation of their lives and their culture. In their eyes, however, Buddhism was a mix of classical textually based doctrine and deeply rooted practices that are more localized and drawn from other imaginings of the natural and supernatural worlds. This complex of religious frameworks and activities has been termed "Villagers' Buddhism" by one commentator, an apt designation for Buddhism as it is actually lived and experienced in northern Thailand. As this excerpt makes clear, it is essential to take Villagers' Buddhism into account if one is to understand how injuries are conceptualized and handled in practice and when the law is deemed relevant or useful. Moreover, as other chapters in the Engels' book make clear, the world of northern Thai villagers was rapidly changing. The practices and beliefs described in this excerpt have been disrupted by global transformations and socioeconomic development, and the role of Buddhism itself has been reconceived to deal with injuries that increasingly occur outside the village or involve individuals who are no longer familiar with the localized practices described in this reading.

> *Law of Sacred Centers in the Village*
> [T]he law of sacred centers radiates outward from a locus having supernatural potency. This system of unwritten customary norms and procedures is strongest at locations closest to the center and becomes weaker and more uncertain at more distant locations. People in Chiangmai remember the law of sacred centers as a feature of village life during their childhood, and they associate it with the traditional practices of their parents and grandparents. We begin our description, therefore, with our interviewees' recollections of the villages and households into which they were born.

The household was historically the sacred center that shaped the identity of Thai villagers from the beginning of their lives. In the past, according to the recollections of many interviewees, individuals in northern Thailand were literally born into houses; this was before hospital birthing became common. The houses were themselves geographical locations constructed around a sacred center, the "auspicious post" that served as "the ritual center of the dwelling."[1] [...]

The identity of each villager was connected from birth to a specific location and a geographically based community of humans and spirits. [...] Injuries, illnesses, and other mishaps were located in relation to the sacred centers and the supernatural beings who presided over them. For example, if a baby cried all night or if a child was sick or injured, the family prayed for the intercession of the ancestral spirits of the rice pot, *pu dam ya dam*. The clay rice pot blackened by smoke from burning wood was a prominent feature of the house's kitchen – a "place" in the geography of the home. [...] Other household spirits required regular propitiation and notification of the family's comings and goings. In exchange, they offered protection against harm: "If you wanted to do anything, you had to consider the household spirits first. They were always watching. People respected them" (interview with Bancha). [...]

Spirits were involved in many aspects of injury practices. Injuries inflicted on a villager could offend the spirits and require propitiatory ceremonies. If individuals behaved disrespectfully, the spirits themselves could cause injuries as a form of punishment. When illness or injury occurred, moreover, the household spirits had the power not only to relieve suffering but to identify the underlying cause. In one such ritual, the family rice pot was covered with a black, long-sleeved shirt, and two women who were traditional healers sat on either side. They would ask the spirits of the rice pot, "What about this person? Where did he get in trouble? What did he do wrong?" A wooden stick, suspended above a large flat bamboo tray filled with grains of rice, would then swing back and forth as the spirits inscribed their answer in the rice (interview with Müang).

Territorial guardian spirits *(jao thi jao thang)* watched over the household, and villagers built shrines to them within each compound. The so-called spirit house is still a familiar feature of most Thai residences – a miniature dwelling, often elevated on a post and positioned outside the house itself. Most

---

[1] Richard Davis (1984), *Muang Metaphysics: A Study of Northern Thai Myth and Ritual* (Bangkok: Pandora), at 49. [Editors' note]

interviewees recalled childhood practices associated with these spirits. Each day, their parents would light incense sticks and candles and would offer sweet and savory foods. The household guardian spirits could reveal the cause of an accident or illness and point the household members toward a solution:

> If someone in the house was ill or injured and didn't get better after seeing a doctor, the elders would make an offering at the shrine of the guardian spirits. They would ask the spirits to enter their dreams and explain why the person was suffering and what needed to be done to get better. They would enter the dreams of someone in the house. It might be anyone. And when we dream, they may come and talk with us, "Oh, you went out and a ghost got you, this ghost or that ghost. A ghost of some dead person. (laughs) A ghost of someone with no relatives [i.e., no one to perform the rituals that would allow the ghost to leave the spot where he had died]." ... If you encountered this type of ghost or failed to show proper respect, if you walked on it or stepped on its head, then you must perform a ceremony to feed it a duck or chicken.
>
> (interview with Bancha)

The intimate relationships of the household were enlarged and replicated at the village level. The word for village, *mu ban*, means literally "a group of households." The village chief in northern Thailand is the *pho luang*, or "big father," suggesting a collective familial relationship within the village. Guardian spirits watched over the entire village, just as they watched over each household. These locality spirits were known by many names, such as *pho ban* ("village father") or *jao ban* ("lord of the village"). In one village we visited, the *süa ban* ("village ancestral spirits") resided in large, houselike shrines, where the villagers made merit during the Thai New Year or when they got married, built a new house, or had a funeral. To invoke the spirits' protection, villagers offered flowers, whiskey, and food, both sweet and savory, and they prayed: "Today we are having a wedding. Please, help and take care of this couple. Keep them from danger" (interview with Bancha). Failure of a villager or a household to propitiate the village guardian spirit could cause misfortune.

Even Buddhist temples had their own (non-Buddhist) guardian spirits, or *süa wat*, which were propitiated by monks and villagers. [Michael R.] Rhum refers to them as "*wat*-protecting spirits."[2] One commentator [Shalardchai

---

[2] Michael R. Rhum (1994), *The Ancestral Lords: Gender, Descent, and Spirits in a Northern Thai Village*. Special Report No. 29, Monograph Series on Southeast Asia (DeKalb: Center for Southeast Asian Studies, Northern Illinois University), at 47. [Editors' note]

Ramitanon] has used the term *villagers' Buddhism* to describe this amalgam of Buddhist and non-Buddhist elements in rural Thai communities.[3] Locality spirits were positioned at the center of village cosmologies that also included Buddhist shrines, temples, monks, and saints.

In short, households and villages were nodes of social and spiritual interconnection. Residence in these communities conferred identity on humans and spirits and gave a place and a meaning to important events, including injuries. [...]

To understand how injuries were conceptualized and handled within communities established around sacred centers, it is necessary to mention some of the key attributes of identity that were familiar to those who resided there. These identity attributes defined the nature of injury itself – what aspect of a human being was harmed when an injury occurred and what remedy or response was most appropriate for the injury victim and the community as a whole. Particularly relevant to an understanding of injuries were the components of identity known as *khwan* and *winyan*.

The first identity attribute, the *khwan*, is a flighty spiritual essence found in all living beings and in some natural objects such as rice fields and mountains. Even automobiles may have a *khwan*. When an individual suffers fright, trauma, or physical injury, it is said that the *khwan* flies out of the body, and a ritual – known as *riak khwan* or, in northern dialect, *hong khwan* – must then be performed to recall the *khwan* and bind it in the body by tying a sacred string or thread around the wrists. Loss of the *khwan* causes the individual to become unwell, both physically and mentally, and the confusion and alienation of the afflicted person was, at least in the past, understood to pose a risk to the entire community. Symbolically, the lost *khwan* was thought to escape from the physical boundaries of the village and enter a realm beyond that of human society. [...]

Recalling the *khwan* of an injured person was seen as essential to repair the fabric of the community. Significantly, the payment made by the injurer was – and still is – referred to as "payment for the *khwan* ceremony" (*kha tham khwan*). This term, even today, is widely used in Thai society to describe the compensation that is paid in an injury case. It is understandable that, in the closely integrated village society of humans and spirits, the entire community would insist that the injurer pay compensation. The injurer's transgression put everyone at risk, and the victim would cease to be a functional member of his family and his village until the *khwan* was recalled and bound firmly into the

---

[3] Shalardchai Ramitanon (2002), *Phi jao nai [Spirits of the Nobility]*, 2nd ed. (Chiangmai: Ming Müang Press) at 34. [Editors' note]

victim's body. Because each injury had this collective aspect, compelling the payment of injury costs was assumed to be essential to the preservation of the village community.

The second component of human identity that is relevant to this discussion of injuries is another type of spiritual essence known as *winyan*. More durable than the *khwan*, the *winyan* leaves the body only at the time of death. Buddhist rituals to make merit for the *winyan* can ensure its progression toward a favorable future life, and ultimately the *winyan* should undergo reincarnation; but when death results from an injury, there is a danger that the *winyan* will remain at the spot of the fatality. When a violent or unnatural death (*tai hong*) occurs, the *winyan* that is allowed to linger at the location becomes the most dangerous type of ghost (*phi tai hong*). It waits until other humans come near to sicken or kill them so that a new *winyan* will take its place and it can continue its normal path in the cycle of birth and rebirth. Thus, when violent or unnatural deaths occur, it is imperative to perform a ritual aimed at preventing this type of dangerous and malevolent ghost from arising. Interviewees recalled that the cost of these merit-making ceremonies in cases of abnormal death was an obligation assumed by the injurer. The entire village had an interest in enforcing this obligation because everyone was put at risk by the dangerous and malevolent *phi tai hong*.

In sum, the remembered law of sacred centers began with traditions located in households and villages. In proximity to those geographical centers, individuals acquired an identity and a status, and they fell under the protection of territorially based authorities – both human and supernatural – who could interpret the cause of injuries, identify the transgressions that caused them, and enforce the payment of compensation. Injuries within the community disrupted social harmony and threatened the well-being of all. The collective interest in redressing this kind of normative violation was voiced by the spirits through various means, such as the ritual to ascertain the views of household spirits and ceremonies associated with spirit mediums, traditional healers, and others. Village elders, including the village or subdistrict chief, served as agents of human authority to compel the payment of compensation. All these practices were understood to be consistent with "villagers' Buddhism," which was actually a heterogeneous mix of Buddhist and non-Buddhist customs and beliefs. [...]

*Injury and Identity Far from Home*
The weakening of the law of sacred centers became more pronounced as individuals traveled farther from home, toward other villages and towns. The highways themselves could be a source of danger because the malevolent

ghosts of accident victims resided along the roadside. When injuries occurred on the highway, the cause was often traced back to the depredations of these ghosts, known as *phi tai hong*. Such ghosts could obscure the vision of a person who came too close or could otherwise try to cause a fatal accident in order to have the victim's *winyan* take the place of the ghost and allow the latter to leave that location and resume its spiritual progression toward a new birth. Such explanations did not necessarily support the assumption that the injured person should receive customary compensation from another human, because the essence of the problem was the ghost rather than the injurer.

The fear of *phi tai hong* made it essential to perform a proper ritual, (*sut thon*) at the place where an abnormal death occurred. [...] Kham, for example, recalled that monks who performed the ritual placed the *winyan* in a bamboo fish trap to remove it from the place where it had fallen at the time of death. He remembered that the lightweight fish trap became extremely heavy once the officiants placed the added weight of the malevolent ghost inside, and it rook four men to lift it and carry it away to be buried at the foot of a sacred bo tree in the cemetery outside a temple. [...] [T]he *sut thon* ritual also involved the placement of miniature sand stupas at the spot where the accident occurred, along with small flags made from colored paper. [...]

Whatever the precise details of the *sut thon* ceremony, villagers believed that it had to be performed to prevent one fatality from leading to other injuries and deaths. The ceremony was associated with a customary law of injuries in that its costs were regarded as the responsibility of the injurer and provided a measure of the compensation to which the victim or the family was entitled. But injuries and fatalities far from home presented another problem: the difficulty of negotiating a remedy. When the claimant and injurer lived in the same village, the village chief or subdistrict chief (*kamnan*) could remind them of the norms and expectations for paying compensation after an injury took place. Because both parties worshipped the same guardian spirits, they were literally brothers and sisters who had to treat one another with respect and generosity. But when injuries occurred on the highway, the disputants were likely to have been strangers to one another and may have found themselves without a mutually acceptable mediator. In such cases, injurers who disagreed about their obligation to pay for the *sut thon* ceremony might discover that there was no authority figure to compel them to change their minds. In legal spaces where authority radiates outward from a sacred center, the more distant a location is from the center that holds significance for the disputants the more problematic enforcement becomes.

*Injuries off the Map: Delocalized Causes of Harm*

We have spoken thus far of injuries that were associated with specific locations: the house, the village, the forest, and the highway. Yet even in the imagined landscape familiar to preceding generations, many causes of injury were not locality based and could not be mapped at all. For example, karmic explanations of injury, which often appeared in combination with other explanations, were not place specific. They referred to the injured person's own misdeeds, either in this life or in an earlier life. The injury was thus a consequence of actions the injury victim had previously directed at the injurer or at another person or even an animal. [...] The effects of these actions later manifested themselves in the form of an accident.

Karmic explanations placed the ultimate causal responsibility on the victim him- or herself. What then of the injurer? A different type of explanation that may be more common in the present than in the past is negligence. The concept of negligence is also "off the map" in that its causal roots are not fixed to any particular geographical location. The Thai word for "negligent" is *pramat* (careless, imprudent), which is also a legal term, but its colloquial meaning in Thai carries some connotations that are lacking in English. When individuals cited the injurer's negligence as one cause of their injury, they usually hastened to add that they themselves had also been negligent. Negligence on the part of both parties – injured and injurer – appear to be linked conceptually in the minds of ordinary people in Thailand.

Injuries occurred because both parties lacked *sati*, or mindfulness. *Sati* is another Buddhist concept, signifying a mind that is focused, calm, aware, and undistracted. *Sati* can be achieved through concentration and meditation as well as a philosophical understanding of the illusory quality of everyday life. Negligence is, in a sense, the opposite of *sati*: "[I]f you are negligent then you don't have *sati*; you are acting without *sati*" (interview with Suwit). The concept of negligence was thus closely connected to the concept we might call "contributory negligence," and both in turn were tied to the Buddhist concept of an undisciplined mind and a lack of spiritual training and awareness. Moreover, the teachings of the Buddha would explain that negligence was a secondary cause of injury, not the root cause. The root cause, from a Buddhist perspective, is karma. The carelessness of both parties and their lack of *sati* have karmic origins.

Karma and negligence were two of the most important "off-the-map" causal explanations for injuries. Neither cause has specific spatial referents; neither has a geographic "place." Interviewees also identified other nonlocalized explanations for injury. The concept of fate or destiny (*khro*), for example, is connected to karma yet distinguishable from it. Women "have *khro*" when their age is an odd number, but men have *khro*, and are therefore more susceptible to injury, when their age is an even number. According to Keyes, *khro* is a non-Buddhist concept of causation "that operates irrespective of the moral actions of people, whereas the Buddhist concept of Karma relates all causation ultimately to moral action."[4] Nevertheless, injury victims in northern Thailand tended to merge the two concepts in a single expression, *khrokam*, and they spoke of their *khro* as the product of bad karma they had accumulated through misdeeds in their current or previous lifetimes. [...]

Injuries sometimes arose from another nonlocalized cause, one's "stars" (*duang*). When a person's stars are in the ascendancy, good luck of all kinds may occur – one may win the lottery, succeed in gambling, and achieve success in all endeavors. But when one's stars are on the decline, bad fortune is likely, and injuries may occur.

Injuries could even be caused by a person's name. One interviewee, for example, complained that his parents did not give him a name that was appropriate for the day, month, and year of his birth. An inappropriate name can bring bad luck and make one susceptible to injuries. At the time of the interview, he was considering a name change to improve his luck and avoid further mishaps. A female interviewee, Saikham, changed her name after her husband was killed in a traffic accident, but this did not protect her several years later from a motorcycle collision that broke her leg. It may, however, have made her accident less serious and saved her life.

All of these delocalized causes of injury – karma, negligence, absence of *sati*, fate, stars, and other forms of bad luck – had one thing in common: None of them, except perhaps the injurer's negligence, was associated with a remedy of any kind, or at least a remedy that the injurer was obliged to provide. If the cause of the injury was the victim's own karma, contributory negligence, lack of *sati*, fate, or bad luck, then why should the injurer take responsibility? In the past, these delocalized causal explanations were familiar and widely accepted, yet they did not necessarily relieve the injurer of an obligation to pay compensation. When injuries occurred in villages near the watchful eyes of the guardian spirits, the delocalized explanations were rarely regarded as the *exclusive* cause of the injury. Causation was multiple, shifting, and overlapping. No single explanation trumped the others. All of them were relevant, and combinations of them were likely to be mentioned when an injury occurred. The village chief could refer to the victim's karma at the same time that he reminded the injurer that he or she had violated local norms and

---

[4] Charles F. Keyes (1977), *The Golden Peninsula: Culture and Adaptation in Mainland Southeast Asia* (New York: Macmillan) at 117. [Editors' note]

> disturbed the well-being of the entire village. Injuries could be simultaneously localized and delocalized. In the normal course of things, injurers were in the end expected to pay compensation.

## III THE ARRIVAL OF "MODERN" LAW AND THE CONCEPT OF SECULARISM

Legal systems based on Western models arrived in Asia during the eighteenth and nineteenth centuries through many pathways. Usually, they were imposed by the imperial powers as part of their colonial political apparatus, but in some Asian countries, most notably Japan and Thailand, they were imported by local elites in consultation with European and American legal experts. These legal systems represented a radical discontinuity with traditional regimes and introduced new models of centralized, "rationalized," and bureaucratized legal orders. A common feature of so-called "modern" legality is the concept of secularism, which in theory split off the legal from the sacred and made it the business of law to set the terms for a separation that was unthinkable under the classical conceptions of law and religion.

A great deal of law and society scholarship has probed and questioned the concepts of modernity and secularism. It would be a mistake to accept what Peter Fitzpatrick (1992) has called "the mythology of modern law" as a literal history or sociology rather than a type of situated discourse that merits careful sociolegal analysis. In this section, therefore, we should ask first what the "project of modernity" (Asad 2003) entailed in different Asian societies and who promoted it. We should then ask what role the sacred played in the imaginings of those who pursued modernity – and what role it played in the actual behavior of rulers and subjects. Finally, we might ask how the concept of secularism, rooted as it was in a specific European cultural history, was interpreted and deployed in Asia. Like modernity, secularism was a "project" that carried different meanings and served different purposes in different social contexts. As Sullivan et al. (2011:1–2) have observed, scholars have come to view secularism and secularization as "highly unstable terms in academic discourse," and recent scholarship has demonstrated the many diverse ways in which religion has remained relevant to law and legal institutions within purportedly secular regimes:

It is now better understood that religion, like secularism, takes plural forms, some of which fit uncomfortably with the liberal modes of thought dominant in Euro-American societies. Some of these deviations from the paradigm of liberal secularism extend the promise of multiculturalism, but some also appear to challenge key assumptions of traditional theoretical models justifying public order and to expose vulnerabilities in the sovereignty of the secular state.

In the readings that follow, therefore, we will not observe the triumph of secularism over an older form of law that had been embedded in religious ideology. Rather, we will see different Asian societies responding in different ways to European concepts of legal modernity while continuing to reflect the profound influence of longstanding sacred practices and beliefs.

## 1.6 The Aborted Restoration of "Indigenous" Law in India, Marc Galanter

The imposition of English law and legal institutions in India aimed to introduce a radical discontinuity with preexisting understandings of justice. The new European-style justice system seemed complex and alien to local sensibilities, but at the same time the classical, Hindu-based *dharmaśāstra* tradition in some ways became irrelevant as a viable alternative. Indeed, the Hindu concept of a legal order based explicitly on social hierarchy and inequality now appeared unjust to many Indians after independence from English colonial rule was achieved. Moreover, efforts to return to village-based justice tribunals, known as panchayats, failed to recapture traditional understandings of local customary law and religion since they were now embedded in the centralized justice system rather than reflecting local autonomy. Although longstanding views of law and religion persisted in India, it was no longer apparent how they could be expressed within a "modern" and secular legal order.

> Traditional law – Hindu, Muslim and customary – has been almost entirely displaced from the modern Indian legal system. Today, the classical *dharmaśāstra* component of Hindu law is almost completely obliterated. It remains the original source of various rules of family law. But these rules are intermixed with rules from other sources and are administered in the common-law style, isolated from *śāstric* techniques of interpretation and procedure. In other fields of law, *dharmaśāstra* is not employed as a source of precedent, analogy or inspiration. As a procedural-technical system of laws, a corpus of doctrines, techniques and institutions, *dharmaśāstra* is no longer functioning. This is equally true of Muslim law. The local customary component of traditional law is also a source of official rules at a few isolated points, but it too has been abandoned as a living source of law. [...]

The dichotomy between the official law and popular legality has been the theme of a continuing stream of criticism from administrators, nationalists and students of Indian society, who have emphasized the unsuitability of British-style law in India. As a scholarly British District Officer plaintively concluded in 1945:

> we proceeded, with the best of intentions, to clamp down upon India a vast system of law and administration which was for the most part quite unsuited to the people .... In Indian conditions the whole elaborate machinery of English Law, which Englishmen tended to think so perfect, simply didn't work and has been completely perverted.[1]

Administrators and observers have blamed the legal system for promoting a flood of interminable and wasteful litigation, for encouraging perjury and corruption, and generally exacerbating disputes by eroding traditional consensual methods of dispute-resolution. The indictment was familiar by the mid-nineteenth century:

> in lieu of this simple and rational mode of dispensing justice, we have given the natives an obscure, complicated, pedantic system of English law, full of 'artificial technicalities', which ... force them to have recourse to a swarm of attorneys ... that is ... *professional rogues* ... by means of which we have taught an ingenious people to refine upon the quibbles and fictions of English lawyers .... The course of justice, civil as well as criminal, is utterly confounded in a maze of artifice and fraud, and the natives, both high and low, are becoming more and more demoralized.[2] [...]

In the nationalist movement, there were similar complaints, issuing in proposals for the restoration of indigenous justice. There was hostility to the courts as an agency of British control, and the civil disobedience movements of 1920–2 and 1931 included attempts to boycott the official courts and to organize truly Indian tribunals which would work by conciliation, relying on moral suasion rather than coercive sanctions. The misgivings of some nationalists about the legal system were succinctly expressed by a Gandhian publicist in 1946, who accused the British system of working havoc in India by replacing quick, cheap and efficient *panchayat* justice with expensive and slow courts which promote endless dishonesty and degrade public morality.

---

[1] Penderel Moon (1945), *Strangers to India* (New York: Reynal & Hitchcock) at 22. [Editors' note]

[2] John Dickinson (1853), *Government of India Under a Bureaucracy* (London: Reprinted and published by Major B. D. Basu, Allahabad, 1925) at 46. [Editors' note]

Existing law, he said, is too foreign and too complex; this complexity promotes 'criminal mentality and crime'. In their place he would have *panchayats* dispense justice at the village level, thereby eliminating the need for lawyers and complex laws.[3]

The Constituent Assembly (1947–9) contained no spokesmen for a restoration of *dharmaśāstra*, nor for a revival of local customary law as such. An attempt by Gandhians and 'traditionalists' to form a polity based on village autonomy and self-sufficiency was rejected by the Assembly, which opted for a federal and parliamentary republic with centralized bureaucratic administration. The only concession to the Gandhians was a Directive Principle in favor of village *panchayats* as units of local self-government. The existing legal system was retained intact, new powers granted to the judiciary and its independence enhanced by elaborate protections. All in all, the Constitution amounted to an endorsement of the existing legal system. [...]

In the late 1950s the Government adopted the policy of community development, whereby elective village *panchayats* were established as instruments of village self-government in the hope that they would increase initiative and participation in economic development. [...]

There is little reason to think of *panchayats* as a reassertion of local norms or institutions. It has been pointed out that administrative *panchayats* have tended to act as downward channels for the dissemination of official policies rather than as forums for the assertion of local interests as locally conceived. It is submitted that this is the case with judicial *panchayats* too. Rather than inspiring a resurgence of indigenous local law, they may serve as agencies for disseminating official norms and procedures and further displacing traditional local law by official law within the village. [...]

[T]he proponents of an indigenous system presented no vivid alternative. Contrast, for example, movements for replacing one language with another, where there is an alternative that is palpable to all and clearly promises advantage, symbolic if not tangible, to many. Here, the proponents themselves were not moved by a lively sense of what the alternative might be. In part this reflected the absence of any plausible candidate – this was a restorationist movement without a believable pretender!

*Dharmaśāstra*, of course, was one alternative, an elaborate and sophisticated body of legal learning. But any proposal in this direction would run foul of some of Independent India's most central commitments. It would violate her commitment to a secular state, insuring equal participation to religious

---

[3] Shriman Narayan Agarwal (1946), *Gandhian Constitution for Free India* (Allahabad: Kitabistan) at 97, 100, 131. [Editors' note]

> minorities. Furthermore, *dharmaśāstra's* emphasis on graded inequality would run counter to the principle of equality and would encounter widespread opposition to the privileged position of the castes. Indeed, the one area where *dharmaśāstra* retained some legal force, Hindu family law, was in the early 1950s being subjected to thorough reform which largely abandoned the *śāstra* in favor of a Hindu law built on modern notions. Thus, it is hardly surprising that none of the documents supporting *nyaya panchayats* even mentions *dharmaśāstra*. While few would condemn it (as had an earlier generation of reformers) claims on its behalf were limited to the symbolic and intellectual levels. It was not an available alternative for practical application.

### 1.7 Smash Temples, Burn Books: Comparing Secularist Projects in India and China, *Peter van der Veer*

The following excerpt addresses secularism in China (portions of the article discussing secularism in India have been omitted). As van der Veer demonstrates, states can institute secular regimes not just by enacting new legislation but also by mobilizing mass demonstrations in opposition to what become characterized as irrational and atavistic religious institutions. The government's emphasis on rationalism across the sociolegal landscape transformed the status of the classical religious traditions within the Chinese state. The article begins with a summary of recent secularism theory by authors such as Jose Casanova, who reject a teleological view of religious decline, secularization, and modernism in favor of a more nuanced examination of how philosophies of religion, secularism, and (we might add) law have been "fused" and/or differentiated in different societies. In other words, it is a mistake to assume that all societies – including those in Asia – have participated in an inexorable march from religious-based legal orders to "rational" and religiously neutral political institutions and practices. To illustrate this point, van der Veer discusses the complex and fascinating interplay of ideas about science, Buddhism, Taoism, and Confucianism in nineteenth- and twentieth-century China. He argues that official Chinese criticism of religion rested primarily on an anticlerical sentiment rather than a formal rejection of underlying religious concepts and beliefs, some of which were actually integrated with "modern" political and legal ideologies. In short, "religious activity seems to be embedded in a fully secular life" in China – and perhaps elsewhere – rather than banished from it. Secularism may have weakened – or at least redefined – the official status of religion within the Chinese state's legal and political framework, but religion remained a robust social phenomenon nevertheless.

"Smash temples, build schools" (毀廟辦學 *huimiao, banxue*) is a particularly telling slogan that was used in a campaign against temple cults and religious specialists during reforms in late Qing at the end of the 19th century. According to the reformists, led by Kang Youwei (1858–1927) and to an extent supported by the emperor, China had to modernize quickly and this had to be done by promoting education and by getting rid of religious superstition. These two elements belonged together, since education should train people in modern, rational thought while superstition and magical thought should be discouraged. Before the Communist victory in 1949 a number of campaigns, first in late imperial China and afterwards in the Republic, destroyed or "secularized," according to one estimate, half of a million existing temples. What the Communists did after 1949 was, to a very great extent, a continuation of these campaigns. While one might have expected that the nationalists in Taiwan with their Confucian nationalism would have had a fundamentally different policy towards religion than the Communists, the opposite is in fact the case. Till the late 1960s the nationalists kept religious activities under a very tight control. All these campaigns against religion should have produced a secular China, but the contrary is true. In Taiwan religious activities are all over the place and with the loosening of the tight controls over religion in the PRC we see religious activity flourishing everywhere. This paradox can be understood by closely examining the nature of these secularist campaigns.

Secularism as an ideology and as a practice in China is in the first place an anti-clericalism. Anti-clericalism has deep roots in Chinese history, but at the end of the 19th century it gained both the attention of the popular media and of intellectuals who grappled with modern, Western ideas. Intellectuals, like Liang Qichao (1873–1929), Zhang Binglin (1869–1936), and Chen Yinque (1890–1969) separated Buddhism and Taoism from their clerical roots and made them into national moralities that could serve the modernization of China. Buddhist leaders such as Taixu (1890–1947) and Daoist modernists like Chen Yingning (1880–1969) made great efforts to bring their religions under the rubric of secular nationalism. The popular press was also not opposed to religion as such, but to Buddhist and Daoist clerics who were described not only as ignorant buffoons, but also as criminals, drunkards, gluttons, and, foremost, as sexually debauched. [...]

Clerics in China were also seen as dangerously violent, since their ascetic disciplines and martial arts that inflict violence on their own bodies can be turned against others for crimes of rebellious purposes. Obviously, this theme gained prominence in the late 19th century during the failed Boxer rebellion. Clerics were able to connect to secret societies that threatened the state monopoly of violence. They combined fighting techniques with magic that made the believers think they were invincible and thus extremely dangerous. The failure of the Boxer rebellion, however, showed Chinese intellectuals that there was no future in using magical means to defeat the imperial powers. Again, the theme of delusion and disguise comes up here with the notion that the illiterate masses are led into meaningless and ultimately fruitless violence by cunning clerics.

Besides a form of anticlericalism Chinese secularism is a form of scientism and rationalism. From a 19th century enlightened and evolutionary perspective it pitches scientific rationality against magical superstition. Secularism is thus a battle against the misconceptions of natural processes that keep the illiterate masses in the dark and in the clutches of feudal rulers and clerics. The term for superstition (迷信 *mixin*) comes from Japanese as many other terms that are employed in the discourse of modernity, like indeed the term "religion" (宗教 *zongjiao*) itself. In using these neologisms it makes a distinction between religion that contributes to the morality of the state and superstition that is detrimental to modern progress. These views are shared by intellectuals of all persuasions, including the nationalists and the communists, but also by many reformist religious thinkers. This is both a discursive and an institutional shift as an aspect of the transition from the ancient regime of the Qing empire to the modern Republic. [...]

Anticlericalism and scientism together were deeply connected to Western, enlightened ideas about progress, in which magic had to be replaced by scientific rationality and by moral religion as basis of national identity. Major currents of western thought, like social Darwinism, neo-Kantianism, and Marxism were absorbed in China. Not only prescriptive thought about society came to stand in the light of rationality, but also descriptive social science, such as sociology and anthropology lost their ability to describe the effects of these ideologies on society since they could not distance themselves from them. Intellectuals played an important role in the secularist projects of nationalizing and rationalizing religion and, crucially, they were part and parcel of large-scale state interventions to produce a modern, national identity. While Buddhism and Taoism were to some extent sources for the creation of national religion, Confucianism was itself being considered as already both national and rational. The attempts to transform Confucian traditions into a civil, national religion were extremely interesting as a form of social engineering, but ultimately failed, largely because Confucian teachings could encompass Daoist and Buddhist teachings but not the social energy that local Daoist and Buddhist cults could mobilize.

One of the great puzzles of China today is not that it proves the secularization thesis wrong, but that despite a century of secularism religion has not been destroyed. In fact we see everywhere in China a more open performance of religious rituals. This raises a number of issues. [...]

Firstly, then, what is the nature of Chinese religion and secularity today? On the one hand we find a general acceptance in China of the idea that religion is not important to the Chinese, that the Chinese have always been rational and secular, and with modernization even more so. This view is not only prevalent among intellectuals, but is also more generally held. And on the other hand, there is a widespread interest in religious practices, in visiting shrines especially during tourist trips, in religious forms of healing. Both in cities and in the countryside communities are rebuilding their temples and have started in awkward negotiations with the authorities to perform their ceremonies again. Religious activity seems to be embedded in a fully secular life, in which job insecurities, health and desire for success and profit create a demand for divine support. With the decline of the "iron rice bowl" of the state this demand has only increased. The same intellectuals who deny the importance of religion pray for their family's welfare wherever they can. The chain of memory, to use Hervieu-Leger's term, however, seems to have been broken and needs to be patched up. In general people who engage in ritual (rather than theology or philosophy) are not very knowledgeable about them but in China this is quite extreme. This is enhanced by the fact that the clergy has been largely exterminated or so much brought under control of the Party that they have lost their liturgical bearings. This situation in itself gives a lot of space for new religious movements in which lay people play an important role, like the many qigong movements.

Secondly, how do we explain the failure of a century of systematic destruction of Chinese religious life? One answer lies in the millenarian nature of Maoism itself. The Party absorbed quite a lot of the social energy that is available in religious movements. Mass mobilization (群众运动 *qunzhong yundong*) for the transformation of self and society has a central place both in Chinese religion and in Maoism. Studying and especially reciting Mao's writings again recall religious chanting. The finding and expelling of class enemies and traitors follow quite precisely the trappings of Chinese witchcraft beliefs and exorcism, even in the giving of black hoods as symbols of evil to the accused. The practice of public confession likewise continues religious practice.

# Religion

> Thirdly, what is the future of secularism in China? As I already indicated secularity is well established in China in daily life as well as in people's self-understanding. Secularism is also certainly still the frame in which clerics have to operate. The Buddhist and Daoist associations are still largely controlled by the state.

### 1.8 Judging in God's Name: State Power, Secularism, and the Politics of Islamic Law in Malaysia, *Tamir Moustafa*

In this excerpt, Tamir Moustafa begins by explaining that precolonial Islamic law in Malaya was highly decentralized, since God's will as expressed in the *shari'a*, though singular and immutable, was interpreted in various ways by different human authorities. In the absence of a centralized church or a unified state, Islamic legal practices and custom (*adat*) were therefore pluralistic and variable. During the colonial period, however, the English rulers created a more unified and centralized "Anglo-Muslim" law, which purported to administer Islamic legal principles through the institutions of the newly established state. This conceptual shift has carried over to the postcolonial Malaysian legal system, in which pronouncements by Islamic legal authorities are no longer mere opinions but carry the binding force of law. Moustafa's analysis concludes with reflections on the nature of secularism. Although Malaysia would appear to be the antithesis of a secular legal regime, he observes that Islamic jurisprudence in Malaysia bears little resemblance to classical understandings of Islamic law as a decentralized and pluralistic system. Paradoxically, this form of religious law is a product of a "modern" Weberian state apparatus, a political form never contemplated by classical Islamic authorities. Moustafa thus joins van der Veer and other contemporary scholars of secularism in calling for a rejection of the conventional binaries of secular versus religious or modern versus traditional in favor of a more nuanced and contextual understanding of the ways in which different societies have drawn on the tropes, methods, and institutions of law and religion to create distinctive understandings of legality in contemporary societies around the world.

> Malaysia ranks sixth out of 175 countries worldwide in the degree of state regulation of religion. Only Egypt, Iran, Jordan, Saudi Arabia, and the Maldives have higher levels of state regulation. State law requires Muslims to attend Friday prayer, to fast during Ramadan, and to abide by dietary

restrictions all year long. Drinking, gambling, and 'sexual deviance' are prohibited, as is interfaith marriage and conversion out of Islam. But over and above these and myriad other substantive rules and regulations, it is the state's monopoly on religious interpretation that is the most striking feature of Malaysian law. Once recorded in the official Gazette, fatwas from state-appointed officials assume the force of law and the public expression of alternate views is prohibited. From this vantage point, Malaysia appears as a religious state, at least for the 60% of Malaysian Muslims who are subject to such rules and regulations. Likewise, if secularism is understood as the strict separation of religion from governance, Malaysia appears to be the antithesis of a secular state.

Few would disagree that aspects of religion and governance are intertwined in contemporary Malaysia, but the simple secular-versus-religious dichotomy tends to obfuscate the ways that religious law is transformed as a result of incorporation as state law. The imposition of select fragments of *fiqh* (Islamic jurisprudence) should not be understood as the implementation of an 'Islamic' system of governance, or the achievement of an 'Islamic state', for no such ideal type exists. Instead, Malaysia provides a textbook example of how core principles in *usul al-fiqh* (Islamic legal theory) are subverted as a result of state appropriation. Malaysia thus provides an important opportunity to rethink the relationship between the state, secularism, and the politics of Islamic law. [...]

1. *The Islamic Legal Tradition*
One of the defining features of Islam is that there is no 'church'. That is, Islam has no centralized institutional authority to dictate a uniform doctrine. For guidance, Muslims must consult the textual sources of authority in Islam: the Qur'an, which Muslims believe to be the word of God as revealed to the Prophet Muhammad in the seventh century, and the Sunnah, the normative example of the Prophet. The absence of a centralized institutional authority inevitably produced a pluralistic legal order. In the first several centuries of Islam, schools of jurisprudence formed around leading scholars (*fuqaha'*) of Islamic law. Each school of jurisprudence (*madhhab*) developed its own distinct set of methods for engaging the central textual sources of authority in an effort to provide relevant guidance for the Muslim community. Techniques such as analogical reasoning (*qiyas*) and consensus (*ijma*), the consideration of the public interest (*maslaha*), and a variety of other legal concepts and tools were developed to constitute the field of *usul al-fiqh*. The legal science that emerged was one of staggering complexity and rigor, both within each *madhhab* and amongst them. Dozens of distinct schools of

Islamic jurisprudence emerged in the early centuries of the faith. However, most died out or merged over time, eventually leaving four central schools of jurisprudence in Sunni Islam that have continued to this day: the Hanafi, Hanbali, Maliki, and Shafi'i.

The engine of change within each school of jurisprudence was the private legal scholar, the *mujtahid*, who operated within the methodological framework of his or her *madhhab* to perform *ijtihad*, the disciplined effort to discern God's law. The central instrument of incremental legal change was the fatwa, a non-binding legal opinion offered by a qualified *mujtahid* in response to a question in Islamic law. Because *fatwas* are typically issued in response to questions posed by individuals in specific social situations, they responded to the evolving needs of particular Muslim communities in their own specific contexts. In this sense, the evolution of Islamic jurisprudence was a bottom-up, not a top-down process.

The Muslim legal community maintained unity within diversity through a critical conceptual distinction between the *shariah* (God's way) and *fiqh* (understanding). Whereas the *shariah* was considered immutable, the diverse body of juristic opinions that constitutes *fiqh* was acknowledged as the product of human engagement with the textual sources of authority in Islam. In this dichotomy, God is infallible, but human efforts to know God's will with any degree of certainty are imperfect and fallible. This norm was so deeply ingrained in the writings of classical jurists that they concluded their legal opinions and discussions with the statement *wa Allahu a'lam* (and God knows best). This phrase acknowledged that no matter how sure one is of her or his analysis and argumentation, only God ultimately knows which conclusions are correct. [...] [D]ifference of opinion was embraced as both inevitable and ultimately generative in the search for God's truth. Adages among scholars of Islamic law underlined this ethos, such as the proverb, 'In juristic disagreement there lies a divine blessing.'[1] In both theory and practice, Islamic law developed as a pluralist legal system to its very core.

The conceptual distinction between the *shariah* and *fiqh* was also critical in defining the relationship between experts in Islamic jurisprudence and lay Muslims. Because human understanding of God's will was recognized as unavoidably fallible, religious authority was not absolute. A *fatwa*, by definition, merely represented the informed legal opinion of a fallible scholar; it was not considered an infallible statement about the will of God.

---

[1] Wael B. Hallaq (2001), *Authority, Continuity, and Change in Islamic Law* (Cambridge: Cambridge University Press) at 241. [Editors' note]

The plural nature of Islamic jurisprudence and the conceptual distinction between the *shariah* and *fiqh* provided for the continuous evolution of Islamic law. Whereas the *shariah* was understood by Muslim jurists as immutable, *fiqh* was explicitly regarded as dynamic and responsive to the varying circumstances of the Muslim community across time and space. [...]

Conspicuously absent from this brief synopsis is any mention of the state. This is because the modern state, as we know it, did not exist for roughly the first twelve centuries of Islam. While specific forms of rule varied across time and place, as a general principle there was no administrative apparatus that applied uniform legal codes in the way that we have become so thoroughly accustomed to in the modern era. [...] Fiqh had thrived, in all its diversity, largely due to the limited administrative capacity of rulers. This would soon change, however, as rulers built modern bureaucracies and expanded their ability to project state power. Beginning in the late 18th century, legal codification and administrative innovations enabled the state to regulate individuals in a far more systematic and disciplined manner.

2. *The Transformation of Islamic Law*

A. *Codification as the Death of Pluralism*

Although Islam spread through the Malay Peninsula beginning in the 14th century, the institutionalization of Islamic law in its present form is a far more recent development. To the extent that Islamic law was practiced in the pre-colonial era, it was part and parcel of *adat* (custom) and was marked by tremendous variability across time and place. [...]

The introduction of codified law, new legal concepts and categories, and English style legal institutions all marked a significant departure from the customary practices that had varied widely across the Malay peninsula. The new legal regime was also incongruent with core epistemological assumptions of *usul al-fiqh*. The term 'Anglo-Muslim' law characterized this peculiar mix of legal traditions. The law was 'Anglo' in the sense that the concepts, categories, and modes of analysis followed English common law, and it was 'Muslim' in the sense that it contained fragments of Islamic jurisprudence that were applied to Muslim subjects. As such, Anglo-Muslim law was an entirely different creature from classical Islamic law. By the beginning of the 20th century, 'a classically-trained Islamic jurist would be at a complete loss with this Anglo-Muslim law', whereas 'a common lawyer with no knowledge of Islam would be perfectly comfortable.'[2] Passages from the Qur'an and Sunna

---

[2] M. B. Hooker (2002), "Islamic Law in South-East Asia," *Asian Law* 4 (3): 213–31 at 218. [Editors' note]

may be cited in court rulings to support particular decisions, but the mode of legal analysis is English common law, not *usul al-fiqh*. Hooker explains, 'it is not fanciful to suggest that the classical syar^i'ah is not the operative law and has not been since the colonial period. 'Islamic law' is really Anglo-Muslim law; that is, the law that the state makes applicable to Muslims.'[3] [...]

Women's rights advocates welcomed many of the provisions in the new Islamic Family Law Act as progressive advances for women. However, subsequent amendments introduced regressive provisions that made it more difficult for women to secure divorce, placed women in a weaker position in the division of matrimonial assets, and provided women with fewer rights in terms of child custody and maintenance. For example, Article 13 requires a woman to have her guardian's consent to marry (regardless of her age) while men have no similar requirement. Article 59 denies a wife her right to maintenance or alimony if she 'unreasonably refuses to obey the lawful wishes or commands of her husband'. Articles 47–55 make it simple and straightforward for a husband to divorce his wife (even outside of court), while a woman is faced with lengthy court procedures to earn a divorce without her husband's consent. Article 84 grants custody to the mother until the child reaches the age of seven (for boys) or nine (for girls), at which time custody reverts to the father. Moreover, Article 83 details conditions under which a mother can lose her right to custody due to reasons of irresponsibility, whereas no such conditions are stipulated for fathers. It should be emphasized that these stipulations are not unambiguously 'Islamic'. Indeed, Muslim women's rights activists field powerful arguments for why these and other provisions must be understood as betraying the core values of justice and equality in Islam. [...]

B. *Naming as a Means of Claiming Islamic Law*
In addition to codification and increased specificity in the law, there was an important shift in the way that Anglo-Muslim law was presented to the Malaysian public beginning in the 1970s. Until that time, Anglo-Muslim family law was understood as being grounded in some substantive aspects of custom and *fiqh* (Islamic jurisprudence), but there was no formal pretense that the laws themselves constituted '*shariah*'. The 1957 Federal Constitution, for example, outlined a role for the states in administering 'Muslim law' as did the state-level statutes that regulated family law. However, a constitutional amendment in 1976 replaced each iteration of 'Muslim law' with 'Islamic law'. Likewise, every mention of 'Muslim courts' was amended to read 'Syariah courts'. The same semantic shift soon appeared in statutory law: the Muslim

---

[3] Hooker (2002), note 2, at 218. [Editors' note]

Family Law Act became the Islamic Family Law Act; the Administration of Muslim Law Act became the Administration of Islamic Law Act; the Muslim Criminal Law Offenses Act became the Syariah Criminal Offenses Act; the Muslim Criminal Procedure Act became the Syariah Criminal Procedure Act and so on.

Why is this important? In all of these amendments, the shift in terminology exchanged the *object of the law* (Muslims) for the purported *essence of the law* (as 'Islamic'). This semantic shift, I argue, is a prime example of what Erik Hobsbawm calls 'the invention of tradition'. The authenticity of the Malaysian 'shariah' courts is premised on fidelity to the Islamic legal tradition. Yet, ironically, the Malaysian government reconstituted Islamic law in ways that are better understood as a subversion of the Islamic legal tradition. That distinct form of Anglo-Muslim law, it must be remembered, is little more than a century old. But every reference to state 'fatwas' or the 'shariah courts' serves to strengthen the state's claim to embrace the Islamic legal tradition. Indeed, the power of this semantic construction is underlined by the fact that even in a critique such as this, the author finds it difficult, if not impossible, to avoid using these symbolically laden terms. It is with the aid of such semantic shifts that the government presents the syariah courts as a faithful rendering of the Islamic legal tradition, rather than as a subversion of that tradition. In this regard, a parallel may be drawn to nationalism. Just as nationalism requires a collective forgetting of the historical record in order to embrace a sense of nation, so too does shariah court authority require a collective amnesia vis-à-vis the Islamic legal tradition. [...]

C. *The State's Monopoly on Religious Law*
One of the most striking features of the Malaysian legal system is the extent to which the state and federal authorities claim a monopoly on religious interpretation. The institutionalization of religious authority can be traced back to the colonial era when state-level religious councils (*Majlis Agama Islam*) and departments of religious affairs (*Jabatan Agama Islam*) were established in most states of British Malaya. According to Roff, these institutional transformations produced 'an authoritarian form of religious administration much beyond anything known to the peninsula before.'[4] This centralization of religious authority continued after independence. [...]

[T]he powers provided to these authorities are extraordinary. Most significantly, the Mufti is empowered to issue fatwas that, upon publication, are

---

[4] William R. Roff (1967), *The Origins of Malay Nationalism* (New Haven, CT: Yale University Press) at 72–3. [Editors' note]

'binding on every Muslim resident in the Federal Territories' [Article 34]. Accordingly, fatwas in the contemporary Malaysian context do not serve as non-binding opinions from religious scholars as in classical Islamic jurisprudence; rather, they carry the force of law and are backed by the full power of the Malaysian state. Moreover, the Administration of Islamic Law Act allows this lawmaking function to completely bypass legislative institutions such as the Parliament. Other elements of transparency and democratic deliberation are also excluded by explicit design. For example, Article 28 of the Act declares, 'The proceedings of the Majlis shall be kept secret and no member or servant thereof shall disclose or divulge to any person, other than the Yang di-Pertuan Agong [Supreme Head of State] or the Minister, and any member of the Majlis, any matter that has arisen at any meeting unless he is expressly authorized by the Majlis.' In other words, the Administration of Islamic Law Act subverts not only basic principles of Islamic legal theory (*usul al-fiqh*), but also the foundational principles of liberal democracy that are enshrined in the 1957 Constitution, by denying public access to the decision-making process that leads to the establishment of laws. [...]

3. *State Power, Secularism, and the Politics of Islamic Law*
This study opened with the observation that Malaysia ranks among the top six countries worldwide in the degree of state regulation of religion. From this vantage point, Malaysia appears to be the antithesis of a secular state and the realization of a religious state, at least for the 60% of Malaysian Muslims who are subject to such rules and regulations. Indeed, former Prime Minister Mahathir Mohammad famously declared Malaysia an 'Islamic state' and government officials have subsequently repeated the claim. Yet despite the fact that aspects of religion and governance are clearly intertwined, the Malaysian case illustrates how the simple dichotomy of 'secular' versus 'religious' obfuscates more than it reveals. As recent work on secularism shows, the secular-versus-religious dichotomy leaves unexamined the troubled genealogy of secularism itself. Most important for our purposes, the dichotomy takes its own starting point for granted and overlooks the ways that both categories were constructed as mirror opposites with the expanding regulatory capacity of the modern state.

The Malaysian case illustrates why the secular-versus-religious dichotomy provides a particularly poor schema through which to understand state incorporation of Islamic law. Perhaps most obviously, the conventional labels of 'religious' and 'secular' impose a binary with zero-sum properties. At any given point, the religious and the secular are imagined to be in an uneasy truce, a state of simmering tension, or an all-out struggle for supremacy. An advance for one is a loss for the other. Indeed, the two most common narratives in studies of Islam and politics in contemporary Malaysia depict an otherwise secular state capitulating to pressure and adopting Islamic law, or, alternately, proactively harnessing Islamic law for political advantage. While both readings capture important dynamics in the competition over religious authority, these sorts of arguments tend to present Islamic law in an 'additive' manner. That is to say, at any given moment Malaysia is understood as being somewhere on a continuum between a 'secular' and 'religious' state. Media frames and popular political discourse cycle through the same tropes ad nauseam, incessantly asking the anxious question of whether Malaysia is, will become, or was ever meant to be a 'secular state' or an 'Islamic state'. This is not to deny the fact that Malaysians have diverse (and often divergent) visions for the future of their country. And this is not to minimize the very real consequences that these political struggles have for individual rights, deliberative democracy, and a host of other important issues. It is only to say that the secular-versus-religious schema too often assumes a unidimensional and ahistorical conception of Islamic law and thus tends to take the state's claim to Islamic law for granted. In other words, anxiety over 'how much' Islamic law is incorporated as state law too often assumes that the outcome is consistent with the Islamic legal tradition in the first place. What drops out of the picture are the specific ways that state incorporation of Islamic law, at least in the fashion documented here, subverts the Islamic legal tradition itself.

As select fragments of *fiqh* (Islamic jurisprudence) are constituted within an emerging field of state law, little or no space is left for *usul al-fiqh*, the interpretive method that undergirds Islamic jurisprudence. Stripped of its methodological underpinnings, these transformations subvert the epistemological approach of classical Islamic legal theory (*usul al-fiqh*) by collapsing the important conceptual distinctions between the *shariah* (God's way) and *fiqh* (human understanding), with the ultimate result of facilitating the state's claim to 'speak in God's name.'[5] But more than this, by monopolizing interpretation, codifying select fragments of *fiqh*, and deploying those laws through state institutions, the Malaysian state is 'judging in God's name'. The religious councils, the *shariah* courts, and the entire administrative apparatus are Islamic in name, but in function they bear little resemblance to the

---

[5] The author notes that he has borrowed both the concept and the phraseology from Khaled Abou El Fadl (2001), *Speaking in God's Name: Islamic Law, Authority and Women* (London: Oneworld Publications). [Editors' note]

> Islamic legal tradition. A deep paradox is therefore at play: the legitimacy of the religious administration rests on the emotive power of Islamic symbolism, but its principal mode of organization and operation is fundamentally rooted in the Weberian state.

## IV LAW, RELIGION, AND CONFLICT IN CONTEMPORARY ASIA

Across the landscape of contemporary Asia, the relationship of law to religion remains highly unstable and varies greatly from country to country. The influence of secularism is everywhere apparent, but there is no uniform commitment to a rigorous separation of the religious and the legal spheres. On the contrary, some Asian countries view the ideology of secularism as consistent with establishing a particular religion as the officially preferred faith. The French concept of *laïcité*, which would in theory prohibit any involvement of the government in religious affairs (and vice versa), has not prevailed in any society except arguably the socialist regimes. But even there, in countries such as China, Vietnam, Cambodia, and Laos, religious practices and beliefs persist and shape the legal consciousness of many in the population. And in some countries, such as Brunei, the government has adopted such a stringent interpretation of a particular religion – in this case Islam – that any deviation or customary practice (such as the worship of local spirit shrines) is deemed a threat to national security. Dominik M. Müller (2015: 341–2) notes that this repressive deployment of religion emerged as a paradoxical result of legal "modernization" during British colonial rule:

> Although the empowerment and expansion of Sharia law in Brunei is locally presented, and might be interpreted academically, as an attempt at postcolonial emancipation, it cannot evade its colonial imprint of modern legalism and bureaucratization, thus presenting a case of uneven, paradoxical continuity. By advising the sultanate on the systematic codification, institutionalization and diversification of its administration of Islam, the British helped to create the institutional and ideational substrate from which the later Shariatization, including the latest legal reform, eventually emerged. Islam became translated into the modern language of bureaucratic legalism, which still continues to shape the postcolonial state's exercise of classificatory power today, as manifested in its sanction-based policies of standardizing truth and deviance.
>
> Considering the political priority given to Islamization policies, and leaving aside sincere beliefs in accumulating divine blessings in this world and the

afterlife for realizing God's legislative will, we may ask who benefits from Brunei's expansion of Sharia law? The Sultan and his political system are the clearest winners, as the SPCO [Syariah Penal Code Order 2013] further consolidates their (literally and figuratively) unquestionable power and divine legitimation. Simultaneously, the SPCO gives to the Islamic bureaucracy what many of its representatives had long hoped for and devoutly believe in, thereby ensuring their support, while simultaneously further cementing the state ulama's monopoly and socio-political influence.

The readings in this section are not a comprehensive survey of contemporary Asia, since the field is too vast and the variation too extensive. Rather, they provide a few examples of the many different dilemmas involving law and religion in Asia today. In Vineeta Sinha's study of Singapore, we see a government struggling to maintain its political commitment to pluralism while at the same time asserting its preference for certain forms of religiosity and its opposition to others. By contrast, in Benjamin Schonthal's study of Sri Lanka, we see a very different government posture toward religion. There, as in a number of other Asian countries, the primacy of Buddhism is enshrined in the constitution, and the government finds itself drawn into pronouncements about proper and improper forms of Buddhist practice even as it asserts a role as protector of religious freedom and pluralism in general. And finally, in John Breen's article about Shinto shrines in Japan, we see a government attempting to defend its stance as a secular regime even as it maintains its ancient connection to sacred Shinto legitimizing practices and institutions that, in modern Japan, can also have disturbing right-wing political overtones.

## 1.9 Theorising "Talk" about "Religious Pluralism" and "Religious Harmony" in Singapore, *Vineeta Sinha*

Vineeta Sinha discusses the passage of Singapore's Maintenance of the Religious Harmony (MRH) Act in 1990. In a small nation composed of multiple ethnic and religious groups, the government adopted a neutral stance toward all religions while insisting that none of them could stir up "ill feelings" toward the others or engage in subversive activities in relation to Singaporean society as a whole. As Sinha points out, the rhetoric surrounding the passage of the MRH Act extolled a mythical past characterized by tolerance, respect, and nonviolence. By contrast, the contemporary era was portrayed as a time of imagined threats of religious-based terrorism and aggressive proselytization. These threats were variously associated with leftist Christian groups, Islamic fundamentalists, and Christian evangelists. Whether such threats were real or not, the legislation provided an occasion for the Singaporean government to reaffirm its policy of strict separation of church and state, even though, perhaps paradoxically, the Act was aimed against certain forms of religiosity that were deemed outside the social mainstream.

*Maintenance of the Religious Harmony Act: A Legislative Solution?*
The 9th November 1990 is significant in the legislative history of Singapore. After more than five years of planning, debating, and deliberation, a Bill to maintain religious harmony was passed by the Singapore Parliament, bringing into effect the MRH [Maintenance of the Religious Harmony] Act. Singapore thus scored yet another 'first', becoming the only country in the world to have a law of this nature. Expectedly, this legislation generated discussions locally and critical sociological commentary from students of Singapore society, highlighting among other things, that this Act was devised to keep the realms of 'religion' and 'politics' separate, realms already pre-defined by the state in specific ways. [Joseph B.] Tamney further states that "Clearly the target of the new law was leftist Christianity (and, to a lesser extent, Islamic fundamentalism). Both the 'Marxist conspiracy' and Christian evangelism awakened the leaders to the political threat of Christianity."[1] [...]

*How the Act Came into Being*
Although the Act came into existence in 1990, different kinds of evidence, including a report prepared by the Internal Security Department (ISD) of Singapore in 1986, set into motion the chain of events that culminated in this unique piece of legislation. Among other details of religious life, the report noted the prevalence of inter-religious tensions in Singapore, coupled with a large-scale incidence of aggressive proselytisation and the exploitation of "religion for political and subversive purposes."[2] The Ministry of Community Development (MCD) then commissioned more detailed studies to investigate religious trends in Singapore. These reports, too, 'confirmed' some of the central findings of the ISD report.

In the face of such evidence the government felt that action was imperative to ensure religious harmony. [...]

Under this law, action can be taken against any religious leader, official or member of any religious group or institution, who causes ill-feelings between different religious groups or promotes a political cause or carries out subversive activities under the guise of propagating or practising any religious belief.

---

[1] Joseph B. Tamney (1996), *The Struggle over the Singapore's Soul: Western Modernization and Asian Culture* (Berlin: de Gruyter) at 36–7. [Editors' note]

[2] *White Paper on Maintenance of Religious Harmony Bill* (1989). Presented to Parliament by Command of The President of the Republic of Singapore, at 13. [Editors' note]

The 'offender' is first issued with a restraining order, with notice, by the Minister of Home Affairs and has the right to make written representations to the Minister and the Presidential Council for Religious Harmony. The latter deliberates on both the order and the written representations of the concerned person and makes recommendations (confirming, cancelling or varying the restraining order) to the President. The President is the final arbiter. He may "... cancel or confirm the order and in confirming may make such variations as he thinks fit" (Section 11). A breach of the restraining order makes the person liable for conviction, which may lead to a fine or imprisonment or both.

*The State's Rationale for Legislation: Singapore Must be Multi-Religious*
In the Singapore State's discourse, religious tolerance is regarded as absolutely necessary for the prevention of religious polarisation and sectarian strife. Excessive religious fervour, missionary zeal, and religious assertiveness are considered undesirable. A situation of religious harmony is a matter of 'national pride', not to mention a good selling point in presenting Singapore as a haven of harmony in the midst of a region characterised by communal differences. The tie between political stability and religious tolerance and moderation is emphasised. The state has an obvious and pragmatic interest in ensuring that religious differences do not lead to conflict, which would be counter-productive to the socio-economic and political security of the nation.

Soon after its separation from Malaya, Singapore's ruling *élite* inherited a multi-religious republic and the responsibility of managing this pluralism. Given the close proximity of different religious communities, religion has been viewed as a sensitive subject and a source of potential social conflict, but nonetheless 'legitimate' and a necessary social feature. Yet, although seen to be potentially problematic, religious differences have not prompted the state to wish for a religiously uniform Singapore. In fact, government ministers consider the idea of a 'religiously homogeneous' Singapore society impossible and absurd. That Singapore is, and must continue to, be defined by diversity and plurality, in its ethnic, linguistic, and religious make-up, is entrenched in all public discussions of social life on the island. Yet, there is a stream of thinking that these irreconcilable differences must be negotiated. With regard to religion, this is clear. According to BG Lee Hsien Loong, "We have to find some way to compromise practically *what is impossible to reconcile theologically.*"[3]

---

[3] *Straits Times*, January 31, 1990 (emphasis added by the author). [Editors' note]

In utterances like these, one notes a fairly serious and problematic admission: religious diversity cannot by itself ensure religious harmony. If anything, it is the reverse. The government's position is that religious diversity and religious differences have the potential to generate misunderstandings among religious communities, but this possibility must be prevented at all cost, through a rational, practical, common-sensical, tolerant approach. According to the Prime Minister, Goh Chok Tong,

> I consider the racial and religious harmony as the most important bedrock of our society. If there is no harmony, there will be no peaceful, prosperous Singapore – as simple as that.[4]

The liberating aspect of the discourse on the MRH Act is that specific statements could be made about inter-religious relations, which were otherwise 'taboo.' The deliberations relating to the Act enable 'talk' of religious disharmony in a context where the overwhelming emphasis is on harmony, whereas inter-religious tensions are experientially real – and not entirely surprising. The Act also supplies a language that enables talk about religious conflict in a discursive context that celebrates religious pluralism, to the almost total denial of tensions. Further interesting is the idea that the tensions are 'new', 'recent', and somewhat anomalous in the otherwise peaceful trajectory of religious co-existence in Singapore since independence. [...] One notes a certain political romanticising (and imagining) of the 'good old days', the glorious, amicable, past of a multi-religious era. [...]

The government's rationale for introducing additional legislation to deal with possible religious disharmony was founded on the following reasons. Firstly, conditions internal to Singapore were cited. The government noted a shift in religious sentiment from 'tolerant co-existence' to 'fervently held beliefs', visible in greater evangelical activity and religious revivalism among Christians, Muslims, and Buddhists. Further, specific instances were noted in which religion had been used as a front for carrying out political activities.... Secondly, government leaders referred to examples of 'other' societies that had been plagued by communal violence. India, Sri Lanka, Fiji, Lebanon, Northern Ireland, the Philippines, Iran, Iraq, Armenia, and Azerbaijan were cited as examples of how communal clashes occurred as a result of religious insensitivity and mixing religion with politics. Finally, the language of the Act alluded to the dangers, negative potentialities, and anticipation of an 'imagined' or 'anticipated' religiously disharmonious situation. According to

---

[4] *Straits Times*, February 24, 1990. [Editors' note]

this logic, Singapore in 1990 continued to be multi-religious, but strewn with seeds of religious tension and disharmony. [...]

One question was whether the proposed Act would infringe the constitutional guarantee of religious freedom. In this discussion, the rights of the individual citizen and these of the collective citizenry confronted each other. While the Constitution guarantees individuals the liberty to practise and propagate religious teachings, including the right to proselytise, the sentiment was also expressed that 'absolute religious freedom' was neither possible nor desirable. Some members of the public called upon the government not only to 'check the activities of people and groups who proselytise in public', but also to ban public propagation of religious beliefs, because religion was a personal affair and should be practised in private.

### 1.10 Securing the Sasana through Law: Buddhist Constitutionalism and Buddhist-Interest Litigation in Sri Lanka, Benjamin Schonthal

In contrast to the strict Singaporean policy of separating church and state, Benjamin Schonthal in the following article discusses a polity – Sri Lanka – with an explicit constitutional preference for one religion, Buddhism, over all others. As Schonthal explains, "Sri Lanka's constitution appears to give the state legal responsibility for the well-being of Buddhism." The "establishment" of one faith as the nation's official religion is by no means unique to Sri Lanka and can be found in differing forms in many countries of Asia and the rest of the world. The result is not necessarily a lack of freedom for other forms of worship, since their rights may also be safeguarded by law; but state support for one officially favored religion can lead to some perplexing constitutional challenges about "what Buddhism is, who should speak for it, and how it ought to be protected." Schonthal describes lawsuits brought by Buddhist leaders to limit commercial appropriation of religious symbols and to oppose proselytization by Catholic organizations that might draw Buddhist worshippers to Christianity. Such litigation places the Sri Lanka Supreme Court in the position of defining what it views as the legitimate nature and role of Buddhism in the nation's public life through its very effort to protect Buddhism's well-being. Schonthal asks why such litigation has been more prevalent in Sri Lanka than in other Buddhist countries, such as Thailand, Myanmar, and Cambodia; and he speculates that the future may bring further efforts to "legalize" questions of religious legitimacy and protection in Sri Lanka and elsewhere. Such efforts would, of course, have significant implications for factionalism in Asian nations, as religious issues have become increasingly politicized across the entire region.

> Sri Lanka's supreme law includes special prerogatives for Buddhism as well as general religious rights. It awards to Buddhism the 'foremost place' and obligates the state to 'protect and foster' the Buddha's legacy in the world, the Sasana, while also assuring rights to freedom of religious belief and practice. [...] Although Sri Lanka's constitution appears to give the state legal responsibility for the well-being of Buddhism, equally important are the ways in which it empowers citizens to make broad and diverse constitutional claims in the name of Buddhism. Buddhist constitutionalism in Sri Lanka has enabled a climate of Buddhist-interest litigation, public legal battles over what Buddhism is, who should speak for it, and how it ought to be protected.
>
> *Buddhist Constitutionalism and the Work of Constitutional Law*
> As a type of constitutional law that privileges a country's most populous religion, Buddhist constitutionalism looks very similar to the constitutional traditions of many other countries. For example, Egypt, Tunisia, Malaysia, Israel, and Denmark all have basic laws that combine special prerogatives for the majority religion with rights and (sometimes) recognition for other religions. These types of constitutions are by no means marginal. By some estimates, approximately 40 per cent of all constitutions explicitly favour a particular religion while also guaranteeing general religious rights and as much as half of the world's population live under constitutional arrangements of this sort. [...]
>
> Constitutional protections for Buddhism have not contained the spread of Buddhist claims on political life nor have they simply authorized the state to act in the best interests of Buddhism. The Buddhism Chapter's more profound effects lie in the way in which it has enabled and incentivized Sri Lanka's citizens – or, at least, those with adequate resources and time – to translate specific disagreements and political concerns into formal contests over the nature of Buddhism and the state's obligations to protect it. Constitutional protections for Buddhism have activated a culture of Buddhist-interest litigation, one that has increased the number and the visibility of grievances about Buddhism, while also making those grievances matters of national concern. Constitutional protections for Buddhism have, counter-intuitively, amplified and multiplied – rather than allayed – public concerns and frustration over the well-being and status of Buddhism. [...]

In 2004 the Supreme Court heard the fundamental rights petition of Ven. Daranagama Kusaladhamma Thero, the head monk of a large Colombo temple. The petition requested that the court issue an order to the inspector general of police to arrest anyone involved in selling 'merchandised Buddha images which defiles and defame[s] Lord Buddha'. The merchandise in question included swimwear manufactured by Victoria's Secret containing 'the image of the Buddha displayed on the breasts and crotch areas', a pair of slippers with Buddha images on them, a candle made in the likeness of the Buddha, and a set of 'Buddha Bar' compact discs (on sale in a Colombo music store). In his petition the monk stated that the products would cause Buddhists to be 'emotionally hurt, annoyed and therefore offended', to be 'gravely provoked', and to be made 'emotionally turbulent.' This would, among other things, contravene Buddhism Chapter obligations to protect and foster the Buddha Sasana.

In his submissions, the monk publicly affirmed a categorical opposition between Western capitalistic imperatives and local Buddhist sensibilities:

> [I]f the Buddha's image is continuously used publicly on bikinis, on slippers, as candles and on music compact discs etc. it would loose [sic] the impact as an image of honour and pilgrimage. Further it would be perceived as a brand like 'Coca Cola', cream soda etc .... Naturally the children teenagers and youth of such religion who are exposed to religious images in such casual and merchandised manner would loose [sic] faith and sincere respect in the philosophy stated by such religious leaders.

The petition accused global manufacturers of transforming the Buddha into a symbol for branding and marketing products. Ven. Kusaladhamma saw this as a significant threat to Buddhism. By using religious imagery as a marketing device, manufacturers (and those who sold their products) contributed to the 'decline in worshiping or observing practices on such religious image or symbol ... [and] this would not only affect the individual per se, it would affect his or her religion in observing and worshiping in the long run'. According to Ven. Kusaladhamma's submissions, reproducing the Buddha's image on common items not only cheapened and degraded the image of the Buddha, it led to the discrediting of Buddhism and therefore to a decline in membership and observance.

The submissions made by Ven. Kusaladhamma invoked the constitutional mandate to protect Buddhism in order to prevent a particular profaning effect of neoliberal commercialism: that of using Buddhist iconography for the selling of commercial products. This, he insisted, was an improper (and unconstitutional) mixing of religion and economics. Similar impulses appear in a second set of court cases. In these cases, litigants invoked constitutional protections to thwart a different kind of mixing between religion and economics. In three cases that were heard by the Supreme Court between 2000 and 2003, petitioners opposed the mixing of economic incentives and religious motives by Christian organizations, arguing that they constituted a threat to Buddhism. Here, however, it was not the commercial degrading of Buddhism that was at issue, but the 'unethical' use of wealth (notably, wealth deriving from foreign sources) to promote conversion to Christianity.

The cases related to attempts by three separate Christian organizations to gain legal incorporation through acts of parliament. (At the time, this was a common procedure for legal recognition of religious groups in Sri Lanka.) In each case, a petitioner, who was affiliated with a Buddhist organization, challenged the proposed incorporation bill, claiming, among other things, that by recognizing the particular Christian group, the government would be contravening its constitutional duties to Buddhism. In 2001, a petitioner challenged the incorporation of an evangelical 'prayer centre' that conducted regular services, faith healing, and charity work. In 2003, two separate petitioners challenged the incorporation of two other groups: one was an independent evangelical ministry whose stated aims included holding 'deliverance meetings', building places of worship, organizing workshops, undertaking social services, and holding religious services; the other was an order of Catholic nuns who ran schools, assisted in medical centres, and undertook other social service activities. [...]

According to the petition, neither the religious activities nor the 'material assistance' specified in the proposed bill alone violated the terms of the constitution. The problem was the mingling of the two. By mixing material and religious imperatives, the petitioners insisted, Christian groups would be able to leverage one against the other, using promises of better jobs, improved health or increased wealth – promises that were underwritten by the perceived wealth and resources of related, international Christian organizations – to draw Buddhists to Christianity. The result was 'unethical' proselytizing.

As with the above cases, litigants associated the profaned (use of) religion with distinct foreign threats. Petitioners pointed out that Christian groups represented not only an alternative faith (to Buddhism), but a different 'culture' and geography as well. The conversion of Buddhists to Christianity, in this view, threatened Sri Lanka's demographic, cultural, and religious uniqueness, and exposed vulnerable local people to powerful 'international' forces.

In 2003, the Supreme Court itself affirmed some of these claims, albeit in terse and evasive language. In the second incorporation case (relating to the incorporation of an evangelical ministry), a Supreme Court majority opinion insisted, without further explanation, that because the ministry seemed to mix economic and religious goals in its charter, its incorporation would be 'inconsistent with the Buddhism Chapter'. In the third case (relating to the incorporation of an order of Catholic nuns), the Supreme Court argued further that not only was such mixing 'inconsistent' with the Buddhism Chapter, a Christian organization of that type might 'impair the very existence of Buddhism or the Buddha Sasana'. No further explanation was given in this case either. [...]

*Expanding and Consolidating Conclusions*
Invoking the Buddhism Chapter in the courts provided a powerful mechanism for expanding the visibility and political importance of protecting Buddhism in Sri Lankan life. While Sri Lanka's courts have not always affirmed litigants' claims about Buddhism, the very act of legal contestation has elevated into matters of public concern questions about the nature of Buddhism, who is authorized to speak for it, and how it ought to be protected. In pursing these questions, courts and litigants have authorized and publicized certain types of religious divisions: between Buddhists and 'anti-Buddhist' governments, between Buddhist monks and laypersons, between orthodox Buddhists and heterodox Buddhists, between Buddhists and non-Buddhists (Hindus, Christians, Muslims, Tamil separatists), and between Buddhism and the corrupting effects of global industry, transnational Christianity, and 'the West'. Litigants and judges have also endorsed the need to protect a variety of objects (for example, temples, educational institutions, practices, monks, texts, archaeological sites, villages, images, and conscience) *from* a variety of threats (for example, government agents, heterodox monks, Tamil Tiger militants, Muslim interlopers, international corporations, foreign governments, and Christian proselytizers).

Since its introduction in 1972, the range of interpretations of the Buddhism Chapter has expanded, keeping pace with and reflecting a growing number of political and social concerns. The very mechanisms designed to expand the availability of public law remedies – protocols of judicial review and fundamental rights jurisdiction inspired by traditions of liberal constitutionalism – have made available channels for making public, constitutional claims about Buddhism. In fact, today one even finds a consistent, almost routinized, legal format for Buddhist-interest litigation. In many cases, litigants use judicial review or fundamental rights petitions to advance specific arguments about how to protect Buddhism: they claim that a certain bill or a certain government initiative contravenes or is likely to contravene the state's duties to

Religion 69

> Buddhism and/or certain fundamental rights; once the case has been granted leave by the Supreme Court, they then use the hearing to publicize and validate particular visions of Buddhism, threats to it, and the ideal nature of the state's relationship with it. This format has been employed frequently. As a result, Sri Lanka has seen a gradually expanding culture of Buddhist-interest litigation.

### 1.11 "Conventional Wisdom" and the Politics of Shinto in Postwar Japan, *John Breen*

Japan's postwar constitution creates a wall between religion and the state, prohibiting the state from engaging in any "religious activity" and from using public moneys "for the use, benefit or maintenance of any religious institution or association." Nevertheless, as John Breen explains in the following reading, Japanese leaders have often engaged in activities at Shinto sites that test these legal boundaries – and the Supreme Court has ruled that some degree of state involvement with religion in such instances is permissible if it does not exceed "an appropriate level." When then-Prime Minister Koizumi Jun'ichirō visited the Yasukuni shrine for the Japanese war dead in 2001, a shrine associated symbolically with Japan's recent imperial past, he triggered an intense debate about the relationship between law, religion, and politics in contemporary Japan. His supporters observed that virtually all Japanese Prime Ministers paid New Year's visits to the Shinto shrine at Ise to venerate Amaterasu ōmikami, the Sun Goddess who was the mythical founder of the Japanese imperial line. Why, they asked, should the Shinto shrine at Yasukuni raise greater constitutional problems concerning the separation of church and state than the Shinto shrine at Amaterasu? Breen's discussion illustrates the extreme difficulty of disentangling religion and the state, even in an Asian polity that has no formally established religion and whose constitution appears to require strict separation. Breen also highlights the extremely volatile politics associated with activities that challenge or arguably transgress the boundaries between church and state.

> The post war Japanese state's relationship to Shinto (and to other religions) is framed in two well-known articles of the Constitution. Article 20 holds both that "freedom of religion is guaranteed to all", and that "no religious organization shall receive any privileges from the State, nor exercise any political authority." Further, it stipulates that "no person shall be compelled to take

part in any religious acts, celebration, rite or practice [and that] the State and its organs shall refrain from religious education or any other religious activity." Then there is Article 89, which forbids the use of public moneys "for the use, benefit or maintenance of any religious institution or association". [...]

The single most important issue in post war state-religion relations has concerned Yasukuni, the Shinto shrine in Tokyo dedicated to Japan's war dead. A small majority of post war Japanese premiers (14 out of 27) have gone to Yasukuni to pay their respects. In doing, they have invited the charge that they breach Article 20, but do they? The jury, it seems, is out. Article 20 clearly guarantees the Prime Minister's right to venerate at Yasukuni as a private citizen, but it does not obviously allow him to patronise, and so privilege, Yasukuni (or any other religious institution) as Prime Minister. For, as such, he represents the state. So when, it may well be asked, is a Prime Minister not a Prime Minister, but a private citizen? Ever since the 1970s, the answer has come to hinge on such niceties as whether he arrives at Yasukuni in an official or private car; whether his shrine offerings come from his own pocket or the public purse, and how he signs himself in the shrine register. [...]

On August 13, 2001, the first year of his premiership, Koizumi worshipped at Yasukuni. He went in an official car, accompanied by his Chief Cabinet Secretary, and signed himself Prime Minister Koizumi; his shrine offerings, however, came out his own pocket. This visit triggered, as surely it was intended to, legal action. The suit that has attracted most media attention was that filed by a citizens' group in the Fukuoka District Court. They sought remuneration from the state for the "spiritual damage" inflicted upon them by Koizumi's act of veneration. In April 2004, Judge Kamekawa granted that the plaintiffs experienced "concern and apprehension", but found no evidence of "infringement of legal interests". Judges in the Matsuyama and Osaka District Courts had reached the very same conclusion in the previous year. What distinguished the Fukuoka suit, however, was that the judge made further comments on the case by way of obiter dictum.

In Japan, unlike Germany say, there are no constitutional courts, and so a plaintiff wishing to get a constitutional ruling in a civil case has to file a suit seeking compensation for infringement of his or her rights. The presiding judge may then choose to refer to constitutional issues, but usually he does not. Judge Kamekawa was thus an exception. The effect of Koizumi's visit to Yasukuni in 2001 was, indeed, he opined, to "aid, assist and promote Yasukuni shrine, a religious institution that disseminates Shinto". "One has to conclude [therefore] that the Prime Minister's Yasukuni visit corresponds to those religious acts prohibited by Article 20". In 2005, the Osaka High Court judge issued another obiter dictum, which similarly deemed Koizumi's actions unconstitutional. Obiter dicta are the judge's "expression of opinion on matters of law, which is not of binding authority". They are thus not "rulings", which of course explains why Koizumi was able to return with impunity to Yasukuni in August 2006. ...

Yasukuni has been at the heart of state-religion issues in the post war period, but there is a justifiable sense amongst some Japanese that the law is applied inconsistently. After all, the prime minister can attend Christian churches and Buddhist temples without a murmur of discontent. Why, it might be asked, is the state's patronage of Yasukuni alone the focus of such keen interest? This question is especially pertinent since prime ministers patronise with impunity the greatest Shinto shrine of them all. I refer to Ise, the shrine dedicated to Amaterasu ōmikami, Sun Goddess and mythical founder of the imperial line. Since the 1970s, it has been the custom for Japanese Prime Ministers of all hues to lead their cabinets to the Ise shrines at New Year. There, they venerate Amaterasu, and pray for Japan's flourishing. The Christian Ōhira Masayoshi, the Socialist Murayama Tomiichi and Hatoyama Yukio of the Democratic Party (incumbent at the time of writing) have all participated in clearly "official" acts of Ise veneration. The media gives this annual event very little critical attention, and so far it has prompted no legal action. Prime Minister Koizumi quite reasonably asked why he cannot venerate at Yasukuni, when he is free to worship annually at the Shinto shrines of Ise? Of course, it could equally well be asked why there is so little controversy over the state's patronage of Ise given the legal problems over Yasukuni? To these two questions, no answers are presently sought. [...]

[W]hat is abundantly clear is that there is a yearning on the part of the Shinto establishment for the type of polity that shaped imperial Japan in the 19th and early 20th centuries. This has been shared, albeit with considerably more caution, by successive LDP administrations. Article 20 and the revised Imperial household law have stood athwart these yearnings, interfering with their reproduction in the post war.

As we have seen, the Shinto establishment idealises a model of state and society in which the imperial institution, the Amaterasu myth, the Ise shrines, and the emperor himself as sacred presence are central. This is the essence of the Shinto spirit that must be located at the foundation of governance. [...]

Yasukuni is above all an imperial shrine. Its war dead died for imperial Japan; its rituals are graced by the presence of imperial emissaries. Those rituals celebrate the imperial virtues the dead exhibited in their dying: patriotism and loyalty and self-sacrifice. No prime minister or cabinet member who worships at Yasukuni can be ignorant of the shrine's powerful imperial symbolism. The shrine and its ritual performances provide a clear and

> unbroken link to the pre-war period, affirming the glories of Japan's imperial past.
>
> This nostalgia for the imperial past, shared by the Shinto establishment and the LDP, encounters Constitutional obstacles – by no means all of them insuperable – at every turn. It is this conflict between the nostalgia and the Constitution that goes a long way to explaining why state-religion, and specifically state-Shinto, issues assume such importance. On these issues is seen to hang the very fortunes of post war democratic Japan.

REFERENCES

**Featured Readings**

Breen, John. 2010. "'Conventional Wisdom' and the Politics of Shinto in Postwar Japan." *Politics and Religion* 4 (1): 68–82. doi: 10.54561/prjo401068b

Davis, Donald R., Jr. 2007. "Hinduism as a Legal Tradition." *Journal of the American Academy of Religion* 75 (2): 241–67. doi: 10.1093/jaarel/lfm004

Engel, David M. and Jaruwan Engel. 2010. *Tort, Custom, and Karma: Globalization and Legal Consciousness in Thailand.* Stanford, CA: Stanford University Press. doi: 10.1515/9780804773751

French, Rebecca Redwood and Mark A. Nathan. 2014. *Buddhism and Law: An Introduction.* Cambridge: Cambridge University Press. doi: 10.1017/cbo9781139044134

Galanter, Marc. 1972. "The Aborted Restoration of 'Indigenous' Law in India." *Comparative Studies in Society and History* 14 (1): 53–70. doi: 10.1017/s0010417500006502

Kirkland, Russell. 2004. *Taoism: The Enduring Tradition.* New York: Routledge. doi: 10.4324/9780203646717-8

Moustafa, Tamir. 2014. "Judging in God's Name: State Power, Secularism, and the Politics of Islamic Law in Malaysia." *Oxford Journal of Law and Religion* 3 (1): 152–67. doi: 10.4324/9781315244624-15

Salim, Arskal. 2008. *Challenging the Secular State: The Islamization of Law in Modern Indonesia.* Honolulu: University of Hawai'i Press. doi: 10.21313/hawaii/9780824832377.003.0006

Schonthal, Benjamin. 2016. "Securing the Sasana through Law: Buddhist Constitutionalism and Buddhist-Interest Litigation in Sri Lanka." *Modern Asian Studies* 50 (6): 1966–2008. doi: 10.1017/s0026749x15000426

Sinha, Vineeta. 2005. "Theorising 'Talk' about 'Religious Pluralism' and 'Religious Harmony' in Singapore." *Journal of Contemporary Religion* 20 (1): 25–40. doi: 10.1080/13537900520003 13891

van der Veer, Peter. 2012. "Smash Temples, Burn Books: Comparing Secularist Projects in India and China." *The World Religious Cultures* 73 (Spring): 17–26. doi: 10.4324/9781315244624-11

**Other Works Cited**

Asad, Talal. 2003. *Formations of the Secular: Christianity, Islam, Modernity.* Stanford, CA: Stanford University Press. doi: 10.1515/9780804783095

Fitzpatrick, Peter. 1992. *The Mythology of Modern Law.* London and New York: Routledge. doi: 10.4324/9780203308943

Geertz, Clifford. 1983. *Local Knowledge: Further Essays in Interpretive Anthropology.* New York: Basic Books.

Müller, Dominik H. 2015. "Sharia Law and the Politics of 'Faith Control' in Brunei Darussalam: Dynamics of Socio-Legal Change in a Southeast Asian Sultanate." *Internationales Asienforum* 46 (3–4): 313–45.

Pirie, Fernanda. 2006. "Secular Morality, Village Law, and Buddhism in Tibetan Societies." *Journal of the Royal Anthropological Institute* 12 (1): 173–90. doi: 10.1111/j.1467-9655.2006.00286.x

Sullivan, Winnifred Fallers, Robert A. Yelle, and Mateo Taussig-Rubbo. 2011. *After Secular Law.* Stanford, CA: Stanford University Press. doi: 10.2307/j.ctvqsfop7

**Suggested Readings**

Bowen, John R. 2003. *Islam, Law and Equality in Indonesia: An Anthropology of Public Reasoning.* Cambridge: Cambridge University Press. doi: 10.1017/cbo9780511615122

Derrett, J. Duncan M. 1999. *Religion, Law and the State in India.* Delhi: Oxford University Press. doi: 10.2307/2754167

Erie, Matthew S. 2016. *China and Islam: The Prophet, the Party, and Law.* Cambridge: Cambridge University Press. doi: 10.1017/cbo9781107282063

Lingat, Robert. 1973. *The Classical Law of India.* Translated by J. Duncan M. Derrett. Berkeley: University of California Press. doi: 10.2307/600926

Oraby, Mona and Winnifred Fallers Sullivan. 2020. "Law and Religion: Reimagining the Entanglement of Two Universals." *Annual Review of Law and Social Science* 16: 257–76. doi: 10.1146/annurev-lawsocsci-020520-022638

Sharafi, Mitra. 2014. *Law and Identity in Colonial South Asia: Parsi Legal Culture, 1772–1947.* Cambridge: Cambridge University Press.

## 2 Legal Pluralism

### Contents

I Evolution of the Concept of Legal Pluralism  77
II Legal Pluralism as State Policy  82
III Legal Pluralism from the Ground Up  101

With the advent of legal modernity across the Asian landscape and the establishment of some form of secularism in almost every Asian country, it became inescapably apparent that state law in contemporary societies always operates in relation to multiple normative systems that structure human interactions, resolve disputes, determine statuses and relationships, and punish wrongdoing. The law codes, statutes, and institutions of the state never hold an exclusive monopoly with regard to these activities.

The state sometimes recognizes, authorizes, or even defers to non-state normative systems; but at other times such systems operate without any acknowledgment by the state. Because the official legal system does not provide a reliable indicator of the existence of non-state legal arrangements, it becomes the task of the law and society scholar to investigate the role and influence of these multiple normative systems from a perspective apart from – or in addition to – that of the state's legal actors and agencies. This undertaking has been called the study of "legal pluralism," and it is one of the oldest and most deeply rooted fields of Asian law and society scholarship.

Legal pluralism "is generally defined as a situation in which two or more legal systems coexist in the same social field" (Merry 1988:870). Legal pluralism scholars study the law of the modern state in relation to many other kinds of normative systems that interact with one another and with state law in a given social space. These include religious law, village or community laws, various forms of "customary" ordering, the internal regulatory systems of companies or other organizations, and the interactional laws that arise from repeated dealings among the same parties over time. Although most legal pluralism scholars use the term "law" broadly to describe a plethora of non-state normative systems, some critics have argued for a narrower definition of "law" and "legal." If norms are unwritten, unrecognized by the state, and enforceable only by social sanctions such as shunning or retaliation, these critics ask, Do they really deserve to be called law (e.g., Roberts 1998)? Are table manners a form of law?

While such definitional issues may be of great importance for legal philosophers, they are not an overriding concern of the majority of legal pluralism scholars, whose aim is to document and analyze actual human behavior in complex, multilayered social contexts. Thus, one of the leading theorists of legal pluralism, M. B. Hooker, emphasizes the importance of supplementing the "prescriptive" view of law adopted by the state with the "descriptive" view of social researchers. Given this broader understanding of what counts as "legal," Hooker (1978:13–14) contends that the societies of Southeast Asia – and, we would add, of Asia as a whole – are characterized to an extraordinary degree by legal pluralism:

> The structure of the South-East Asian legal systems is pluralistic in nature. The municipal laws of the colonial powers, and now those of their successor states in South-East Asia, claim an absolute monopoly of source of law, legal machinery, and political support within the nation-state. A consequence of this is that laws may be valid on two levels; if the state insists, as it must, upon its absolute right to determine what is law through the machinery of the municipal law system, then only those laws so determined are prescriptively validated. A breach of valid prescription requires the application of sanction. In municipal law this is the standard way of working and it operates perfectly well in the homelands of South-East Asia's European laws, but it does not work so well in South-East Asia itself because large sections of the population do not know the contents of municipal law or, if they do, choose to regard them as not binding. They prefer the traditional status-type laws which have a descriptive validity. Whether or not one wishes to accept that informal law is 'law properly so called' is really beside the point; such laws actually do determine personal obligation, in some cases to the extent that municipal-law institutions, such as local courts, are forced to take account of them. The result is at best an internal conflict of principle or, at worst, a complete disregard by the population for the formally valid law.

What was true of colonialism and legal pluralism in Southeast Asia was equally true of colonial regimes elsewhere in the world. To cite a very different example described by Paolo Sartori (2017:16–17), Russia's colonization of Central Asia also led to a situation in which the colonizers were forced to acknowledge the continued existence of Muslim legal traditions within their jurisdiction in order to limit their salience:

> [They] blended the purported preservation of the status quo with a broader vision of institutional and social change. On the one hand, they claimed to have maintained nearly intact the core of indigenous judicial institutions ruling according to *sharia*, which were presided over by *qādīs* (Muslim judges); on the other, they effectively reformed the procedure of appointment to the position of judge by establishing a system of popular elections: where *qādīs* had once been designated by the head of a Muslim principality, "native judges" (*narodnye sud'i*) were, under Russian rule, to be chosen by voting representatives of local communities. Furthermore, Russians restricted severely the jurisdiction of Islamic law courts, thus removing, for instance, murder cases and highway robbery from their purview.

These new arrangements in colonial Central Asia led to an openly pluralistic legal world in which, according to Sartori, both Muslim law and Russian law were maintained but altered through their interactions with one another.

Scholarship on legal pluralism takes at least two forms. The first is what Keebet von Benda-Beckmann (2001, cited in Benda-Beckmann and Turner 2018:263) has called a "legal political" conception of legal pluralism, which focuses on the *"recognition* of one legal system by another legal system – usually that of the nation state." For example, Hooker (1975:464–6) himself explored the quite different ways in which French, Dutch, and English colonial governments recognized the multiplicity of normative orders over which they asserted their authority:

> [T]he French version of civil law could not admit the coexistence of another legal system within the same politically determined boundary, unless, by an act of the French state, such a system was acknowledged to exist. [...] In the Dutch colonial territories, ... [t]he population was divided into racial groups each retaining its own law. The conflicts of law which arose were settled according to 'interracial private law', the principles of which were developed by the colonial courts. [...] In British colonial law, on the other hand, [...] [t]he relationship between English law and a local law is not usually one of conflict between systems but of the incorporation of indigenous principles into the great body of the common law. The incorporation may retain an indigenous principle, but, although it changes its form and effect, it is truly a part of the general law.

In this first type of legal pluralism scholarship, researchers aim to document and analyze the approaches taken by "modern" states as they attempt to operate their justice systems in socially and culturally complex environments.

A second type of legal pluralism scholarship proceeds inductively, as scholars describe what they see "on the ground" when they observe human conduct in a variety of social fields. Based on their observations, these scholars construct empirically based theories about the normative orders that actually shape behavior – their interaction with one another and their interaction with state law. As Janine Ubink (2018:141) has observed, this second approach to legal pluralism is "a response to legal centralist ideology that law is and should be the law of the state and that other normative orderings are hierarchically subordinate to state law." The aim of these scholars, as Hooker would put it, is descriptive rather than prescriptive, and their stance toward state law is agnostic and often skeptical with respect to its claims of authority and exclusivity.

## I EVOLUTION OF THE CONCEPT OF LEGAL PLURALISM

Legal pluralism as a field of sociolegal study emerged with clarity in the second half of the twentieth century, but its theoretical roots extend back much further. Max Weber, for example, recognized that the exercise of what he called "legal coercion" was not the "monopoly of the political community" but was distributed more widely among a variety of social actors who were prepared to enforce physical or psychological sanctions in particular situations (Weber 1978:17). Scholars of Asian law adopted early versions of a legal pluralism framework during the colonial era, most notably in Indonesia, where von Vollenhoven and others in the so-called Adat School attempted to document and analyze non-state legal orders rooted in Islam and in village-level custom. Similarly, Leopold Pospisil (1958), conducting fieldwork in Papua New Guinea in the 1950s, emphasized the importance of observing and analyzing the multiple "legal levels" that can be found in any society.

In East Asia, shortly after the end of World War II, Masaji Chiba initiated an influential effort to develop the concept of legal pluralism with reference to Japanese law and society. Noting that the postwar Showa legal system claimed exclusive authority and denied recognition of premodern, customary, patriarchal, and sacred laws, Chiba nevertheless insisted that the sociological realities of Japanese legal culture did not match the ideology of its modern legal structure. He observed (Chiba 2002:46) that, "Among the real structure of the Japanese state law, there are various indigenous laws existing whether officially or unofficially." Chiba's fieldwork in mid-century Japan documented legal pluralism, for example, with reference to the continuing significance of "shrine communities" and of *iemoto* laws – traditional family-like norms and structures found in numerous Japanese social groupings and organizations, including large corporations and even criminal societies (Chiba 2002:49–53). Chiba's work in East Asia reinforced scholarly efforts in Southeast Asia – and in other world regions – leading to a surge of interest in the theory of legal pluralism and in fieldwork projects designed to document the coexistence of official and unofficial laws in many Asian societies.

## 2.1 Legal Pluralism, Social Theory, and the State, Keebet von Benda-Beckmann and Bertram Turner

Keebet von Benda-Beckmann and Bertram Turner, in the excerpt that follows, provide a useful overview of the origins and theory of legal pluralism.

*Legal Complexity in Early History*
Although a fairly recent concept in the social sciences, the phenomenon of legal pluralism has persisted throughout history. It has provided the very "condition of possibility" for pre-modern empires and thus has been part of a normative logic of statehood. Such a model of statehood also referenced the diversity of its constitutive people in terms of normativity. All early empires recognized this and dealt with it in pragmatic ways. In a post-Westphalian world order, two entangled strands of politico-legal development gained momentum, the nation state and its political counter-part, the imperial and colonial state. This development entailed the axiomatic shift from "where there is society, there is law" to "where there is state, there is law." Only with the establishment of nation states and ideologies that canonized the state-people-law nexus in the nineteenth century, the prevalence of legal pluralism came to be seen as problematic. This coincided with theories of modernity and evolutionist conceptions of social organization, development and linear progress, and that included imperialism and colonialism. While emerging nation states sought to eliminate all traces of legal pluralism in domestic legal ideology, though it continued to exist unabated in practice, in colonial states, the realities of legal pluralism needed to be acknowledged, not least as an administrative necessity.

In this context, colonial empires began to distinguish "modern" law from customs, tradition, and "primitive" law. In line with evolutionist thinking, scholars began to systematically collect and compare "precursors" of modern law. But this issue was not merely of theoretical interest. It was also of high political relevance, because according to legal doctrine, customs and tradition – in contrast to customary or traditional law – could be disregarded at the whim of the administration. Colonial experiences incited lawyers and administrators to consider whether existing normative orders in the colonies could be characterized as law or as mere custom. Scholars of different provenience also developed an interest in local laws. There was greater "disciplinary job sharing" among scholars of different disciplines than today.[1] Most scholars

---

[1] Bertram Turner (2017), "Translocal, Faith-Based Dispute Management: Moroccan-Canadian Struggles with Normative Plurality," in *Multireligious Society: Dealing with Religious Diversity*

adopted evolutionary theories aimed at a universal theory of law. These theories presumed that early models of order had been based on feuds and retaliation, genealogical relationships, and on communal ownership. These evolved into hierarchical societies with property regimes based on individual ownership. But it was only with the emergence of states that law assumed its full role of maintaining order. [...]

*From Colonialism to the Postcolony*
At the turn to the twentieth century, new fields and methods of inquiry emerged with growing interest in what constituted law in daily social and economic interactions. A holistic approach was supposed to guarantee the study of all aspects of social life. Anthropological fieldwork entailed full immersion in a society to allow the researcher to see how law was used in daily practices. Societies with relatively loose forms of institutionalization and flat hierarchies were studied without interrogating the effects of colonial rule. Such research nevertheless helped understand how law could function in societies without specialized institutions for legislation and law enforcement, and to what extent social organization relied on reciprocity and on community as a public forum. That line of research embraced functionalist perspectives, and paid special attention to the social function of law and customs.

Parallel to this development, as legal scholars began to engage in empirical research, emergent disciplinary boundaries between social and legal sciences were blurred. In the Netherlands, Van Vollenhoven argued that a deep understanding of customary law was essential for the Dutch colonial government. Misunderstanding its character led to illegal expropriation of land and other resources. His interest in the diversity of laws, their similarities and differences across the Malay Archipelago, was genuinely academic, notwithstanding his political motivation. The relations between local and colonial laws and the manner in which colonial courts determined how local laws were interpreted were key to his analyses.

Colonial administrative activity itself contributed to the complexity and diversity of plural legal configurations. Parts of local legal registers interacted with the legal order of the colonial state as they were acknowledged and codified by the colonial state. In this way, they became entangled with the dynamics within traditional and religious normativity. The result was that the borders between state and other-than-state law were sometimes barely

*in Theory and Practice*, edited by Francisco C. Gonzalez and Gianni D'Amato (Abingdon: Routledge) at 291–5. [Editors' note]

recognizable. Similar diversity would later be rediscovered both in the post-colonial and the industrialized colonizing states.

The pioneers of this era, among them, anthropologists Bronislaw Malinowski and Richard Thurnwald, as well as Eugen Ehrlich, a legal scholar, built the foundation for the modern anthropological work on law through various trajectories. Primarily interested in law as an organizing principle of society that ensured social cohesion, they paid relatively little attention to conflicts and disputes. Pioneering the study of local laws in relation to the state and its law, however, Van Vollenhoven argued that adat (customary) law inevitably undergoes change when colonial courts and administrative institutions use it, which Anglo-American legal anthropology did not take into account until the 1970s. His analytical concepts underscored his criticism towards the colonial government, which systematically, and often intentionally, misrepresented the character of adat regimes and thereby violated its promise to fully recognize adat law. Careful academic analysis thus had profound political implications, for it showed that the government's expropriation of large tracts of land for economic development was largely illegal.

That brought forth the insight that more knowledge of "unadulterated customary law" was needed, a trajectory that allowed legal anthropologists to step out of the shadow of the colonial state. Thus, the focus on law as organized in registers that inevitably share basic features and allow for a comparative analysis did not go unchallenged. Pioneers in the African colonial context, such as Max Gluckman and his Manchester School, put customary law center stage, advancing the notion that customary law was best understood through the study of disputes by means of the extended case method. However, the disadvantage of this very method was that they lost sight of the state. In fact, many authors interested in customary laws in this period show a remarkable lack of interest in the state.

Eventually, a paradigm shift could be noted in the last phases of colonialism, roughly between the 1940s and the 1970s, when legal anthropologists took to conceptualizing customary law devoid of the state. [ ... ]

*Critique at "Customary Law"*
Increased emphasis in anthropological research on disputing in colonial settings led to a reconsideration of the character of customary law. Critical analysis showed that customary law, too, was pluralized and transformed over time by colonial state law and reinvented as neo-tradition. This critique revealed how deeply interwoven dispute analysis was with state normativity, be it the state as the leviathan against which informal conflict processing takes

shape, or entailing the involvement of state officials in conflict processing outside the framework of state institutions, often also wearing the hat of local informal grass roots legal agents. Customary law allowed chiefs endowed with colonial authority, for instance, to enhance their power and stewardship over land at the expense of women's rights to land, a creative, still ongoing practice that entails combining state law with custom. [...]

*The Concept of Legal Pluralism*
Deeper insights into disputing processes showed for one, that people in colonial settings often had a choice to opt for one legal system over another, and secondly, that the state was not a passive onlooker but an active agent in the construction of multiple legal orders. Thus debate about legal anthropological concepts and categories to identify and spell out links between normative orders was spurred by a heightened interest in the state. Legal anthropologists now needed an analytical framework to accommodate a conceptual inclusion of the state, its judiciary and legal institutions into their analyses of legal situations at local level.

The legal sociologist Gurvitch first used legal pluralism to denote co-existing legal orders. But it was the Belgian lawyer Vanderlinden who first used the term in an analytical sense. Legal pluralism, according to him, referred to a situation in which people could choose from among more than one co-existing set of rules. Legal plurality, by contrast, denoted the co-existence of multiple (sub-)legal systems within one state, to cater to different categories of persons who had no option to choose from among these bodies of law. For example, if commercial law was applicable for merchants, civil law was applicable for other citizens. The term legal pluralism initially met with considerable resistance and there were opposing views about what the term law signified. Over the years, many alternative terms were coined to deal with this discomfort. The nineteenth-century modernist notion of the nation state as the sole source of law dominated, whereby only state law and not normative orders deserved to be labeled as law, as the codified, differentiated, institutionalized and legitimized expression of the state sovereignty and monopoly of power. This understanding of law continued to be widely accepted by lawyers, economists, and social and political scientists throughout the twentieth century. [...]

In this period, two main conceptions of legal pluralism proliferated, especially in debates on the relationship between legal pluralism and the state. Even if scholars who considered law as standing for state law did not necessarily reject the notion of legal pluralism, they accommodated legal plurality only if and to the extent the state legal system recognized other forms of law. [...]

Or more concretely, legal pluralism is understood here as deriving from the recognition of one legal system by another legal system – usually that of the nation state. Keebet von Benda-Beckmann calls this a legal political concept of legal pluralism that has developed into what scholars interested in law at the trans-national and global level today understand as "normative legal pluralism."

However, other scholars considered a state-centric position inconsistent, because most proponents of this view acknowledged the existence of religious law as law, despite the fact that it was not enacted by the state. It was therefore not appropriate for the social scientific study of law that aimed at understanding the social working of law.[2] The second strand places the formal legal system principally on a more or less equal footing with all or some of the other legal orders constituting a plural legal constellation. Here the relationship is qualified, for instance, as "deep," "strong," "real"[3] or as "factual" legal pluralism.[4] An implicit or explicit agency of diverse legal regimes (customary, religious) is often assumed. The term "co-existence" then translates into an arrangement of normative orders, each with its own legitimacy and validity. Here the existence of law irrespective of what the state declares to be law is emphasized. People may refer to a normative register even if it is not recognized by the state.

## II LEGAL PLURALISM AS STATE POLICY

Under colonial regimes, official recognition of legal pluralism helped Europeans exercise control over Asian populations. Particularly when it came to personal or family laws, the colonial authorities often sanctioned different rules and norms for different population groups, rather than attempting to

---

[2] Franz von Benda-Beckmann (1979), *Property in Social Continuity: Continuity and Change in the Maintenance of Property Relationships through Time in Minangkabau, West Sumatra* (The Hague: Martinus Nijhoff). [Editors' note]

[3] John Griffiths (1986), "What Is Legal Pluralism?," *Journal of Legal Pluralism and Unofficial Law* 18 (24): 1–55. [Editors' note]

[4] Anthony H. Angelo (1996), "Self-Determination, Self-Government and Legal Pluralism in Tokelau. Is Decolonisation Imperialistic?," in *International Yearbook for Legal Anthropology*, vol. 8, edited by Rüdiger Kuppe and Rüdiger Potz, 1–10 (The Hague: Martinus Nijhoff). [Editors' note]

enforce uniform laws concerning marriage, divorce, inheritance, and the like. In doing so, they were able to satisfy and control legal subjects who held sharply diverse – often religious-based – views. Thus, legal pluralism in colonial times was an effective instrument of state policy.

In postcolonial regimes, on the other hand, states seeking to consolidate their power and instill a spirit of nationalism typically strove for uniformity across the entire civil law corpus rather than administer arguably unequal or discriminatory laws in patchwork fashion. Although Künkler and Sezgin (2016:988) note that "the unification of legal systems became a major pillar of many postcolonial nation-building projects," they go on to observe that this policy of legal uniformity gave way over time to a large-scale return to state-sponsored legal pluralism. "No fewer than 50 countries today recognize separate family laws for separate ethnic or religious groups of the population. This phenomenon ranges from countries that recognize only one group's religion-based family law (Indonesia) to countries that do so for multiple groups" (Künkler and Sezgin 2016:988).

In this section, we present three studies of state-sponsored legal pluralism in contemporary Asian societies. They illustrate the tension between "modern" legal ideals of equality and uniformity on the one hand and deference to religious freedom and cultural autonomy on the other. Ironically, perhaps, it is often the case that the power of the state is actually strengthened when it abandons its effort to impose uniform laws on all population groups and permits pluri-legal systems to flourish. But doing so can sometimes mean the sacrifice of important normative principles or constitutional mandates that the state should in theory guarantee to all citizens.

## 2.2 Global Doctrine and Local Knowledge: Law in South East Asia, Andrew Harding

In this article, Andrew Harding describes how Southeast Asian states have for many years dealt with the issue of legal pluralism. Although he focuses primarily on contemporary recognition of Islamic personal law within otherwise secular legal systems, he also emphasizes the multilayered character of Southeast Asian law. Like the great temples of Southeast Asia, he notes, Southeast Asian polities integrate local traditions and legal precepts drawn from Hinduism, Buddhism, and Islam as well as from contemporary global legal regimes. In Harding's words, "The history of law in the region, as well as the history of everything else, is distinguished by the ability of South East Asia to embrace the best of that which is foreign without destroying that which is authentically local." That being the case, however, each state is faced with the difficult challenge of ascertaining local traditions – in this article, traditions associated with Islam – and administering them within the framework of secular law. And, at the same time, each state must continue to absorb influences from beyond its borders. Where does "local knowledge" come from, and to what extent does the state distort or even destroy the very traditions it purports to preserve? In this characterization, legal pluralism constantly evolves, presenting each Southeast Asian polity with a continual challenge to recognize and integrate disparate legal concepts, norms, and procedures.

> Let us now try to paint a more general picture of the region's legal pluralism, and how it has dealt with the problems of global doctrine and local knowledge which have so exercised the English judiciary, the Dutch scholars, and the Muslim jurists. Legal pluralism may be represented by several geological strata, which still remain visible to us due to tectonic movements. This matter is deeply related to the culture of the region, whose principal characteristic has been to absorb foreign influences in such a way as to develop rather than obliterate its own genius. The great temples of Borobudur and Ankor Wat stand as wondrous testaments of this fact. The history of law in the region, as well as the history of everything else, is distinguished by the ability of South East Asia to embrace the best of that which is foreign without destroying that which is authentically local. As in food, architecture and religion, so in law. It is therefore as difficult to describe the essential character of South-East Asia's law as it is to describe the essential character of its food; but perhaps the effort may nonetheless be instructive.
>
> First there was the custom or 'native' law of the aboriginal inhabitants, which is still recognised by the courts as positive law in several parts of the region. Then came several strata of transplanted law: *adat* (Malay custom), which was based on the *rumah gadang* (long house); in *adat perpatih*, the customary law of the Minangkabau matrilineal society, property passed along the female line; Hindu and Buddhist law from South Asia, uniquely amalgamated, and operating at the rarified level of the *kraton* (court); Islamic law from the Middle East, which mingled with *adat* and formed the basis of personal law in maritime South East Asia; and Chinese law via immigration and imitation. All these not only had great influence but influenced each other in interesting ways. Beginning as long ago as the eleventh century CE custom began to be written down in codes such as those of Java, the *Undang-Undang Melaka* (civil and constitutional law), and the *Undang-Undang Laut* (maritime law) of Malacca in the fifteenth century, and the Thai Law of the Three Seals in 1805. It was also described by scholars, such as the industrious Dutch who institutionalised *adat* into nineteen adat-areas; this crystallisation

resulted eventually in its decline as a form of living law, and at independence the Dutch civil law was preferred by the Indonesian state in the interests of modernisation. *Adat* is still however enforced in the courts of Malaysia and Indonesia along with Islamic law in certain respects.

The reception of Islamic law in South East Asia represents the geographical zenith of the most significant and thorough transplant of global doctrine in legal history, surpassing even that of Roman law in Europe. It spread throughout Malaya, Indonesia, and parts of Thailand and Philippines. In all these countries Islamic law represents a separate sub-system of personal law, enforced by separate courts, as well as affecting, in some cases, aspects of general criminal, commercial, and constitutional law. The Islamic legal tradition is still developing through its interaction with local knowledge as well as with technology and the advance of global commerce and culture, and the need in practice to accommodate other legal traditions.

From about 1500 colonialism formed another stratum. The Portuguese and Spanish civilian traditions were brought to what became the Catholic parts of the Malay archipelago, such as East Timor and Philippines. The English common-law tradition, with a heavy dose of the great Anglo-Indian codes, was imposed in Burma and the Straits Settlements and later in Malaya, Brunei, Sabah, and Sarawak, while its American cousin became a permanent legal influence throughout the twentieth century in the Philippines. The French civilian tradition was imposed in Indo-China and also, along with German, Swiss, and Japanese models, influenced Thailand; and Dutch law was imposed in Indonesia. As a result all the legal systems of South East Asia, even that of Thailand, which was not colonised, have a clearly European-style framework, and all modernised their legal systems and their criminal, civil, and commercial laws with European-style codes just before or just after the turn of the twentieth century, or a little later. The distinction between the civilian and common law systems remains valid and important even today, although its importance is declining even as it declines in Europe. Indonesia's Company Law of 1996, for example, smoothly integrates both Dutch and common-law ideas in pursuit of the modern requirements of corporate governance.

The period since 1945 has seen two further phases. The first was the period of decolonisation and independence, in which it was assumed that the logic of 'law-and-development' would result in the convergence of all Asian legal systems along Western lines, a view which sat easily with a juristic orthodoxy which saw all legal systems as path-dependent.

This was the period in which 'new states' were to prevail over 'old societies', led by economic-development law and democratic constitutions: Malaysia and Singapore are the prime examples of the success of this approach. The socialist states of Indo-China provide a comparable model, albeit with different socio-economic objectives, importing Soviet and Chinese 'socialist' law. In South East Asia, the notion of the 'Asian developmental state', characterized by social stability, authoritarian governmental structures, and long-term economic planning, has been seen as continually relevant to the understanding of post-colonial law in the region. Thus the centrality of law to development has been remarked upon but hardly ever actually studied.

A new phase since about 1990 embraces globalisation-law, which has been driving much of legal development and transplantation in South East Asia in the field of international business and commercial law, for example relating to foreign investment and intellectual property. These developments have had a knock-on effect on organic laws, even public and constitutional law. The interesting outcome of this phase as regards legal studies is a renewed emphasis on culture and society as guides to the analysis and understanding of law. The recent economic crisis in South East Asia has also renewed emphasis on the rule-of-law, civil society and the empowerment of legal institutions as the way forward. Thus 'new state: old society' has given way to 'old state: new society';[1] in this phase it is expected by many that Asian legal systems, propelled by people-power and international commerce, will finally reach a kind of legal Fukuyama-land, in which local knowledge will finally be counted out. [...] Huge question-marks over these developments hang suggestively in the region's development-polluted skies. The influence of legal transplants continues, but is becoming more varied: when Malaysia enacted its cyberlaws in 1997–8, it used models from the United States, England and Singapore. The new Thai Constitution displays many disparate influences (France, Germany, and England, for example) as well as some purely home grown elements. Legal influence is moving in many directions. Comparative law has become an industry. Global doctrine and local knowledge are fusing in such a way that it becomes hard to see where one starts and the other ends.

What this brief summary reveals, if it is correct, is that, inside the concept of law in South East Asia lies, as a result of historical experience, an accretion of layers of law and legal culture, as distinct from a monolithic 'progression' from one conception of law to another, as some would have it. The achievement of law in South East Asia has been to construct out of these disparate elements of legal systems which, while pluralistic in their origins, have, to a greater or lesser extent, become syncretic or unified, and which represent a tradition of

---

[1] Benedict R. O'G. Anderson (1983), "Old State, New Society: Indonesia's New Order in Comparative Historical Perspective," *Journal of Asian Studies* 42 (3): 477–96. [Editors' note]

> accommodation of differing or even conflicting conceptions of law. This is something from which non-South East Asians can certainly learn. They are, it is true, institutionally imperfect systems, in which the rule of law itself is a competing value-system rather than a basic condition; but they have replaced pluralistic abandon with what the anthropologist Clifford Geertz's phrase usefully calls a 'working misunderstanding'.

### 2.3 Beyond Democratic Tolerance: Witch Killings in Timor-Leste, Rebecca Strating and Beth Edmondson

Timor Leste is one of the world's newest states, having achieved independence in 2002. In its short modern history, it has faced a serious policy question – how should a constitutional democracy deal with legal pluralism and, specifically, how should a predominantly Catholic country deal with the problem of witchcraft? As Strating and Edmondson explain, the killing of witches is a longstanding practice in some regions of Timor Leste and in other nearby states, sanctioned by customary legal norms and practices that are familiar to many citizens. It has been suggested, whether accurately or not, that a majority of the population may endorse this practice. Yet the newly enacted constitution would clearly outlaw the extrajudicial killing of women who are considered witches, and international legal norms would condemn the practice as a form of gender violence. This article asks whether, in a constitutional democracy, a state should defer to the concept of legal pluralism and allow a serious violation of state law (and of international law) to go unpunished because it is at least arguably sanctioned by custom and by majority sentiment.

> In traditional East Timorese society, two types of leaders exist within each *suku* (village): a spiritual leader, who is responsible for the "cosmos," and a *liurai* (political leader), who is responsible for "jural order."[1] *Lian nains* (masters of the word) also carry moral authority in East Timorese society and enforce social norms derived from spiritual beliefs. Their roles as "custodians and

---

[1] Tanja Hohe and Rod Nixon (2003), *Reconciling Justice: "Traditional" Law and State Judiciary in Timor-Leste* (January) (Washington, DC: United States Institute of Peace) at 14–15. [Editors' note]

interpreters of indigenous Timorese animistic cosmology" sees them "dispense justice according to spiritually derived behavioural norms."[2] Unlike in modern liberal-democratic states, where the laws emphasise the separation of church and state, in Timor-Leste the political leader is subservient to the spiritual leader according to customary law. Timor-Leste's "multiple and diverse societies" remain rooted in these "traditional" social systems.[3]

For the East Timorese, adjusting to a new democratic culture means recognising the authority of the state over that of local leaders and ascribing the political realm primacy over the spiritual realm. As a new liberal democracy, Timor-Leste is experiencing a new emphasis on individuals and a corresponding shift in recognition away from community-located views of citizens/subjects. Social and legal relationships have become redefined as part of the democratising process. [...]

Witchcraft remains a feature of local justice measures in some East Timorese regions. An important role of the *lain nain* is to draw upon their "localised, spiritual authority," especially in "prosecution[s] for witchcraft."[4] In Timor-Leste the *nahe biti* (literal translation is "stretching out the mat") customary dispute resolution mechanism is underpinned by two key principles: a willingness to come together and the voluntary confession of culpability.[5] These are consistent with customary justice in exchange societies where compensation ("replacing social values") and *badames* (forgiveness or reconciliation) are ways of restoring social order. Although each *suku* interprets *nahe biti* differently, *nahe biti* usually results in a violent punishment in dispute resolutions involving accusations of witchcraft. As in other states, such as Papua New Guinea (PNG), violent punishments of witches are targeted towards women in contexts of highly unequal power relationships.

Since Timor-Leste's successful independence referendum, reports have periodically emerged concerning the punishment or killing of accused witches. The Early Warning and Response group recorded 32 sorcery-related conflicts in Timor-Leste from October 2011 to February 2014 across 16 of 65 sub-districts. It appears that sorcery-related violence is not isolated, either in frequency or geographical incidence, and that state institutions struggle to

---

[2] Andrew Marriot (2010), "Leaders, Lawyers and Lian Nains: Sources of Legal Authority in Tijmor-Leste," in *Understanding Timor-Leste: Democracy and Localism*, edited by Michael Leach, 159–63 at 160 (Melbourne: Swinburne University Press). [Editors' note]
[3] Hohe and Nixon (2003), note 1, at 7. [Editors' note]
[4] Marriot (2010), note 2, at 160. [Editors' note]
[5] Mateus Tilman (2012), "Customary Social Order and Authority in the Contemporary East Timorese Village: Persistence and Transformation," *Local-Global* 11: 192–205 at 194. [Editors' note]

prevent it. Yen and others observe that the apparent sightings of "witches" and other phantasms occur more frequently during periods of political and social uncertainty. For instance, during the international state-building mission, allegations emerged that a group of men had tortured and killed an elderly woman they had accused of witchcraft in the eastern Los Palos district. Additionally, most instances of witches being tortured or murdered occur in districts that are geographically removed from the administrative heart of Dili – that is, areas where the reach of state agencies remains limited. [...]

The difficulties in having parallel and sometimes competing legal systems became apparent in the international state-building phase. In one example, a local man who complained that another man had accused his daughter of witchcraft was directed by a United Nations police officer "to deal with it in a traditional way."[6] The United Nations police officer rightly acknowledged that he had "no authority to deal with accusations of black magic." According to Herriman, "the complainant returned and advised the UNPol officer that he had done as told, and dealt with the problem using traditional means; he killed the accuser."[7] The complainant was then arrested for murder. In this problematic case, *ema halo* (black magic) was viewed as being beyond the purview of the police officer. Nevertheless, the police office recognised the continuation of pre-existing social structures, wherein "traditional" socially sanctioned retribution might be possible.

A spectrum of customary punishments exists whereby punishments are imposed according to the "severity of witchcraft involved."[8] Toohey maintains that Timor-Leste "dresses itself up as a Catholic nation," but culturally and politically embedded animism runs "deeper than all that."[9] Following independence, the national newspaper *Suara Timor Lorosae* carried reports of the torture and killing of witches in 2003, 2006, and 2008. In January 2007 three women in the Liquiça district unsuccessfully attempted to heal an injured teenager (and distant relative), who then reported seeing the women in a feverish dream. The women were subsequently accused of witchcraft, hacked to death with a machete, and burned along with their houses; the child died

---

[6] David Mearns (2001), *Variations on a Theme: Coalitions of Authority in Timor-Leste* (Sydney: Australian Legal Resources International) at 20; Nicholas Herriman (2009), "The Case to Intervene and Stop East Timorese Killing Witches," 2009 *East Timor Law Journal* 7. [Editors' note]

[7] Herriman (2009), note 6. [Editors' note]

[8] Warren Wright (2012), "Murder and Witchcraft in Timor-Leste," *East Timor Law and Justice Bulletin*, 22 December. [Editors' note]

[9] Paul Toohey (2007), "Witchhunt," *The Bulletin*, 125, 6562, 24. [Editors' note]

14 days later. Another suspected witch reportedly died after hot coals were placed on her back.

A debate emerged in the *Timor-Leste Law Bulletin* concerning the "democratic" nature of these customary punishments, primarily between Nick Herriman and Warren Wright. Wright expressed concerns regarding the extrajudicial nature of these killings and the challenges they pose for Timor-Leste's democratic institutions. He contends that:

> Many anthropologists who lack a comprehension of the concepts of democratic secular law and justice, are ardent supporters of traditional justice systems even though they posit supernatural hypotheses for the explanation of the realities of social disharmony and criminal conduct and impose corporal punishments and worse tortures on citizens accused of the impossible crime of witchcraft.[10]

In response, Herriman argues that his fieldwork demonstrates that:

> Killing "sorcerers" [...] was the wish of almost all local residents – often the "sorcerers" own family, friends, and neighbours. In the sense that it is the will of the majority, it is thus democratic. If a trial by jury were established, I strongly suspect that "sorcerers" would be similarly condemned. I suspect that most villagers in Timor Leste would also wish to kill witches. To the extent that his is true, it appears that democracy is not antithetical to witch killings.[11]

This debate over the democratic nature of these killings points to the challenges the East Timorese state faces in achieving authority over customary law, including laws concerning the punishment of witches. Controversies concerning issues of legitimate jurisdictional capacities highlight the importance of reconciling diverse views of the public regarding the relationship between citizens' identities and roles, and engendering widespread recognition of the authority of state structures and agencies. [...]

Scholars have increasingly recognised the sociological reality in many political communities of legal pluralism. In dealing with diverse sources of law, some have advocated "hybrid" legal systems whereby democratic political and judicial institutions are reconciled with features of customary practices. Peacebuilding missions often fail due to a lack of local legitimacy. In democracies laws must generally be obeyed due to a belief that the universalised application of a state-based rule of law is preferable to other legal systems.

---

[10] Wright (2012), note 8. [Editors' note]
[11] Herriman (2009), note 6. [Editors' note]

Such views are underpinned by a belief in the moral claims of state agents in their legitimate exercise of authority. Expectations and acceptance of codified moral claims are key components of a democratic rule of law that does not rely upon citizens perceiving self-interest or fear in order to comply. Under these conditions legitimacy creates a "voluntary pull toward compliance" that enables consolidated liberal democracies to become politically self-perpetuating.[12] Such beliefs derive from the relationships, structures, and institutions that both enable a generalised rule of law to be exercised and encourage recognition of the legitimacy of government decisions. It is not an easy or rapid process for citizens to adapt to a new sociopolitical organisational system, particularly in parochial and fragmented societies such as Timor-Leste.

In Timor-Leste an irreconcilable clash of worldviews is evident: certain communities believe witchcraft is a legitimate crime, but a "rational" state rejects the power of sorcery and thus has no need to protect the community from it. Even if acts of violence against accused witches are an acceptable part of "traditional" or "customary" law in Timor-Leste, they are not based on reason and thus cannot be tolerated by new democratic state structures – otherwise, the authority of democratic government and its ability to establish a universal rule of law would be challenged.

Arguments that seek to preserve customary practices for their own sake are problematic for democratic equality in newly independent states for a number of reasons. They can encourage conflict resolution methods that do not conform to acceptable democratic practices or support new citizenship rights. [...] One of the key advantages of state-based legal systems is that they apply equally to all citizens within a territory and correspond with democratic rights established in the constitution, including "the inviolable right of hearing and defence in criminal proceedings."[13] [...]

Nevertheless, there are hurdles to reconciling state-based and customary law without undermining democracy. Problematically, the state-based legal system is not as popular as local systems are. This makes it difficult to legitimise the state-based system while simultaneously relying upon customary systems to fill in the gaps. In Timor-Leste's remote, rural societies there is a lack of knowledge about state-based legal systems and laws, which means that traditional justice is often administered by the *lian nain*. In these cases, moral

---

[12] Allen Buchanan (2004), *Justice, Legitimacy and Self-Determination: Moral Foundations for International Law* (Oxford: Oxford University Press). [Editors' note]

[13] Matthew Libbis (2012), "Witchcraft, Conflict and Resolution," *East Timor Law and Justice Bulletin*, 24 December. [Editors' note]

order – derived from spiritually based behavioural norms – informs the application of customary law. [...]

In Timor-Leste prioritising customary forms of dispute resolution such as extrajudicial punishments for witches may require disregarding gender equality provisions guaranteed in the Constitution. As Swaine demonstrates, women are excluded from playing a substantive role in local justice hearings, and the cultural beliefs and prejudices held by the administrators of justice regarding the status of women in society influence their legal findings. Traditional justice mechanisms do little to protect women from violent and hazardous situations, including accusations of witchcraft. This again reflects the key issue that administrators of justice such as the *lian nains* are guided by own cultural beliefs which are not supported by the "rational" modern state.

Most problematically, culturally relative arguments permit dishonest claims to "cultural" practices, including those that undermine efforts to reduce incidences of gender-based violence. This is a particular issue in Timor-Leste, where rates of domestic violence have been used to reify the idea that such violence is embedded in the "culture" or "tradition."

## 2.4 Muslim Mandarins in Chinese Courts: Dispute Resolution, Islamic Law, and the Secular State in Northwest China, Matthew S. Erie

Do democratic and authoritarian states differ in their approach to legal pluralism? The answer to this question is not obvious, as we saw in the previous reading by Strating and Edmondson on accused witch killings in Timor Leste. Under one theory, principles of equality and fairness would require a truly democratic state to administer a unitary legal regime with no room for contending – and potentially undemocratic – legal systems to operate apart from state law. Under a different theory, however, democracies should strive to protect religious freedom and preserve non-state norms and procedures within the framework of state law – an explicit recognition of legal pluralism within the democratic system. It is not self-evident, in other words, whether legal pluralism is consistent or inconsistent with democratic principles.

When it comes to authoritarian states, the picture is no clearer. In the following article, Matthew S. Erie examines the legal pluralism policies of the People's Republic of China, particularly as they pertain to the 10.6 million Chinese Muslims (known as the Hui). As this case study demonstrates, authoritarian regimes do not necessarily adopt strict policies of proscription when it comes to non-state legal orders, such as Islamic law among the Hui. To the contrary, the PRC has explicitly recognized some of the legal traditions of its minority populations. During his ethnographic fieldwork in Northwest China, Erie interviewed local officials, Muslim "mandarins," and others to understand how state law integrates Muslim authority figures and normative orders, particularly through officially recognized People's Mediation Committees, thus making legal pluralism an important principle of state law. In the process, as Erie demonstrates, state law is modified and "pluralized," but at the same time Islamic law is inevitably transformed as it becomes part of the official legal regime.

## GOVERNING PLURALISM

One of the defining features of the Chinese legal culture is the presence of multiple sources of law and authorities that coexist or compete with state law. China's extreme pluralism is a result of the diversity of communities, distinguished by faith, ethnicity, lineage, profession, and geography, which are subsumed within the modern nation-state. The rules that regulate behavior in these communities cannot be reduced to law. Ethical, moral, and customary rights and obligations interact with formal law in a number of settings, whether familial, commercial, or penal. Some of these sources are law, however, which I define, following Brian Tamanaha, subjectively. Hui, for instance, call Islamic law *jiaofa*, meaning "law of the teaching" or "religious law," and follow its rules for both social relations and devotional matters.

The PRC has responded to pluralism by taking a bifurcated approach to the formal recognition of nonstate procedures and substantive nonstate law as applied to minorities who both practice transnational religions and inhabit sensitive borders areas (e.g., Hui, Uyghur, Tibetans, and Mongolians). This approach affects the institutional design of dispute resolution mechanisms. On the one hand, the Constitution of the PRC and a number of religious regulations guarantee freedom of religion. Clerics have rights under these regulations, and official recognition has implications for the party-state's collaboration with clerics, as I discuss below.

On the other hand, the secular state dissociates religion from religious law. PRC law does not officially recognize religious law or the legal systems of ethnic minorities. PRC civil procedure law and conflicts of law exclude mention of religious law. Unlike US law, for instance, which recognizes Islamic law as foreign law, PRC legislation concerning choice of law remains in its infancy. The demarcation of religious and state authority is particularly fraught with secular anxieties in the postsocialist context. Economic transitions after socialism may conflict with ideological bulwarks against religion in the public domain.

Official PRC discourse omits discussion of Islamic law, but state law does allow for the limited recognition of the category Hui customary law (Huizu xiguanfa), an ethnicized and depoliticized concept, as interpreted by Marxism-Leninism. Customary law is the term applied to the law of each of China's fifty-five ethnic minorities. Whereas minorities in southeastern China have codified their customary law, and whereas people's courts in Amdo Tibet (i.e., Qinghai, Sichuan, and parts of Gansu and the Tibetan Autonomous Region) may refer to Tibetan customary law in making decisions, the Hui have been unable either to codify their law or to enforce it in the courts. Though Hui customary law is referred to in official and academic sources, it is limited primarily to ritualistic matters, including dietary law, prayer, and ablutions. It largely excludes the body of Islamic law on social relations (mu'āmalāt). Only in recent years have PRC scholars begun writing about Islamic law, although most such treatments apply to Islamic law outside of China.

In addition to the state's relegation of Islamic law to customary law, the party-state established regional ethnic autonomy jurisdictions in the early 1950s that ostensibly permitted minorities residing therein to adjust national legislation to local circumstances. In practice, however, the people's congresses of autonomous regions (ARs) are legislative doldrums. Although two of the five ARs have significant Muslim populations (i.e., the XUAR and the NHAR), they have limited capacity to enact laws in accordance with Islamic law. Whereas relevant laws empower the legislative bodies of autonomous region governments to enact both autonomous regulations (zizhi tiaoli) and individual regulations (danxing tiaoli), to date, autonomous regions have not enacted a single autonomous regulation. [...]

[The article goes on to discuss state-sponsored mediation practices, in which Muslim mandarins – such as clerics, leaders, and elders – play a prominent role. People's Mediation Committees defer to some Hui norms and authority figures but formalize and inevitably transform them by incorporating them into the state law framework. After an extended description and analysis of mediation by Hui elders within the PRC legal structure, Erie concludes, "In sum, the form of dispute resolution routinizes the charisma of Muslim mandarins, severs Muslim authority from Islamic law, and reproduces the party-state's version of Islamic orthodoxy." The article then turns from state law's influence on Hui legal practices to the influence of Hui leaders and practices on state law itself.]

## THE INFORMALIZATION OF ADJUDICATION

Whereas sociolegal studies have theorized the state's integration of informal law and ADR, they have given less attention to the effects of such integration on the formal legal system itself. The case of Islamic law under party-state governance provides an inroad to addressing this question. In addition to the formalization of mediation, another type of collaboration between Muslim mandarins and their counterparts in the local party-state is what I call the *informalization of adjudication*. This type of collaboration, most prominent in Linxia but apparent also in other areas of Gansu and Qinghai, points to the primacy of personalistic ties between judges and Muslim mandarins over formal law. If, during adjudication, a Hui litigant makes an oral argument based on Islamic law that is integral to the matter under dispute or uses Islamic law as a basis of evidence (e.g., a wife arguing that because she and her husband had an Islamic marriage contract, they were validly married under Islamic law), a state judge may turn the case over to a Muslim mandarin. This process, which operates in the gray area of PRC procedural law, both results from existing social networks and further informalizes the judiciary.

In Hui communities, when disputes arise between family members or neighbors, they often seek mediation by a Muslim mandarin who applies Islamic law, but sometimes they go to the neighborhood office that has government-appointed mediators who apply state law. Only rarely does an unresolved dispute involve litigation in a basic-level people's court. If the judge is Hui and a disputant invokes Islamic law during the proceedings, the judge, who cannot opine on a matter of religious law, may use what could be called a *cleric hotline*; he or she calls a cleric to come and mediate the dispute. Once the cleric takes over, Islamic law becomes the relevant law. The procedural law of judicial mediation is ambiguous concerning the legality of remanding a case to a nonstate authority. Given that the trial's record of speech (*tanhua bilu*) strikes any reference to Islamic law and that case records omit any use of clerics, court procedure suggests that the use of religious law contravenes civil procedure law.

A young cleric I shall name Nasim receives many of these cases. The process by which Nasim became a Muslim mandarin illustrates the informalization of adjudication. Nasim's knowledge of Islamic law and his personal charisma stem from both his own lineage (he is a third-generation cleric) and his study abroad. Upon returning to Linxia from Saudi Arabia in the 1990s, through sermons and mediating disputes, he began teaching his mosque community the importance of following Islamic law. Over the years, he gained a reputation as an expert in Islamic law that has spilled over into official arenas so that the local government took notice of his standing in the community. The provincial traffic police hired him as a supervisor. Whereas other clerics in Linxia are hired by different public security and judicial organs on a temporary basis, Nasim's role is permanent, and he proudly shows a license proving his official status.

Officially, his expertise is limited to advising the provincial traffic police on vehicular accidents, but representatives from a variety of bureaus come to the mosque to consult him on matters touching on Islamic law that they encounter in their work. In return, Nasim, who is never paid for his services, has acquired a reputation as a resource for the party-state's bureaucrats along with other benefits, such as having his mosque selected for a visit by high-ranking party leaders. Judges also consult him on cases that touch on Islamic law. Sometimes he is invited to court to mediate, and sometimes the judge asks the disputants to seek Nasim at his mosque. Or they meet in a neutral environment, such as a restaurant. Usually, the referring judge is Hui and knows Nasim personally. Of the ninety-two cadres in the Linxia City People's Court, forty are Muslim. Social ties among coreligionists transcend the party-state's attempt to demarcate secular and religious domains. Government offices are zones of atheism, and Hui cadres cannot pray at work. However, when these cadres call on their cleric, they do so both as representatives of the party-state and as members of the mosque community. Nasim relates:

> I may come across issues relating to inheritance, marriage, and divorce. The procedure of referring a case back down to the local religious authority is, in fact, illegal. The case should not be taken out of the state venue. Once the complaint is lodged there, it should be decided by that authority. This has been going on for many years. Official PRC court decisions will not only exclude any mention of religious law, but there will be no instances of even remnants of Islamic law in decisions, or references of any kind, however vague.

Here there is a direct conflict between informal and formal law. Nasim characterizes as unlawful the use of a cleric as temporary judicial mediator, but the cleric is used despite the law's prohibition. Article 95 of the 2012 amended PRC Civil Procedure Law allows a court to invite (*yaoqing*) a governmental unit or individual to assist (*xiezhu*) with mediation. Though it is unclear whether a cleric can be considered an individual, the statute indicates that the court is still in charge of the mediation.

Furthermore, according to Article 33 of the 2010 Mediation Law, the relevant people's court may review the agreement that results from mediation by a PMC. Judicial oversight does not occur in the informalization of adjudication, however. Rather, the Muslim mandarin takes over the case. Nor do

Muslim mandarins draft a mediation agreement; the entire process circumvents any recording. Complicating the notions of the authorities' "legalization" of interpersonal and wider social conflicts, the referral of cases to religious specialists shows the dramaturgical purpose of law. Law provides a veneer for the thick personalistic ties that otherwise blur the divide between official and unofficial legal venues.

The informalization of adjudication is characterized by relationships between the Hui elite and government officials that are marked by discretion rather than transparency or official record. The work of mediating disputes is done "backstage," to use Erving Goffman's apt phrase. The "back room," not the courts, is often the site for brokering power between stakeholders. As Ling Li has written, "[m]ore seems to take place behind courtrooms than in them in litigation in China." Meanwhile, the courtroom is the venue for the public performance of the law. In this sense, the formal legal institutions of secular rule of law are dependent on the informal authority of Muslim mandarins and their capacity to mediate in accordance with Islamic law.

Although the informalization of adjudication cannot be officially recognized, it is an open secret, a conspicuous indirection. Within this arrangement, Nasim seeks to educate his mosque community and others about Islamic law. Linxia Muslims of all teaching schools come to his quarters to ask him to mediate problems. Thus, since secular law and its institutions depend on Islamic authority, Muslim mandarins use the social capital conferred through such delegations to spread Islamic law consciousness.

Nasim's visibility to both Muslim followers and officials (overlapping pools of clients) brings with it no small degree of danger. He whispers:

> The CCP cannot know that I am explaining Qur'ānic law to members of my mosque. And it's not even enforcing Qur'ānic law, but merely explaining it. Much of Qur'ānic law is at odds with state law. If they knew I was doing this, they would say I was interfering with the judiciary.

From the view of the party-state, Nasim can work only to put disputants back on a course where they can negotiate their own problem. In this, his work parallels that of a *qadi*, the crucial difference being that clerics cannot enforce the law. Consequently, Islamic law operates here not through implementing institutions, but through continual education, instruction, sermon, and prayer.

As many commentators have observed, weak courts remain the Achilles heel of legal reform in the PRC. Most critics point to the CCP's oversight of people's courts as invalidating their independence. Courts have another set of relationships, specifically, their reliance on local authority figures to mediate claims. As a normative point, although such relationships deviate from

Western rule of law prescriptions, it is arguable whether such reliance is a weakness or a strength. Indeed, scholars have analyzed connections between the CCP, lawyers, and judges as political embeddedness. Such social connections have generally been viewed as a net good, as a resource and means of protection for lawyers. So, too, do Muslim mandarins accrue benefits from collaborating with local officials.

However, Muslim mandarins must be wary of being perceived as too close to cadres and thereby losing credibility in the eyes of nonelite Hui. In serving two masters – the followers of the Prophet and the members of the party – they must toe a line that is continually shifting. [...] The potential for violence percolates beneath collaborations, creating suspicion of both Muslim mandarins and their official counterparts. The ability of Muslim mandarins to straddle the demands of the party-state and those of their communities is even more precarious among Uyghurs. For instance, on July 30, 2014, Juma Tahir, the *imam* of the largest mosque in the XUAR and head of the Kashgar Islamic Association, was stabbed to death allegedly by radicalized Uyghur teenagers who believed the imam owed loyalty more to Beijing than to his own people.

Though partnering with cadres may benefit Muslim mandarins, their collaboration with the party-state, through political embeddedness, may actually work as a means of government control. The informalization of adjudication operates to keep tabs on those Muslim mandarins who are gifted based on their character, achievements, kinship ties, and regional reputation, and thus might be seen as threatening to the regime. Conversely, as state law is not a privileged basis of legitimacy in China, connections with those who have the capacity to influence others are powerful sources of maintaining legitimacy. In other words, authoritarianism is not simply top-down coercion, but operates through a number of nodes of authority. In Hui communities, the local party-state thus relies on Muslim mandarins.

THE DYNAMISM OF INFORMAL LAW: THE CHINA MODEL?
The treatment of informal legal orders, such as that of Islam, under state secular laws is one of the central questions of the post-9/11 period. The perceived incompatibility of Islamic law with liberal norms in the West has incited intense intellectual efforts at accommodation that are at the center of designing institutions to incorporate Islamic law into secular justice systems. The arbitration model, used in the United Kingdom and Canada, for instance, has proven controversial, as women's rights activists have raised questions about gender equality under such institutions. Likewise, Tamir Moustafa has argued that the binary and mutually exclusive way in which Islamic law and liberal law are conceived in Malaysia is more a factor of

institution building than of any inherent conflict. India has devised a "semi-confessional system" whereby secularly trained Anglo-Indian judges apply the Islamic law of personal status in civil courts, although the enactment of a Uniform Civil Code that would abolish such state-enforced legal pluralism is hotly contested.

In China, socialist doctrine fails to recognize Islamic law. Hui disputing reveals that it is not formal institutions that do the work in reconciling state law from above with Islamic law from below, but rather systemic informal relationships. Whereas Islamic PMCs function to reproduce state power at the local level and do not reconcile Islamic law with socialist state law, the informalization of adjudication is the process through which cadres and clerics determine the scope and applicability of state versus Islamic rules. The kinds of relationships between judges, police, and judicial bureaucrats, on the one hand, and Muslim mandarins like Nasim, on the other, are not purely ad hoc, nor do they necessarily fall within the ambit of official responsibilities from positions within the Yi-Xie or CPPCC; rather, they gain traction in dispute resolution largely beyond official responsibilities and entitlements by law or regulation, where *guanxi* or unofficial connections take over.

*Guanxi* is routinely criticized as inviting corruption, particularly in the current anticorruption campaigns led by General Secretary of the CCP, Xi Jinping. Whether or not personalistic relationships are bad or good for legal development depends to some measure on whether arrangements attain their goals. The formalization of mediation addresses local conflicts and keeps disputes out of courts by mobilizing Muslim authorities. [...] A secondary function ensures that such disputes are not resolved with respect to Islamic law. The process appears to achieve success in obtaining these respective aims. Likewise, the informalization of adjudication takes disputes out of courts and delegates mediation to clerics like Nasim. The crucial difference is that Nasim uses such delegation to apply Islamic law rather than state law. [...]

Addressing disputes and keeping them out of the formal court system may not necessarily be a means to justice, however, particularly from the vantage of Muslim piety where Islamic law is controlling. The formalization of mediation and the informalization of adjudication have different effects on informal law. In the former, dispute resolution conducted by Islamic PMCs is emptied of Islamic law substance. The latter process valorizes the capacity of Islamic law to address conflicts, all the while maintaining its exclusion from official recognition. Each process involves secular law and policy actively shaping Islamic law – by occluding it from gaining traction in the public sphere but using it (in some instances) to minimize social conflict. In the informalization of adjudication, skilled mediators can apply Islamic rules, but enforcement depends, elliptically, on the piety of those who seek such forms of redress.

ADR-like institutions in Northwest China are one instrument of the party-state's rule over Muslim minorities. The study of dispute resolution in Hui com- munities points to the soft power aspects of mediation in the course of the state's regulation of nonstate authorities. [...] The case of Muslim mandarins shows power running in multiple directions and its benefiting or constraining multiple parties.

The case of Hui disputing sheds light on the relationship between state law and informal law, more generally. Writing over forty years ago, Sally Falk Moore demonstrated that where multiple regulatory regimes interact in the same social field, "legal, illegal, and non-legal norms all intermesh." The sociologist Boaventura de Sousa Santos has called this process "structural interpenetration." In Hui disputes, however, normative pluralism is not as pronounced as procedural blurring, particularly in the informalization of adjudication. Much of the disputing is driven by the deep pragmatism of the state's legal and judicial bodies. In short, human agency produces the relationship between state law and Islamic law, however complicated by a state ideology or the letter of the law that refuses to give legal status to religious law.

The codependence of formal and informal law in Northwest China thus relies on social connections and pragmatic decision making of actors on the ground. The ways China approaches disputing and governance, more broadly, in plural societies has practical importance. An arena for increasing empirical research is collaborations between Western states and domestic Muslim leaders in communities that feature a large number of Muslims for purposes of dispute resolution, surveillance, and information gathering. Police in US cities, for instance, have looked to *imams* and elders as "relationship-building leaders" in "community-policing" programs. A concern in recent years has been homegrown terrorism perpetrated by nationals who have been influenced by antistate propaganda, often in the form of online media, as allegedly motivated the killer of the Uyghur *imam* Juma Tahir. In such community-policing programs, relationships may transform law's categories. Although the Hui are not directly the object of state counterterrorism policies as is the case of the Uyghurs, the preexisting relations cadres have with Muslim mandarins are nonetheless mobilized for purposes of collecting information about developments within Muslim communities in China. Some well-educated clerics opt out of the system for a number of reasons, including discontent at being accessed by the local party-state.

# Legal Pluralism

The ADR processes I have discussed suggest that in the grayed-out margins where formal law meets informal law, collaborations may transform formal law. In the example of the informalization of adjudication, procedural requirements that a case cannot be remanded to a nonstate authority once it has been lodged within a people's court are ambiguous, and human actors who are under pressure from seniors to address grievances further informalize rules by handing over disputes to Muslim mandarins. When social ties shape the practice of law, such arrangements are flexible and may benefit parties to the dispute; however, they can also potentially encourage abuses of justice in a race to the bottom.

More research is needed on the effects of secularist policies and their pragmatic concerns of public safety and security for Muslim communities and their rights under both state law and informal legal orders, such as that of Islam. Placing the China case in a comparative reference, informalization of law may signal a race to the bottom as counter-radicalization programs erode due process and formal rights. In other words, rather than China adopting Anglo-American legal standards, in the case of governance of Muslim minorities, Western democratic states may be becoming more like China. Although the formalization of mediation confirms sociolegal theory about the state's colonization of informal law and dispute resolution processes, future research can determine the extent to which the informalization of adjudication has equally colonized official law in the post-9/11 period of anxious collaborations between the state and Muslim authorities.

## III  LEGAL PLURALISM FROM THE GROUND UP

As we have noted, research on legal pluralism does not necessarily adopt a state-centric approach. Rather than focusing on the ways in which state law accepts or rejects non-state legal orders, some pluralism scholars use their powers of observation, description, and analysis to identify the systems of law (broadly defined) that they actually can see operating within a particular social space, and they describe how people invoke, ignore, reject, or manipulate them. In such accounts, state law may or may not have a prominent position, depending on the research findings in each instance. Moreover, even when state law is conspicuous, its observable operations – the law in action – may differ greatly from its idealized depictions – the law on the books. Thus, studies of legal pluralism "from the ground up" offer certain advantages over state-centric approaches, since they give greater prominence to the multiple normative systems people actually experience, and they allow us to see more accurately how state law operates in complex, multilayered social environments.

## 2.5 Gender, Power, and Legal Pluralism: Rajasthan, India, Erin P. Moore

This study by Erin P. Moore of a rural community in Rajasthan, India, exemplifies research on legal pluralism "from the ground up." The author's perspective does not make state law or state legal institutions central to her analysis. Indeed, the article begins with a description of dispute resolution through magical performance by a village elder, a *maulavi* (Muslim religious teacher and healer). The disputants seek his intervention precisely because they wish to avoid the cost and unpredictability of local or state-level legal institutions. Moore goes on to describe the multiple "systems of normative ordering" that are operative in villagers' lives. These include some official institutions sanctioned by the state, but more often they consist of other "legal" systems, not just consultations with the maulavi but also caste or village panchayats and hearings conducted by the *grampanchayat* (known to the villagers as the "committee" – which is meant to serve as a bridge connecting local traditions with lower-level regional authorities). Moore's account thus provides a fascinating map of overlapping and intersecting systems of law and dispute resolution. The reader cannot escape the impression that, for the villagers, the most accessible and useful of these in their everyday lives is the *maulavi*. Moore notes that, for women in particular, the local healer offers a unique avenue to present grievances and to "make the body the locus of complaint," such that treatment of a "somatized complaint" – "convert[ing] a social distress into a physical distress" – is much more likely than litigation to deliver justice.

An older man in a rumpled coat and full loose pants leans over the white-bearded maulavi, or Muslim religious teacher, and complains that his uncle, his father's younger brother, took his two-and-a-half-acre parcel of land, sowed it, and refuses to give it back. The maulavi is busy writing, in a light yellow ink on the shell of an egg, *"Bismillah ir -Rahman ir- Rahim"* ("In the name of God, the Merciful, the Compassionate"). The egg is for a woman who has borne only daughters. The maulavi does not look up from his work, but he nods as he listens to the old man. Then he again turns his attention to the woman: "Eat the egg with salt tomorrow, wear this around your waist [he hands her a length of purple yarn that he has just knotted at two-inch intervals], and drink a glass of water with a clove and a *naqas* every day for the next 30 days." He gives her two handfuls of crumpled papers the size of large raisins; they are naqas', small pieces of folded paper that contain sacred writing in the maulavi's script. The prescription is not repeated. An impatient crowd presses in around the maulavi, and for the first time he looks up at the man who has lost his land. The maulavi does not ask any questions but gives the man six naqas'. Five of these are to be put into the well on his land, and one is to be buried under the path where his uncle walks. There is no further communication, and the man turns to leave without placing even a rupee note, as others have done, on the rope-strung cot where the maulavi sits. I stop the man and ask if he will not call a village council to help him retrieve his land. "No," he replies. He is a poor man and his uncle is rich; the council would not listen to him. It would be the same in the courts. He walks away; this is the solution available to him. The maulavi is already engaged with his next patient, exorcising spirits from a young married woman. [...]

What do the three petitioners – the man seeking the return of his land, the woman who has borne only female children, and the young married woman possessed by spirits – have in common? Why do they seek the help of the maulavi? To answer these questions, I will examine the dispute-processing alternatives that are available to the rural villager in northeastern Rajasthan, India, showing how these alternatives are shaped by power and resistance.

In theory, the Rajasthani villager has a variety of options available for the public airing of a grievance. There are dispute-processing forums that represent the ideological interests of religion, the dominant caste within the village, and the state. Each forum has different economic-political origins, represents a different philosophy of justice, and has its own procedural and substantive laws: state, village "customary," or religious. Each forum represents a different manifestation of patriarchy. In secular India, the voice of religion that once dictated the rule of state now finds its public forum for dispute resolution limited to caste panchayats. (The religious traditions that dictate the personal laws for Hindus and Muslims in the state courts have been severely limited.) In this area of Rajasthan, however, caste (*jati*) panchayats are no longer active in the settlement of conflicts. The state courts and the village panchayat (the community council of the dominant caste) are the two main dispute-processing forums used by the villagers. The villagers theoretically have one other forum, the "committee." The committee, a statutory creation of the state government, was designed for village administration and the resolution of petty conflicts at the village level. However, this forum too has been co-opted by the village power structure.

The range of sources of the law and their associated institutions is referred to as legal pluralism. Starr and Collier note, "Legal orders should not be treated as closed cultural systems that one group can impose on another, but rather as 'codes,' discourses, and languages in which people pursue their varying and often antagonistic interests."[1] There is a continuing negotiation among the systems, and a villager may use a variety of forums in the course of any one dispute.

While there is competition and contradiction among the systems, in reality these legal arenas are almost exclusively the domain of the powerful. Behind-the-scenes bribing and politicking limit their value to others. In the village, the cultural construction of power focuses on combinations of money, family lineage, caste, and gender. Education and connections in town add to the power currency of the younger village men. Women and most poor or low-caste men are not heard in the legal arenas. They manage conflict and negative feelings in other ways. Sickness, spirit possession, flight from the affinal village, violence, and suicide are some of their avenues for the resolution of conflict.

It is not surprising that the young women and the old man described above should have met at the maulavi's cot. They are in similar positions of political weakness in relation to the village dominants. In the opinion of the old man, his claims go unaddressed because he is poor and powerless. For justice, he turns from the courts and panchayats to the maulavi of Nagina. The young bride and the woman with too many daughters also fit into this paradigm, in which law is understood as social control. The rural peasant women of north India do not have a dispute-processing forum to curry their loyalty. Like the old man, they have no one who will listen to their complaints. North Indian women marry outside their natal villages and, at least for several years after marriage, are under the control of a mother-in-law who is the domestic head of the extended family. Lonely, tired, overworked, and sometimes undernourished, these women become sick and often possessed by spirits. [...]

[T]he Indian women who fall ill or become possessed and then visit a maulavi are responding to their oppression in ways culturally consistent with their subordinate female status. It is not expected that they will protest in a court or panchayat. Instead, they may convert a social distress into a physical

---

[1] June Starr and Jane F. Collier (1989), "Introduction: Dialogues in Legal Anthropology," in *History and Power in the Study of Law*, edited by June Starr and Jane F. Collier, 1–30 at 9 (Ithaca, NY: Cornell University Press). [Editors' note]

# Legal Pluralism

distress. This is what I call the "somatization of conflict." In such cases, getting "sick" is a mode of seeking justice. [...] [T]he body becomes an instrument for the expression of distress and alienation; it becomes a locus for control and resistance. Rajasthani women's anger and frustration challenge the patriarchal social structure. Voicing their complaints in the language of the body, the women are able to stop work, leave their affinal villages, and perhaps find justice in an appeal to their God. [...]

[Here,] I offer an introduction to the pluralistic systems of normative ordering in rural Rajasthan, India, presenting the villagers' experiences of the central legal institutions, the councils and courts, as a framework in which to understand the maulavi at Nagina. By considering this spirit healer as part of the legal system, I break the usual sociolegal boundaries of the "law." The study of cross-cultural conflict and legal pluralism most often focuses on statutory law, courts, and councils, not on healers, although it sometimes examines witchcraft or religion as an alternative remedy agent. In research that does explore healing and dispute processing, the healing ceremony is considered the dominant mode of resolution rather than an alternative for the powerless. The resort to traditional healers ought to be examined within a sociolegal framework.

By understanding the political context of health complaints, we broaden the legal field to reembrace issues ceded to the medical field: stress, somatization, and the role of traditional healers. In northern India, villagers see the lawyer and the healer as parts of a continuum of options. At the legal end of this continuum, issues are addressed in the social arena of family, caste, or village, and the stated goal of the petitioner is "justice." At the medical end of this continuum, the "trouble case" is seen as an individual, and often physical, issue that is unconsciously incorporated into the body. The social subaltern seeks a personal solution offered by a healer, and the goal is health. Justice and health are different names for the same aim: harmony, peace, and order. [...]

Attention to the maulavi's spirit healing not only broadens our perspective on dispute-processing forums and on indigenous meanings of justice but also provides insight into victimizations by the state and village laws. In patriarchy, legal institutions play a significant role in maintaining systems that subordinate and oppress women; law is used to define and control women's sexuality through the regulation of marriage, divorce, paternity, and so on. In addition, courts and councils feminize poor and low-status male plaintiffs by silencing them. But this does not mean that the disenfranchised play no important part in the local legal culture. One form of female resistance to patriarchy is the visit to the maulavi. This is resistance that can be understood only in light of cultural constructions of gender and the multipositional role of the maulavi.

Attention to body rituals of complaint may help scholars understand women's unique responses to the law and their roles in legal change promoted by protest and resistance. [...]

[Moore goes on to describe her extended fieldwork over a ten-year period in a rural village in northeastern Rajasthan, which she calls Nara. Nara's population includes Hindus and Sikhs, but the community is dominated by the Meo caste, which is Muslim. The men from all three religious groups "believe that it is their duty to control the women of their lineage," and they monitor the women's movements and restrict their interactions with others. Most married women come from outside the village and are brought in as brides, which adds to their vulnerability and isolation. Moore notes that "Younger women counter the isolation of life in the affinal village with visits or flights home, where they are pampered by their mothers and seek the support of their fathers, brothers, and uncles in their battles in the affinal village." In Moore's account, patterns of disputing and dispute resolution must be understood within a social context crosscut by religious and cultural differences and by rigid gender roles and power disparities. Next, Moore turns to a map of the "landscape of disputing" in the village.]

*[T]he Landscape of Disputing*
**village forums: panchayats** The dispute-processing forum used most frequently by the villagers is the panchayat. The word panchayat (*panca:yat* is derived from the Sanskrit root *panc*, meaning five, but Nara villagers refer to any community meeting of any number of men (women are not invited) as a panchayat. Even in terms of disputes, the Nara panchayat is not one thing. It is a form of flexible membership for male community input: to witness the repayment of a debt, to collect evidence, to air grievances, or to work toward a compromise in a dispute. A process more than a single event, the panchayat usually entails a series of meetings with differing degrees of privacy, leadership, and consultation with various members.

This council is discussed in the literature as one of two types: a caste panchayat or a village panchayat. In Nara, the distinction between them is not always clear. All panchayats include men from a variety of castes, but in intracaste disputes, particularly those involving domestic issues, the caste whose members are in conflict controls the panchayat. In intercaste disputes, the Meos dominate.

**caste panchayats** At one time caste panchayats promoted caste solidarity, unifying the people of dispersed villages under one social institution that regulated the behavior of individual caste members. The caste panchayat dealt with the infringement of caste rules, particularly in personal matters (such as marriage and divorce), sexual offenses, and the maintenance of service relationships. Almost every modern account of caste panchayats ends with a comment on the decline in their power. Some scholars attribute the decline to the establishment of British courts, while others believe that caste solidarity has gradually been replaced by village solidarity. In either case, the replacement of caste authority by village or state authority is the result of concerted political action to eliminate competing spheres of authority.

Multivillage caste panchayats seldom convene in northeastern Rajasthan. "Who has five or six thousand rupees?" one caste elder asked rhetorically. Today the caste may gather at a funeral feast, a wedding, a celebration over the birth of a son, or a festival, taking that opportunity to discuss a variety of issues: elections, the set fees for caste-related village services, government benefits, education, dowries, or proper moral conduct. Disputes are seldom discussed. Caste-men complain that it is almost impossible to enforce caste rules today. The state has forbidden outcasting under both the defamation laws and the Indian Untouchability Act. Villagers fear that they would be fined and put in jail for outcasting a fellow caste member. At the same time, the caste is not united as it used to be. The village watercarriers told me that several years earlier the caste had ostracized a watercarrier; he had eventually paid 1,000 rupees to the watercarriers in a neighboring state, and they had accepted him. In addition, the dominant castes in the villages control dispute settlement in their territories. The head of the leatherworkers for the 210 villages of their panchayat said that he was no longer asked to settle disputes. In the Ahir villages, the Ahirs (a landowning caste) settled the cases themselves, and in the Meo villages, the Meos had the village as a whole settle them. [...]

Nara women do not expect to find justice in the panchayats or the courts. These are the men's forums. "Where does a woman find justice?" I asked. A Meo woman responded: "If there is any dispute or you are angry, you are just angry within yourself and keep on working. You don't go anywhere." Another Meo woman said: "You don't go anywhere. Women are not panches; if you go to a neighbor woman and tell her about your trouble, it will create more trouble." A sweeper woman, whose caste was the lowest in the village and was represented by only one household, said: "If someone curses me, I say go ahead and curse me. I don't care." If she was not paid her wages, she did nothing about it. She had no options. [...]

*the "committee"* To combat village partisanship and extend the powers of the state under the guise of "democratic decentralization," the Indian federal constitution mandated that each state recognize the panchayats and endow them with state powers enabling them to act as authorized units of self-government. Under state law, Nara is governed not by the village (Meo) panchayat but by representatives elected from Nara and the three surrounding villages, a population of about 3,000. This body is officially called the *gram* panchayat (literally, the village council), but the villagers refer to it as the "committee" (using the English word). I will do the same. The lowest level of a three-tier organization of regional government with administrative and judicial authority, the committee was envisioned as a union of what was believed to be the best of both the village panchayats and the low-level state system. In its judicial role, the designers hoped it would afford easy access to inexpensive, informal justice because it would rely on an elected leadership, a government secretary, mandatory female and untouchable caste representation, and statutory rules of law and procedure.

In Nara the committee functions, if at all, like the village panchayat. Neither women nor untouchables are invited into this multicaste, male bastion. Instead, an attendance book is sent to the required representatives, wherever they may be working, and the impression of their thumbprints is to suffice as proof of their presence to the auditors. At the time of my fieldwork, the village panchayat was usually the villagers' choice of dispute-processing forum. If one or both of the disputing parties happened to be Hindu, they would try to interest Nara's Hindu sarpanch, the elected committee chair, and ask him to join the village panchayat. Generally, he sat to one side of the gathering and listened silently even when goaded to give his opinion. A Hindu in a Meo-dominated village, he respected the jurisdiction of the powerful Nara elite. He too relied on Meo reciprocities. The Nara sarpanch had been the chair for the past 30 years but did not believe that the committee, *his committee*, could dispense justice. In his opinion, the vote divided people and the committee members supported only those villagers who voted for them. "There is only this 'party politics,'" he said, using the commonly employed English words. Baxi and Galanter point out that because the committee is the conduit for community development funds and grants for the needy, the elections for the sarpanch are hotly contested and the dominant sections of the village often capture power for their own ends. This has been the experience of the Nara villagers. Nara's wealthiest villager commented:

> The panches [here, the men of the committee] say, "You do my work and I'll do yours.".... The panches take money; they are not impartial. The panches and sarpanches that take money are like dogs eating shit. They settle the cases with partiality; they do not give true justice .... They fill their stomachs.

Because the committee is co-opted by the powerful of the village, villagers who want to circumvent the powerful may turn to the state courts.

***state courts*** One of the most noted achievements of British rule in India was the formation of a unified national legal system. In all matters except personal laws (laws relating to marriage, divorce, inheritance, adoption, and so on), uniform territorial rules were established. Attention to the individual and the enforcement of standards without reference to the group meant that the new court system might offer new avenues for mobility and advancement for both the powerful elite and the village underclasses.

In Nara, I found that the majority of upper-caste men had had some experience with the state legal system. Generally the women had only had experience through their husbands. Still, Nara villagers complained about the corruption in the courts. "With money you can buy any result you want; if you put the skull of a man whom you have killed into the palm of your hand and lay five or ten thousand rupees on top of that, you will be set free," an untouchable man told me. This story was repeated by other villagers. The courts are seen as an arena of and for the powerful. The police are feared for their liberal use of the stick against both sides, the complainant and the respondent. Lawyers are feared for their verbal skills, which can turn truth into lies, and all the actors-witnesses, lawyers, judges, and police-are vulnerable to bribes. [...]

In practice, state forums are little different from the panchayats in their treatment of Nara village women. State laws are written to give women their say in village government (on the committee), but in Nara the women are excluded and the attendance books are brought to them for their thumbprints. State courts, too, often fail to protect women. [...]

***negotiating forums*** The choice of dispute-processing forums has very specific consequences on relationships within the village. There is significant pressure from the powerful elders to use the village forums for dispute processing. To bring a dispute involving villagers before the panchayat is said to give honor to the community. In fact, it preserves the community power structure. As Mullings observes in discussing Ghanaian medical healers, to choose the traditional system (whether healer or dispute-processing forum) is to reaffirm the lineage, the collectivity, respect for the elders, and local reciprocity.[2] The state court system undermines village hierarchies and limits the area of dispute to the individual and the particular conflict. As a result, a villager can choose to minimize or maximize his or her local worth by the choice of forum. India has no jury system; a petition to the court asks for a

---

[2] Leith Mullings (1984), *Therapy, Ideology, and Social Change: Mental Healing in Urban Ghana* (Berkeley: University of California Press). [Editors' note]

decision by one man and for a state-defined solution, both alien to the panchayat. [...]

The majority of Nara women told me they did not believe that either the village panchayats or the state courts would offer them justice. Village women have few sanctioned means of redressing perceived injustices. There is no dispute settlement forum that welcomes their complaints, and the men often fail to see women's domestic issues as actionable. The local male culture would not consider it unfair to harass a young woman who bears only female children, who is sterile, or who claims equal rights in divorce, parenting, and inheritance. Those with issues that concern parties of unequal power, or issues that involve people who do not have the power to interest the panches in gathering, seek their justice elsewhere.

Villagers and judges alike repeated the refrain that real justice came only from God. They rolled their eyes upward, lamenting today's corruption. If the panchayats functioned according to local ideology, the panchayats too would offer God's wisdom. But they do not. As everyone reminded me, now is the kali yuga, the dark age (one of the cyclic ages in the Hindu calendar) when people are dishonest, selfish, and thieving. Some villagers turned their gaze to the God within. A leatherworker man said optimistically: "Today justice is in your heart and nowhere else. You don't find it outside. If you are true to the world, then the whole world is true to you." For the disempowered, the choice to remain silent in the face of conflict is born of necessity. [...]

I argue that the appeal to the maulavi in Nagina is one form of female resistance. When young brides suffer and leave the village for care, they are expressing gender conflict in terms of sickness. Women's complaints are re-formed in the discourse of the maulavi. His is a medical discourse; he is not a counselor or a judge but a healer. An excursion to the maulavi may be the Nara women's distinctive form of work stoppage. The visit usually requires an overnight stay, meaning that the woman and often her husband or brother are pampered at the home of a relative; they buy gifts for the children at home (adding excitement and expectation to their homecoming); and she enjoys a needed break from the routine of daily work and a mother-in-law. In addition, the maulavi's cures often require that the patient drink a quarter kilo of warm, sweetened milk and take a warm bath daily. These would be mandated luxuries for a woman in Nara. The maulavi's cure always involves a naqas that is to be worn forever. But the naqas becomes polluted and must be replaced, requiring a return visit at least once a year.

Judging whether the women are resisting or merely surviving their circumstances calls for sensitivity to both a gendered and an Indian notion of resistance. Cultural variability is not adequately discussed in the literature on

# Legal Pluralism

resistance. Instead, when Abu-Lughod describes resistance among the Bedouin women of northern Egypt she suggests that the ethnologist turn from explaining resistance to "us[ing] resistance as a diagnostic of power." She draws upon Foucault's insights on power to say, "where there is resistance, there is power."[3] A focus on resistance should lead the investigation back to relationships of power and their methods of oppression. In north India, the active use of the maulavi in dispute processing and the extensive treatment of women for spirit possession and gender-specific ills call attention to female repression and the exclusion of women, as well as other weak members of society, from the legal arena of courts and panchayats. When men petition the maulavi they can discuss their social conflicts in a legal discourse. Women, more often, must mask their complaints against the patriarchy in a medical discourse. They somatize the complaints.

## REFERENCES

### Featured Readings

Benda-Beckmann, Keebet von and Bertram Turner. 2018. "Legal Pluralism, Social Theory, and the State." *The Journal of Legal Pluralism and Unofficial Law* 50 (3): 255–74. doi: 10.1080/07329113.2018.1532674

Erie, Matthew S. 2015. "Muslim Mandarins in Chinese Courts: Dispute Resolution, Islamic Law, and the Secular State in Northwest China." *Law & Social Inquiry* 40 (4): 1001–30. doi: 10.1111/lsi.12137

Harding, Andrew. 2002. "Global Doctrine and Local Knowledge: Law in South East Asia." *International and Comparative Law Quarterly* 51 (1): 35–53. doi: 10.1093/iclq/51.1.35

Moore, Erin P. 1993. "Gender, Power, and Legal Pluralism: Rajasthan, India." *American Ethnologist* 20 (3): 522–42. doi: 10.1525/ae.1993.20.3 .02a00040

Strating, Rebecca and Beth Edmondson. 2015. "Beyond Democratic Tolerance: Witch Killings in Timor-Leste." *Journal of Current Southeast Asian Affairs* 34 (3): 37–64. doi: 10.1177/186810341503400302

---

[3] Lila Abu-Lughod (1990), "The Romance of Resistance: Tracing Transformations of Power through Bedouin Women," *American Ethnologist* 17 (1): 41–55 at 42. [Editors' note]

## Other Works Cited

Benda-Beckmann, Keebet von. 2001. "Transnational Dimensions of Legal Pluralism." In *Begegnung und Konflikt – eine kulturanthropologische Bestandsaufnahme*, edited by Wolfgang Fikentscher, 33–48. München: Verlag der Bayerischen Akademie der Wissenschaften, C. H. Beck Verlag.

Benda-Beckmann, Keebet von and Bertram Turner. 2018. "Legal Pluralism, Social Theory, and the State." *Journal of Legal Pluralism and Unofficial Law* 50 (3): 255–74. doi: 10.1080/07329113.2018.1532674

Chiba, Masaji. 2002. *Legal Cultures in Human Society: A Collection of Articles and Essays*. Tokyo: Shinzansha International.

Hooker, M. B. 1975. *Legal Pluralism: An Introduction to Colonial and Neo-colonial Laws*. Oxford: Clarendon Press. doi: 10.2307/2800821

——— 1978. *A Concise Legal History of South-East Asia*. Oxford: Clarendon Press.

Künkler, Mirjam and Yüksel Sezgin. 2016. "The Unification of Law and the Postcolonial State: The Limits of State Monism in India and Indonesia." *American Behavioral Scientist* 60 (8): 987–1012. doi: 10.2307/844595

Merry, Sally E. 1988. "Legal Pluralism." *Law & Society Review* 22: 869–96. doi: 10.2307/3053638

Pospisil, Leopold. 1958. *Kapauku Papuans and Their Law*. New Haven, CT: Yale University Publications in Anthropology, No. 54. doi: 10.1525/aa.1959.61.4.02a00340

Roberts, Simon. 1998. "Against Legal Pluralism: Some Reflections on the Contemporary Enlargement of the Legal Domain." *Journal of Legal Pluralism and Unofficial Law* 30 (42): 95–106. doi: 10.1080/07329113.1998.10756517

Sartori, Paolo. 2017. *Visions of Justice: Sharīʿa and Cultural Change in Russian Central Asia*. Leiden and Boston: Brill. doi: 10.1163/9789004330900

Strating, Rebecca and Beth Edmondson. 2015. "Beyond Democratic Tolerance: Witch Killings in Timor-Leste." *Journal of Current Southeast Asian Affairs* 3: 37–64. doi: 10.1177/186810341503400302

Ubink, Janine. 2018. "Introduction: Legal Pluralism in a Globalized World." *UC Irvine Law Review* 8: 141.

Weber, Max. 1978. *Economy and Society: An Outline of Interpretive Sociology*. Translated by Guenther Roth and Claus Wittich. Berkeley: University of California Press.

## Suggested Readings

Benda-Beckmann, Franz von. 2002. "Who's Afraid of Legal Pluralism?" *Journal of Legal Pluralism and Unofficial Law* 47: 37–82. doi: 10.1080/07329113.2002.10756563

Griffiths, Anne. 2011. "Pursuing Legal Pluralism: The Power of Paradigms in a Global World." *Journal of Legal Pluralism and Unofficial Law* 43: 173–202. doi: 10.1080/07329113.2011.10756674

Griffiths, John. 1986. "What Is Legal Pluralism?" *Journal of Legal Pluralism and Unofficial Law* 24: 1–55. doi: 10.1080/07329113.1986.10756387

Santos, Boaventura de Sousa. 2002. *Toward a New Legal Common Sense: Law, Globalization, and Emancipation*. New York and London: Routledge. doi: 10.1017/9781316662427

# 3 Disputing

Contents

| | | |
|---|---|---|
| I | Dispute-Based Fieldwork | 116 |
| II | Dispute Processing and Litigation | 120 |
| III | Alternative Dispute Resolution | 129 |

As the field of law and society began to flourish worldwide in the 1960s and 1970s, one of its primary foci – some would say its signature research paradigm – was the study of disputes and dispute processing. There are several reasons for the ascendancy of dispute analysis among law and society researchers during the second half of the twentieth century.

The study of law across the nations of the world had long been dominated by comparative law specialists and their analysis of "families of law" – civil law, common law, and socialist law – as they operated in different countries. But this type of analysis was not well-suited to the interests of law and society researchers, particularly those who studied Asian societies. Comparative law scholarship was primarily doctrinal and not empirical. It focused on law texts and the opinions of high court judges. Since it emphasized the "top down" study of laws and legal institutions that had been transplanted from Europe and North America, its methods were somewhat limited in their capacity to probe deeper into the actual workings of law within the societies and cultures of Asian countries. Lacking the sociological dimension that was so important to law and society scholars, the field of comparative law seemed to mask or ignore the cultural dimensions of law – its meanings, its everyday uses, and its actual consequences for the peoples and societies of Asia.

But if the methods of comparative law scholarship were too limited for law and society scholars, what alternative set of methods could they adopt? The question became particularly pressing with the recognition by law and society scholars of the universality of legal pluralism, as described in Chapter 2. How could researchers escape the straitjacket of top-down doctrinalism if they wished to study the multilayered, multicentered legal systems in countries throughout the world? The answer that emerged during the formative years of the law and society field was the study of disputes. Every society – indeed, every level and location in every society – had disputes and developed distinctive ways to deal with them. If the dispute became the unit of scholarly analysis, there would be no built-in bias toward official versus non-official legal institutions or Western versus non-Western concepts of law and legality. Even the distinction between civil and criminal justice systems would become contingent, since the shaping and definition of most disputes as civil or criminal cases depends as much on extrinsic social factors as on their intrinsic features. Thus, researchers began to base their inquiry not on doctrinal categories, law texts, or families of law, but on the dispute itself. They asked what the dispute was about, how it arose, where it went, how it was handled, and whether various forms of official law became relevant, remained dormant, or were avoided altogether. Dispute analysis could encompass formal law and legal institutions – some disputes, but certainly not all of them, did end up in court – but it did not make formal law its central or exclusive focus or even its starting point. The centrality and the importance of official law in a given dispute became an empirical question and was never simply assumed. In short, researchers came to regard disputes as the atoms out of which all legal matter was constituted.

It is impossible to overstate the importance of the dispute paradigm in the emergence of law and society as an academic field.[*] Although some of the features of dispute processing scholarship now appear dated – or overly positivistic – it left a lasting impression, and its influence remains strong. Scholars such as Laura Nader, Richard Abel, Marc Galanter, and Sally Falk Moore published important theoretical pieces on dispute analysis that guided much of the empirical work. Nader's (1965) classic comparison of two villages in Lebanon and Mexico, for example, led her to theorize that disputes are more likely to be filed as lawsuits in state-run courts when communities are "divided into two endogamous groups" as compared to less sharply divided communities, which tend to resolve disputes internally without formal

---

[*] Dispute-based law and society researchers tended to avoid using the term "dispute resolution" and instead spoke of "dispute processing" or simply "disputing." This was because of the recognition that many disputes went unresolved and instead persisted or branched into new and different forms of grievance. It was the handling of the disputes that interested researchers rather than some imagined finite outcome.

litigation. Abel (1973) theorized that the handling of disputes is shaped by the nature of the third party "intervenors." The more they are "differentiated" culturally, socially, and professionally from the context of the dispute and from the disputants themselves, the more formalized, rationalized, bureaucratized, and "legalistic" the dispute resolution process. Moore (1973) theorized that the concept of the "semi-autonomous social field" explained why legal norms partially but not completely shaped the handling of disputes in particular social settings. Galanter (1974) called attention to the advantages enjoyed by "repeat players" in dispute processing and explained why they tend to come out ahead of "one-shotters" both in the short term and in the long run.

Influenced by these and other theories, fieldwork studies of dispute behavior in many different societies proliferated. Even studies of litigation and court caseloads rested largely on a foundation of dispute analysis, as law and society scholars attempted to track disputes that found their way to court in comparison to those that did not. Some researchers undertook large scale surveys of disputing in different countries, based on the assumption that meaningful comparative conclusions could be drawn if scholars working in each society adopted the dispute as the common unit of analysis (Trubek et al. 1983; Genn and Beinart 1999; Michelson 2007; Matsumura and Murayama 2010).

Readings in this chapter illustrate some of the recent applications of dispute analysis by law and society scholars working in Asia.

I DISPUTE-BASED FIELDWORK

One of the most time-honored approaches to the study of dispute processing by law and society scholars is to choose a particular community or locale and to ask how local residents handle instances of conflict. Very often, answering this question requires the researcher to explore a variety of local level procedures and institutions, including mediation by respected elders or local leaders. The case study method is typically favored in this type of close-textured study of dispute processing. The following excerpt from an ethnographic study by Fernanda Pirie in Ladakh, in the Kashmir region of India, illustrates this approach particularly well.

3.1 Conflict in the Village, *Fernanda Pirie*

Pirie's fieldwork in the village of Photoksar revealed that strong moral disapproval attached to villagers who engaged in disputes, argumentation, and fights: "The phrase used to describe people who got into quarrels was usually *tsokpo*, a general word meaning bad or dirty but also used to signify strong disapproval" (2006:70). Anger in itself was regarded as an undesirable

# Disputing

character trait, as were selfishness and lack of dedication to social harmony and the welfare of the community as a whole. Conversely, emotional self-discipline was highly valued, even in the face of personal affronts such as marital infidelity. In this regard, Pirie's findings in Ladakh may remind us of Nader's description of the "harmony ideology" among the Zapotek, who also disfavored conflict within the community. According to Nader (1990:309), "What resulted is a peace at any price culture that is a social success, sometimes at a cost to individual Zapotec. Harmony comes at a price." Nevertheless, disputes inevitably arose in Photoksar from time to time. Pirie describes the process through which the *goba* (village head) and the *yulpa* (meeting of village men) could become involved. As she explains, their efforts were usually directed at suppressing conflict and restoring harmony rather than adjudicating the rights and wrongs of a situation. Nevertheless, in some situations they imposed punishment on a perceived wrongdoer.

> When anger leads to a quarrel but the protagonists walk away or make up their differences then the incident remains merely a talking point in the village. If animosity remains active, however, it becomes a village concern. An unresolved dispute is an ongoing problem for the households involved and, ultimately, for the village as a whole. It is primarily the *goba*'s duty to engineer a form of resolution. Whenever we discussed the role of the *goba*, both in Photoksar and other villages, people always also mentioned dispute resolution, very often first, among his list of duties. The primary concern of his intervention is to restore good relations between the individuals, *shakhs choches*. One day, for example, one of the village women came in a state of high indignation to talk to Paljor, who was then village *membar* [a village official]. She had just had a quarrel with her daughter-in-law's mother, a woman from another village. Paljor listened and a few days later accompanied the *goba* to a meeting to resolve the problem. Choron told me that the two women had argued and thrown stones and that the meeting was to make them shake hands so that they did not throw stones any more. She also used the expression *chams chug*. *Chug* means 'to cause' and *chams* was explained to me in terms of the affection that family members feel for each other. A relationship of *chams* was to be restored between them. No-one could tell me what the quarrel had actually been about, however. That was not the point. It was the argument that was the problem and Paljor's responsibility, as village *membar*, was to ensure that good relations were restored.
>
> For the villagers, disputes are events of public significance and *shakhs* (mediation) is a conscious, deliberate process. It is a widely discussed village practice which follows a hierarchical pattern culminating in the meeting of the *yulpa*, the village's ultimate judicial authority. There are two phenomena

here, which could be distinguished as 'differences' and 'disputes'. The words used to describe disputes are roughly translatable as 'shouting', 'flinging abuse', 'arguing', 'quarrelling' and 'fighting', in other words overt forms of antagonism. Their public nature means that disputes affect the whole community. Mere differences that do not result in overt antagonism, by contrast, are dealt with as practical problems. On the border between differences and disputes are those bad relations between individuals who, nevertheless, avoid an open quarrel. [...]

Differences or disputes that do not involve violence might be resolved by employing the services of a mediator, a *barmi*. As already mentioned, shortly after I arrived in the village Tsewang, Paljor's younger brother, had had an argument with his wife, Yangzes, during the course of which he had hit her. It was reported to me that she had then 'become angry', *sho yongse*, and returned to Wadze, her natal home. In the days that followed there was much contact between the families. Meme Sonam, Gyaltsen and Morup from Khangltakh all went to Wadze to ask her to come back but she said that she did not want to return. Tsewang did not go and there was much shrugging of shoulders about his attitude. Maybe he did not want her back. Eventually they called in the *onpo* to act as mediator. According to Morup, he 'talked wisely'. At first he told Tsewang to go and bring Yangzes back but Tsewang said he did not want to do so. The *onpo*, therefore, consulted Yangzes who also said she did not want to return. So he suggested a divorce: one of the two children should belong to Khangltakh and the other to Wadze. Later they drew up an agreement which included the payment of half a yak from Khangltakh to Wadze. The whole issue was resolved within a month. Tsewang and Yangzes remained on bad terms but the continuation of good relations between the two households was assured by this settlement.

Although the resolution of disputes is ultimately the *goba's* responsibility, others can, thus, act as mediators. There are no individuals who are particularly qualified to assume this role, however. It is generally older men who are asked to do so but, as with other matters of village politics, there is no status of 'village elder', or the like. It is considered to be more important that the mediator should know the parties and, therefore, the background to the dispute. [...]

There was a perceived need to restore good relations, *chams*, in all these cases and in all of them the mediation of the *goba* and *yulpa* was ultimately successful. Lingering antipathy might have remained, as it did between the father and brother and between Tsewang and Yangzes, but workable relations were restored, most importantly between their respective households. Village life, with its networks of cooperation and assistance, could, therefore, continue

# Disputing

as normal. Similar attitudes towards the restoration of good relations were expressed in conversations I had about disputes with informants from all over Ladakh. One striking example is reported by Kim Gutschow from Zangskar.[1] A case of rape, which had resulted in the death of the girl, was dealt with entirely internally to that village. The girl's father merely demanded and obtained, against an admittedly guilty party, a donation to the monastery and a payment for a *sangs*, purification ritual. Gutschow comments on the way in which the following year the father and his daughter's attacker were again working side by side in the fields without any apparent residue of animosity between them.

The resolution of fights in Photoksar can involve an element of punishment by the community of the individuals involved, with the protagonists called to justify themselves before the village meeting and fines being paid to the village, 'for the fight'. When we were discussing the mediation carried out by the *yulpa*, for example, Paljor was quite specific about the sort of fines they would impose in different cases. In a bad case of fighting the protagonists would have to give *khatags* and *yal* and a fine of between Rs6,000 to Rs9,000, but the fine would only be around Rs1,000 if the case was less serious. If it was just an argument then they would only have to give *khatags* and *yal*. I never encountered any cases of theft but Paljor said that if they caught a thief then the *goba* and *membars* or the *yulpa* would beat him. [...]

The villagers effectively preclude the expression of individual rights by concentrating on the course of the disruption and expression of anger and antagonism. What could be analysed as a clash of interests is, rather, described as a disturbance to order. This is what marks the distinction between differences (clashes of interests that require a pragmatic solution) and disputes (overt antagonism that requires reconciliation). It is the latter that disturbs the village order and requires the most immediate and deliberate remedy.

According to this epistemology, all overt antagonism is a danger to the order of the community requiring resolution and the ceremonial restoration of good relations. This is supported by the local scheme of morality according to which all such behaviour is reprehensible on the part of the individuals involved, who are labelled *tsokpo*.

---

[1] Kim Gutschow (2004), *Being a Buddhist Nun: The Struggle for Enlightenment in the Himalayas* (Cambridge, MA: Harvard University Press) at 140–2. [Editors' note]

## II DISPUTE PROCESSING AND LITIGATION

This section illustrates how some scholars explain litigation choices by situating courts in the broader context of dispute institutions in society. As we have seen in Chapter 2, studies of legal pluralism played an exceptionally important role in shaping law and society as a field. Pluralism scholars have demonstrated that every society contains multiple, overlapping systems of law and legality to deal with issues such as land and property, marriage, violence, inheritance, and the like. Official state law represents but one of many legal systems operating in the same geopolitical space, and the legal pluralism paradigm has expanded researchers' focus to include various forms of customary and religious law as well as the laws and legal institutions of the state. Very often religious and customary systems of legal regulation are unwritten and cannot be studied through law books or case compendia. Legal anthropologists sometimes attempted to record oral traditions in written form as a kind of customary code, but such attempts tend to reduce vibrant and flexible systems to mechanical and lifeless written compilations that fail to capture the true dynamics of the "law in action." Dispute analysis appeared to offer a better methodology for studying plural legal systems and for situating formal litigation in its broader societal context.

Consider, for example, an influential article by one of the leading scholars of legal pluralism, Keebet von Benda-Beckmann. Writing in 1981 about legal pluralism in a Minangkabau village in West Sumatra, Indonesia, von Benda-Beckmann carefully describes a multitude of institutions with overlapping "jurisdictions" that were available to villagers in the region where she conducted her fieldwork. Some of them "derive their legitimation from *adat*, the indigenous Minangkabau system of normative rules and usages, others from the national – formerly colonial – legal system." In von Benda-Beckmann's analysis, these plural legal systems became active through the choices made by villagers to "forum shop" their disputes to the institutions most likely to favor their claims. By the same token, she points out that the institutions associated with each of the plural legal systems also engaged in an analogous type of "shopping" for particular kinds of disputes that they could acquire and process to further their own political interests. In this richly detailed description, von Benda-Beckmann shows that the movement of disputes – whether "pushed" by the disputants or "pulled" by the fora themselves – is the dynamic force underlying legal pluralism in Minangkabau.

## 3.2 "What He Did Was Lawful": Divorce Litigation and Gender Inequality in China, *Ke Li*

Much of the law and society research on dispute processing has attempted to situate government courts within the larger array of official and unofficial institutions and practices in which disputes are handled, resolved, reshaped, and at times passed on to other dispute resolution fora. By adopting this perspective, such studies attempt to explain why cases do or do not flow into the courts and why judicial dispute resolution is or is not effective. Even though the law and society perspective on dispute processing is multicentered, pluralistic, and often bottom-up rather than top-down, courts nevertheless are a recurring preoccupation for scholars in the field. The following article about Chinese divorce litigation by Ke Li is, therefore, representative of the use of dispute analysis by law and society researchers to explain how cases are channeled and shaped and why in some instances they may be marked by inequality and injustice.

The rise of divorce is a fairly recent phenomenon in Chinese history. Under imperial laws, women faced much higher barriers to marital dissolution than men. It was only in the early 1930s that Chinese law, for the first time, granted women and men nearly equal rights to divorce. Soon after the Chinese Communist Party came into power, it formally instituted the principle of equality between women and men in family life by promulgating the 1950 Marriage Law. Despite that, divorce remained rare for the most part during the Mao years (1949–76). The reform era, however, witnessed a rapid increase in divorce. Crude divorce rate, measured by the number of divorces per one thousand individuals, soared nearly tenfold from 1978 to 2008.

In rural China, a similar trend has been emerging in the past decade. Survey research conducted in twenty-three villages across five provinces in 2002 and 2010, respectively, found that in both years, divorce was the leading dispute type going into the legal system in the countryside. The same surveys also indicated that divorce had remained the leading reason for rural residents to contact lawyers, justice assistants, and judges for help.[1] As divorce becomes increasingly common in the countryside, rural residents nonetheless continue to face a shortage of licensed lawyers, a phenomenon well documented in the Chinese press. An article published in *Procuratorial Daily* in 2005, for example, lamented that nationwide, 206 counties did not have a single

[1] Research findings by Ethan Michelson shared with the author. [Editors' note]

lawyer.[2] Five years later, this number ascended to 213, according to an article that appeared in *China Daily*.[3] A more recent news report published in *Legal Daily* reduced this number to 174 counties, and the vast majority of those lawyer-less counties were located in western rural areas.[4]

Indeed, in China's vast countryside, it is often another group of law practitioners who attend to rural residents' struggles with divorce. These law practitioners, also known as basic-level legal workers (*jiceng falü gongzuozhe*), make a living by handling rural residents' legal problems. Without any public funding, they usually make elaborate efforts to retain clients and business. In that sense, they are bona fide market players, just like licensed lawyers. [...]

In 2001, China's highest legislative body passed much-awaited amendments to the Marriage Law. The revised law reiterated the principle of equality between women and men in marriage and family life. In the area of divorce, the amendments introduced important changes by codifying concrete grounds for divorce and putting in place a system intended to deal with blameworthy marital conduct such as domestic violence, spousal abandonment, and bigamy. These legislative changes were widely viewed as the state's renewed efforts to protect women's rights and well being. In the following decade, more marital regulations were passed, with mixed responses from government agencies, scholarly communities, and society at large. [...]

[D]ispute over child custody was a recurring theme during the initial face-to-face interactions between marital disputants and legal workers: twenty-two out of the sixty interactions involved a disputant demanding child custody and/or support upon divorce. A careful examination of legal workers' responses exposed a stark contrast: while female disputants were frequently subjected to overt or covert obstruction from legal workers, male disputants rarely encountered similar impediments to their pursuit of child custody.

Upon learning of female disputants' intentions to contend for child custody, legal workers launched various efforts, not to help them realize custodial rights, but to block their attempts at legal mobilization. Two strategies deployed by legal workers warrant close scrutiny: status-based stereotyping and manipulative interpretation of state law. The example below illustrates how a legal worker used the first strategy to discourage a mother from seeking child custody. During a meeting, a young woman revealed that her husband

---

[2] Shenjian Xu (2005), "Why 206 Counties Do Not Have a Single Lawyer," *Jiancha Daily* (Beijing). [Editors' note]

[3] Yan Zhang and Yan Wang (2011), "Lawyers Have Been Assigned to 213 Lawyerless Counties," *China Daily* (Beijing). [Editors' note]

[4] Engshu Li (2014), "134 Counties Ended the History of Having No Lawyers," *Legal Daily* (Beijing: Fazhiwang). [Editors' note]

# Disputing

recently had an affair, leaving another woman pregnant. Disillusioned with the marriage, she was determined to divorce the husband and raise her daughter on her own. To this end, the woman set up a beauty salon in Shenzhen, a coastal city in south China. After months of preparation, she was finally ready for a divorce. Soon after the legal worker learned about the basic contours of the case, he called into question the woman's suitability for parenting:

**Legal worker:** It'll be hard [for you] to secure child custody. Once you're divorced, you will have no housing, no stable income.
**Female disputant:** I live in Shenzhen now. And I do have stable income.
**Legal worker:** What kind of "stable income" do you have?
**Female disputant:** Well, I don't have my own apartment right now, but I will get one later.
**Legal worker:** If you want child custody, you have to prove that you have residence of your own as well as stable income. The two conditions are important. If your daughter is to stay with you, you can't expect her to roam around with you. I had a case before. Both parties insisted on child custody. Then I told the wife, "you have no housing of your own, and you are now working as a migrant worker. So does that mean your daughter will crash at one place in Beijing today and another place in Nanjing tomorrow?"

[Later, the legal worker further spelled out his reservation about the woman's pursuit of child custody.]

**Legal worker:** Although divorced, you're still young. You're unlikely to remain single for the rest of your life.
**Female disputant:** That's not necessarily true. It depends.

**Legal worker:** You'll be better off letting him [the husband] raise the kid ...

From the legal worker's perspective, the woman squarely fell into two status-based categories. First, she was a "migrant worker" (*dagong de*), a condescending term describing peasants who leave the countryside to work in the urban labor force. Labeling the woman as a "*dagong de*" instantly led the legal worker to a conclusion: she must have few resources and move around constantly, and her daughter would inevitably live an unanchored life. Apart from being a "*dagong de*," the woman was on her way to becoming one of "the divorced" (*lihun de*), another status-based category that invites stigmatization and discrimination. Though the legal worker tactfully commented on the woman's situation (she was about to be "divorced," "still young," and "unlikely to remain single"), behind such diplomatic expressions is a profoundly ingrained stereotype in Chinese society: divorced women are further depreciated on the marriage market if they bring children from previous relationships into new ones. Adding insult to injury, the children would become "*tuoyouping*," a derogative term for those who follow divorced mothers into remarriages. In line with this cultural logic, the legal worker announced: "you'll be better off letting him [the husband] raise the kid."

What happened in this case was hardly an exception. When female disputants in the observational sample raised concerns about child custody, half of them were subjected to status-based stereotyping. Age, rural origin, employment status, and residence arrangements were often cited as the grounds for their lack of suitability for parenting. By contrast, none of the male disputants in the sample were exposed to such scrutiny. Behind legal workers' differential treatment of women and men's pursuit of custodial rights is the profoundly ingrained patrilineal tradition in rural China. According to this tradition, children, and especially sons, should be raised by their biological fathers and, in turn, carry on family lineage. Acutely aware of the importance of family lineage in the rural context, legal workers often align themselves with the patrilineal tradition in their divorce law practices. The following example further illustrates how the rural context shapes legal workers' disputing strategies in divorce litigation.

At the center of this case was a young couple's custody battle over a teenage daughter and son; both parties were committed to the fight for child custody. The husband gained the upper hand early on, as he successfully mobilized his kinship networks to secure an experienced lawyer. The wife, however, was unable to do so. Instead, she relied on a junior legal worker with whom she had no family connections. What further tipped the playing field was the fact that the husband's lawyer had close ties with the local court (he came from a law firm whose founder happened to be the father of a judge). Soon after the legal worker learned what he would be up against in the court, he started pressuring his client to give up child custody. To this purpose, he cited the woman's age, employment status, and prospect of remarriage as the grounds for concession. All these efforts were to no avail. Then the legal worker said:

**Legal worker:** Even if the court ruled in favor of your claim on child custody, it would not enforce the decision. In principle, the rights of the person are unenforceable. If he [the husband] refused to let go of the kids, the court would not do anything.

[Later, the legal worker spelled out what he meant by saying "the rights of the person are unenforceable."]

**Legal worker:** You have to trust the law. The law says that the rights of the person are unenforceable. [It means] what the court can forcefully enforce, for example, are rulings over debt. Suppose you were a debtor, and the court ruled that you were entitled to certain money. In that case, the court could physically execute the ruling. But [regarding child custody], it falls into the scope of the rights of the person. It is unenforceable.

Throughout the meeting, the "rights of the person" (*renshen quanli*) appeared seven times in the legal worker's talk. Again and again, he tried to drive home the same message: custodial rights, as part of the "rights of the person," were beyond the scope of the court system's "forcible enforcement" (*qiangzhi zhixing*). If the husband refused to cede physical custody to the wife, the court would not take any action to remedy the impasse. In this account, the law was portrayed as toothless, and the court as utterly incompetent. Yet, a close look at the court system's operation on the ground reveals much more complicated realities. Existing laws remain unclear whether or not the court system can forcefully enforce its rulings on child custody, and judges continue to debate the issue. In practice, judges do not have to resort to forcible enforcement, for they have plenty of discretion in their handling of custody battles. Recent studies of Chinese courts indicate that judges routinely exercise formal and informal influences on disputing parties in order to facilitate divorce settlements, thereby bypassing formal trials. As disputing parties enter settlements, there will be a relatively small chance for them to turn to the courts for forcible enforcement. In other words, only in worst-case scenarios will the courts consider physical force to execute rulings on child custody. By exaggerating the difficulties associated with enforcement, the legal worker projected a bleak prospect of the custody battle. Knowing that his opponent had strong ties with the local court, the legal worker backed down and pressured his client to drop claims on child custody. In the end, the woman lost custody of both children to the husband.

This example illustrates the second strategy – manipulative interpretation of state law – legal workers regularly used in their face-to-face interactions with female disputants. [...] [T]his strategy was exclusively imposed on female disputants but not on male disputants. This gender disparity mirrors a general pattern in divorce law practices in the countryside. Due to the persistence of patrilocal residence in rural China (that is, women are expected to relocate from their natal families and communities to live with the husband's family and community), married women often find themselves isolated at home and in conjugal communities. Rural men who have stayed close to their natal families, by contrast, tend to stand a better chance of mobilizing ties with local elites, such as village cadres, government officials, and judges. The gender differences in social networking can have serious consequences for disputing and litigation: in view of the husband's strong ties with the local court, the legal worker readjusted his disputing strategies by urging the wife to give up child custody. Seen in this light, the persistence of patrilineal and patrilocal tradition in rural China has distinctive effects on legal workers' interactions with female and male disputants. As Landon argued, for those who practice law in rural contexts, community characteristics often serve as the prior and fundamental source of structuring for their disputing strategies.[5] [...]

Finally, the *initiation stage* featured no shortage of grievances against abusive spouses. Among the sixty face-to-face interactions in the observational sample, there were sixteen cases of a female disputant speaking of her sufferings at the hands of the spouse. As those women explained to legal workers why they were seeking divorce, accounts of verbal abuse, physical violence, and coerced sex surfaced. Upon hearing female disputants' complaints of domestic violence, none of the legal workers conducted thorough investigations. No advice was given to the women with regard to evidence collection, and no information was provided to inform them of their rights as victims of domestic violence, despite the Marriage Law's express stipulation on this matter. Instead, legal workers often glossed over women's experiences of domestic violence. To this purpose, they deployed several strategies in their face-to-face interactions with the women. The most frequently used strategy was diversion, namely, abruptly shifting the direction of the conversation in order to keep the issue of spousal abuse at arm's length. [...] [E]ight out of the sixteen interactions witnessed legal workers applying this strategy in response to female disputants' complaints of domestic violence.

Another strategy derived from legal workers' ability to eviscerate the meanings of spousal abuse, thereby clothing it with a layer of normality. I call this strategy "normalization." The following example illustrates how this strategy operates in everyday conversations in the legal workers' office. In this case, a female disputant vividly depicted the verbal, physical, and emotional abuse she had suffered. Note the words she used to describe her victimization: "torture" (*zhemo*), "violent beating" (*baoli daren*), "threaten me with a knife" (*yong dao*

---

[5] Donald Landon (1990), *Country Lawyers: The Impact of Context on Professional Practice* (New York: Praeger). [Editors' note]

*Disputing*

*bi wo*), "stab me with a knife" (*cuo dao wo*), "he scares me" (*wo pa ta*), and "I really can't stand it anymore" (*wo shizai shoubuliao le*). As far as the disputant was concerned, what happened in her marriage was anything but "normal." Yet, the legal worker put a drastically different spin on the disputant's marital experiences. At one point, the disputant mentioned that the couple once worked at a factory and many coworkers saw the husband beating her up in public. Alerted by this revelation, the legal worker looked into the incident:

**Legal worker:** Did anyone at the factory know you two once fought?
**Female disputant:** Yes, they [coworkers] knew what happened.
**Legal worker:** Can you find evidence to prove that you two quarreled?
**Female disputant:** My sister could prove that.
**Legal worker:** Well, ask your sister to approach the manager, so you can get a statement from the factory to prove that you two routinely quarreled and fought with each other.

Rather than unequivocally naming the husband's abusive conduct as an example of domestic violence, the legal worker repeatedly chose words, such as "fighting" (*dajia*) and "bickering" (*chaojia*), to characterize the violence inflicted on the wife. A close scrutiny of the legal worker's selection of words indicates that he did not adopt any of the verbs used by the disputant herself (e.g., torture, beat, threaten, stab, scare, etc.). Instead, he consistently stuck to a language that was devoid of gender, physicality, and emotionality – a language that omitted the woman's agonies over spousal abuse – and ultimately, a language that denied her rights as a victim of domestic violence. Toward the end of the meeting, the legal worker instructed the disputant to gather evidence, not to establish her legal status as a victim, but to merely prove that she did not get along with the husband.

Diversion and normalization allowed legal workers to surreptitiously keep victims from voicing their grievances against abusive spouses. Legitimization, the third strategy, was different in that it enabled legal workers to defend domestic violence in broad daylight. The following case presents a powerful example. During a meeting, a woman in her midforties bitterly recalled her sufferings in her marriage. Out of jealousy, the husband put her through months of sexual abuse. This experience tormented the woman so much that she compared her relationship with the husband to the one between a prostitute and a client: "I'm not his wife anymore; now, he is treating me as if I were one of those who sell their bodies." At some point in the conversation, the woman revealed that one night she was subjected to forced sex, and the legal worker immediately picked up on the issue:

**Female disputant:** Ever since I came back from Chengdu, we have been arguing day after day. Even if I were done with poker games and went home at two or three o'clock in the morning, he would pick a fight with me. Then he would [pause]. Well, last night, I didn't go out for poker games. I figured that I would go to bed earlier. Still, he would not let it go. Well, he forcefully insisted on sleeping with me. The thing is that I don't have feelings for him anymore.

**Legal worker:** So he insisted on sleeping with you? Did you two have a marriage certificate?

**Female disputant:** Yes, but.

[The legal worker interrupted the disputant.]

**Legal worker:** Well, [in that case] what he did was lawful.

In this case, the legal worker tackled the disputant's complaint head on by pointing out how the official justice system perceived sexual aggression within marriage. As the couple was legally married, the wife had obligations to cohabitate with the husband, including having sex with him. The husband's sexual conduct toward the wife, coercive or not, was therefore lawful. The legal worker's unsympathetic interpretation of the situation was partially in line with the existing legal framework and practice. To this day, no legislation in China has specifically outlawed marital rape. In practice, marital exemption – a legal doctrine recognized by the country's highest court in 2001 – continues to dominate the court system's handling of rape within marriage. According to this doctrine, a husband cannot be charged with rape of his wife, unless the couple had previously filed for divorce. What the legal worker failed to mention is that, despite the lack of legal grounds for the wife to build a criminal case, she did have a choice to pursue civil action against the husband. The Marriage Law clearly stipulates that victims of domestic violence are entitled to damages at the time of divorce. Yet, the legal worker did not inform the wife of her rights to pursue damages from the abusive husband. In the end, the wife walked away from the meeting with the impression that the husband's conduct was entirely "lawful" and there was no legal redress for sexual aggression within marriage.

In-depth interviews with legal workers and lawyers further exposed the legal profession's stereotypes about domestic violence. For example, when asked about male aggression in Chinese families, some in the legal profession denied the severity of the problem outright, a viewpoint contrary to existing evidence. Some blamed victims for having a "backward" mentality, which held them back from speaking up about domestic violence. Victim blaming

# Disputing

> was also invoked to explain the difficulties in building lawsuits against abusive spouses. As one lawyer put it, rural women typically harbored a "weak consciousness in evidence collection" (*quzheng yishi bu qiang*), and therefore, were ill prepared for legal battles over domestic violence. These accounts flatly negated the reality that women disputants often went to great lengths to seek legal assistance for their victimization.

## III ALTERNATIVE DISPUTE RESOLUTION

As the dispute processing paradigm consolidated itself in the 1960s and 1970s, the findings of law and society researchers caught the eye of policy-makers in the United States and elsewhere, who began to ask whether the forms of nonjudicial dispute resolution described in Asian and African societies could be transplanted to North America and Europe. Instead of conflictual, expensive, zero-sum litigation, why couldn't disputes in the so-called "developed" countries be handled through more harmonious, inexpensive, and mutually satisfying procedures similar to those researchers had found in non-Western village moots or religious courts? In the 1970s, the concept of "alternative dispute resolution" (ADR) emerged and was quickly endorsed by bar associations, courts, and legislatures as a way to divert cases from overburdened judicial systems into less formal dispute institutions. ADR was then exported from North America and Europe to Asia in a kind of reverse migration back to the source. ADR was, ironically, billed as a new and progressive legal development and was met with enthusiasm in many Asian countries.

Many law and society scholars were disturbed by the emergence of ADR, including some – such as Laura Nader – whose work was cited with approval by ADR supporters. These scholars were suspicious of the motives of ADR enthusiasts, who appeared too ready to sacrifice the legal rights of disputants, particularly in so-called "minor disputes," by channeling their claims to forums without legal protections or substantial remedies. ADR mediators often lacked legal training and placed the highest value on producing a settlement rather than promoting justice. Critics also feared that cases diverted to ADR were viewed as less important because the disputants were persons of lesser means or lower social status, thus reserving the official court system for the wealthy or socially prominent. Furthermore, they pointed out that traditional nonjudicial dispute processing of the kind described by law and society scholars was deeply rooted in communities with shared social and cultural norms. Its success depended on the parties' familiarity with those norms and on multiple, overlapping connections among the disputants and the third-party mediators. Modern versions of ADR lacked such culturally embedded features and could never replicate the harmonious, community-affirming outcomes that law and society scholars had discovered in their fieldwork. Some critics therefore claimed that ADR promoters had hijacked the findings of law and society researchers and applied them in ways that would exacerbate injustice and inequality rather than ameliorating them.

### 3.3 Community Mediation as a Hybrid Practice: The Case of Mediation Boards in Sri Lanka, *Sepalika Welikala*

Despite these cautions and criticisms, ADR has become a prominent part of the official dispute resolution process in most countries in Asia – and throughout the world. The following article by Sepalika Welikala illustrates how law and society researchers have attempted to study ADR as a now-familiar feature of the legal landscape.

> A news headline that was widely publicized in Sri Lanka in 2013 was the case of a 13-year-old schoolgirl being arrested and produced in a magistrates' court for stealing eight coconuts from a neighbour's garden. The girl claimed that she stole the coconuts because her family was unable to provide the Rs. 800 (approximately US$6) contribution demanded by her school towards painting the classrooms. This case was discussed at various fora as to how a minor was arrested, produced in a magistrates' court, and released on bail when the police should have followed proper legal procedure by referring the case to the local Mediation Board (MB). The legal blunder committed by the police and the local magistrate brought to light a socio-legal entity known as the MB that exists in contemporary Sri Lankan society as a mechanism to resolve local disputes. They were established by an Act of Parliament and at present there are more than 300 of these state-sponsored community mediation programmes that were conceptualized and modelled along the lines of Alternative Dispute Resolution (ADR) to function in parallel with the formal courts of law. The MBs were established as an alternative mechanism to the formal courts on the promise of being more effective and efficient by allowing the local community to settle their own disputes. Yet the confusion highlighted in the coconut-stealing case suggests that MBs occupy an ambiguous space within the local dispute resolution system, raising questions that need to

be examined from a sociocultural perspective such as: How do individuals engage with the MB? Where is the MB located conceptually within society? Is it within formal laws or popular justice? Can this be seen as a representation of the plural nature of legal ordering where law is defined broadly as a normative system? How do the different normative systems interact? [...]

The concept of community mediation has a long history in Sri Lanka going back many decades, if not centuries. There are records of local-level dispute settlement through the Gamsabha (village tribunal/council) system that can be traced as far back as the fifth century BC, referring mostly to the pre-colonial Sinhala village organizations. The Gamsabha was an adjudicatory body chaired by the village headman and its membership was drawn from the traditional rural leadership. After a period of decline beginning with the Dutch period, the British tried to replicate a similar local dispute settlement mechanism through the Village Communities Ordinance of 1871. Although these Village Tribunals were seen by British officials as "resurrecting ancient village institutions," as they maintained the status quo vis-it-vis the powers of the traditional elite, these were opposed by other upwardly mobile communities.[1] In the post-independence era, "obsession with the Gamsabhavas continued to haunt the post-independence legal reformists"[2] and another attempt was made in the form of the Conciliation Boards through the Conciliation Boards Act No. 10 of 1958. The Conciliation Boards can be seen as a precursor to the present MBs. In addition, as described by Tiruchelvam, the government's foray into popular tribunals in the post-independence Sri Lanka was to create "social consciousness" that was consistent with the socialist development ideology of the governing elite. By de-professionalizing the form and process of conflict resolution, the Conciliation Boards were expected to encourage the participation of the ordinary people in its work. However, they failed to achieve their objectives and instead have displayed a close resemblance to the Gamsabha that sought to settle disputes through the normative standards of the existing social order. The Conciliation Boards, though not intended, comprised the village leadership and elites who used social pressure to mediate between disputants by applying the values and norms of the existing social structure. Due partly to the politicization of the mediation process and lack of competent mediators, the Conciliation Boards became less effective and were rejected by the local communities. As a result,

---

[1] John D. Rogers (1987), *Crime, Justice and Society in Colonial Sri Lanka* (London: Curzon Press) at 56. [Editors' note]

[2] Neelan Tiruchelvam (1984), *The Ideology of Popular Justice in Sri Lanka: A Socio-Legal Inquiry* (New Delhi: Vikas) at 34. [Editors' note]

the Conciliation Boards Act was repealed in 1978. However, in yet another attempt to formally revive the idea of community mediation, the current MBs were established ten years later with the objective of "facilitating the voluntary settlement of minor disputes using interest-based mediation."[3] The trajectory of the concept of community mediation in Sri Lankan society thus shows its unique position within the judicial landscape.

Currently, MBs exist in almost all parts of the island and is believed to be the third largest mediation system in the world. As at December 2013, there were 324 such MBs in operation, with over 7,000 trained mediators actively engaged in the mediation process. Officially, MBs function under the Ministry of Justice and are governed by the Mediation Boards Act No. 72 of 1988, amended by Act No. 15 of 1997, Act No. 21 of 2003, and Act No. 7 of 2011. The Act defines the duties of the MB as:

> by all lawful means to endeavour to bring the disputants to an amicable settlement and to remove, with their consent and wherever practicable, the real cause of grievance between them so as to prevent a recurrence of the dispute, or offence. [Section 10]

The primary objective of MBs was to offer an alternative mechanism of dispute resolution for local and minor conflicts outside the framework of the overburdened state legal system. They were thus expected to ease the case-load placed on the courts and to improve people's access to justice by offering a locally mediated settlement. [...]

From the physical location of the MB to the actual mediation sessions by individual panels, there are many instances of structured formalities that mimic the formal legal system, as Merry has discussed in her analysis of ADR and popular justice.[4] This replication is evident in the ritualistic start to the MB as well as in the physical layout where clear boundaries are maintained between the mediators and disputants similar to a court of law. It also extends to the individual panels as well, where mediators and disputants sit on opposite sides with mediators directing the process. According to the mediators' training manual, the only mention about seating is that there should be adequate space between the disputants in order to prevent any tension, and also that mediators should maintain equal distance from the disputing parties. However, in the MB, there is clear maintenance and

---

[3] Michelle Gunawardana (2011), *A Just Alternative* (Colombo: The Asia Foundation). [Editors' note]

[4] Sally Engle Merry (1988), "Legal Pluralism," *Law & Society Review* 22 (5): 869–96. [Editors' note]

# Disputing

reinforcement of the social differentiation which can be translated as the power differentials that exist in the mediation process.

The physical layout and the operational aspects of the MB clearly illustrate the duality that exists in terms of formal and informal protocol while reinforcing the existing social differentiation and power relations of the community. [...]

When mediators are appointed by the Mediation Board Commission, they are given formal training in mediation. According to the training manual, mediation is seen as positive social work based on the principles of self-determination, co-operation, respect, justice, equity, respect, empowerment, and flexibility. The mediators are expected to follow certain methods and techniques of dispute resolution in keeping with the principles mentioned above. However, in actual practice, the mediators use various techniques such as social pressure based on values and norms existing in society to conform disputants to compromise on a settlement. For example, the following dispute clearly shows the use of social pressure to conform to the values held by the mediators in trying to reach a compromise.

> The dispute involved a marital issue between 27-year-old Kapila and his 18-year-old wife, Sonali, who has left him and now lives with her mother. The dispute was referred to the MB by the police on a harassment complaint made by Sonali's mother, Pushpa, who claims that Kapila was harassing Sonali, demanding that she return to him with their child. Kapila on the other hand claims that Pushpa is turning Sonali against him.
>
> The panel listened to both parties, including Pushpa, who was clearly angry with Kapila for "getting Sonali pregnant and ruining her future." There was a lot of argument between Pushpa and Kapila and the mediators constantly asked the parties to stay calm and discuss the matter in a "civilized" manner. When Sonali was asked to give her views, she said she does not want to return to Kapila and wished to stay with her mother. The panel however tried to persuade her to return to Kapila, as there is a child involved. They also reminded Sonali repeatedly that society will not look at her favourably if she separates from her husband. The panel made it sound as if Sonali has no choice and that she should return to Kapila with their child. The panel also asked Pushpa to let Sonali and Kapila decide what they want to do. After a lengthy discussion, the mediators asked both parties to come back in two weeks for another session. In the meantime, the parties were asked to think about the situation seriously and try to come to some reconciliation.

This application of social pressure is perhaps reflective of the gender bias that exists in society. The rights of Sonali were not considered by the mediators, who approached the dispute from the normative standard of the local community. Sonali's rights were almost non-existent in the discussions. The gender dimension of community mediation in Sri Lanka as discussed by Jayasundere and Valters shows that mediators' desire to settle disputes sometimes discriminates against women, since they impose their interpretation of gender equality and status of women in society.[5] This could in turn discriminate against women who seek mediation under great social barriers. In the case discussed above, the mediators' own gender bias is evident when they refused to acknowledge Sonali's wish to separate from her husband. By referring to the adverse reactions by the community towards such situations, the mediators used social pressure as a means to reach a compromise in the dispute. [...]

The rhetoric of anti-formal courts is used widely by mediators in persuading disputing parties to compromise. This is often presented as the dichotomy between formal and informal mechanisms of settling disputes. In the case below, mediators express their views on the efficiency and effectiveness of the mediation process in opposition to the formal courts of law.

> The parties involved were a father and son (Ravi), and another young male (Namal). The parties are from adjoining villages. The dispute was referred to the MB from the police as it was a case of assault complained by the first party.
>
> Ravi said he went to see a musical show in his village where Namal was present. During the show, a fight broke out and, as Ravi was injured, he went to the police to make a complaint against Namal who was involved in the fight. However, according to Namal, he was not directly involved and that there were about 50 others involved in the fight. Namal claims that he has been unfairly singled out.
>
> The panel explained that, if this goes to courts, the parties will have to spend a lot of money and that it would be better to settle it amicably there. Both Ravi and Namal were willing to settle the case and were therefore issued certificates of settlement. The panel advised them to stay out of fights and that it would cost them a lot of money if these disputes are taken to courts.

In a dispute involving a husband and wife, the mediators yet again attempt to persuade the aggrieved party to compromise instead of proceeding with a

---

[5] Ramani Jayasundere and Craig Valters (2014), *Women's Experience of Local Justice: Community Mediation in Sri Lanka* (London: The Justice and Security Research and Asia Foundation). [Editors' note]

divorce. The mediators in this instance intervened by advising against divorce, saying it will be a tedious legal process.

The first party in the dispute was a 34-year-old Kala who complained to the police about her husband Piyal who had assaulted her. Their pre-teenage son was also present, but the panel asked him to wait outside the room.

While giving her side of the story, Kala got hysterical, saying she has to endure physical assault by her husband every time he gets drunk. The panel tried to calm her down while Piyal admitted to his misbehaviour. The mediators told Piyal that the fault is entirely with him and that he needs to change his behaviour. However, Kala was adamant that she wants to initiate divorce proceedings and that she needs the non-settlement certificate for the assault case. The panel advised Kala that a divorce is a tedious process, going through courts and lawyers and that, since there is a child between them, she should try to reconcile with Piyal. However, even after repeated attempts by the panel to dissuade Kala from proceeding to courts, she was not willing to compromise. The panel told her that any case in the courts is cumbersome. They even called the son inside in an attempt to get Kala to compromise. Yet there was no compromise on her part. [...]

*Conclusion*
Community mediation in Sri Lanka as a form of ADR exists as a hybrid practice that combines elements of formal procedures with informal social processes. [...] The mediation setting involved the use of symbols, ideologies, and procedures resembling the formal legal system. There is replication or reproduction of the formal courtroom setting with clear demarcation drawn between the mediators and disputants. However, in keeping with the ideology of popular justice and non-adversarial dispute resolution, the members of the Board are individuals without any legal background whose only qualification to be a mediator is his/her social standing within the community. The setting therefore represents an amalgamation of different normative orders. In addition, the process of mediation also can be seen as a conflation of both systems. For instance, the conceptual space within which mediators and disputants operate is context-specific and based on how mediators define the situations.

Yet, the physical setting and the manner in which the mediators inquire and position themselves vis-à-vis the disputants show a tendency towards the formal legal procedures. This can also be seen as a marker of power incongruence within the mediation setting. Even though the relationship between mediators and disputants seem straightforward, it can be discerned from the disputes presented that this too is fluid and context-dependent, borrowing

> from different normative systems. Moreover, the mediation process as seen in the disputes uses social pressure to get the disputing parties to compromise, thereby giving legitimacy to the bargaining process. The mediators' desire to settle disputes by imposing a compromise theoretically contradicts the principles of community mediation as espoused by the ADR movement. Yet, by limiting the number of times disputants are permitted to seek mediation, the MB clearly sets their boundaries of operation. The MB in H therefore represents a duality in both its setting and procedure where the formal legal system and the local normative order are fused together to construct an alternative which can be seen as a hybrid practice.

## REFERENCES

### Featured Readings

Li, Ke. 2015. "'What He Did Was Lawful': Divorce Litigation and Gender Inequality in China." *Law & Policy* 37 (3): 153–79. doi: 10.1111/lapo.12034

Pirie, Fernanda. 2006. *Peace and Conflict in Ladakh: The Construction of a Fragile Web of Order*. Leiden and Boston: Brill. doi: 10.1163/ej.9789004155961.i-238

Welikala, Sepalika. 2016. "Community Mediation as a Hybrid Practice: The Case of Mediation Boards in Sri Lanka." *Asian Journal of Law and Society* 3 (2): 399–422. doi: 10.1017/als.2016.32

### Other Works Cited

Abel, Richard L. 1973. "A Comparative Theory of Dispute Institutions in Society." *Law & Society Review* 8 (2), 217–348. doi: 10.2307/3053029

von Benda-Beckmann, Keebet. 1981. "Forum Shopping and Shopping Forums: Dispute Processing in a Minangkabau Village in West Sumatra." *Journal of Legal Pluralism* 19: 117–59. doi: 10.1080/07329113.1981.10756260

Galanter, Marc. 1974. "Why the 'Haves' Come Out Ahead: Speculations on the Limits of Legal Change." *Law & Society Review* 9 (1): 95–160. doi: 10.2307/3053023

Genn, Hazel, and Sarah Beinart. 1999. *Paths to Justice: What People Do and Think about Going to Law*. Portland, OR: Hart. doi: 10.5040/ 9781472558886

Matsumura, Yoshiyuki, and Masayuki Murayama. 2010. "Hosihiki to Hunso Kodo" [Legal Consciousness and Disputing Behavior]. In *Gendai Nihon no Hunso Shori to Minji Shiho* [Dispute Resolution and Civil Justice in Contemporary Japan], edited by Yoshiyuki Matsumura and Masayuki Murayama. Tokyo: University of Tokyo Press.

Michelson, Ethan. 2007. "Climbing the Dispute Pagoda: Grievances and Appeals to the Official Justice System in Rural China." *American Sociological Review*, 72 (3): 459–85. doi: 10.1177/000312240707200307

Moore, Sally Falk. 1973. "Law and Social Change: The Semi-Autonomous Social Field as An Appropriate Subject of Study." *Law & Society Review* 7 (4): 719–46. doi: 10.2307/3052967

Nader, Laura. 1965. "Choices in Legal Procedure: Shia Moslem and Mexican Zapotec." *American Anthropologist* 67(2): 394–9. doi: 10.1525/aa.1965.67.2 .02a00060

———. 1990. *Harmony Ideology: Justice and Control in a Zapotec Mountain Village*. Stanford, CA: Stanford University Press. doi: 10.1525/ae.1994.21.4 .02a01900

Trubek, David M., Joel B. Grossman, William L. F. Felstiner, Herbert M. Kritzer, and Austin Sarat. 1983. *Civil Litigation Research Project: Final Report*. Madison: University of Wisconsin Law School. doi: 10.1111/j.1467- 9930.1980.tb00227.x

**Suggested Readings**

Abel, Richard L. 1982. "The Contradictions of Informal Justice." In *The Politics of Informal Justice, Vol. 1: The American Experience*, edited by Richard L. Abel, 267–320. New York: Academic Press. doi: 10.2307/ 1410181

Felstiner, William L. F., Richard L. Abel, and Austin Sarat. 1980–1. "Emergence and Transformation of Disputes: Naming, Blaming, Claiming ... " *Law & Society Review* 15: 631–54. doi: 10.4324/ 9781315236353-12

Fitzpatrick, Peter. 1993. "The Impossibility of Popular Justice." In *The Possibility of Popular Justice: A Case Study of Community Mediation in the United States*, edited by Sally Engle Merry and Neal Milner, 453–74. Ann Arbor: University of Michigan Press. doi: 10.1525/ae.1995.22.2 .02a00450

Greenhouse, Carol J., Barbara Yngvesson, and David M. Engel. 1994. *Law and Community in Three American Towns*. Ithaca, NY: Cornell University Press. doi: 10.7591/9781501725012

Mather, Lynn, and Barbara Yngvesson. 1980. "Language, Audience, and the Transformation of Disputes." *Law & Society Review* 15: 775–821. doi: 10.2307/3053512

Tiruchelvam, Neelan. 1984. *The Ideology of Popular Justice in Sri Lanka: A Socio-Legal Inquiry*. New Delhi: Vikas. doi: 10.2307/840140

# 4 Legal Consciousness

## Contents

| | | |
|---|---|---|
| I | National, Local, and Global Dimensions | 141 |
| II | The Role of Traditional Practices | 153 |
| III | Rights Consciousness | 161 |
| IV | Relational Legal Consciousness | 176 |

As the readings in Chapters 1 through 3 have made clear, states never succeed in establishing a legal monopoly despite their best efforts – not in Asia or in any country of the world. When it comes to matters where the law might play a role, people always have their options. But how do they choose among them? What is it that leads people to use state law in some instances and reject it in others – or seek recourse in non-state legal alternatives? And in what situations do people "bargain in the shadow of the law" or simply "lump" their losses?

To explain how people selectively invoke the law, law and society scholars have increasingly turned to the concept of "legal consciousness." *Consciousness* in this context refers not only to cognition but also to behavior – the practices of people who are involved with situations in which law could play a role. Although legal consciousness research focuses on the subjective aspects of people's behavior in relation to the law, it is not just a study of attitudes or opinions; it is also a study of decision-making and behavior.

Legal consciousness scholars explore the absence as much as the presence of law. They try to explain not only why people turn to the law but also why they reject it, misunderstand it, or have no knowledge of it at all. Law and society researchers have demonstrated that law holds different meanings for people in different situations. At times, the law may appear promising and even alluring, but at other times it may seem remote from everyday life, intrusive, or threatening. For most legal consciousness researchers, "law" or "legal" refers to the law of the state, and they have found that people tend to view state law as useful in facilitating certain kinds of transactions or claims but potentially destructive of relationships or of valued traditions in other circumstances, capable of turning cooperation into adversarialism and hostility.

For law and society scholars, legal consciousness research is not just the study of individuals; it entails the study of broader cultural phenomena and of the social and political currents that shape people's thoughts and actions. Moreover, researchers have begun to extend their understanding of "consciousness" itself to include its relational aspects and not just its individual manifestations.

Legal consciousness research in Asia has proliferated in recent years and has become one of the fastest growing areas of law and society research. Indeed, Asia-based studies of legal consciousness have led the way in raising new questions and proposing new frameworks for understanding the law-related thoughts and practices of individuals and groups. In this chapter, we trace the origins of legal consciousness research in Asia as well as the frontiers that are now being mapped by law and society researchers.

Legal consciousness research can be grouped into three schools: Identity, Hegemony, and Mobilization. They are described in Chua and Engel (2020:187–8):

> The Identity school views legal consciousness as an ongoing process of constructing the self in relation to law and legal rights. Typically relying on biographical or autobiographical narratives, researchers examine how the relevance or irrelevance of law to a person's experience connects to the process by which that person's identity – or sense of self – takes shape, making legal norms and institutions appear naturally suited in some instances and inappropriate in others. Identities are fluid and people's relationship to law continually shifts and changes. [...]
>
> The Hegemony school treats law as a pervasive and powerful tool of state control that can shape the categories, values, and assumptions of individuals even when it is not applied directly and instrumentally. Researchers using this framework aim to reveal the workings and the often invisible effects of law in the thoughts and actions of ordinary people. They trace the dominance of law and legal institutions in everyday life, and they also examine whether and how individuals resist law's power. According to the Hegemony school, however, even when individuals try to resist the law, they cannot overcome its inescapable

reach. Their acts of resistance inevitably operate within law's logic and understandings, rather than outside its framework, and reinforce or leave intact law's superordinate power.

The Mobilization school investigates how legal consciousness promotes – or fails to promote – the role of law and the efficacy of rights in transforming social conditions, particularly to achieve justice or protect disadvantaged populations. Mobilization researchers focus on the relationship between processes of social change and the experiences, perceptions, and actions of individuals who choose to use or avoid the law. Some Mobilization scholars study people's legal consciousness to gauge the extent of social change that has occurred, whereas others study it to explain how and why those people have turned to the law to transform their circumstances. In either case, studying legal consciousness helps Mobilization scholars to view social change through the lens of human agency, thereby augmenting the more typical research on social change that tends to adopt an aggregate and distanced perspective.

Law and society scholars of Asia have generally adopted either the Identity or the Mobilization approaches to legal consciousness research, giving relatively less attention to the Hegemony approach. This preference will be reflected in the readings presented in the remainder of this chapter.

I NATIONAL, LOCAL, AND GLOBAL DIMENSIONS

The earliest research on Asian legal consciousness attempted to define traits that were thought to be shared at the national level. Subsequently, these portraits of national legal consciousness attracted criticism and no longer carry much weight among scholars. Nevertheless, the role of the state in organizing legal regimes and administering legal institutions remains very much a part of contemporary legal consciousness research, and state-level legality is typically viewed in relation to localized legal practices that researchers identify in Asian villages, urban neighborhoods, corporate life, and even within the legal profession itself.

Nowadays, researchers have exhibited an increasing awareness that legal consciousness is also shaped by transnational actors and institutions. Thus, many researchers attempt to account for the global dimension of legal consciousness, even when they conduct their research at the level of the individual or in face-to-face communities. In short, contemporary legal consciousness research has become quite complex, exploring the interaction of phenomena at multiple levels simultaneously and attempting to explain how changes in legal consciousness – even within the day-to-day experience of individual actors – can take place as a result of shifts or transformations in one or more of these levels.

## 4.1 Kawashima and the Changing Focus on Japanese Legal Consciousness: A Selective History of the Sociology of Law in Japan, *Masayuki Murayama*

As this article by Masayuki Murayama makes clear, the roots of law and society scholarship in Japan extend back more than a hundred years, and the study of legal consciousness appeared as a central concern of Japanese researchers almost from the beginning. Japanese legal scholars in the early twentieth century focused heavily on the disparity between "social practice" and the new Japanese civil code. They drew inspiration from the work of Eugen Ehrlich, the Austrian theorist who advocated the study of what he called "the living law" rather than an exclusive focus on the written law, as well as the work of the American scholar Roscoe Pound, whose *sociological jurisprudence* distinguished between the "law in books" and the "law in action." By the 1920s, Izutaro Suehiro, "a civil law professor who later became the early founder of the sociology of law in Japan," began to study the living law in Japan and later in north China. Other law professors followed his example, most notably Takeyoshi Kawashima, who, like Suehiro, also conducted research among rural villagers. After World War II ended, Kawashima emerged as the preeminent law and society scholar in Japan. Kawashima viewed legal consciousness as key to understanding the living law in Japan. Moreover, as Murayama explains in his article, Kawashima considered it essential to transform Japanese legal consciousness so the Japanese people would embrace democratic legal principles and processes.

Perhaps the most enduring – and most controversial – aspect of Kawashima's work is his characterization of Japanese legal consciousness as distinctively law-averse. His research was understood to stand for the proposition that Japanese people – more than people in western societies – avoid asserting their legal interests because they prefer to resolve issues through non-adversarial processes. Later scholars challenged what John Haley (1978) called "the myth of the reluctant litigant" in Japan and pointed to features of the legal profession or of the law itself to explain the country's low litigation rates. Others argued that there is nothing distinctively Japanese about law avoidance. Nevertheless, as Murayama demonstrates in this excerpt, Kawashima's exploration of the concept of legal consciousness and the debates sparked by his work have had a profound impact on the course of law and society research in Japan and elsewhere in Asia.

Less than a year after the end of the war, Kawashima published an uncompleted paper in which he contrasted the traditional Japanese normative consciousness with the modern legal consciousness in the West. He argued that

Japanese people widely failed to comply with economic regulation law even during the war, because the law required, in order to function, a modern legal consciousness, which Japanese people did not have. He strongly urged Japanese people to make the modern law epitomised in the post-war Constitution 'our living law', in order to democratise Japan. In this and a later revised paper, Kawashima presented a model of 'modern legal consciousness', drawing upon the Kantian notion of morality with specific reference to the categorical imperative. Concerning the Japanese pre-modern normative consciousness, Kawashima presented the social relationships between tenants and landlords in farming and housing as social conditions that bred the traditional consciousness, while pointing out differences between the modern law and the Japanese consciousness in such legal areas as ownership, contract, family, public law and international law. During the 1940s and 1950s, he devoted himself to critically analysing traditional social norms in relation to their social backgrounds.

Kawashima continued to write on incongruities between the institution of law, in particular litigation, and the Japanese legal consciousness. The best-known article in English is 'Dispute Resolution in Contemporary Japan' and the one in Japanese is Nihonjin no Ho Ishiki [Japanese Legal Consciousness]. However, in these works, the focal point of argument clearly changed from the normative to the empirical. He compared the US and Japanese statistics of litigation cases in traffic accidents and argued that the Japanese pre-modern normative consciousness was a much more important cause of the small number of litigation cases than the cost and delay of litigation.

His empirical argument proved to be more controversial than his normative one, inviting criticism from Japanese and foreign scholars, as we will see in the next section. Although the phrase 'legal consciousness' was used as a direct translation of the Japanese words Ho Ishiki in the English translation of his argument on contract, Kawashima did not use the words 'legal consciousness' in his own English article. He later pointed out that the English words 'legal consciousness' were misleading, as he meant to include the subconscious as well as the conscious. He also noted that his idea of legal consciousness, Ho Ishiki, presupposed a theoretical framework of cultural sociology or anthropology, but included psychological elements such as emotional/affective response, desire/volition and value judgment.

However, Kawashima wrote about not only the Japanese pre-modern attitudes but also the social structure that supported such attitudes. He seemed to believe that subsequent social changes brought by further industrial urbanisation would produce a transformation of the Japanese legal consciousness and eventually an increase in litigation. He considered that there were various factors which would influence the legal control of a society and that consciousness was not the ultimate fundamental determining factor of legal phenomena. But he argued that the reason for focusing on legal consciousness was that legal consciousness not only affected law-related behaviour, but also was the factor closest to law-related behaviour among relevant factors. Crucially, Kawashima argued that legal consciousness was the most powerful predictor of legal behaviour, but that legal consciousness had a social foundation and would change as its social foundation changed. [ ... ]

Though Kawashima maintained his normative model of law, he later integrated it into a comprehensive model of law in his search for the distinctively legal. He emphasised adjudication as the focal part of the distinctively legal. But empirical research on adjudication itself has scarcely been conducted since. Rather, it was Kawashima's arguments on legal consciousness which foreshadowed the enduring concerns of Japanese scholars with comparing law and practice as well as contrasting Japan and the West.

Kahei Rokumoto applied Kawashima's normative scheme to the legal resolution of civil disputes, and conducted an interview survey in Tokyo in 1968. He found that the social changes of Japanese society had increased demand for legal services, which was often satisfied by pseudo-lawyers, and that the use of formal legal machinery seemed determined by one's occupational position and particularistic social networks.

Rokumoto also worked on the empirical aspect of Kawashima's argument. Ever since Kawashima made his argument about Japanese legal consciousness, one of the challenges has been how to measure legal consciousness. How we could understand the relationship between Kawashima's normative model and empirical model also seemed to remain a question. It is difficult not only to identify what the legal consciousness is, but also to operationalise it in order to measure it empirically. Rokumoto refined the concept of legal consciousness into a narrow sense of legal consciousness, on the one hand, and legal conception, on the other. The former consists of three elements: knowledge about law, attitudes toward law and opinions about law; while legal conception is a framework to perceive law. Rokumoto explained that the narrow sense of legal consciousness would be the 'general sense of justice' in English, more or less the equivalent of KOL (Knowledge and Opinion about Law), while the legal conception would be the 'idea of law' or 'Rechtsvorstellung'. The point of the distinction between the narrow sense of legal consciousness and legal conception is that the former can change for a rather short period of time, while the latter tends to persist. Rokumoto argued that the Japanese normative conception 'giri' was the ordering principle of pre-modern Japanese society and formed the founding element of Japanese legal culture.

Though not based on Rokumoto's framework, surveys of opinions and attitudes about the law have been conducted several times since the 1970s. The surveys of Nihon Bunka Kaigi tried to measure characteristics of Japanese legal attitudes and found that respondents tended to have little interest in laws, expect flexible applications of legal norms, and split into punitive and lenient groups. These findings were understood to support the view that Japanese people have attitudes towards the law that are different from the West. In contrast, Masanobu Kato suspected that anecdotal episodes that Kawashima used as examples to show distinctive Japanese legal attitudes were misleading, and did not find peculiarly Japanese attitudes towards contracts in their international survey results.

The latest survey of Japanese legal attitudes was conducted in 2005 as a part of a large research project, The Civil Justice Research Project. The survey asked about legal attitudes and knowledge as well as social attitudes towards norms and disputes. It also replicated the survey of Nihon Bunka Kaigi almost thirty years later. They found that Japanese attitudes had not changed significantly except for becoming more punitive. However, full analyses of the survey results are yet to come.

Scholars who studied under Rokumoto or [Takeo] Tanase also addressed the issues Kawashima raised, but findings differed. Ichiro Ozaki, in his research on disputes among residents in eleven condominiums in a residential district of Yokohama, found that disputes tended to deteriorate to emotional exchanges, without much possibility of communication based on reason. But Kiyoshi Hasegawa conducted fieldwork on private agreements among residents, also in Yokohama, and found that residents could behave as rational actors who used the law in a reasonable way in their attempts to preserve residential environments. Yoshitaka Wada, based on his research on disputes between tenants and house owners, argued that the meaning of dispute resolution had been changing in urban society from restoring harmonious relations to handling immediate disputes while letting a conflicting relation continue, and found that people mobilised the law as a strategic weapon to pursue their self-interests. Masaki Abe conducted field research on how local residents invoked the law for the purpose of environmental protection and found a similar tendency to that found by Wada: people mobilised the law as one of the instruments available to achieve their purposes.

These four studies were conducted as qualitative research to contribute to both empirical and theoretical understandings of the use of the law, rather than identifying overall patterns of behaviour in Japanese society. Yet, these studies seemed to show that the actual behaviour of Japanese people could be different from and more varied than that which Kawashima described in his empirical arguments. They also seemed to limit the validity of his normative arguments.

It would be fair to note here that Kawashima's empirical arguments of legal consciousness began to be directly and frequently critically assessed by foreign as well as Japanese scholars from the late 1970s. The central issue of the debate was whether the Japanese normative consciousness was the main cause of a small number of litigation cases, though the theme was not always shared and the way of conceptualising the issue was different among scholars ([John O.] Haley; [Masao] Oki; [Frank K.] Upham; [J. Mark] Ramseyer; [Takao] Tanase; [Christian] Wallschaeger; [Kahei] Rokumoto).

The Civil Justice Research Project (2003–2008), directed by Masayuki Murayama, conducted three kinds of nationwide research to cover the whole process of problem-solving behaviour, from experience of a problem to the use of litigation. The first survey, the Disputing Behaviour Survey, consisted of a Consciousness Survey, which was discussed above, and a Behaviour Survey that enquired into problem experience and subsequent behaviour. The second survey, the Advice Seeking Behaviour Survey, focused on how people sought advice from various agencies and how they evaluated it. The samples of these surveys were randomly chosen from among Japanese people from twenty to seventy years old. The third research, the Litigation Behaviour Survey, took data from randomly chosen litigation cases at the district courts and then asked questions of the litigants and their lawyers.

The *Disputing Behaviour Survey* found little evidence to support the perception that Japanese people experienced few legal problems and that they were reluctant not only to make claims but also to reject claims. Patterns of behaviour in these early stages of problem-solving were surprisingly similar between Japan and the US, and significantly affected by the types of problem that people experienced. These findings raise questions about Kawashima's presumption that legal consciousness defines disputing behaviour and, even if legal consciousness did matter, to what extent and how it mattered concerning behaviour.

The *Litigation Behaviour Survey* found, contrary to the popular view, that litigants were less satisfied when litigation ended in settlement than when litigation ended in judgment.

For Kawashima, the need to study legal consciousness arose from his perception of a dramatic disparity between "modern law" as it had been enacted in Japan and longstanding social practices and customary law-ways that still shaped the behavior of many Japanese people. As he sought to explain why the living law differed so markedly from the written law, Kawashima and others generalized very broadly about legal consciousness as a national phenomenon. Although the concept of legal consciousness remains dynamic in Asian law and society scholarship, most scholars today address it in a more particularized and contextual way. Rather than writing about imagined national traits or characteristics, they explore legal consciousness within particular social groups.

Nevertheless, even in the most recent studies of legal consciousness in Asia, the role of the state – and of state law and legal institutions – remains important. Legal consciousness is typically viewed in relation to state law – as people embrace it, acquiesce to it, resist it, avoid it, or simply ignore it. Indeed, scholars have given attention even more broadly to transnational factors that shape the legal consciousness of particular individuals or groups. The impact of globalization on legal consciousness is the subject of some of the most recent studies and has generated debate among scholars. On the one hand, some have argued that the forces of globalization tend to produce a convergence in the legal consciousness of diverse peoples around the world, as they increasingly view their experiences in terms of similar liberal rule of law concepts. On the other hand, others contend that globalization has quite a different effect on legal consciousness. It may reinforce distinctive, locally based worldviews or may bring about transformations in worldviews that lead to avoidance of law in all of its plural forms. The latter view is reflected in the following article on globalization and legal consciousness in Thailand.

## 4.2 Globalization and the Decline of Legal Consciousness: Torts, Ghosts, and Karma in Thailand, *David M. Engel*

In this study, Engel compares the legal consciousness of injury victims in Northern Thailand before and after a series of dramatic socioeconomic changes associated with globalization. His research in and around the Chiangmai Provincial Court in 1975 had revealed relatively low levels of litigation in injury cases and a preference for traditional village-level remedial systems. When these customary systems broke down, however, some injury victims in the 1970s were willing to litigate in order to force their injurers to come to terms and provide customary compensation or sponsor rituals that would make them whole again.

In the years that followed Engel's first study, Chiangmai's economy was transformed by global investments and industrial development. New ideas and images became familiar to the people of Chiangmai, along with new political, cultural, and religious ideologies. Increased tourism led to contact with visitors from around the world, and local residents also traveled far beyond the borders of their villages. The question this article explores, then, is how these global transformations had, by the turn of the twenty-first century, affected the forms of legal consciousness that had been apparent in 1975. Did globalization produce an increased tendency to adopt rule-of-law concepts, as many scholars would predict? Engel argues that, at least with respect to practices involving physical injuries, the answer is no. Even as traditional remedial systems began to atrophy, injury victims did not replace them with remedies afforded by state law nor with concepts associated with liberal legalism. Tort litigation was, if anything, less frequent than before, references to legal rights were all but nonexistent, and injury victims were left without any remedy whatsoever.

The article centers around the injury narrative of a middle-aged woman, "Buajan" (a pseudonym), whose leg was seriously injured in an accident. As she stood near a roadside stand, she was run over by an old man she calls "Uncle." He lost control of his car, seemingly because of the malicious intervention of a ghost inhabiting a nearby mango tree. As Buajan recovered in the hospital, Uncle visited her and promised to pay all her expenses as long as she didn't press charges.

Buajan lists multiple causes for her misfortune, including karma, fate, spirits, ghosts, the old man's negligence, and her own negligence – by which she meant that she must have lacked the Buddhist quality of mindfulness (*sati*), and if she had been more alert she would not have been hurt. She was especially conscious of the workings of karma, because she had beaten a dog that entered her house and broken its leg. It was no coincidence that her own leg was broken when Uncle ran her over. Moreover, she believed that, in a previous life, she had injured Uncle, and her karma caught up with her in this lifetime.

After the injury, Buajan pursued various measures to remedy her situation and make herself whole. She performed a traditional *khwan* ceremony to restore the vital essence that had fled from her body as a result of the trauma. She offered food to the Buddhist monks to make merit and rectify her karmic imbalance. And she attempted in various ways to negotiate a settlement with Uncle. These negotiations proved highly unsatisfactory, resulting in a minimal compensatory payment that barely covered her medical costs and totally failed to address her lost wages and pain and suffering. Buajan suspected that intermediaries in the negotiation process – the subdistrict officer (*kamnan*) and the police – had been bribed by Uncle, leaving her with no viable options.

Buajan sees herself as the victim of a gross injustice, and does not view the law as offering any hope for ordinary people like her:

> Whenever I've used the law, I've gotten nothing. The police, for example. Law and the police. The law is loose and leaky. That's how it is here. Especially if we're poor, we can't rely on the police for help. Money is more important. That's why I don't rely on the law; I rely on myself. [...] No matter how holy the law is, I have no hope of using it. I don't stand on the law, I stand on my own two legs, even though one of them is broken.

The article concludes with some general observations about the impact of globalization on legal consciousness in northern Thailand from 1975 to the end of the twentieth century. According to the author, injury victims do not exhibit a greater attachment to liberal legalism than they had before. In fact, the reverse appears to be the case. Law in all of its forms – official and customary – has receded in importance and left injury victims like Buajan with the sense that they now have no recourse of any kind.

> The effects of globalization are evident throughout the injury narratives of Buajan and others. Had globalization not had an impact on northern Thailand, we might imagine that Buajan, instead of moving to the city of Chiangmai, would have remained in the farming village where she was born. With fewer motor vehicles on the road, her chances of being struck by a car would have been sharply reduced; and with a less-extensive highway system, she might never have traveled to the butcher stand where she was injured. Had she suffered an injury in her own village, Buajan's case would have been of intense interest to the entire community. Since her injurer would most likely have been a fellow villager, the injury would have been seen as a matter of concern to the local spirits, and the injurer would have been required to pay damages. Buddhist precepts, spirit worship, and the intervention of community leaders would in all likelihood have produced an agreement that conformed to Buajan's sense of justice – and probably that of her injurer as well. If the injurer did not agree to pay compensation, however, and if he was somehow beyond the reach of local systems of social control, Buajan might have been among the small number of individuals who chose to pursue a traditional remedy (in this case, *khaa tham khwan*) in the Chiangmai Provincial Court. There, formal legal procedures would probably have compelled the very same injury payment that community pressures alone could not produce.

Because of globalization, however, Buajan's life changed, and so did the type of legal consciousness evident in the injury narrative that she recounts. As a result of globalization, her life was marked by mobility, separation from her birth community, economic uncertainty, frequent interactions with strangers in unfamiliar locales, elevated levels of risk, and increased disparities of wealth and power. With these changes came others that affected the conceptualization of her injury and the range of options she could imagine in response. Media reports and popular discourse increasingly emphasized rights and the rule of law, but at the same time "mediascapes" and "ideoscapes" disseminated new forms of religious thought. They presented Buajan and others with familiar religious ideas in new packaging – Buddhist beliefs and practices that are no longer embedded in particular localities and connected to the animist practices associated with those localities. Buddhism has assumed a more universal form, located as much in the mass media and in translocal and transnational networks as in the village temple or in local connections between Buddhism and animism. Religion divorced from geography has great appeal to individuals who have become separated from the villages and communities where they grew up. Belief in spirits and ghosts remains strong, but the attachment to village-level remedial systems has weakened, and the close linkages between Buddhism and locality spirits have become attenuated. These developments have important implications for the role of law in the lives of ordinary people.

Injury narratives such as Buajan's reveal a complex form of legal consciousness marked by ambiguity and a degree of uncertainty. Buajan clearly considered herself an aggrieved party and a victim of unfair treatment. She thought that the elderly driver who ran into her should have offered considerably more money than he did, but she found no interpretive frame that could express her claim in terms that he would understand and accept. References to payment for the *khwan* soul – a traditional form of compensation that she might once have obtained without difficulty – proved useless, since the two of them now disagreed about the essential meaning and purpose of such payments. [...] References to spirits or shared community interests were no longer possible, since she and "uncle" lived in different worlds subject to different social and supernatural forces. Locality-based remediation systems were no longer available to resolve their differences and facilitate an agreement. References to the intervention of an authority figure who might produce a settlement were also ineffective, since the social distance separating the two parties was so great that only the police might conceivably act as mediators. For Buajan, the police were part of the problem of power and wealth that put her at a disadvantage. She did not view them – or the legal system as a whole – as part of the solution.

In the past, when local remediation systems broke down, a small but consistent number of injured persons pursued traditional remedies in the courts. But the option of litigation, even as a hypothetical possibility, is now conspicuous by its absence from the injury narratives. It no longer represents an alternative means to enforce village-level practices ensuring injury payments, since such practices have become unfamiliar to most local residents. The risks and costs of litigation are seen as comparable to the risks and costs of police mediation, and a further disadvantage is the loss of control over one's own claim once it is in the hands of a judge. Yet these risks and costs were also present 25 years ago, when litigation rates per injury were higher than they are today. It appears that injury victims in Chiangmai now tend to view their belief in Buddhism as inconsistent with an aggressive insistence on a remedy. As the close linkage between Buddhism and village customary laws has been broken, the abstract norms of Buddhism are no longer connected to any remedy system and, instead, seem to counsel against the pursuit of a claim for compensation. Karma caused the injury, and karma will determine its consequences. The cycle of injury and suffering can be brought to an end only by forgiveness and not by the "selfish" pursuit of money damages.

But what about the effects of globalization on legal consciousness? Why has the "compression of the world"[1] not made individuals more familiar with liberal legalism and the language of rights? Why has the transnational dissemination of rule-of-law ideology – evident in the Thai "People's Constitution" of 1997, in the activities of numerous international agencies and NGOs that operate in Thailand, and in ubiquitous news reports and commentaries on national and international events – not made people like Buajan more inclined to conceptualize their injuries in legal terms and more ready to turn to the law for redress?

Perhaps Western observers are prone to exaggerate the influence of their own ideologies on people in other parts of the world. In modern Thai society, it is true that public discourse frequently refers to rights, the rule of law, and constitutionalism. Significant political mobilization around these concepts has indeed altered the course of Thai history over the past several decades. Yet references to rights and liberal legalism, like other symbols of "globalization," must be interpreted with some restraint. Although such references indicate important developments in Thai society at the national level or in Bangkok, and although the English-language media may emphasize this type of discourse

---

[1] Roland Robertson (1992), *Globalization: Social Theory and Global Culture* (London: Sage) at 8. [Editors' note]

when offering accounts of contemporary Thailand, that does not necessarily mean that a broad-based transformation of Thai legal consciousness has occurred in the everyday lives of ordinary citizens throughout the country.

In other regions of the world, we have seen a resurgence of the great religious traditions, in part as a response to the effects of globalization in its many forms. This study of a particular locality in Thailand may illustrate how and why such dynamics can develop, as global influences change local circumstances for ordinary people. Buddhism is as fundamental to Thai culture today as it has been for centuries, yet it appears that its essential qualities have changed in some respects. If the injury narratives provide a reliable indication, the effects of globalization have contributed to a separation of Buddhism from locality-based beliefs and practices. Buddhism in Thailand is increasingly a universal religion whose norms can influence belief and action without regard to the location of the believer. Separated from the local systems of social control to which it was formerly linked, which had routinely compelled injurers to pay damages, Buddhism's general precepts now guide injury victims away from the pursuit of compensation and toward a quest for selflessness, nonaggression, and forgiveness.

Injury victims no longer view the legal system as a viable alternative through which to pursue culturally acceptable goals by a different means, nor do community pressures encourage the aggressive pursuit of a remedy. Rather, the legal system increasingly represents the antithesis of deeply held religious and cultural beliefs about injuries and appropriate responses. Although injured persons may in some overtly political contexts have considerable respect for the language of rights, they do not view their mishap in terms of a potential rights claim. The language of rights is nowhere to be found in the injury narratives, and in any event, it is not evident to the narrators how their own rights can be safely and effectively vindicated. At the same time, ordinary Thai citizens appear to view law as existing in tension with their religious convictions, and they perceive the Buddha's teachings as morally superior to the ideology of liberal legalism. Although globalization may indeed have transformed legal consciousness in Thailand, the accounts provided by injury victims suggest that the end result – somewhat unexpectedly – has been an atrophy of locality-based remediation systems, a further diminution of the role of law in everyday life, and a heightened sense that justice for the ordinary person is more likely to be achieved through self-abnegation than through the pursuit of rights.

Legal Consciousness 153

## II THE ROLE OF TRADITIONAL PRACTICES

In Asian contexts, legal consciousness is typically shaped by the interaction of "modern" legal institutions and processes on the one hand and longstanding social practices on the other. It is never enough simply to ask how people think and act in relation to state law. Rather, it is essential to ask how customary norms and practices influence the way people perceive situations in which the law might play a role – particularly when the law is seldom invoked or even considered. Some of the most impressive studies by law and society scholars in Asia have explored legal consciousness by considering the extent to which traditional practices persist or are transformed or supplanted. The following article is an example.

### 4.3 Legal Consciousness of the Leftover Woman: Law and *Qing* in Chinese Family Relations, *Qian Liu*

In this article, Qian Liu addresses the legal consciousness of Putianese family members with regard to issues of marriage and the obligations children owe their parents and ancestors. Because of China's one-child policy, which was modified relatively recently, and prohibitions against sex-selective abortion, many families ended up with no male descendants. By custom, when the daughters in one-child families married young men, they became obligated to support their husbands' parents and ancestors but not their own. In this sense, marriage of a daughter could create serious problems for her parents and ancestors. If a daughter remained single for a long time, however, she became known as a "leftover woman," a stigmatized social status. A customary Putianese solution to this dilemma is the practice known as *lianggu*, an agreement between husband and wife to support both lineages equally: "Under *lianggu*, the married couple supports all parents and ensures that the next generation will carry on the family names of both sides as a way to continue both family lines. Additionally, the couple is responsible for ancestor worship of both families, which includes visiting ancestors' graves on Tomb-Sweeping Day and on the anniversary of the death." Young women's parents viewed *lianggu* as a way to ensure their own support and well-being, even after death, while still allowing their daughter to marry and start her own family. Whether the young man's family would acquiesce to this customary practice was another matter.

As they navigate their way through these complex and sometimes contradictory frameworks, the 72 "leftover women" interviewed in Liu's study draw on the concept of *qing* to inform their choices to embrace, avoid, or resist the law. In her article, Liu skillfully weaves together the various strands of state law and customary practice as she explains the thoughts and actions – the legal consciousness – of so-called leftover women and their Putianese families.

To understand the legal consciousness of ordinary Chinese people and the interactions among individuals in Chinese society, it is not enough to consider their relationship to law alone, but also law's connection to *qing* in people's thoughts and actions. As a long-standing and supremely important concept in China, *qing* is loosely translated as a sense of humanity, human instinct, human nature, and human relations. In traditional Chinese legal culture, the concept of *qing* refers to human nature and the normal feelings or attitudes of the public in particular contexts and circumstances. For example, people's desire to enjoy a healthy and wealthy life together with their family members is considered the *qing* of ordinary people, because it is human nature to long for health, wealth, and the wellbeing of their loved ones. Chinese people believe that law should respect the desires and needs shared by ordinary people and that law should be consistent with *qing* (法合众人之情).

Ordinary people in China typically look to *qing*, rather than state law, to distinguish right from wrong. Historically, Chinese jurisprudence emphasized that *qing*, *li* (理, reasonableness), and *fa* (法, law) should exist in unity, and that all three of these elements formed an indistinguishable whole. People are well advised that, when a conflict arises, the first thing to be considered is *qing*, and "only when all such avenues are exhausted does one turn to *li* ... If this too proves unavailing, one is then forced as a last resort to invoke *fa*."[1] In other words, ordinary Chinese people's primary emphasis is on *qing* and only secondarily on *fa* and *li*. [...]

The primary aim of this article is to investigate how law and *qing* interact in different ways to shape ordinary Chinese people's legal consciousness. In my research, I observed two broad categories of interaction between law and *qing* – namely, law in opposition to *qing* and law in alliance with *qing*. To be specific, I identify four forms of legal consciousness when state law is in opposition to *qing*: (1) avoidance of state law when it conflicts with *qing*, (2) invocation of *qing* to mitigate undesirable results of state law, (3) resistance of state law to protect *qing* and (4) dismissal of state law when breaking the law conforms to *qing*. On the other hand, when it is perceived that state law is – or should be – in alliance with *qing*, the legal consciousness that emerges from the interaction of *qing* and law may be of two kinds: (1) embrace of state law when it enforces *qing* and (2) perception of state law as too weak when it fails to transform "old" understandings of *qing*.

---

[1] Randall P. Peerenboom (1993), *Law and Morality in Ancient China: The Silk Manuscripts of Huang-Lao* (Albany: State University of New York Press) at 268. [Editors' note]

My theory of how the interaction of law and *qing* shapes ordinary Chinese people's legal consciousness in everyday life is based on my study of the legal consciousness of "leftover women." "Leftover women" is a term of recent origin that refers to Chinese women who fail to follow the practice of marrying at an early age. The state media, as well as the public, often regard these women as "leftover" products in the marriage market. I use this discriminatory term in this article to emphasize that the society has imposed a significant pressure on single women to marry. [...]

### 4.1 Law in Opposition to *Qing*
In this section, I use Putianese leftover women's legal consciousness as an example to show how people engage with state laws that are considered contrary to *qing*. My findings show that, when people believe state law is in opposition to *qing*, they hold negative attitudes towards state law and choose to avoid, resist, and dismiss state law, and they invoke *qing* to mitigate the consequences when the law has already caused undesirable results. [...]

#### 4.1.1 *Avoidance of State Law When It Conflicts with* Qing
While some Putianese women mention that they felt anguished both physically and emotionally when their parents forced them to break up with boyfriends who refused to practise *lianggu*, they never think of deploying state law to protect their rights, nor are they eager to advocate for a legal reform to ensure Putianese women's freedom of marriage. None of my interviewees chose to exercise their legal right to marry in order to stop their parents from forcing them to leave their boyfriends. Likewise, nobody sued their parents for interfering in their marriage, nor do they consider their parents' actions to be domestic abuse or violence. Quite the opposite: the women I interviewed repeatedly invoked the concepts of love, duty, reciprocity, traditional virtue, family harmony, and filial piety. All these concepts are considered significant components of *qing* with respect to family relations between daughters and parents. Putianese women's emphasis on these concepts reflects the fact that they prioritize the relationship with their parents over freedom of marriage. [...]

This is especially the case in a city with influential patriarchal culture, such as Putian. If a woman marries into a Putianese man's family without choosing *lianggu*, she is not supposed to spend money on her own parents. Otherwise, her parents-in-law and husband will be very upset. [...] Therefore, the requirements of being a Putianese wife in a traditional Putianese family make it extremely important for parents who do not have sons to have at least a daughter to practise *lianggu*. For these parents, their daughter's refusal to practise *lianggu* would mean the possibility of having no one to support or take care of them when they are in their old age. Even worse, it is likely that no one will visit their grave to sweep away the dirt after their death.

As supporting one's parents in old age or being a filial daughter is considered a requirement of *qing*, my interviewees believe that the custom of *lianggu* is what they should respect and follow. They perceive a conflict between a woman's right to choose her own marital partners and the need to protect the interests of her parents. Although the marriage law emphasizes freedom to choose one's partner and prohibits coercion by a third party, my interviewees hold that it is undesirable to invoke the law against their parents to assert this right. It is true that Chinese society still considers being leftover in the marriage market a mark of shame for both the woman and her family, but leftover women's insistence on *lianggu* shows that being leftover is more acceptable to them than acting against *qing* to fight for their rights. [...]

### 4.1.2 *Invoking Qing to Mitigate Undesirable Results of State Law*

State law is not completely irrelevant in shaping Putianese people's legal consciousness. For example, state law has a significant impact on people's understandings of local custom in the interaction of *lianggu* with China's population policy – a form of state law that changed people's family structures substantially in recent decades. China's birth policy has experienced three important turning points in recent history: the implementation of the one-child policy, the relaxation of the one-child policy, and the shift from the one-child policy to the two-child policy. The one-child policy was first implemented in 1979 in China to curb population growth. Each couple in urban areas was allowed to have only one child with very few exceptions, while, in rural areas, a married couple had the opportunity to give birth to a second child if the first one was a girl. In 2009, all provinces in China allowed couples to have two children if both parents did not have siblings and, in late 2013, the policy was further relaxed in many provinces to allow families to have two children if one of the parents was an only child. The two-child policy replaced the one-child policy in late 2015. In effect since 1 January 2016, the two-child policy allows all married Chinese couples to have two children.

Born and raised under the strict one-child policy, all my interviewees in Putian started their descriptions of the local custom of *lianggu* by pointing out the impact of the one-child policy on ordinary Putianese people's family structures and attitudes towards marriage. The legal framework is so influential that all women I interviewed in Putian maintain that there is a close linkage between China's population policy and their choices in marriage and childbearing. The most significant influence of China's population policy, according to these women, is that it has made *lianggu* a popular practice in Putian. In her interview, Lu, a 29-year-old civil servant, told me that, after the implementation of the one-child policy, many families in urban areas of Putian ended up having a single daughter, while many families in rural areas had two daughters. The lack of a son made it necessary to have a daughter to practise *lianggu* in order to take care of the old and carry on the family name and property. [...]

In this case, China's population policy contributes to the prevalence of *lianggu* by transforming ordinary people's family structures, familial relationships, and understandings of the local custom of *lianggu*. At the same time, following the custom of *lianggu* represents Putianese daughters and their parents' strategy to mitigate one of the most unfortunate consequences of the one-child policy, namely having no male descendants to support the older generation. As the one-child policy ignores *qing*, Putianese daughters and their parents must invoke *qing* themselves to deal with the undesirable outcomes caused by this form of state law.

In order to mitigate this negative result of the one-child policy, Putianese daughters choose their partners strategically. Being the eldest daughter of her family, Tian stated that she would ask the man at the very beginning of their relationship whether he could accept *lianggu*, because she would not want to waste her time on those who could not. For Tian and some other leftover women in Putian, being leftover in the marriage market is more acceptable than being a daughter who turns down her parents' requests to provide old-age support. Tian takes it for granted that it is her responsibility to practise *lianggu* in order to secure the interests of her parents and make them happy. According to Tian, choosing *lianggu* is almost the best thing she can think of to show how grateful she is to her parents. In fact, virtually all of my interviewees tended to show sympathy for their parents who were deprived of the chance to have a male descendant because of the one-child policy. Their willingness to follow the practice of *lianggu* offers their parents a sense of security regarding their eldercare. Therefore, choosing *lianggu* illustrates a form of legal consciousness in which *qing* directly redresses negative social outcomes arising from state law.

### 4.1.3 *Resistance of State Law to Protect Qing*
China's one-child policy makes it difficult for parents to continue their family lines if they do not have male descendants. *Lianggu* improves the situation by requiring a couple to carry on the family line of both sides. In order to achieve this end, it is ideal for each married couple to have at least two children. In most cases, Putianese women who choose *lianggu* will give birth to two children, regardless of whether it is legal or not. [...]

Before the shift to the universal two-child policy, choosing to work for private companies or finding a non-permanent job in order to have two children was a popular strategy for Putianese women who wished to follow *lianggu* and fulfil their filial duty by passing down their family names. Some women chose to quit their government job shortly before they gave birth to the second child. The legal consciousness of [such] women who strategically engaged with the law to have more children exemplifies yet another form of legal consciousness: resistance of the law to protect *qing*.

One important feature of this third form of legal consciousness is that people are quite willing to accept responsibility for the consequences of violating the state law. These women emphasize that taking responsibility for one's own actions is required of any good citizen. Nonetheless, *qing* justifies their violation of law from two aspects. First, as the population policy has not taken account of *qing*, ordinary people prioritize local custom over state law to guide their behaviour. Second, since being responsible for one's own actions is a vital requirement of *qing*, people do not try to escape punishment for their direct resistance of state law. *Qing* explains how Putianese women can reconcile their lawbreaking behaviour and their perceptions of themselves as law-abiding citizens. In this sense, a focus on the role of *qing* clarifies the legal consciousness of women by highlighting not only their reluctance to use the law, but also their direct resistance to it.

4.1.4 *Dismissal of State Law When Breaking the Law Conforms to* Qing
Shun illustrates another form of legal consciousness by focusing on the limited efficacy of official efforts to enforce the law that prohibits childbearing out of wedlock. While China's current population policy encourages each married couple to have two children, relevant laws and policies still deny leftover women's reproductive rights and constrain childbearing within marriage. In rural China, however, villagers consider a couple as married once they invite their relatives and friends to a wedding banquet. Thus, it is not unusual for the couple to live together after the wedding banquet and have babies without going through the legal process of getting married. Shun argues that law's restrictions have only a limited impact on childbearing out of wedlock, and therefore she concludes that obedience to the law is unimportant when the majority do not think breaking it is against *qing*. She says:

> Quite a few couples in Putian have already had a child or even several children before they are legally married. Many friends of mine did not go through the legal process of marriage when they gave birth, and the local cadres did not mind as long as they were engaged or had a wedding banquet in the village.

# Legal Consciousness

In Shun's opinion, the state law is not effective, as many people manage to give birth outside marriage without being punished. Indeed, in most cases, local cadres are themselves members of the village society, and they share a similar understanding of *qing* with villagers. Village cadres are reluctant to report those who break the law if the actions of these villagers are compatible with *qing*.

Thus, the legal consciousness of Shun, her friends, and the village cadres reflects the old saying that "law should not, and could not penalise the majority" (法不责众). This saying means that, if the majority breaks a particular law out of the belief that doing so conforms to the requirements of *qing*, then *qing* should prevail and the law should not punish them. As long as many people participate in the practice, the majority has justice on its side. The main feature of this form of legal consciousness is that, when state law is against *qing*, ordinary people's beliefs about what the law should be are more influential than state law itself in shaping people's legal consciousness.

To summarize, these four forms of legal consciousness illustrate that, when people hold negative attitudes towards state law, they tend to use *qing* rather than the law to guide their behaviour – and they believe *qing* can fix the undesirable consequences of the state law.

## 4.2 Law in Alliance with *Qing*

In a society that is undergoing dramatic economic, cultural, and legal changes, it is not surprising for *qing* to differ from what it used to be. The fact that people believe law is secondary to *qing* does not necessarily mean that people do not expect the law to reinforce *qing* or promote new understandings of *qing* as conditions change. Putianese women's legal consciousness shows that, when law is – or could become – congruous with *qing*, people anticipate that law should play a more important role in enforcing *qing* or transforming old understandings of *qing* to help it catch up with social changes.

### 4.2.1 *Embrace of State Law When It Enforces* Qing

Although Putianese people consider it normal for a couple to give birth without going through the legal process of getting married, people still attach a stigma to single mothers and assume that women who give birth out of wedlock are immature, irresponsible, and lacking in the ability to control their own bodies. Even some leftover women themselves share this belief, which serves as the principal barrier to their childbearing in Chinese society. It is predictable that people may develop a more inclusive attitude in the future towards mothers who are single by choice. At this moment, however, childbearing out of wedlock goes against Putianese people's understandings of *qing*, as the majority still believes it is immoral for a single woman to become a mother. [...]

[Women who adhere to this belief] demonstrate a distinctive form of legal consciousness with regard to official Chinese population policy prohibiting childbearing out of wedlock: embrace of the law when it enforces *qing*. These women believe that, if a single woman becomes a mother, she will have to suffer from abandonment or discrimination, and thus state law should protect them by constraining childbearing within marriage. Indeed, my interviewees fail to acknowledge that women have the right to choose any kind of family structure, including a single-parent family. Their legal consciousness, however, reflects a prevalent belief among ordinary people that state law should protect its citizens by punishing those who act against *qing*. One important feature of this form of legal consciousness is that state law has been considered a source of support for *qing* and not in opposition to it.

### 4.2.2 Perception of State Law As Too Weak When It Fails to Transform "Old" Understandings of Qing

A final form of legal consciousness is evident among interviewees who view law as potentially useful in promoting new understandings of *qing*. Unfortunately, in their view, state law falls short of achieving the desirable transformation of social and cultural norms regarding leftover women. For example, Yue, a 27-year-old medical laboratory scientist, was the only Putianese women in this study to suggest that single women should be granted reproductive rights. According to Yue, some women desire for valid reasons to become single mothers by choice, but the current social environment makes it difficult to do so. She herself would probably not choose to be a single mother, even if it were legalized, because it might endanger her relationship with her father, a traditional Putianese man, who firmly believes that it is immoral to give birth outside marriage. Yue argues that law's refusal to legalize single women's reproduction reinforces the widespread belief that becoming a single mother by choice is morally unacceptable.

In Yue's view, the law is rather weak in protecting single mothers from the pressure imposed by family members as well as by society in general, as many people do not consider leftover women's reproduction as consistent with *qing*. But Yue views people's understandings of *qing* as malleable – they may change at different times and under different situations. Yue believes that state law needs to shoulder the responsibility of helping to challenge social discrimination against single mothers. This distinctive form of legal consciousness, therefore, perceives the law as too weak, when it could potentially be more useful to help transform *qing*. People such as Yue may adopt this form of legal consciousness when local customs and other social norms are not inclusive enough to accommodate the needs of people who disagree with the dominant understandings of *qing*. They may then look to state law to transform *qing* to ensure social justice – but the inability of law to achieve this goal generally leaves them disappointed and even disillusioned.

To summarize, by exploring the legal consciousness of ordinary Putianese women born and raised under the one-child policy, I have detected two broad ways in which the interaction of law and *qing* relates to Chinese people's thoughts and actions. I argue that these variations of legal consciousness result from the dynamic relationship between *qing* and legal orders – both state and non-state. Ordinary Chinese people invoke *qing* to form their own ideas of justice and fairness and decide whether they should prioritize a particular legal order over others. If people consider a particular legal order as conflicting with *qing*, they choose to avoid or resist it. At the same time, they may turn to other legal orders that meet the demands of *qing*. When the outcomes of state law endanger their interests, people may deploy *qing* to confront the problems arising from state law. When the majority considers breaking a certain official law is consistent with *qing*, people will dismiss state law and view those who violate it as law-abiding citizens. On the other hand, when state law supports and reinforces *qing*, people embrace it and expect it to protect the citizens. As the meanings of *qing* are subject to the ever-changing social environment within which people form their understandings of it, people expect that state law should play a positive role in transforming *qing* in order to create harmony, respect, and justice in society.

## III RIGHTS CONSCIOUSNESS

The concept of legal consciousness implicates a broad range of human activities and relationships. As the previous reading by Qian Liu suggests, the legal consciousness perspective helps us to understand issues of family life, parent–child relationships, and marriage. It is also useful for researchers who study transactions of various kinds – commercial exchanges, consumer activities, landlord–tenant relationships, and others. And the legal consciousness perspective has also proved useful in studying the work of lawyers, judges, and other actors within the formal legal system.

Perhaps the most frequent application of the legal consciousness perspective, however, has been in the area of legal rights – the entitlements each individual can claim under law to guarantee his or her freedom, autonomy, and fair treatment. Researchers have time and again attempted to explain when, why, and how the intended beneficiaries of legal rights actually invoke them. In some cases, rights-holders decide to make formal legal claims. In other cases, they may assert rights informally – in conversations with others or by referring to them within institutional procedures and structures as employees, customers, and so forth. In still other cases, individuals may be aware of their rights but choose not to invoke them. And, for many individuals, rights may remain dormant because individuals simply do not know they exist.

The readings in this section directly address issues of rights consciousness and demonstrate that the existence of rights "on the books" tells us little about the situations in which rights actually become active in people's lives. To understand the pathways that rights follow, the authors turn to the theories and methods of legal consciousness research. Readers should note that this portion of Chapter 4 deals with rights *consciousness*. In Chapter 5, we will address studies that examine the different ways in which rights are *mobilized*.

## 4.4 (Un)Becoming a Man: Legal Consciousness of the Third Gender Category in Pakistan, Muhammad Azfar Nisar

In its response to claims of discrimination by gender nonconforming individuals, the Supreme Court of Pakistan held that such individuals have constitutional rights entitling them to freedom from discrimination. Subsequently, the government agency that issues legal IDs in Pakistan made it possible for citizens to self-identify not just within the binary categories of male or female but with a third gender category, which the agency chose to call Khawaja Sira, thus identifying third-gender individuals in Pakistan with a well-known supportive community that many of them joined. Despite this apparent legal breakthrough, however, very few people have chosen to self-identify as Khawaja Sira in official contexts or to invoke the rights established for them under law. In this article, based on interviews with fifty members of the Khawaja Sira community in Lahore, Muhammad Azfar Nisar explores the legal consciousness of the so-called Third Gender in Pakistan with particular attention to the issue of rights.

Nisar's article exemplifies research within the Identity School of legal consciousness, although he also draws on literature and concepts associated most closely with the Hegemony School. Nisar demonstrates that only by understanding how identity is constructed can one explain how rights become active or remain dormant. Moreover, identity construction cannot be achieved by law alone but is also affected by culture and religion, as Nisar's analysis makes clear. In particular, cultural norms associated with parent–child relationships and customary inheritance practices tend to inhibit individuals from formal assertion of transgender rights; and religious norms and practices strongly influence transgender women to identify as men, despite their legal right to categorize themselves as third gender. Insofar as most social institutions and practices continue to adhere to a traditional gender binary – either male or female – the new legal right to claim a nonconforming gender identity holds little attraction for the individuals Nisar interviewed. The article thus provides a striking example of the ways in which legal consciousness comes to be associated with a diminished role for legal rights.

> *Family and Legal Thirdness*
>
> The other day three Khawaja Sira came to my house. They looked just like women and even had the [sex realignment] operation done. They said, "Sister we have to get the ID as a man!" I said, "But you look just like women, why don't you register as Khawaja Sira?" to which they replied, "No Sister! Our uncle will kill us if we do that." ... I think if there was less family pressure, more among us might register as Khawaja Sira.
>
> (Salma, 45, unemployed, an influential Guru)
>
> The new ID introduced by the government can only be issued ... in the name of the Gurus. We want our name to be included with the name of our parents. Our parents gave us birth, our mother carried us in her womb for nine months, our father did hard labor for us. They took care of us in our childhood. How can we erase their name?
>
> (Katrina, 33, unemployed)
>
> These two narratives indicate the multiple ways in which family influences the legal consciousness of the Khawaja Sira community. Many families keep tabs on the members of the Khawaja Sira community and actively discourage a public display of their feminine identity even after they leave or are thrown out of their homes. For example, one research participant was brutally beaten by her family members after her interview aired on a local news channel about the rights of the Khawaja Sira community, as she was thought to have brought shame on the family. Another was taken to her family home on a false pretext and her long hair was forcibly cut short to minimize her overt femininity. This anxiety over family honor reaches its peak when the families come to know that their "son" is going to register as a Khawaja Sira. Consequently, various strategies – like admonition, threat of violence, and withholding family verification (mandatory for getting a legal ID) – are used to dissuade family members from choosing the legal third gender.

However, family influence on the legal consciousness of the Khawaja Sira community is not always in the form of external coercion. As noted in the context of welfare stigma, individuals often internalize negative stereotypes associated with being a welfare recipient. This internalization, in turn, results in refusal to participate in welfare programs even if one is eligible to receive benefits. Many of my research participants had also internalized the social discourse that choosing the legal third gender meant abandoning their parents. This was partly because most members of the Khawaja Sira community believe that an integral part of choosing the legal third gender is to replace their father's name with that of their Guru even though this is legally not possible. That is why most members of the Khawaja Sira community call the ID with the masculine gender as the *family card* and one with the third gender as the *Khawaja Sira card*.

Even though most of them had been forced to leave their homes, formally abandoning family remained a taboo as obedience to parents and psychological connection to family are idolized in Pakistani society. To them it seemed as if choosing the third gender legally would make their disconnect from family "real," and they ended up choosing the masculine gender because they thought it would keep them, at least symbolically, connected to their families. Nargis, who is 56 years old, summarized this sentiment the best when she said, "There is no use of it [legal third gender]. People say get it, get it. How can one forget one's family, one's parents?" Among my research participants, only those who had experienced especially bad breaks from their families or whose parents had died wanted to choose the legal third gender. In fact, a couple of these participants even demanded that they be allowed to use their Guru's name instead of their father's to make the disconnect from their families formal.

*Religion and Legal Thirdness*
Religion plays an important part in the governance structure of Pakistan – a country that takes pride in being created as a self-proclaimed Islamic state. That is why religious scholars hold a great deal of influence in molding public opinion on different social issues. While traditional sources of Islamic Law are mostly silent about the Khawaja Sira identity, most contemporary religious scholars rely on the dominant social construction in Pakistan that gender–sex disjunction is not possible and that the only authentic third gender/sex is congenital and biologically determined. Such scholars believe that the Khawaja Sira are men only pretending to be women and should, therefore, perform their religious duties only as men.

Paradoxically, while the Khawaja Sira community contests social discourses that deem their femininity to be illegitimate, when it comes to religion they conform to the dominant patriarchal discourses. Most members of the Khawaja Sira community believe that for God, they are (ontologically) men and should perform all religious rituals as men; otherwise, those rituals will remain imperfect. From Naghma's observation that "we are born as boys in our parents' homes" to Neelo's opinion that "we will be resurrected with men at the day of judgment" and that she wants to be "standing in the Prophet's row [implying the row of men] on the day of judgment," it was the most consistent finding about the religious beliefs of the Khawaja Sira community. This is somewhat surprising since most other narratives of the Khawaja Sira community about their self-identity are based on the idea that they have a feminine soul inside a masculine body. I would have assumed (perhaps naively) that religion should be concerned with the soul and not the body. But when it comes to religion, the soul paradoxically takes a back seat for the Khawaja Sira community and the body takes over.

This religious belief becomes important for the Khawaja Sira community when they travel to Saudi Arabia for religious pilgrimage (umrah or hajj). Most members of the Khawaja Sira community believe that they will either not be allowed to enter Saudi Arabia or must perform religious rituals like women if they choose the legal third gender. Both options are unacceptable to them. My research participants narrated multiple incidents where their Khawaja Sira friends were not allowed to travel to Saudi Arabia. These fears were augmented when multiple news outlets reported last year that Saudi Arabia had banned all members of the Khawaja Sira community from traveling to the country. While this news was soon denied by officials from the Saudi embassy in Islamabad, the Khawaja Sira community is still apprehensive about choosing the legal third gender or traveling internationally dressed in feminine clothes. As one participant noted, "No one registered as a Khawaja Sira can go for Umrah. Those [Khawaja Sira] who have long hair and breasts can't go for Umrah either [even if they register as men]. Some Khawaja Sira went to Umrah [in recent months] but they cut their hair short and all of them had ID as men." Overall, it is always easier for members of the Khawaja Sira community to travel to Saudi Arabia as men even if there is no official policy that bans their travel. The uncertainties regarding travel to Saudi Arabia also highlight the difficulties inherent in introducing legal third gender in the international governance context. Even if Pakistan recognizes third-gendered individuals, they still must conform to the binary gender system while traveling internationally.

*Costs and Benefits of Legal Thirdness*

For many members of the Khawaja Sira community, the choice of the masculine legal gender also is motivated by more utilitarian concerns. In a patriarchal sociolegal system, there are tangible economic benefits associated with becoming a "legal man," which one must forego to choose the third gender legally. For example, men get a higher share of inheritance than women in Islamic and Pakistani law. Many members of the Khawaja Sira community believe that by choosing the legal third gender, they will not be entitled to the share of men and will instead get the share reserved for women (or "non-men"). Simran, 47 years old, unemployed and a Khawaja Sira rights activist, stated:

> I always say that we should get IDs as men otherwise we will be counted as women [for legal purposes] and instead of getting a larger (12 anay) share [equal to a man] we will be given a smaller (4 anay) share in inheritance as they [our brothers] would say that since we registered as Khawaja Sira, we are now equal to sisters. That's why I advise everyone [in the Khawaja Sira community] to get IDs as men ... to claim complete [and due] share in inheritance.

Such narratives associating legal third gender and a lower share of inheritance circulate widely among the Khawaja Sira community and produce powerful effects. Like Simran, other participants also mentioned inheritance as one of the main reasons they legally chose the masculine gender. In many cases, their primary concern was not about *what* their share was in inheritance but whether they got *any* share at all. As noted by the Supreme Court in its decision, the Khawaja Sira community is generally denied any share in their parents' inheritance. This denial is generally justified on the premise that the Khawaja Sira do not need to save or care for anyone other than themselves (as they do not have any spouse or children). For example, when one participant asked her father the reason for her exclusion from his will, he said incredulously, "What use would you have for the property?" Members of the Khawaja Sira community registering as men are holding on to the hope that legally identifying themselves as men may persuade their parents (and siblings) to let them have their due share in inheritance.

While there are tangible benefits associated with the masculine legal identity, there are hardly any benefits associated with the legal third gender. Even though the Supreme Court had ordered the government to take special measures for socioeconomic inclusion of the Khawaja Sira community – for example, provision of jobs and educational opportunities – none of them have subsequently been implemented. Moreover, most institutions in Pakistan have different policies for the collection of gender-related information, none of which associate any material benefits with the legal third gender. As Naima, 37 years old and employed, noted:

> What good is [adding the third gender on] the ID for us unless "third gender" is added to all forms, for example, related to transfer of property, ... on certificates, on forms for admissions to schools. On these forms, there is never written man, woman, Khawaja Sira. We just have to write man or woman. unless a third category is added everywhere, how can we get our place and our dignity [*izzat*]? [...]

In the context of Pakistan, it is important to note also that most public institutions – including schools, hospitals, and banks – are segregated along gender lines with separate spaces reserved for men and women. Even though a third gender category has been created, there have been no associated changes in these institutions. Ironically, even in the NADRA offices, no separate lines exist for the Khawaja Sira, who must stand with either men or women to apply for legal IDs. [ ... ]

*Conclusion*
[...] My research highlights that there are multiple institutional and discursive factors that influence and constrain the legality of the third gender category for the Khawaja Sira community. Therefore, I am hesitant to call the general reluctance of the Khawaja Sira community to choose the legal third gender as an act of resistance. [...]

I contend that at a deeper level, this choice of the Khawaja Sira community problematizes patriarchy and the hegemony of law in several ways, and the legal consciousness of the Khawaja Sira community should be conceptualized as a strategic "patriarchal bargain"[1] based on a personal cost–benefit calculus. The salient aspects of this bargain are as follows: First, my research highlights that most members of the Khawaja Sira community do not consider the formal legal system to be the arbiter of their self-identity. Before starting my fieldwork, I expected that the symbolic benefits of legal third gender – legal legitimacy of their thirdness – would be an important incentive for the Khawaja Sira community to choose it. However, I gradually realized that when their mere presence in a room or a workplace is enough for others to label and ostracize them – even when they do not want to disclose their real gender identity – there is limited, if any, utility in the legal third gender for

---

[1] Deniz Kandiyoti (1988), "Bargaining with Patriarchy," *Gender & Society* 2 (3): 274–90. [Editors' note]

most members of the Khawaja Sira community. It is not as if registering as men will prevent them from living their lives as third-gendered individuals. Society already considers them to be charlatans, and even if they choose the legal third gender that social assessment is unlikely to change. Hence, to the extent possible, they decide to strategically use the patriarchal legal order for their own benefit.

Second, a very important qualifier in the present context is lack of tangible material benefits associated with the legal third gender. If the government associates economic benefits – like social welfare – with the third gender, more members of the Khawaja Sira community will likely adopt the legal third gender as the strategic benefit will be higher. Paradoxically, as allocation of governmental resources is often based on the numerical strength of different groups, unless a critical mass of individuals chooses the legal third gender, the government is unlikely to associate any economic benefits with it. For example, a provincial minister in Punjab recently noted that since the number of officially registered Khawaja Sira was very small, the government was unable to fix any separate job quota for them. Hence, after the creation of the legal third gender, there is no perfect choice for the Khawaja Sira community: the choosing of the legal third gender means accepting social and religious stigma and foregoing the benefits associated with the masculine identity, while choosing to register as men potentially compromises their long-term agenda of symbolic and material inclusion.

That is why it is critical to keep in mind Molyneux's distinction[2] between *strategic* (long-term, group based, deductively articulated) and *practical* (immediate, need-based, inductively articulated) *gender interests*. For the Khawaja Sira community – most of whom live in extreme poverty – the practical (material and religious) interests that are served better by choosing the masculine gender legally are more urgent and important. On the other hand, there is no guarantee – at least in the short-term – that their strategic gender interests (like social acceptance and material inclusion) will be served by choosing the legal third gender. The Khawaja Sira community, therefore, makes a purposeful patriarchal bargain by choosing the masculine legal gender to take advantage of the privileges associated with the masculine identity in a patriarchal sociolegal order while foregoing the symbolic benefits associated with the legal third gender.

Therefore, in addition to improving our understanding of the legal consciousness of gender-nonconforming individuals, this analysis cautions against

---

[2] Maxine Molyneux (1985) "Mobilization without Emancipation? Women's Interests, the State, and Revolution in Nicaragua," *Feminist Studies* 11 (2): 227–54. [Editors' note]

> considering the introduction of the legal third gender as an unambiguously positive step for the inclusion of gender-nonconforming individuals. My research also problematizes the assumption that gender-nonconforming individuals would uncritically adopt the legal third gender because of its symbolic benefits. My findings further suggest that if the legal third gender is to become a viable option for social integration of gender-nonconforming individuals, governments, especially in developing countries, must associate with it tangible material benefits – such as improved job opportunities or dedicated welfare programs – to offset the social costs that individuals must bear by choosing the legal third gender.

### 4.5 Islamic Law, Women's Rights, and Popular Legal Consciousness in Malaysia, *Tamir Moustafa*

Although legal consciousness research typically relies on ethnographic and interpretive methodologies, in this article, Tamir Moustafa adopts a different approach in his study of women's rights consciousness in Malaysia. He prepared a telephone survey questionnaire, which Malaysia's leading public survey research group administered nationwide. The survey tested the views on Islamic law held by a random stratified sample of 1,043 Malaysian Muslims, with particular attention given to the question of women's rights.

Based on the results of this survey, Moustafa concludes that Muslims in Malaysia tend to misunderstand Islamic law and believe erroneously that it denies women their rights or narrowly circumscribes them. In fact, Islamic law consists of both *shari'a* and *fiqh*, the former referring to the immutable word of God and the latter to human interpretations. Since humans are fallible and far from omniscient, their efforts to interpret the law are never conclusive or free from errors. Thus, most of the Islamic legal canon is dynamic, ever-evolving, and open to debate. It is not binding as state law, nor should challenges to it be regarded as sinful. Nevertheless, as Moustafa's survey reveals, most Malay Muslims believe their narrow view of women's rights is a fixed and immutable aspect of Islamic law and therefore beyond debate, regardless of women's status under state law or international law.

For a more detailed and grounded discussion of Islamic law in modern state regimes, readers are referred to readings by Arskal Salim and by Tamir Moustafa in Chapter 1 of this Reader.

In most Muslim-majority countries throughout the world, the laws governing marriage, divorce, and other aspects of Islamic family law have been codified in a manner that provides women with fewer rights than men. Yet despite this fact, the Islamic legal tradition is *not* inherently incompatible with contemporary notions of liberal rights, including equal rights for women. This divergence between Islamic law in theory and Islamic law in practice is the result of how Islamic family law was written into state law in the nineteenth and early twentieth centuries throughout the Muslim world. A growing body of scholarship suggests that the process of legal codification was both selective and partial. Far from advancing the legal status of women, legal codification actually narrowed the range of rights that women could claim, at least in theory, in classical Islamic jurisprudence.

As a result, some of the most promising initiatives for expanding women's rights in the Muslim world today lie with the efforts of activists who explain that the Islamic legal tradition is not a uniform legal code, but a diverse body of jurisprudence that affords multiple guidelines for human relations, some of which are better suited to particular times and places than others. This approach represents a new mode of political engagement. While women's rights initiatives were almost invariably advanced through secular frameworks through most of the twentieth century, efforts to effect change in family law *from within the framework of Islamic law* have gained increasing traction in recent years. To varying degrees, women have pushed for family law reform within the framework of Islamic law in Egypt, Iran, Malaysia, Morocco, and many other Muslim-majority countries, opening up a new terrain for popular discourse and, in some cases, producing concrete and progressive legal reforms.

When women's rights organizations push for the reform of family law codes, however, they almost invariably encounter stiff resistance due to the widespread but mistaken understanding that Muslim family laws, as they are codified and applied in Muslim-majority countries, represent direct commandments from God that must be carried out by the state. As leading Muslim women's rights activist Zainah Anwar explains: "Very often Muslim women who demand justice and want to change discriminatory law and practices are told 'this is God's law' and therefore not open to negotiation and change."[1] For many lay Muslims, the state's selective codification of Islamic law is understood as the faithful implementation of divine command,

---

[1] Zainah Anwar (2008b), *Wanted: Equality and Justice in the Muslim Family* (Selangor, Malaysia: Musawah) at 1. [Editors' note]

full stop. As a result, rights activists cannot easily question or debate family law provisions without being accused of working to undermine Islam. As a further result of this dynamic, the laws concerning marriage, divorce, child custody, and a host of other issues critical to women's well-being are effectively taken off the table as matters of public policy. Popular (mis)understandings of core conceptual issues in Islamic law therefore have a tremendous impact on women's rights.

This difficulty faced by women's rights activists is symptomatic of a larger problem with which scholars of Islamic law have been concerned for quite some time. Specialists in Islamic jurisprudence and Islamic legal history are often dismayed by the disjuncture between Islamic legal theory and popular understandings of Islamic law. In its classical form, Islamic legal theory (*usul al-fiqh*) was marked by its flexibility, its commitment to pluralism, and, most notably, the fact that Islamic law was not binding as state law. Yet in contemporary political discourse, large segments of lay Muslim publics are swayed by the notion that Islamic law is uniform and static, that it should be enforced by the state, and that neglecting such a duty constitutes a rejection of God's will. These informal obstacles to family law reform underline the critical importance of "legal consciousness," defined by Merry as "the way people conceive of the 'natural' and normal ... their commonsense understanding of the world."[2] [...]

The survey confirms that there is a significant disjuncture between fundamental conceptual principles in Islamic legal theory and how those concepts are understood among lay Muslims in Malaysia. [... ]

Shari'a *versus* Fiqh: *Conflating Divine Will with Human Agency*
The first statement presented to respondents was, "Islamic law changes over time to address new circumstances in society." As previously explained, this statement represents a core concept in Islamic legal theory. Yet those surveyed were divided in evaluating the statement, with only slightly more respondents agreeing (50.5 percent) than disagreeing (48 percent). The next statement in the survey approached the issue in a more direct and strongly worded fashion: "Islam provides a complete set of laws for human conduct and each of these laws has stayed the same, without being changed by people, since the time of the Prophet (s.a.w.)." An overwhelming 82 percent of respondents agreed with the statement, a remarkable result given that Muslim jurists and historians would strongly dispute the claim. A third statement was designed to probe the

---

[2] Sally Engle Merry (1990), *Getting Justice and Getting Even: Legal Consciousness among Working-Class Americans* (Chicago: University of Chicago Press) at 5. [Editors' note]

TABLE 1. *The Nature of Islamic Law in Popular Legal Consciousness*

| Statement | Agree | Disagree | Do Not Know |
|---|---|---|---|
| Islamic law changes over time to address new circumstances in society. | 0.505 | 0.479 | 0.015 |
| Islam provides a complete set of laws for human conduct and each of these laws has stayed the same, without being changed by people, since the time of the Prophet (s.a.w.). | 0.820 | 0.176 | 0.005 |
| Each of the laws and procedures applied in the *shari'a* courts is clearly stated in the Qur'an. | 0.785 | 0.153 | 0.059 |

same issue in more grounded terms: "Each of the laws and procedures applied in the [Malaysian] *shari'a* courts is clearly stated in the Qur'an." It is striking that 78.5 percent of respondents agreed with the statement, while only 15.3 percent disagreed. [...] [V]ery few of the laws and virtually none of the procedures applied in the Malaysian *shari'a* courts are found in the Qur'an; rather, the laws applied in the *shari'a* courts are at most a codified version of *fiqh*, which itself is not uniform on most principles of law and is the product of human reason, not direct divine command. In their answers to all three questions, the understandings of a large percentage of lay Muslims diverge sharply from both the historical record and core axioms in Islamic legal theory (see Table 1).

These misconceptions are not merely significant in a religious sense. Because Islamic law is used extensively as an instrument of public policy, popular misconceptions about basic features of Islamic jurisprudence have significant implications for democratic deliberation on a host of substantive issues, of which women's rights is just one important example. When the public understands the *shari'a* courts as applying God's law unmediated by human influence, people who question or debate those laws are likely to be viewed as working to undermine Islam. Indeed, it is the presumed divine nature of the laws applied in the *shari'a* courts that provides the rationale for criminalizing the expression of alternative views in the Shari'a Criminal Offenses Act. As a result, laws concerning marriage, divorce, child custody, and other issues critical to women's well-being are difficult to approach as matters of public policy. The Malaysian women's rights organization Sisters in Islam has identified public misunderstanding of core principles in Islamic law as the most formidable obstacle that it faces in its pursuit of progressive family law reform. For this reason, Sisters in Islam conducts a variety of public education programs with a central focus on reconstructing the critical distinction between *shari'a* and *fiqh* in public legal consciousness.

*Islamic Law As Legal Method or Legal Code?*
A second and related set of survey questions probed whether Malaysian Muslims conceive of Islamic law as uniform in character, with a single "correct" answer to any given issue or, alternatively, whether Islamic law is understood as providing a framework through which Muslims can arrive at equally valid yet differing understandings of God's will. Perhaps the best way of approaching this issue is by assessing popular understandings of the convention of the *fatwa*. Among scholars of Islamic law, a *fatwa* is readily understood as a nonbinding opinion by a religious jurist on a matter related to Islamic law. For any given question, jurists are likely to arrive at a variety of opinions, all of which should be considered equally valid if they follow accepted methods of one of the four schools of jurisprudence. But do lay Muslims understand the institution of the *fatwa* in the same way?

To explore this issue, respondents were asked a series of questions focused on the convention of the *fatwa*. First, respondents were asked: "If two religious scholars issue conflicting *fatwas* on the same issue, must one of them be wrong?" The majority (54.2 percent) of respondents answered yes while 39.5 percent answered no. In one sense, this majority response is in harmony with Islamic legal theory: most *fiqh* scholars believe that there is a correct answer to any given question, but that humans can never know God's will with certainty in this lifetime. However, in another survey question the same respondents were asked: "Is it appropriate in Islam for the *'ulama* to issue differing *fatwas* on the same issue?" On this question, 40.5 percent answered yes while the majority, 54.2 percent answered no. Taken together, responses to the two questions suggest that most respondents believe that there is a single, "correct" answer for any given issue *and* that religious scholars can and should arrive at the same answer in the here and now. In other words, most lay Muslims in Malaysia tend to understand Islamic law as constituting a single, unified code rather than a body of equally plausible juristic opinions. (See Table 2.)

The finding that most lay Muslims understand Islamic law as a legal code that yields only one correct answer to any given religious question, rather than a legal method that is capable of producing equally plausible opinions from different scholars, is a testament to how comprehensively the modern state, with its codified and uniform body of laws and procedures, has left its imprint on public legal consciousness. Only about 40 percent of the population appears to conceive of the possibility that two or more opinions can be simultaneously legitimate on any matter in Islamic law, a remarkable

TABLE 2. *Uniformity or Plurality of Islamic Law in Popular Legal Consciousness*

| Question | Yes | No | Do Not Know |
|---|---|---|---|
| If two religious scholars issue conflicting *fatwas* on the same issue, must one of them be wrong? | 0.542 | 0.395 | 0.062 |
| Is it appropriate in Islam for the *'ulama* to issue different *fatwas* on the same issue? | 0.405 | 0.542 | 0.050 |

divergence from core axioms in Islamic legal theory. As with the previous set of questions, this finding has deep implications beyond private religious belief. Because important matters of public policy are legitimized through the framework of Islamic law, the vision of Islamic law as code rather than Islamic law as method narrows the scope for public debate and deliberation.

This dynamic is again illustrated in concrete terms by the challenges faced by women's rights advocates in Malaysia. The nongovernmental organization Sisters in Islam works to advance women's rights within the framework of Islamic law by drawing on the rich jurisprudential tradition within Islam. Rather than accepting the specific codifications of *fiqh* that have been enacted as state law, Sisters in Islam examines the variety of positions in Islamic jurisprudence on any given issue, in the context of the core values of justice and equality that Islam affirms. For example, Sisters in Islam has lobbied the government to permit women to stipulate, in their marriage contract, the right to a divorce should their husband marry a second wife. While the Shafi'i *madhhab* does not afford women the opportunity to make such stipulations in the marriage contract, the Hanbali *madhhab* does. Why, Sisters in Islam asks, must Malaysian family law conform to the Shafi'i *madhhab* on this point of law when the Hanbali *madhhab* affords a more progressive opportunity to expand women's rights? These women's rights advocates highlight the fact that *fiqh* is not a uniform legal code. Rather, it is a diverse body of jurisprudence that affords multiple guidelines for human relations, some of which are better suited to particular times and places than others. In a state where Islamic law has been codified as an instrument of patriarchal public policy, Sisters in Islam thus engages conservatives on their own discursive terrain. The common response to women's rights activism that "this is God's law" is thus challenged by the powerful rejoinder that, on most questions of law, Islam simply does not provide a single legal opinion.

Unfortunately, this approach is again stymied by popular misconceptions of Islamic law. To the extent that Islamic law is understood as a fixed and uniform code, with only one correct answer for any particular issue, women's rights advocates face an uphill battle in convincing the public about the possibilities for legal reform, even within the framework of Islamic law. The fact that 78.5 percent of lay Muslims in Malaysia believe that each of the laws and procedures applied in the *shari'a* courts is clearly stated in the Qur'an, which Muslims consider the direct word of God, indicates the public's weak grasp of Islamic legal principles as well as their weak knowledge of the basis of Malaysian public law. The collapse of the distinction between *shari'a* and *fiqh* in popular legal consciousness makes it extremely difficult to propose alternative interpretations, even when they are equally legitimate in Islamic law. [...]

*Conclusions*
[...] The data suggest that there is a significant gap between the epistemological commitments of Islamic legal theory and how Islamic law is understood among lay Muslims in Malaysia. The findings indicate fundamental misunderstandings of basic principles in Islamic jurisprudence – misunderstandings that blur the distinction between *shari'a* and *fiqh*. Whereas Islamic jurisprudence is marked by diversity and fluidity, Islamic law is understood among most Muslims in Malaysia today as singular and fixed. Implementation of a codified version of Islamic law through the *shari'a* courts is understood as a religious duty of the state, and indeed it appears that most Malaysians believe that the *shari'a* courts apply God's law directly, unmediated by human agency. Likewise, unquestioned deference to religious authority is assumed to be a legal and religious duty among most Malaysians.

Given the nature of popular legal consciousness in Malaysia, it is no wonder that women's rights activists have encountered such difficulty in mobilizing broad-based public support in their efforts to reform Muslim family law codes. It is also not surprising that they often find themselves on the losing end of debates with conservatives, regardless of the strength of their arguments. Women's rights activists, even those operating within the framework of Islamic law, are easily depicted by their opponents as challenging core requirements of Islamic law, or even Islam itself. Conversely, the discursive position of conservative actors is strengthened by popular misunderstanding of epistemological commitments in Islamic law. Religious officials, political parties, and other groups wishing to preserve the status quo can easily position themselves as defenders of the faith, given popular understandings of Islamic law as singular and fixed. [...]

Despite the fact that a smaller share of the general public understands Islamic law as plural, flexible, and shot through with human agency, the survey data provided some reassurance that popular legal consciousness is not monolithic. More importantly, the survey data can provide valuable

> insights into how popular legal consciousness varies across levels of income, education, age, sex, region, and urban-rural divides. Armed with such data, women's groups can target their limited resources more effectively. Moreover, they can use this data as a public education opportunity by helping to highlight the myths and realities of Islamic law, women's rights, and public policy in contemporary Malaysia.

## III RELATIONAL LEGAL CONSCIOUSNESS

Studies of legal consciousness in non-Asian settings have typically adopted a linear model influenced by the "naming-blaming-claiming" framework set forth in Felstiner et al. (1980–81). In this model, individuals initially experience an inchoate sense of injury that may lead to the perception that someone else's wrongful action is responsible – and, in a few cases, the assertion of a claim against the perceived wrongdoer. Legal consciousness plays a key role in this linear progression from an initial perception of harm toward claiming, leading some individuals but not others to sharpen their feeling of misfortune and transform it into a demand that things be made right – a demand that can bring law, legal rights, and legal institutions into play.

Legal consciousness research in Asia has raised important challenges both to the linear qualities of this model and to its emphasis on individual decision-making. Scholars of Asian law and society have found that the ultimate goals being pursued may have little to do with rights claims but rather the strengthening or repair of important social relationships. Arguably, every study of legal consciousness incorporates some relational features. Therefore, Lynette Chua and David Engel (2019:346–7) have suggested that the relational aspects of legal consciousness research can be placed on a continuum. At one end of the continuum are "studies that view the self as essentially autonomous and independent, not entirely divorced from social relationships yet functioning primarily on its own" in terms of problem perception and decision-making. In the middle region of the continuum "we find legal consciousness studies that retain the individual as the appropriate object of study but treat other individuals as co-creators of consciousness rather than mere external variables." And, at the far end of the continuum, "is a concept of relationalism that rejects the individual as the unit of analysis and views legal consciousness as a fully collaborative phenomenon."

Research on legal consciousness in Asia, including the following article by Hsiao-Tan Wang, has explored the fully relational aspects of legal consciousness and has challenged the more individualistic bias inherent in much of the earlier legal consciousness literature.

## 4.6 Justice, Emotion, and Belonging: Legal Consciousness in a Taiwanese Family Conflict, *Hsiao-Tan Wang*

The following excerpt from an article by Hsiao-Tan Wang illustrates the new insights provided by a relational perspective on legal consciousness. The article centers on a dispute within a Taiwanese family concerning wealth, inheritance, and the roles and responsibilities of parents and children. The dispute does not transition from generalized feelings of wrongdoing to the sharp and explicitly rationalized assertion of a claim. Instead, the disputants jockey for position in the family unit and pursue the goal of *zìjǐrén* – belonging and acceptance as a proper parent or child. Facts are falsified and reality is distorted in the struggle to establish one's position in the family. To complicate this painful story even further, the second son – who is most unhappy with the situation – comes to embrace a more individualistic, even a legalistic, view of his rights than do the other family members. Even though his view may differ from theirs, however, his goals are largely relational, and it never occurs to him to engage in "claiming" to vindicate his rights rather than seeking acceptance within the family.

Mother Lee and Mr. Lee had three adult children – two sons who married and lived on their own, and a daughter who lived with her parents. The eldest son was favored by his parents and, after Mr. Lee retired, received their financial assistance to enable him and his wife to pursue graduate education abroad. The parents took out a mortgage on their house to pay the educational expenses, but at the same time they asked the second son and the daughter for financial support. For two years, the second son gave Mother Lee two-thirds of his salary, while the first son enjoyed a luxurious lifestyle abroad. Even after the first son returned to Taiwan, Mother Lee continued to support him financially, while expecting the second son to provide some support. The family gathered for dinner each month, but never discussed finances.

Because of his profligate spending, the eldest son continued to incur debts and even persuaded his parents to take out a second mortgage after the first was paid off. The second son objected to no avail and eventually confronted Mother Lee about her unfair treatment. She responded, "When we are older, your elder brother will take responsibility for us. You do not need to worry about us. All you have to do is have dinner with us sometimes." Shocked by her words, and unable to discuss the matter directly with his brother, the second son curtailed his involvement with the family and, when his father died, made no attempt to claim his share of the inheritance. Taiwanese law requires that each child should inherit equally unless the deceased parent has stipulated otherwise.

*Interpreting the Lee Family Conflict*
When Mother Lee told her second son that he only had to have dinner with them sometimes and falsely claimed that the eldest son did not take any money, she was implying that she was unhappy about not being identified as a good mother. At this point, she was clinging to her impression of the bonds she shared with the first son, and thus, took the second son's complaint about his brother as an attack on her. If the second son had accepted her version of reality, he would have sent her the message that he respected her as a good mother, bringing them both emotional balance while creating more affinity between them. However, his reaction in refusing to accept her version of reality meant that he was not identifiable as a good son; this only estranged him further from his mother, and in turn, the family. For Mother Lee, the alienation of her second son in this manner was a sacrifice that she was making for her first son, which ultimately put more pressure on him to comply with his filial duties in the future. The second son, however, was forced to capitulate and retreat, leaving his relationships with his mother and brother "shrunk or terminated" and his sense of self greatly transformed.[1]

Rather than Mother Lee's fear of aging inspiring her to explicitly communicate her feelings to her children about her future needs, she constructed a version of the facts that favored her first son as the most *zìjǐrén*. In making use of the family resources to pursue a psychologically friendly and responsive relationship with her eldest son, she simultaneously secured elder care and most importantly living arrangements for her and her husband in their older years. She may have been acting in the interests of reducing the risk of embarrassment or the "loss of face" that would be caused by eventually taking this issue to the public courts to claim her legal right to elderly maintenance (Article 1117 of the Civil Code), but she was aware that the laws in place did not necessarily serve her and her specific goal of not living alone. Indeed, it may seem as if this was a rational or calculated process but, for Mother Lee, it was more an attempt to bring balance to her emotional sense of self as a form

---

[1] William L. F. Felstiner (1975), "Avoidance as Dispute Processing: An Elaboration," *Law & Society Review* 9 (4): 695–706 at 695. [Editors' note]

of justice which depended on her intuitive sense that others identified her as morally good with regard to her social roles.

After Mother and Father Lee finally moved into their eldest son's apartment, the second son's interpretation of the event changed as he applied individualistic contractual logic to frame what he finally understood as an economic exchange between his mother and brother. He also recognized that his mother had used him as leverage to bring about a form of justice that served her so that the eldest son would be indebted to her in exchange for her sacrifices. In the end, his final interpretation of the event, his legal consciousness, even provided a position of agency for his mother in her struggle to find her best approach to aging. Not claiming his inheritance rights and avoiding the law after Father Lee passed away afforded him a greater opportunity to keep up minimum contact with his mother in the years that followed. Mother Lee's legal consciousness had also transformed; her identity had shifted to be more individualistic and independent which better served her. Her words explicitly implied that she came to believe it to be her personal right to do as she pleased within the family and insist on the deference she was owed as a mother and as *zìjǐrén*. [...]

*Adoption of Law Driven by Emotion and Cultural Concepts*
[Qian] Liu's unique work has indeed opened the discussion about the effect that *qíng* has on the formation of legal consciousness; however, the effect of identity or one's relational perception of others is not emphasized, and the true degree of power that *qíng* has over people's thoughts and actions is not described. The Lee family conflict puts a spotlight on this by identifying *qíng* as much more than a norm and suggesting that it is actually a catalyst for one's perception of reality, and subsequently for one's reactions to situations. The ubiquitous practice of *qíng* is constituted through the plural, dynamic, and complex process of interpersonal interactions between people who are striving for an identity as "belonging" emotionally to a family or other social group rather than standing apart from others. In everyday Taiwanese life, the bonds of *zìjǐrén* are provided by the establishment of mutual identification or *rèntóng* (認同), a term connoted with personhood (i.e., identity, identification, or identify). Although this promotes affection and self-worth, these bonds are constantly tested, shaped, and reformed as a result of power and negotiation. Chua and Engel argue that "individual personhood is subsumed within other social relationships, [and that] there is a possibility that these relationships are unequal and maintain existing social hierarchies."[2]

---

[2] Lynette J. Chua and David M. Engel (2019), "Legal Consciousness Reconsidered," *Annual Review of Law and Social Science* 15: 335–53. [Editors' note]

It follows then that the role of identity – one's own self-perception (personal identity) and the perceptions of others (social identity) – involves the acknowledgement and setting of conceptual boundaries that shift and change throughout a lifetime as an individual's self has experiences with others in society. Within the context of local Taiwanese practices and traditions, the sense of self or self-other relationship is characterized by a constant interplay between *rèntóng* and *zìjǐrén*, a combination of personhood and relational self-positioning and positioning by others. This implies that the sense of self in Taiwan is not based on what sets individuals apart but rather on the similarities that place them within a group and the exchanges that happen therein. As Chua and Engel's "relational model" suggests, the understanding of and decision to adopt the law or not may emerge within "the porosity of boundaries between individual cognition and relationships with others." This article shows that legal consciousness is more than likely to be highly dependent on one's connections with varying social groups, how one feels they are identified by the members of these groups, and the interactions that take place within them.

Embodied subjectivity, relational affinity, and culturally embedded life course patterns and practices intensify or shift broader forms of hierarchy and inequality, which has the power to reshape identity and reorient the boundaries between inclusion and exclusion. Justice in this broader sense is usually presented through the perception of reality and thereafter reactions toward each other. Emotion (*qíng*) in Taiwanese contexts does not merely refer to personal emotion such as anxiety, anger, and alienation, but also encompasses the sense of belonging that one pursues as a life goal or a way of life. To feel included (*zìjǐrén*) or identified with (*rèntóng*) can bring one a sense of balance that determines the relevance of law in everyday thoughts and actions. When wronged by loved ones, the feeling of closeness and remoteness can bring to light the many variations in how one perceives and interacts with others. Legal consciousness in this context may be transformed along with the fluid boundary of inclusion and exclusion while one strives to gain acceptance and be respected by a perceived group.

*Conclusion*
[...] The case study of the Lee family conflict presented in this article demonstrates that legal consciousness is dependent on emotions that are deeply connected to one's perception of the self-other relationship, the level of affinity shared with others, and the life objectives of all those involved. As the conflict heightened, the Lee family had different and contrasting interpretations of the situation; while emotionally contesting the boundaries of belonging in their daily social practices, they tended to avoid, fabricate, or

selectively utilize underlying facts, at times with references to law as an interpretive framework to assess their relationships with one another. As the disputants emotionally negotiated for mutually satisfying arrangements regarding the issues of filial piety, the distribution of resources, future elder care, and ultimately inheritance, they also constructed their identities as based on whether they felt included or excluded, or accepted and respected, by the group.

Their adoption of law was at times absent, at others influential, but always shaped by Chinese concepts like *zìjǐrén*, which constitute the emotional complex of belonging in Taiwan and serve as the major determinants of how reality, justice, and belonging are perceived. When in conflict, this cultural patterning is the driving force behind a disputants' pursuit of an identity that places them on moral high ground as a form of justice. In this approach to the study of legal consciousness, an understanding of the culture or social group to which one relates can potentially foster accurate predictions of how disputants are going to react to certain situations. However, such predictions have a limited half-life because as an individual's position within a group changes, so do their feelings toward the situation, those involved, and thereby the law. Comparative studies in other cultural and social contexts are needed, in and outside of Taiwan, in order to contribute further to our understanding of how emotion and the need for relational affinity shape legal consciousness.

REFERENCES

**Featured Readings**

Engel, David M. 2005. "Globalization and the Decline of Legal Consciousness: Torts, Ghosts, and Karma in Thailand." *Law & Social Inquiry* 30 (3): 469–514. doi: 10.1111/j.1747-4469.2005.tb00351.x

Liu, Qian. 2018. "Legal Consciousness of the Leftover Woman: Law and Qing in Chinese Family Relations." *Asian Journal of Law and Society* 5 (1): 7–27. doi: 10.1017/als.2017.28

Moustafa, Tamir. 2013. "Islamic Law, Women's Rights, and Popular Legal Consciousness in Malaysia." *Law & Social Inquiry* 38 (1): 168–88. doi: 10.1111/j.1747-4469.2012.01298.x

Murayama, Masayuki. 2013. "Kawashima and the Changing Focus on Japanese Legal Consciousness: A Selective History of the Sociology of

Law in Japan." *International Journal of Law in Context* 9 (4): 565–89. doi: 10.1017/s174455231300030x

Nisar, Muhammad Azfar. 2018. "(Un)Becoming a Man: Legal Consciousness of the Third Gender Category in Pakistan." *Gender & Society* 32 (1): 59–81. doi: 10.1177/0891243217740097

Wang, Hsiao-Tan. 2019. "Justice, Emotion, and Belonging: Legal Consciousness in a Taiwanese Family Conflict." *Law & Society Review* 53 (3): 764–90. doi: 10.1111/lasr.12422

**Other Works Cited**

Chua, Lynette J. and David M. Engel. 2019. "Legal Consciousness Reconsidered." *Annual Review of Law and Social Science* 15: 335–53. doi: annurev-lawsocsci-101518-042717

———2020. "Legal Consciousness." In *The Routledge Handbook of Law and Society*, edited by Mariana Valverede, Kamari Clarke, Eve Darian Smith, and Prabha Kotiswaran, 187–91. London and New York: Routledge. doi: 10.4324/9780429293306-38

Felstiner, William L. F., Richard L. Abel, and Austin Sarat. 1980–1, "The Emergence and Transformation of Disputes: Naming, Blaming, Claiming ..." *Law & Society Review* 15 (3–4): 631–54. doi: 10.4324/9780429293306-38

Haley, John. 1978. "The Myth of the Reluctant Litigant." *Journal of Japanese Studies* 4 (2): 359–90. doi: 10.2307/132030

**Suggested Readings**

Engel, David M. 2016. "Blood Curse and Belonging in Thailand: Law, Buddhism, and Legal Consciousness." *Asian Journal of Law and Society* 3 (1): 71–83. Revised and reprinted in *Thai Legal History: From Traditional to Modern Law* edited by Andrew Harding and Munin Pongsapan, 89–99. Cambridge: Cambridge University Press. doi: 10.1017/9781108914369.008

Gallagher, Mary E. 2006. "Mobilizing the Law in China: 'Informed Disenchantment' and the Development of Legal Consciousness." *Law & Society Review* 40 (4): 783–816. doi: 10.1111/j.1540-5893.2006.00281.x

Miyazawa, Setsuo. 1987. "Taking Kawashima Seriously: A Review of Japanese Research on Japanese Legal Consciousness and Disputing Behavior." *Law & Society Review* 21(2): 219–42. doi: 10.2307/3053520

Young, Kathryne M. 2014. "Everyone Knows the Game: Legal Consciousness in the Hawaiian Cockfight." *Law & Society Review* 48 (3): 499–530. doi: 10.1111/lasr.12094

# 5 Legal Mobilization

Contents

| | | |
|---|---|---|
| I | Scope of Legal Mobilization | 185 |
| II | Legal Mobilization Tactics | 192 |
| III | Legal Mobilization Effects | 208 |

Legal mobilization occurs "when a desire or want is translated into a demand as an assertion of rights" (McCann 1994, quoting Zemans 1983:700). A large law and society literature based on this concept of mobilization grew out of influential studies by Scheingold (1974), McCann (1994), and other law and society scholars working largely in American settings. More recently, the concept of legal mobilization has been applied to Asian settings as well. Writing about Southeast Asia, Lynette J. Chua (2022) describes rights mobilization as a phenomenon that occurs when people "make sense of and express their problems in a language of rights. Co-labouring in groups or working individually, they interpret and adapt rights to fend off attacks, push back restrictions, recoup losses or fight for admission into institutions previously denied to them. They also use rights to empower others to participate in rights mobilisation" (p. 7).

The concept of legal mobilization is closely related to legal consciousness, which is the subject of Chapter 4. We might say that legal mobilization is a form of legal consciousness manifesting in actions, words, and thoughts. It can be as simple as interpreting or articulating a problem to a confidante in rights or other legal terms. An individual or group could take up legal mobilization for themselves or do so to benefit others. Of course, legal consciousness is also defined as action and not just cognition, so the two concepts overlap in many ways, and some scholars would even view legal mobilization research as a subset of legal consciousness research. These two law and society fields, in short, have developed in close proximity to one another with frequent crossovers.

Readers also should note that "rights mobilization" and "legal mobilization" tend to be conflated in the law and society literature. For the most part, law and society scholars use the two concepts interchangeably. However, there may be situations in which the two concepts are not interchangeable, where law is mobilized without specific reference to rights, for example, when using a criminal provision to prosecute somebody; and, in that sense, legal mobilization is arguably the broader of the two.

The degree to which "rights mobilization" and "legal mobilization" become interchangeable depends on the way in which a given scholar conceptualizes "rights" and "law." As we learned in the Religion and Legal Pluralism chapters (Chapters 1 and 2), different systems of normative ordering – both state and non-state – feature different worldviews and different understandings of people's experiences and interactions with one another, with governments, and with other groups and holders of power. These differing norms can generate distinctive ideas about "rights" and about law itself. They can shape legal consciousness and the mobilization of various forms of law in response to people's problems and grievances – whether couched in terms of rights or not.

The existence of pluralism further suggests that rights can have diverse genealogies. Each normative order offers different pathways for individuals to come to their own appreciation of rights. All contemporary Asian states have formal legal orders, influenced to varying degrees by their histories of pre-colonial empires and kingdoms, colonial rule, or even armed conflicts. Almost every state has a constitution, maybe different versions over the years, and they enshrine constitutional rights, at least on paper. Internationally, there are peremptory norms, such as prohibitions against torture, genocide, and slavery, that are meant to bind all states, rights treaties ratified by Asian states, such as the International Convention on Civil and Political Rights and Convention on the Elimination of All Forms of Discrimination against Women, and the ASEAN Human Rights Declaration, the only Asian-based regional human rights instrument.[*] Furthermore, localized customary laws may contain their own systems of rights, although the terminology may vary

---

[*] The signatories are the ten members of the Association of Southeast Asian Nations (ASEAN), Brunei, Cambodia, Indonesia, Laos, Malaysia, Myanmar, Philippines, Singapore, Thailand, and Vietnam.

considerably from one society to the next. Law and society scholars have engaged extensively with these multiple normative systems and have recognized that their pluralities and contingencies result in a situation in which rights – and law itself – can mean different things to different people and thus manifest differently.

In short, in law and society studies, the subjects and meanings of legal mobilization and the use of rights are informed by the empirical context. Questions of what rights and law mean are important points to bear in mind as we make our way through this chapter's readings. The readings feature some studies that focus on rights claims as well as other studies in which the research subjects do not explicitly refer to rights but engage the law with reference to other terms as they press for social justice or change.

I SCOPE OF LEGAL MOBILIZATION

Litigation does, of course, occur in every Asian country, but a great deal of legal mobilization takes place away from formal mechanisms of the state. Frequently, mobilizers litigate in conjunction with other tactics, or after years of building support painstakingly at the grassroots and shoring up expertise and resources. From law and society literature on Asia and beyond, it is clear that legal mobilization need not be directed at courts or other formal institutional mechanisms. Nevertheless, we might come across definitions of legal mobilization that confine the concept to actions directed explicitly at formal institutional mechanisms. This kind of narrow approach is rather unfortunate, because it leads to only a partial understanding of law in the Asian context in which one is interested. It also runs contrary to the law and society tradition of investigating the workings of law and overlapping layers of power in all facets of life, not merely where and when the state takes center stage.

The inclusive scope of legal mobilization goes hand in hand with a broad construction of law's power, especially that of rights. Certainly, rights possess instrumental power to compel or prevent action, for example, when they are enacted in legislation or effected by court order. Legal mobilization scholars, however, take the view that rights can do more, regardless of and in addition to their instrumental power. Informed by cultural anthropology, legal mobilization scholars conceptualize rights as social practices, a set of culturally conditioned beliefs or a symbolic framework with which to formulate, think about, and react to one's troubles and other encounters (Geertz 1964). Thus, rights become cultural resources that people can draw upon to bargain, rally, empower, and organize.

## 5.1 Constructing SSLM: Insights from Struggles over Women's Rights in Nepal, *Margaret Becker*

In this article, Becker refers to "support structure for legal mobilization" (SSLM), a concept denoted by Charles Epp (1998) as the significant resources – such as advocacy groups, lawyers, and financing – needed to successfully undertake rights mobilization through the courts. A concept related to SSLM is "legal opportunity structure," which consists of features of a legal system, such as court rules, existing laws, judicial precedents, and potential alliances, that encourage or discourage rights litigation (see, e.g., Anderson 2006; Arrington 2021). Becker, however, goes beyond litigation, and, consequently, captures a wider range of legal mobilization that emerged as the women from two Nepalese organizations responded to and targeted different sources of power emanating from state and non-state normative orders.

> *"Opening the Iron Gate": Mobilising for the Rights of Widows*
> Lily Thapa – a highly educated, high-caste woman from a large, highly respected Kathmandu family – is a veteran of agitating for women's rights in Nepal, having founded Women for Human Rights – Single Women Group (hereafter WHR) in 1994. WHR is primarily concerned with the issues and rights of widows in Nepal. Because of the stigma associated with the word "widow" WHR passed a national declaration in 2001 to use the term "single women" instead of the word "widow". For Hindu women in particular, to be widowed is to face a social death, although the severity of the experience of widowhood is greater for high-caste women. Her status as a widow means that she is no longer regarded as a "good woman" by her family and community. A local moral order based on Hindu religious ideologies drawn from Brahmanical writings and teachings, the notion of the "good woman" refers to the ideal life path of women. In this life path, the woman's roles are focused on the family and the most cherished characteristics are those that support the patriarchal family.
>
> Marriage, particularly, is central to this ideal life path, as prolific Nepali academic and women's activist Acharya notes: "marriage becomes the overwhelming factor determining all her life options. This [is] reinforced by all round social norms and legal structures, everything else is secondary to marriage". Those women whose husbands die before them are thus seen as deviating from the ideal life path of the "good woman". Indeed, a widow is regarded as an aberration, as someone with bad fate and bad luck and she is

often blamed for her husband's death. Regarded as invisible, she is relegated to the margins of society where she typically faces discrimination, prejudice and abuse.

It was Lily's own experience of being widowed that was the impetus for WHR. Following the death of her husband in 1990, Lily's life changed dramatically as her status quickly shifted from respected married woman to widow, as someone to be treated with suspicion and disdain, as she highlighted during one of our conversations:

> When my husband was alive everybody not dare to do anything to the wife. The dignity, respect and everything... I get that while my husband is alive, no? The second, the minute after my husband's death I would not get that auspiciousness, honour.

In 1992, two years after her husband's death, Lily initiated an informal weekly support group for widows in order to provide a space in which they could openly express their sorrows and difficulties. In the beginning, seven widows gathered to share their grievances and provide support for each other. The number gradually increased to up to 50 widows and in 1994 the group was formally registered as an NGO. Currently WHR is one of the largest women's NGOs in Nepal with more than 100,000 members. The organisation is far reaching with over 1,550 groups in 73 of the 75 districts of Nepal.

WHR's focus on the formal recognition of the rights of widows was apparent during my first meeting with Lily Thapa at the organisation's headquarters in Baluwatar – an affluent area of Kathmandu. Lily talked at length about WHR's legal action in relation to expanding widows' rights, pointing to numerous human rights articles and instruments such as CEDAW and United Nations Security Council Resolution 1325. It was immediately clear that WHR was working within the global discourse of rights, and further, that Lily Thapa was highly conversant in the language of human rights, including the numerous human rights instruments. She noted the way in which "things appear to be good for women on paper – provisions are made however this is only on paper – in reality things are not like this. WHR tests these things in court".

As a result of the organisation's litigation efforts: (i) widows no longer require the consent of their adult sons and unmarried daughters to sell or hand over property ownership; (ii) widows do not need to reach the age of 35 to inherit their husbands' property; (iii) there is no longer government policy to award money to men who marry a widow; and (iv) widows no longer need permission from a male family member to obtain a passport. WHR's litigation record highlights the organisation's experience with the judiciary which, in turn, constitutes a key resource for the SSLM. Indeed, Epp has underscored the way in which the presence of "repeat players" – in terms of extensive experience with the court system – forms a key element in the SSLM needed to access and utilise the judiciary.

In order to engage in litigation, WHR draws on a range of resources including staff, legal advocates, far-reaching supporters and extensive networks. These form an important part of the support structure necessary for the organisation to pursue rights for widows through the judiciary. WHR employs 35 staff members, comprising 11 widows, 18 female staff members who are not widows (described by WHR as non-widows) and 6 male staff members – of whom many are highly educated. [...]

Critical to WHR's capacity to provide SSLMs to widows are the organisation's numerous and wide-ranging connections including "partners", "contributors", advocates and supporters – ranging from large international donor organisations and local Nepali businesses to both Nepali and foreign academics and women's rights advocates. Indeed, the organisation is well funded, thereby providing it with the necessary economic resources to litigate [...] Here we see the importance of a proven funding track record to an NGO's financial resources, which in turn impacts on an organisation's capacity to litigate. As a "repeat player" in terms of both litigation and receiving financial backing, WHR has the capacity to provide the necessary SSLMs to pursue single women's rights causes through the courts.

WHR is also well resourced in terms of the current global discourses on rights, including international law and the various human rights instruments and treaties, and Nepali law with respect to laws pertaining to women. Further, WHR's public acknowledgment of the government's ongoing support highlights the organisation's connections with the upper echelons and power brokers within Nepali society. Given that WHR has long been lobbying the government for change at the policy level – particularly in regard to legislation pertaining to the rights of widows – these connections are not surprising. Lily Thapa (email communication, June 2012) highlighted the importance of such connections, noting: "in our country where there are more influences from political party [sic], it will not be possible without mobilising them that's why we sensitise them a lot on issues".

While WHR mobilises its doctrine of anti-discrimination and improved status of widows through litigation, it also employs a range of other strategies to support this legal action and to achieve changes in attitudes towards widows. These strategies include awareness campaigns through newspaper and magazine articles, books, pamphlets and newsletters, forums and focus group discussions. Since 2001 WHR has conducted national workshops aimed at "institutionalising the concerns and issues of single women" through the narratives of widows from all regions of Nepal. Government officials and media representatives attend these events, thereby significantly increasing the visibility of WHR and the plight of widows in Nepal. WHR also engages in capacity building programs, research studies on the status of widows, regional workshops, workshops relating to access to justice, and organisational development aimed at formulating strategies to identify future work and potential partners. WHR has hosted two international conferences aimed at developing agendas and forums in order to provide a platform for voicing the issues of widows based on international human rights instruments. At the conclusion of the 2010 conference, WHR promulgated its own advocacy tool, "The Kathmandu Declaration", aimed at raising awareness at the government level about the needs of widows. [...]

*Women's Rights at the Local Level*
The NGO that forms the focus of the next case study was a world away from the context of WHR, even though its head office was located only 20 minutes away by taxi. Sangam was relatively unknown within women's development NGO circles and in the wider sector of development in Nepal more generally – to which I had access through friends and acquaintances. Nevertheless, despite its obscurity, Sangam was also "doing development", and successfully so. Yet this NGO operated at a markedly different level from that of WHR. As a volunteer organisation, Sangam worked at the ground level – in the community and social spaces where women live. Sangam focused on the health and nutrition of pregnant women, young children under 3 years of age, and their mothers through its nutrition program. Nevertheless, the "empowerment" of women was a key component of its Kathmandu-based nutrition program and it is this aspect that I will be focusing on. [...]

Within the nutrition program there was a range of different activities running across 11 wards in Kathmandu Metropolitan City, including growth monitoring, awareness programs (one targeting men specifically), volunteer training and savings groups, among others. For this discussion I draw on data collected during home visits, a key activity of the program that entailed Sangam staff members and volunteers visiting the home of a child that had been identified as underweight at a growth monitoring session. Simply providing a family with information about food and nutrition did not always result in an increase in the weight of an undernourished child. Sangam recognised that there was typically a link between the weight of the child and the physical and emotional well-being of the main caregiver, which in most families involved with the NGO was the mother. Sangam described this as the psychosocial situation of a family. During home visits the NGO focused on "listening to women" to find out about the constraints and difficulties that prevented a mother from adequately caring for her child. Developing a trusting relationship with the mother was the central focus, as it was the first step in enabling the mother to open up and express her problems and concerns. It was found that once these difficulties were raised – and, ideally, addressed – by Sangam staff it would then be possible to facilitate the feeding and hygiene of the child. Thus, these visits were a key strategy aimed at empowering women. [...]

Home visits were also a way in which Sangam disseminated rights discourse, although in terms that resonated with the mothers. "Rights talk", in the sense of the overt, global notion of human rights that permeates the language used by WHR, did not feature in these interactions. [...] Rather, talk focused on the local level and the ways in which the situation (i.e. defending or enforcing a particular right) could be resolved using local informal mechanisms such as intra- and inter-family mediation or quasi-judicial forums, which points to the emphasis on local forms of justice. In particular, Sangam strongly promoted the importance of women's citizenship rights during program activities and interactions with women in the community. Many women in Nepal do not have proof of citizenship and remain unaware of its importance and the implications for claiming rights, including access to education, formal sector employment, affordable healthcare, marital property and inheritance. Proof of citizenship is also fundamental to pursuing rights causes through the courts. Sangam staff provided information and practical support to enable women to obtain the necessary paperwork – including a birth certificate (often held by the woman's family in rural areas) and a bank account (by joining Sangam's savings group). Sangam also provided women with access to a female lawyer, which in Epp's terms constitutes one of the support structures necessary for legal engagement, but according to a Sangam staff member, women rarely (or possibly never) accessed this service for fear of the social consequences legal action might bring. As Meena's story below highlights, many women did not consider legal channels to be a tangible option.

Meena was a woman I encountered during home visits with Sangam. Meena's situation could have applied to any number of women living in this community – a middle to low socioeconomic area of inner Kathmandu. Women here appeared to have very limited life choices due to a lack of education and skills, often as a result of poverty and/or early marriage. This story brings to the fore the social and cultural constraints women confront in trying to realise their rights through legal frameworks. Meena was introduced to me at her home as a woman experiencing many difficulties. While this was my first visit to her home with Sangam, Meena had long been interacting with the NGO staff. Meena was the second of three wives – all of whom were married to the same man. While polygamy is illegal in Nepal, it is still widely practised in both urban and rural areas. Meena had a young son with her husband while her husband's 22-year-old son from his first wife was also living with them. Life in the home had deteriorated badly, particularly for Meena. Her husband's son from the first wife regularly beat Meena, but her husband refused to intervene. On numerous occasions Sangam staff had spoken with the husband in an effort to improve the situation, but the husband believed that Meena was deserving of such beatings, describing her to one Sangam staff member as lazy around the house and slack because she did not regularly cook his food on time. Thus, Sangam's intervention at the familial level proved futile in improving Meena's situation.

On the day of our visit Meena was desperate to escape her increasingly difficult situation. Sangam staff talked with Meena about her options, suggesting that she should not tolerate violence. She could get a divorce, she could work outside the home, and now that the laws had changed she would be entitled to a share of her husband's property. Staff recommended a lawyer who would be able to assist Meena, but for Meena, divorce was out of the question. Meena's husband had already threatened that she would never receive anything, including any property, if she divorced him. When Meena had asserted that she had rights in relation to divorce and property, her husband had laughed, telling her that he had good connections within the community to support him and prevent Meena from receiving the property. Even though Meena could choose to engage in legal action against her husband in an effort to enforce her formal right to property, the wider implications prevented her from doing so. As the notion of the "good woman" highlights, a woman's status is in relation to men. Marriage, therefore, is extremely important to a woman's social and economic status. Divorce would mean that she was no longer a "good woman", thereby bringing dishonour to her family and resulting in ostracisation from her family and stigma within the community. Asserting her rights and seeking property through the courts would have a similar effect. Engaging in legal action might also result in further violence and abuse. In addition, Meena was illiterate and lacked skills outside the home, which further limited her options. Without marriage and property, Meena would not have economic security or social standing, thereby rendering her vulnerable to other forms of discrimination.

Meena's story highlights the way in which women's rights in this context are relational – something that women themselves realise. Claiming one right may impact on other rights, in which case it may mean that seeking to enforce a particular right could be counterproductive, even dangerous. Here we see the tension between global rights and norms and beliefs in this context – between the "rights-bearing individual" and the notion of the "good woman". Knowledge of their rights does not necessarily mean that women have the capacity – or the desire, particularly if their claim is in opposition to the norms to which they are subject – to assert those rights. Nevertheless, Meena's story exemplifies the symbolic power of legally enshrined rights – as something to aspire to and to call upon when conflict arises. For instance, you can work outside of the home, you have recourse in domestic violence situations, and you have the right to property and to seek divorce. Thus, justiciable legal frameworks do work at a certain level in this context, even if it is only at an aspirational level, thereby enhancing the effectiveness of promoting women's justice.

## II LEGAL MOBILIZATION TACTICS

The readings in this section further explore legal mobilization tactics. They draw attention to how legal mobilizers devise and implement tactics based on their social positions and relationships, their intended targets, and their comprehension of the sources of power and normative orders operative in their contexts. When a person takes up legal mobilization, whether on their own or in collaboration, they are capable of producing meanings about law, which can morph with each interaction. Hence, legal mobilization scholarship shows that legal (and rights) meanings are plural and contingent. The elite and marginalized, and the powerful and weak, can all partake in legal mobilization and the meaning-making of law.

### 5.2 The Politics of Love in Myanmar: LGBT Mobilization and Human Rights as a Way of Life, *Lynette J. Chua*

We begin with rights adaptation, a common tactic whereby the chosen discourse of rights is unfamiliar to the people whom mobilizers hope to convince or otherwise engage. In her book, *Human Rights and Gender Violence* (2006), Sally Engle Merry describes such adaptation processes as translation and vernacularization. Lynette J. Chua's research on the LGBT rights movement in Myanmar focuses on what Merry might consider to be the grassroots level of adaptation. However, Chua also draws influence from the study of law and emotions, sociology of emotions, and social movement studies to incorporate emotions into her analysis.

> Before LGBT activists can galvanize queer Burmese to fight for human rights together, they have to first empower them. And to do that, they have to change the way queer Burmese feel about themselves, so that they abandon feeling rules built on inferiority, stigmatization, and resignation.
>
> Changing self-understanding entails, first and foremost, making human rights resonate with queer Burmese. Although Aung San Suu Kyi, Myanmar's most famous pro-democracy activist and leader, advocated for human rights in her speeches and writings, ordinary Burmese in Myanmar had little access to human rights discourse during military rule. The movement's founding and recruitment stories in the previous chapter show how human rights activism was suppressed. Before joining the LGBT movement, Pyae Soe had not heard of Aung San Suu Kyi. Nor did he realize what was wrong with the forced portering and labor that he and his family experienced in their village. Those incidents were simply part of their lives, the way things had always been. Tin Hla did not understand the 1988 protests or its aftermath. Most Burmese like him were unfamiliar with, even fearful of, human rights.
>
> But LGBT activists have a rich cultural schema: the suffering of queers and other ordinary Burmese: "Our people know human rights from their suffering .... The human rights concept comes from their lives. It comes from their real life, real suffering" [said Tun Tun, the movement's pioneer]. All through their lives, whether it was suffering caused by family, other people around them, or state actors such as police, queer Burmese have felt pain, fear, and despair. Pyae Soe, Kyaw Kyaw, Aung Aung, and many other LGBT activists have experienced them in their own lives. [...]
>
> To make human rights relevant, LGBT activists evoke the emotional power of suffering. Emotions such as pain, fear, and despair are the antithesis of having human dignity, *lu gone theit khar*, a central tenet of human rights to LGBT activists. Hence, in Tun Tun's words above, Burmese people understand human rights by feeling what it is like to live in their absence. When queer Burmese experience the pangs of suffering, they lose human dignity, robbed by the violations of human rights. Although LGBT activists are informed by the UDHR, such as Article 1's reference to the equal entitlement of human beings to dignity, by "human rights violations," they do not mean claims according to the formal standards of international law. Rather, they

mean human rights offer queers and other Burmese what they are deprived of, which has caused them to feel the emotions of suffering. [...]

Although he was shouting for "human rights" during the 1988 protests, Tun Tun admitted he did not really understand what that meant at the time. After joining the rebel army, in "jungle university" along the Myanmar-Thailand border, he came across a UDHR booklet donated by an international organization to their camp library. "I started reading [the booklet] and compared it with the life in Burma. We don't have human rights, but we have violations of human rights [laughs]!"

While LGBT activists do not delve into major events of political oppression at every workshop, they usually encourage participants to share their encounters with oppression to summon the emotional power of suffering. At one workshop, Pyae Soe asked, "What are your experiences?" In response, the participants talked about feeling "pressed down" – being beaten, disinherited, or kicked out of the house by family elders, bullying, verbal harassment, police abuse, expulsion from school, and dismissal from work – personal stories reflecting the grievances of queer Burmese described earlier. Sometimes they watch a movie before sharing their stories. The movies, such as *The Wedding Banquet*, *Happy Together*, *Stonewall Inn*, and *Boys Don't Cry*, are not Burmese, but the participants see past their ostensible foreignness to find similarity in the prejudices that the characters encountered. In addition, since their first celebration in 2009 in Ranong [Thailand], LGBT activists recount the discrimination and violence that queer Burmese face as part of their IDAHO celebrations. Usually they screen a video or give speeches that deliver a message to such effect. At IDAHO 2016, for instance, one activist told the audience about a gay student who "committed suicide because of discrimination from his family and school." A lesbian followed to tell her story: her parents sent her to a mental institution because they disapproved of her same-sex relationship.

Having evoked the emotional power of suffering, associating queer suffering with the absence of dignity, and construing it as the result of human rights violations, LGBT activists ask these fellow Burmese to imagine the opposite: what enjoying dignity and thus human rights would feel like when they are free from the pain of abuse, feel safe, and experience joy and happiness. Pyae Soe and other activists link the stories that workshop participants share to the UDHR (and sometimes the Yogyakarta Principles) to explain what it entails to have human rights. They take participants through the clauses in these international documents, which provide for rights to equality, life, personal security, fair trial, and education and illustrate them with relevant grievances mentioned in participants' stories. For example, they say, being detained under the Police Act just because they are *apwint* is a violation of "the right to life, liberty and security of person" under Article 3 of the UDHR.

*From Shame to Blame: Shedding Negative Feeling Rules*
By characterizing their suffering as human rights violations, LGBT activists try to help queer Burmese shed negative feeling rules, another necessary step to transform self-understanding. Steeped in stigmatization, feelings of inferiority, and resignation, negative feeling rules breed self-hatred, shame, and fear of being queer. Therefore, LGBT activists urge queer Burmese to jettison the internalized beliefs about karma to which Yamin referred earlier – that is, people are reborn queer due to bad karma from past lives and are expected to endure ill treatment and low social status. They remind them that prejudicial norms, state laws, authorities who abuse power, and other social actors are to blame for the pain, fear, and despair they feel. Their suffering should not be accepted or explained away on the basis of bad karma, for they are the fault of these other people and conditions, which violate their rights and human dignity.

LGBT activists explain that queers deserve human rights, just like everyone else. They again call upon human rights' promise of dignity. They point to human rights documents, such as the UDHR and Yogyakarta Principles, to persuade queer Burmese they are not inferior but are worthy of human dignity, regardless of their sexuality or gender and regardless of their past. In workshops and interviews, activists ranging from long-time VIVID leaders to new grassroots organizers consistently stress that LGBT rights are the same as human rights and that they are asking for the same treatment.

The appreciation of human dignity – and thus human rights – by LGBT activists contains the meaning of a transformed sense of self as someone as deserving as other human beings. Chan Thar, like many others who recounted their experiences to me, described his amazement and wonder: "I felt like I was in a foreign country, seeing all the new things .... It was like when I went to Bangkok and saw the MBK shopping center. 'Whoa, it really exists!' That kind of feeling." He could not believe it when he first learned about human rights at VIVID's workshops. He remembered breaking down and crying as he rejoiced that he, a queer person, was entitled to human rights.

It would be easy to read LGBT activists' interpretation as a demand for the rights of LGBT persons to be recognized as human rights, akin to the efforts of international activists in the early 1990s. However, I find that it carries the much more significant meaning that queer people are equally deserving of rights. This meaning cannot be taken for granted in the Burmese context, for

> LGBT activists have to counter entrenched beliefs about karma and the related views on social hierarchy. I was particularly struck by the observations and interviews that contain statements along the following lines. At the movement meeting before IDAHO 2013, Tun Tun asked grassroots organizers how they would explain to local media the slogan for the event, "LGBT Rights Are Human Rights." Gyo Kyar, one of the earliest grassroots organizers, stood up and said, "We are all human beings, so there should not be discrimination of LGBT people." When asked what he had learned about human rights, Min Min, a grassroots organizer who joined in 2013–2014, answered, "We are equal like other human beings. And we being like this doesn't mean that we are lower than other people."

### 5.3 Labour Law and (In)justice in Workers' Letters in Vietnam, Tu Phuong Nguyen

Nguyen's analysis of letters written by Vietnamese factory workers documents a form of legal mobilization known as "rightful resistance." First coined by O'Brien and Li (2006), "rightful resistance" refers to a type of mobilization that is individual or uncoordinated, and noisier and more confrontational than everyday resistance yet short of rebellion. It "entails the innovative use of laws, policies, and other officially promoted values to defy disloyal political and economic elites; it is a kind of partially sanctioned protest that uses influential allies and recognized principles to apply pressure on those in power who have failed to live up to a professed ideal or who have not implemented some beneficial measure" (O'Brien and Li 2006:2–3). In the letters analyzed by Nguyen, the workers complained about their employers' illegal conduct and held the government accountable for their plight, appealing to labor rights legislation as well as the communist party's representation of itself as the vanguard of equality and progress.

> I had a chance to know Mrs Nguyên thanks to her engagement in a legal-aid project, previously funded by Oxfam. With assistance from a labour lawyer, Nguyên managed to compose a complaint letter and appeal directly to the labour inspector against her management's illegal conduct. Despite facing a labour institution that has been notoriously skewed against workers' interests, the

legal knowledge she has gained [from legal aid workers] confirmed her conviction that her struggle was legitimate and that her demands should, by law, be met. It is not surprising that her letter is dense with evidence and legal accusations against the company's misconduct, and argues straightforwardly for a proper enforcement of labour law. Below is a substantial portion of her accusations:

> According to the legal regulations, the company has to raise wages for employees every year. We have worked here for many years but our wage has been raised only once from 1.67 to 2.01 [the wage level]. This will affect employees' rights and interests when we retire. We raised our question but the company said that, if we wanted to have a wage increase, we had to take a skill examination to show that we can make a certain quantity of clothes in a certain time. ... Such conduct is *against the law*, as the company is evading its responsibility to employees [author's italics].

The reference to "rights and interests" constitutes both legal and moral claims. Legally, the pensions that workers receive each month must be calculated based on their basic wage at the time of their employment, and therefore a low basic wage would later allow for little retirement benefit. Yet it also implicates a moral obligation of employers, derived from their legal responsibility, to ensure employees' welfare and livelihoods. The way Nguyên framed her argument demonstrates an awareness not just of workers' legal benefits, which have been infringed upon by the management, but also of the longer-term ethical consequences borne by the workers.

In 2015, Nguyên also sent a hand-written letter to the provincial authorities, in which she evoked the Communist Party's rhetoric, its moral authority, and its campaigns concerning cadres' conduct. The language and sentiment expressed in her personally composed letter are different from the predominantly legalistic language in her previous complaint letter. It seems that, when legal reasoning was exhausted to no avail, she decided to opt for an emotional appeal to justice. Nguyên herself is not a Communist Party member, yet she derived her judgement from the party's political campaigns that she believed have established the grounds for one's legal and moral behaviour. I shall hereby quote the letter in full to do justice to its extraordinary nature:

> During this time, all citizens and party members across the country, including Đồng Nai province, are following the law, self-educating and self-training according to the moral lessons of Hồ Chí Minh, in order to make certain achievements ahead of the Party Congresses at the local levels. Unfortunately, there is an enterprise that violates the law, despite

being awarded the title "hero in the reform era" and having a party cell. Within the party cell, there are party cadres that have verbally abused and humiliated employees. Yet those cadres are always nominated reward and are holding the positions of the union chairman or vice chairman in the company. So, who will demand equality and legitimate rights and interests for employees?

Once more, with all respect, I urge the leaders of all state agencies of Đồng Nai province to promptly intervene to save our lives. We are genuine employees who have no rights, lack equality, but experience a lot of coercion by the business.

Because of the wish to demand fair rights and interests for employees, I have sent my petition letters, which have been handled by the state authorities and especially the labour inspectorate. However, those cadres only addressed my complaints in a cosmetic manner and protected the business; they also forced me to sign a meeting memo in which I have to confirm that I will stop sending my complaints and denunciations. Such command has given grounds for the company to punish and repress me in a brutal manner.

I am wondering if there is no justice or equality in our lives, in our society. I guess that I might remain in agony and pushed to my death before my letters are resolved.

As mentioned at the start of the article, Nguyên's letter bears resemblance to the type of rightful claims made by aggrieved citizens in China, who mobilize official discourse and legal institutions in a hope to curb the power of corrupt and abusive elites. Nguyên arrived at her plea by extensively drawing upon political rhetoric, which has been ironically betrayed by the people who are supposed to act upon its principles, given their position and status. Her sorrowful claim that employees "have no rights" while experiencing "a lot of coercion" implies a breach of both ethical and legal standards on the part of the business and, indirectly, of the state, for condoning the business's conduct. She does not just draw on extra-legal claims in a tactical way to justify the authority's attention, facilitate their intervention, or push the state to deliver legal justice, as has been the case with the American citizens who wrote to the Department of Justice in the Depression era. She also draws upon these claims because she has faith in the values underpinning them and conveys a hope that her letter might ultimately reach a good-hearted official.

As such, despite the legally adept complaint language in the type-written complaint letter, her appeal to justice overall is not so different from that of other letter writers: she also holds the state authorities accountable for the workers' plight and stretches the boundary of law and legal rights to push for

# Legal Mobilization

an honouring of workplace ethics. More importantly, in connecting workers' grievances to (the lack of) justice and equality "in our society," Nguyên has eloquently wedded her aspiration for workplace ethics to the fundamentals of the Vietnamese state's socialist vision of equality and progress.

## 5.4 Pragmatic Resistance, Law, and Social Movements in Authoritarian States: The Case of Gay Collective Action in Singapore, *Lynette J. Chua*

Chua's study of gay rights activists in Singapore uncovers legal mobilization tactics that she describes as "pragmatic resistance." These tactics partially resemble the everyday resistance of individuals (Scott 1984) – who hide their intention to challenge the dominant power – but, unlike Mrs. Nguyên's lone petition, are coordinated and collectively performed. Through in-depth interviews with activists, observations of movement activities, and analysis of movement-related documents, media reports, and government statements, Chua shows how pragmatic resistance disguises the activists' intention of challenging state power directly, avoids coming across to state actors as confrontational or threatening, and settles for small, creeping gains.

Because gay activists in Singapore start out with repressive conditions that limit civil-political liberties, they initially adapt their strategy away from tactics that are public, overt and confrontational. Then they go through [a cycle] with each subsequent tactic, refining and improving their [strategic] dance. Even though this dance resists and challenges power, it is a pragmatic one with features that resemble everyday resistance. It has an eye on survival, and avoids direct confrontation with the state, or being seen as a threat to existing arrangements of power. Most of the time, these activists focus on immediate gains that change practice and informal policies, but not formal laws and regulations. On the rare occasions when they do seek legal reform, they also perform pragmatic resistance. The goal is to stay alive and advance with skirmishes, rather than court demise with open warfare declared on grander principles. Hence, whilst they fight the battle to improve conditions for gays in Singapore, they do not wage war for greater rights and democracy. With each tactical performance, they vary the dance a little to advance the movement, but do not transform it into a completely different dance altogether.

Dancing pragmatic resistance, thus, entails striking a balance between "pushing boundaries," and "toeing the line," terms that activists use to describe their tactics. Imagine the two as overlapping forces pulling in opposite directions. The challenge is to stay within the area where the two forces overlap. Boundary pushing expands the cultural norms to accommodate more challenges of authority and possibilities of achieving change, whereas line toeing adheres to the limits of those norms to ensure the movement's survival. Toeing the line too much will achieve little progress, whereas pushing too aggressively on the other end may provoke state retaliation.

To strike this balance, gay activists execute a dance repertoire of moves that weave legal restrictions and cultural norms together. They obey the law so as to play to the norm of legal legitimacy; they get around legal restrictions to bring their actions beyond the law's reach, and thus avoid transgression. Or, they deliberately make use of legal restrictions and procedures, a move that plays to legal legitimacy, and enables them to do what they want within law's confines. They tend to focus on specific decisions or immediate issues, and thus avoid publicly questioning the larger order, or the repressive laws that curtail civil-political liberties. This plays to the norm of nonconfrontation, and preservation of the ruling party's monopoly. But when they do ask for legal reform, they usually downplay confrontation, and play up other norms, particularly social stability. Adherence to the law is an important move, but it is not the sole determinant of finding balance. These activists understand the state to tolerate some rule bending, even contraventions. As a whole, so long as their tactics do not threaten the appearance of hegemonic control, the state tolerates them, and reciprocates by dancing to the socially constructed understandings of pragmatic resistance as well. [...]

[Chua goes on to analyze pragmatic resistance tactics from the early days of the movement up to more recent times, exemplified by Pink Dot below.]

Since the year 2000, as part of the state's effort to contain dissent, public speaking at Hong Lim Park's "Speakers' Corner" has been exempted from license application. In September 2008, the legislature extended the exemption from public speaking to cover "performances" and "exhibitions." The news caught [gay rights activist] Nelson's attention: why not hold a gay pride parade at the park? After rounds of debates, Pink Dot was born. Unlike the pride parades familiar to San Francisco, London, and Sydney, nevertheless, Pink Dot did not march down public streets but confined itself to the exempted park. People wearing shades of pink gathered to picnic, enjoy musical performances, and form a "pink dot" in the center of the park. From a hotel with a vantage point, photographers captured the formation on film, and organizers circulated the videos and photos online. In 2009, about 2,500 gay and straight people participated. In 2010, 2011 and 2012, it was reprised with an estimated crowd of 4000, 10 000, and 15 000 respectively.

# Legal Mobilization

Pink Dot's men and women play to, and earn the event cultural legitimacy by intentionally confining it to the exempted park, and following legal conditions. By obeying the law, they make use of it to push the boundaries of the norm against confrontation. Before Pink Dot, an affirmative, public gathering of gay people was perceived to be transgressive. Pink Dot organizers, as Winston points out, recognize the tokenism of Hong Lim Park, but they creatively use it to nudge the boundaries outward.

> [Hong Lim Park's] about restricting the space available for free speech to this tiny corner. So in conceptualizing Pink Dot, we wanted to reverse all that. We wanted to do something that was in a way visually stunning, so that it breaks out of the confines of that space, something that's memorable, something that's in a way iconic.
> (Interview, Winston, 30s, public school administrator, Singapore, June 2009)

Meanwhile, they play to the norm of social stability to deflect negative reactions from the state and the counter movement. Neither portraying Pink Dot as a demonstration, nor using it as a platform to demand for rights, they toe the line by minimizing perceptions of outright confrontation. Further, they carefully craft a publicity campaign to convey the message that acceptance of diverse sexualities strengthens rather than polarizes society, and to avoid potential accusations by opponents that they impose Western values. For example, they circulated promotional videos on the Internet featuring local celebrities who identify as straight. They also crucially reinterpreted the meaning of the color pink. Instead of making the color's symbolic connection to discrimination or gay pride, they link it to a localized notion of diversity through the idea of pink as the product of mixing Singapore's national flag colors of red and white. They then point out that the color – the result of accepting diversity – is already part of what it means to be Singaporean, as it is also the color of identity cards issued only to citizens.

## 5.5 Performing Artivism: Feminists, Lawyers, and Online Legal Mobilization in China, *Di Wang and Sida Liu*

Compared to the more cautious and restrained acts of pragmatic resistance, Wang and Liu demonstrate that legal mobilization can be confrontational and performative in the face of severe threats of repression. Drawing from Erving Goffman's theater metaphor and Judith Butler's theory of subversive disruption, Wang and Liu analyze how "artivists" perform conspicuous spectacles on the "front stage," in the public eye to expose the Chinese state's illegal or repressive backstage actions, or to promote values and norms alternative to the official ideology. Simultaneously, with their savvy use of social media, artivists take advantage of the temporal delays of censorship to spread their messages virally and create an Internet trail, which is impossible to expunge completely. As a result, artivists gain access to the front stage, usually monopolized by the authoritarian regime, to generate opportunities for social change. In their study, Wang and Liu compare the artivism of feminists and lawyers. Feminists, who are younger, less politically connected, and thus more vulnerable to state repression, enjoy less access to the courts and start with street protests. By contrast, lawyers begin in the formal legal system and then move onto the streets in their mobilization.

*Performing Feminist Artivism: From Silent Performers to Disruptive Audiences*
In the most widely shared "Bloody Bride" image, there were three young feminist activists wearing blood-spattered wedding dresses, holding signs with anti-domestic violence slogans, and looking determinedly into the distance. In the grey and red-themed background was Qianmen Street, a busy commercial street and popular tourist site in downtown Beijing, less than a mile from Tiananmen Square. This "Bloody Bride" image not only showed that violence could happen in any intimate partnership but also that young Chinese women were "marching" to combat it. The action attracted national and international media attention and marked the collective coming out of this new generation of Chinese feminist activists. Other examples of similar actions include the "Bald Girl" action for equality in higher education in 2012; the "Occupy Men's Restroom" action for equal public facility distribution from 2012 to 2016; and the "Homophobia Kills Lesbians" action against sexuality-based violence in 2013. By shaving one's own hair in public, taking over men's restrooms, and kissing each other in public all around Beijing, these young feminist activists challenged normalized gender inequality and made their demands visible to the public by producing viral online images.

While the streets were their primary battlegrounds, feminist activists also extended artivism to the courthouse. One high-profile legal case that they supported was the Li Yan case, in which the defendant Li Yan was initially sentenced to death for killing her husband after suffering years of his violence and abuse. In 2013, when the Supreme People's Court reviewed and approved Li Yan's death penalty, Chinese feminist activists and lawyers petitioned the courts and hosted online discussions to draw national and international attention to the case and demand for the suspension of Li's death penalty. On February 3, 2013, echoing these demands, feminist activists wrapped themselves with white cloth and laid down in front of courthouses across China, with a sign "I don't want to become the next Li Yan". These images highlighted both the imminence of Li's execution and the possibility that, under the current legal system, every woman could end up in her situation.

These feminist activist actions visualized the argument that Li Yan's case was a consequence of a flawed legal system that first failed to intervene in domestic violence cases and then punished women for fighting back against their abusers. According to the ADVN, from 2009 to 2012, the media had reported forty-eight cases similar to Li Yan's situation, and only twenty-eight of them were reported with details on their sentences, and 64 percent of these defendants were sentenced severely, ranging from ten years of imprisonment to the death penalty. Like many of these women, Li Yan also sought support from the local police and the ACWF's local branch but did not get any effective state intervention. As her lawyer told the New York Times, when Li Yan asked for support, they advised her to simply "bear it (*rennai*)."

Although feminist activists have no access to the judicial decision-making process on the backstage (compare with activist lawyers, discussed in the next section), their artivism spotlighted the life-threatening consequences of the lack of legal protection for domestic violence survivors in China. By laying outside courthouses and symbolizing the imminent death of Li Yan with cloth-wrapped bodies, feminists disrupted the state's frontstage performance by unveiling the social reality outside of many people's evidential boundary – that is, domestic violence survivors are systematically constrained by law and social norms in China. The visual contrast between the majesty of the courthouse and the precarious condition of Li Yan questions whether the Chinese legal system can deliver justice when handling domestic violence cases. As a participant of the feminist action in Guangzhou told a reporter, "in a society where a victim cannot receive effective assistance, Li Yan is worthy of [our] sympathy. Li Yan's death sentence is not only a tragedy for all domestic violence victims, but also a tragedy for this society due to its absence of relevant law." [...]

*Performing Lawyer Artivism: From Courtroom Warriors to Online Activists*
[...] In both the Li Zhuang case [high-profile trial of a lawyer for criminal perjury] and a few subsequent cases in 2011–12, the courtroom was the main site of lawyers' artivism. Li Zhuang's first trial in 2009–10 was highly dramatic because Li was not only defiant in his self-defense throughout the case but also

used a "hidden poem" (*cang tou shi*), a literary legacy of Imperial China, in one of his final statements in court to send out the message that the Chongqing authorities had forced him to confess. In this six-sentence statement, the first and last Chinese characters of each sentence formed the anagram: "[I was] forced to admit guilt to get probation, once released [I would] firmly appeal" (*Beibi renzui huanxing, chuqu jianjue shensu*). Although Li was still sentenced to eighteen months in prison in 2010, the courtroom drama generated nationwide attention on his case and marked the beginning of lawyers' use of artivism to fight against procedural illegality and other abuse of state power in the judicial process. Such courtroom drama is a good example of subversive disruption as it exposed the state's backstage actions in front of the public eye and forced the state to adjust its performance.

Soon after the trial of Li Zhuang was concluded in 2011, some activist lawyers began to use Weibo to organize "lawyer groups" (*lüshi tuan*) to collectively and vigorously defend lawyer colleagues and other criminal defendants – they labeled themselves "die-hard lawyers" (*sike lüshi*) because of their stubbornness over legal procedure and courage to challenge the state authorities. In the Xiaohe case in 2012, for instance, four die-hard lawyers had heated arguments with judges and were expelled from the courtroom. One of them, Chi Susheng, had diabetes, and she fainted on the way out. Thanks to Chi's status as a representative of the National People's Congress (NPC) and the dramatization of her fainting by her lawyer colleagues on Weibo, the incident generated an online uproar and led to a five-month-long trial suspension. In both of these examples, courtroom drama was only effective when it was combined with the surrounding gaze on social media. Indeed, the formation of die-hard lawyer groups was made possible through Weibo. In the Beihai case in June 2011, in which four lawyers were detained by the local police, the activist lawyer Yang Jinzhu posted the case materials on Weibo and called for the formation of a lawyer group to go to Beihai, a remote city in southwest China. A week later, six lawyers flew to Beihai from Beijing, Shandong, and Yunnan to assist the detained lawyers. The total number of lawyers joining the group reached thirteen by mid-July, and many of them had never met in person and only got connected through their interactions on Weibo. Facing the increasing surrounding gaze online, the Beihai police released three of the four lawyers soon afterwards. [...]

The primary site of artivism for die-hard lawyers soon shifted from inside the courthouse to the outside. While lawyers must follow legal procedures and professional etiquette in the courtroom, their code of conduct on the streets becomes similar to that of feminist activists. [...]

One of the most creative performances by die-hard lawyers was made by Yang Jinzhu and Li Jinxing, the lawyer who was taken to the hospital during the Beihai case. In January 2013, Yang and Li were retained by the family members of a criminal defendant who had been detained for twelve years without a judicial sentence and asked to represent him in his second trial at Fujian Provincial People's High Court. However, the court did not permit the defendant to change his legal counsel and refused to accept Yang's and Li's letters of attorney. In response, Yang and Li bought some sweet potatoes from a grocery store, put on their lawyers' gowns, and began to march around the courthouse carrying the sweet potatoes. The idea originated from an old Chinese saying: "If an official did not deliver justice for the people, he'd better go home to sell sweet potatoes" (*Dangguan buwei min zuozhu, buru huijia mai hongshu*). A few hours after photos of their march were posted on Weibo, the court invited them in and approved their representation of the defendant. The conspicuous spectacle of lawyers marching in gowns carrying sweet potatoes, as well as the strategic combination of street and web theaters, worked brilliantly in this case as a means to expose the illegality of backstage judicial behavior.

### 5.6 Litigation Dilemmas: Lessons from the Marcos Human Rights Class Action, Nate Ela

Domestic activists sometimes build alliances with international NGOs or foreign governments to create a boomerang effect (Keck and Sikkink 1998), such that the international entity or foreign government would apply pressure on their political leaders (see, for example, Tsutsui 2017). It is uncertain, though, whether external pressure can move a recalcitrant state, or a totalitarian and isolated regime such as North Korea (Yeo and Chubb 2018). In Nate Ela's study, activists filed a class action lawsuit under the American Alien Tort Statute (ATS) against former Philippine president Ferdinand Marcos for human rights abuses. Marcos was living in the United States after he was ousted from power in the Philippines. Ela, therefore, examines the tactic of litigation. By conducting and analyzing in-depth interviews with litigants and lawyers, Ela discerns three types of litigation dilemmas that troubled anti-Marcos activists – participation, representation, and settlement – and shows that legal mobilizers who share the same cause are not a monolithic group but experience internal contestations and divisions. The excerpt below covers the first dilemma, participation.

In March 1986, the People Power Revolution ousted Ferdinand Marcos from the Philippine presidency. Robert Swift, a partner in a Philadelphia plaintiff-side class action firm, read the news in the New York Times. Marcos had fled to Hawaii, and when Swift learned of the abuses that had occurred under the Marcos regime – thousands of dissidents reportedly detained, tortured, and disappeared during a period of martial law that lasted from 1972 to 1981 – he realized it might be possible to use the ATS to build a mass tort class action. He bought a ticket to Manila.

Before Swift's arrival, anti-Marcos activists had not heard of the ATS, or contemplated suing Marcos in a US court. This changed when Swift met with board members of SELDA, a social movement organization that advocated for martial law detainees and victims. Although established in 1985, SELDA had become active only since the fall of Marcos. Its founding members included former political detainees – prominent journalists, labor leaders, and dissidents. [...]

These activists had to decide whether to help Swift build a case and continue the struggle against Marcos in a US court. SELDA leaders appreciated that either filing a case, or not doing so, involved risks. The respondents who were involved with SELDA's decision making told me that they did not expect to win. Several described the case as *suntok sa buwan* – an expression that roughly translates as "shooting the moon."

Jovelyn, a longtime SELDA leader who was familiar with the board's deliberations, told me that winning economic damages was not the priority:

> The board very clearly stated to [Swift] that the objective was for the Filipino nation and the world to know that Marcos really violated the rights of Filipinos during martial law . . . . We wanted a documentation of these violations because to our minds there really was no systematic documentation, and the government's attitude was for us to forget – forget about the brilliant struggle, the shining struggle of the Filipinos.

Rizal, a friend of several board members, put it more frankly. The case was "primarily for propaganda," he told me, adding that many activists "did not expect that they would win the case or that they would get anything. Some people took it as a joke . . . . It's more put it on record, preserve the evidence for propaganda purposes." The lawsuit was not only a propaganda mission, of course; multiple appeals and three separate jury trials – addressing liability, compensatory damages, and punitive damages – confirmed its firm legal and factual bases.

SELDA's board members, like the pay equity activists described by [Michael] McCann, were not "duped by either myopic lawyers or the liberal myth of rights." To the contrary, their use of litigation was politically sophisticated. They saw it as a way to "win through losing" – using a sure-loser case to score symbolic and political points.

SELDA's leaders, part of a movement with a strong critique of US imperialism, recognized the incongruity of this approach. "To us it was ironic that we would be filing the case in the US," Jovelyn recalled. Yet she also felt it was "savvy," since a case could not have been filed in the Philippines. Rizal felt more strongly. "It offends my sense of national pride to go to an American court," he told me. "Why should we go there for court? The thing is to fight for rectifying the justice system in this country. This is really a mess, but we have to do it – in our country, through our efforts."

Seeking monetary compensation was also problematic. "We were aware that Swift was in this for the money," Jovelyn said, "and the board members thought, that, you know, the money thing was not in complete coalition with the objectives that our board members have." They decided to think of the money as "just a bonus." But the notion of such a bonus troubled Rizal. "We were not fighting for ourselves," he told me. "We were not fighting for material gains. And so I don't feel nice about being personally compensated."

SELDA's board ultimately chose to help Swift build a case. But Jovelyn's and Rizal's accounts illustrate how SELDA leaders grappled with a dilemma. If they did not litigate, they risked losing out on opportunities to shape the historic record and tell their story through the media – propaganda opportunities. But by filing suit in the United States, they risked appearing to be mercenaries rather than freedom fighters, and passing on a chance to push for reform in the Philippine justice system. ATS litigation offered an opportunity to continue the struggle, but at least some activists saw potential downsides to its boomerang effects. Nevertheless, the opportunities afforded by litigation, despite expectations the case would lose, appear to have convinced SELDA's leaders to work with Swift.

SELDA's decision making suggests why activists might tend to resolve the participation dilemma by deciding to litigate. The litigation process creates opportunities to advance the interests of social movement activists, at least in the short run, even if in the long run the case seems likely to be lost. [...] Although nothing compels activists to file an ATS case, one can see why leaders of an organization like SELDA could feel pulled toward doing so.

> This aligns, at least in part, with how McCann dismisses the "lure of litigation" proposition. McCann describes this as the idea that "reformers beguiled by the liberal myth of rights ... tend to undermine their own efforts through reliance on lawyers and litigation." Based on his study of the pay equity movement, McCann argues that litigation is less likely to produce setbacks when movement activists and cause lawyers see it as just one tactic among many. Extending McCann's approach to a transnational context, [Cheryl] Holzmeyer argues that we should see activists' use of the ATS in a similar light: rather than being beguiled by human rights, activists use the ATS strategically, to make possible other pressure tactics.
>   SELDA's experience confirms that litigation can be alluring. However, it is not necessarily the myth of rights that lures radical activists into filing suit. The political possibilities offered by pursuing an ATS claim can themselves be quite beguiling. Opportunities to score symbolic points can convince sophisticated activists to file a case, even when they appreciate the risks involved in doing so.

## III LEGAL MOBILIZATION EFFECTS

Law and society research finds that the effects of rights mobilization are equivocal and varied. The overall takeaway is perhaps the idea that rights are paradoxical (McCann 2014; Chua 2022). Rights can vindicate and empower the oppressed, but they can also fail to protect them, and even disempower or disillusion those who look to rights for protection. In this section, we read selections that illustrate different degrees to which rights mobilization have produced positive and negative outcomes.

At the heart of law and society's debate over the efficacy of legal mobilization is a methodological issue. How a scholar approaches the study of legal mobilization and their consequences is deeply connected to how one conceptualizes the power of law. In the classic "rights debate," based on legal mobilization research informed by the American experience, "myth of rights" proponents argue that rights fail to live up to their promises of vindicating wrongs and preventing rights-offending behavior. Rosenberg (2008), in his well-known study of landmark US Supreme Court decisions, contends that major court verdicts did not bring about social change, not without the intervention of the legislature and administration. Rosenberg's position is based on the instrumental might of rights and explores whether rights can achieve tangible wins, such as damages and the prohibition or compulsion of actions.

For Asian law and society research, we suggest additional considerations for the downside of legal mobilization. Fieldwork by some scholars demonstrates that rights do not necessarily resonate with local populations. Consequently, NGOs or activists may find that rights lack efficacy if they try to encourage local populations to redress their grievances by making rights claims (see, e.g., Engel 2012). Others caution that rights mobilization attracts retaliation from the state or other powerful opponents. Or, they conclude that appealing to rights, especially when it involves adaptations to suit local norms, ends up pandering to the status quo and causing a movement or challenger to lose their transformative edge. Several earlier readings in this chapter – Becker on Nepalese women's rights organizations, Wang and Liu on Chinese artivists, and Ela on the anti-Marcos litigation – offer glimpses into these potential problems. Still other scholars are drawn to arguments of Third-World Approaches to International Law (TWAIL). According to TWAIL scholars, (human) rights are another form of imperialism that exacerbates unequal distribution of power. They point out that international NGOs and funders from the Global North require good governance in order for their economic assistance to be implemented properly, and impose requirements in the guise of human rights projects to prescribe top-down changes to the recipient country's legal and political institutions, with little regard for local contexts and alternatives.

On the other side of the classic rights debate, legal mobilization scholars account for the symbolic power of rights, which we discussed in Section I. In this broader view, rights as social practices have not only instrumental value but also the ability to fashion cultural changes – alter the way people understand their social interactions, who they are, and their place in society, motivate the marginalized to speak out, bring people together, and inspire collective action. Cultural changes can be imperceptible, taking place quietly person by person, but they can snowball and cumulate bigger consequences for the future. We saw hints of such possibilities in the readings by Chua on pragmatic resistance and Becker on Nepalese women's rights activists.

The differences in law and society research on the effects – both positive and negative – of legal mobilization could be due to the theoretical orientation of the scholar and what appeals to the scholar (for example, is the scholar an optimist who sees a glass of water as half-full or a pessimist who sees the glass as half-empty?), but they are also due to the empirical context, the research design, and the data. Context matters deeply in all law and society research, of course, and definitely so for rights mobilization. In response to criticisms that rights are too moderate and play within existing arrangements of social relations, as Chua (2019) noted on the Burmese LGBT rights movement, whether or not rights mobilization is radical depends on the context, in that case, Myanmar: "While it is not radical in the revolutionary sense of toppling regimes or eradicating structures, it challenges deeply rooted beliefs and the social hierarchy and organization of relations founded on them" (142).

The following four readings illustrate the divergent effects of legal mobilization and engage with the paradox of rights to varying degrees. We start with readings that present critical views and move toward those that project more sanguine outlooks.

### 5.7 Indigeneity and Legal Pluralism in India: Claims, Histories, Meanings, *Pooja Parmar*

Parmar's ethnography examines the protracted dispute over a Coca-Cola plant on the lands of the indigenous Adivasis in India. The Adivasis played a prominent role in initiating and sustaining protests against Coca-Cola. Other parties, including non-Adivasi activists and lawyers, joined the resistance subsequently and organized litigation against the company. In the excerpt below, Parmar scrutinizes the effects of litigation on the Adivasis to discover that they had disappeared from the formal legal narratives, and that the lawsuits excluded their most pressing claims of tribal rights.

> The legal issues identified by all the lawyers I spoke with relate to the conflicting positions of Coca-Cola and Perumatty Panchayat over the use of groundwater for the company's operations, and involve the question of whether and to what extent the decision of the Kerala High Court undermines a panchayat's ability to make decisions at the local level. For most the central legal issue that needs to be decided by the Supreme Court is the role and powers of a panchayat in the decentralized system of governance envisaged under Part IX of the Constitution of India, in general, and the Kerala Panchayat Raj Act, in particular. Related questions, emphasized to varying degrees by each of them, are those of determination of rights over groundwater and environmental pollution. Resolution of these issues and questions calls for a definitive interpretation of constitutional guarantees, property rights, and the various statutes invoked by all parties to the litigation. The energies of the lawyers are therefore focused on presenting the best arguments based on legal enactments and precedents in support of the respective positions of their

# Legal Mobilization

clients, that is the Perumatty Grama Panchayat, Local Self-Governance Department, Kerala Pollution Control Board, state of Kerala, NGOs, individually named activists, and a farmers' organization. [...]

Raising complex questions of dispossession, displacement, and legal and social processes through which Adivasis have been impoverished, when [...] the law does not often recognize these as violations, cannot be sound litigation strategy. Even though related, the "social" and the "legal" thus remain external to each other. The "social" presents the dispute but does not determine the "questions of law," which are determined by and in the language of the law that requires the translation of the specific into abstract. The legal violations are named and framed by the law. Thus framed, the questions are also then determined by applying the law. There is no room here for the complex issues invoked by the expression "tribal rights." Issues and questions that a court cannot recognize are considered best left out. [...]

In Kerala, as in other parts of the country, the most important issue that Adivasis continue to face is that of dispossession and displacement. And yet the lawyer, who acknowledged during our conversation that the Adivasis in Plachimada are concerned over the protection of their traditional sources of water, thinks it prudent to not raise such questions of "tribal rights" in the Supreme Court. Precedents like *State of Kerala v. PUCL* show that reliance on tribal rights to land or arguments based on Adivasi connections to their traditional lands stand no chance when weighed against statutes. The state law does not recognize any tribal right to maintain connections to traditional lands in perpetuity. In a situation where those lands are required for national progress and development, such tribal rights do not, as the lawyer pointed out, "cut much ice."

The violation experienced by Adivasis in places like Plachimada, when recognized, creates issues that require questions of law and justice to be framed differently than they currently are. The "tribal question" cannot be successfully translated into familiar "questions of law" for courts. The kind of translation that the Adivasi accounts call for – the practice of "hearing-to-respond," the recognition of the limits of the existing legal language and processes, and the courage to commit to a different vision of the future – is not common. Unfamiliar and messy questions that are inseparable from long and complicated histories of social, economic, and political exclusion offer neither the comfort nor the stability of the familiar categories and narratives of law. For the lawyers, greater possibility of success therefore, lies in translating claims into a language the court can recognize and respond to, that is, in formulating arguments that can be grounded in existing statutes and legal categories of harm, not in the realm of tribal rights. This is especially so when these rights seem to be diverging from the currently imagined future of the nation.

### 5.8 The Paradox of Vernacularization: Women's Human Rights and the Gendering of Nationhood, *Sealing Cheng*

Building on Merry's (2006) idea of vernacularization, Sealing Cheng traces the adaptation of international norms about human trafficking and women's human rights in South Korea, and finds that American diplomatic maneuvers, the South Korean state, and the South Korean women's movement have conflated human trafficking with sex trafficking and narrowed anti-trafficking concerns down to prostitution. Although efforts to localize women's human rights in anti-prostitution reforms may challenge the state and propel reforms, Cheng argues that they may also corroborate state nation-building and reinforce a statist notion of national culture and womanhood.

Through her case studies of the translation of human rights ideas in campaigns against violence against women in such diverse sites as Fiji, India, and Hong Kong, Merry found that vernacularization of the rights framework challenges deep-seated ideas of gender violence as a normal and natural social practice. Yet Merry's approach seems to have side-stepped one important discussion: for whose good and to what extent do women's human rights get vernacularized? [...] While the state, national elites, and middle-class activists may all pledge their commitment to women's human rights, they often disagree on what constitutes violation *and* the protection of these rights, whether patriarchy is the main culprit, as well as what to do about it. In addition, those who are the subjects of these rights' intervention may reframe their own experiences in human rights terms that deviate from and even contradict the understanding of those who speak on their behalf. [...]

*Authentic Victimhood and the Nation*
"Victim" is the operative word in the new framework for state responses to prostitution as provided by the Punishment Act and the Protection Act passed on March 22, 2004. The introduction of the term "victims of prostitution" marked a new era in state regulation of prostitution in South Korea, as well as a new subject position for women in prostitution to make claims on the

state while reinforcing a particular discourse of women's sexuality in the nation. [...]

The new laws continue to criminalize sex workers – since uncoerced engagement in prostitution continues to be a crime. Those who do not qualify as victims – such as women who work in prostitution without debts, or work independently outside of brothels, or manage other sex workers and sell sex at the same time – are criminals. It is significant that this distinction between "victims" and "criminals" existed even in the proposed legislation tabled by the National Solidarity. According to Kim Hyunsun, they did not try to argue for complete decriminalization because Korean society still stigmatized women who sell sex. Creating the category of "victims of prostitution" was a first step to protecting the human rights of women in prostitution. The unsaid was that "prostitutes" would remain criminalized. In fact, the gendered logic of nationalism also ensures that the hypothetical "second step" of complete decriminalization of sex workers is unlikely to happen.

With the introduction of the term "victims of prostitution" and its silent counterpart "prostitutes," the laws highlighted that only innocent women who have been coerced deserve protection from the state, distinguishing between good women who are worthy of help and the bad ones who need to be punished. The laws thus perpetuate the stigma of prostitution and the virgin/whore dichotomy. The protection offered by the new laws is therefore only for "authentic" victims – whose sexual purity has been violated.

Authentic victimhood has been a well-rehearsed basis for competing claims on state recognition and protection by women who are sexually suspect as prostitutes in South Korea. It is not just a competition of who "suffered most," but also of who is least responsible for one's own suffering. As figures of female deviance in moral and legal discourses, prostitutes are "fallen women" who need to be contained and regulated, if not criminalized and rehabilitated. As symbols in nationalist discourses, however, they are the rallying points for outcry against foreign encroachment and the struggle for authentic Korean culture. The figure of the prostitute ravaged by foreign aggressors has been an allegory of the nation's misfortune as a divided and a subjugated nation in literary, political, and activist discourses. Premised on the feminine ideal of purity, the figure invokes a strong sense of honor and dignity lost as well as virtues and propriety violated, engendering the emotional and historical weight of women's sexuality in nationalist imagination. [...]

In the absence of foreign aggressors as villains, therefore, women catering to a Korean clientele are conceptually removed from any claims of victimhood. Korean women activists resolve this tension by representing prostitution as a "foreign evil" – a product of military aggression and capitalist patriarchy. In this narrative, prostitution is a product of Japanese colonialism (1910–1945), and then of US military occupation since 1945, subsequently proliferating with the globalization of western sexual mores and capitalism. Cho Young-sook, Secretary-General of the KWAU, stated that "Prostitution was closely related with foreign invasion," with the "first 'brothel'" established by the Japanese in 1920s and the build-up of "camp town prostitution" for the US military after the war. The prostitute thus becomes an emblem of women's subordination in Korea, bearing the symbolic burden of women's oppression in both nationalist history and capitalist patriarchy. In this view, prostitution is not indigenous to Korean society and culture, and can therefore be purged. [...]

*Rights for Good Daughters Only: No Sex Workers Need Apply*
The process of redefining the authentic sexual victim simultaneously produces the real whore, reinforcing the boundary between "good" and "bad" women and limiting rights claims to worthy victims whose purity has been violated. Challenges to the laws arose most importantly from the women whom these laws intend to protect. Satisfied neither with being victims nor whores, women in prostitution organized to claim their rights first as citizens, and subsequently as sex workers. The responses of the women's movement and the state to their claims, however, reveal the goal of restoring a monolithic set of feminine ideals to modern Korea. [...]

[I]n these mainstream activists' paradigm of women's human rights, women who demand a recognition of their right to work in prostitution are *persona non grata* who blatantly defy the victim subject endorsed by the women's movement and the new laws. Putatively attributing all claims of sex work by women in prostitution to brothel owners' manipulation, Korean feminists like Cho eliminate the agency of all women to consent to sex work as well as to engage in public protests. On the same premise, Korean feminists have dismissed any reference to "sex work" as a call for state-regulated prostitution, harking back to the system of legal prostitution under Japanese colonial rule. To these ardent women activists, their understanding of prostitution is *the* truth of prostitution in Korea. Elimination of prostitution is the only way to achieve women's rights because, according to the director of *Dasihamkke*, the biggest anti-prostitution NGO in Seoul, it is a historical responsibility: "If we don't fight for the criminalization of prostitution, then more young women would enter prostitution. In this perspective, women who refuse to leave prostitution are willful deviants who endanger *other* women (young women of the future as well as women in general) by perpetuating the institution of prostitution. This perspective leaves intact the historical and contemporary symbolic burden of the prostitute, essentializing prostitution as inherently a form of masculine domination of women and thus an assault on women as a whole. Eradicating prostitution is therefore a project of both restoring "tradition" and enforcing the "modern" – female virtues of pre-colonial Korea and gender equality of a democratic nation-state. [...]

[Cheng goes on to describe the vernacularized framework of trafficking as giving "the Korean state moral and legislative powers – as the modern state committed to combating trafficking, the democratic state that embrace women's rights, and the benevolent state that upholds traditional virtues" (497).]

Firstly, since the anti-trafficking initiatives focus solely on prostitution, these laws that are supposed to deal with human trafficking are incapable of addressing abuses suffered by migrant workers in other sectors. The status of illegal migrant workers has generated human rights abuses by both employers and the state. According to an Amnesty International report published in August 2006, at least 360,000 migrant workers were believed to be working in Korea in June 2006. Of this total, 52 percent, were "irregular" migrant workers, most of whom suffered a range of financial and physical coercion. The similar structural vulnerabilities of migrant workers in the entertainment industry, factories, and domestic work have made it possible for employers to withhold salaries, impose arbitrary fines, deductions, and long working hours, and threaten or employ the use of violence. All migrant workers are exposed to potential sexual violence. [...]

Secondly, the new laws fail to generate empowering conditions for migrant women to report abuses, as the law turned them into disposable instruments of investigation and prosecution without due protection of their rights. Article 13, "Special Provisions for Foreign Women" in the Punishment Act, stipulates that those who file reports or are being investigated as victims of trafficking into forced prostitution would be temporarily exempted from deportation in order to file suits and claim damages. They have to leave Korea eventually, usually within three months. No service provision (except for two shelters for foreign women), allowance or work permit is provided. Even if a woman is being investigated as a victim, she would not have any means to make a living during the period of investigation or trial. Even women who have won favourable verdicts may not get damages from clubowners, since they are required to leave Korea. It is doubtful how these migrant victims may benefit from prosecution.

5.9 Mobilizing the Law in China: "Informed Disenchantment" and the Development of Legal Consciousness, *Mary E. Gallagher*

In her study of urban Chinese workers, Mary E. Gallagher found that the complicated result of mobilizing state labor laws was "informed disenchantment," a manifestation of legal consciousness that embodied efficacious feelings about the law accompanied with disappointment and frustration with the inequities and dysfunction of China's legal system. Based on sixteen months of research at a legal aid center and in-depth interviews with plaintiffs, Gallagher observed that workers entered the formal legal process with high expectations about the possibility of protecting their rights while possessing only a vague knowledge of legal procedure and their actual codified rights. Through the process of legal mobilization, the workers increased their individual efficacy and competency but at the same time felt more than ever that the legal system was unfair and ineffective.

> Informed disenchantment of these legal aid plaintiffs is captured in three separate realms of the legal mobilization process: the acquisition of strategic knowledge, feelings of inclusion into a social network, and the post-dispute impulse to become a "little expert" – to transmit one's knowledge and experiences to friends and family. While many plaintiffs were frustrated and angry, disappointed with many aspects of the process, nearly all respondents emerged from the process with a much stronger sense of their legal rights and a more strategic and realistic view of the legal process. They had, in effect, learned how to play the state's new game. What is perhaps most surprising is that despite the heightened feelings of disappointment and cynicism, the vast majority of the plaintiffs were willing to play the game again should they experience another employment dispute.
>
> *Acquiring Strategic Knowledge*
> Most legal aid plaintiffs came to the process with a strong but vague sense that their rights had been violated. Exposed to the campaign slogans of labor law dissemination and media coverage that tended to highlight successful cases, they came to the process with a strong sense of their rights but little exact knowledge about how those rights would be protected or reclaimed in the legal process. In the cases of many older workers from the state sector, they even believed (erroneously) that the law would prevent their termination or layoff from the company that had employed them for several decades. While some of the high expectations of workers are caused by the way in which rule of law is transmitted in China, in some cases, as with these workers from the

state sector, high expectations are related to a sense of confusion over what the legal responsibilities of employers are. In a time of transition from an "iron rice bowl" system of employment, it is not surprising that many older workers tended to believe that they would be grandfathered into the old system. But this was not the case; China's labor laws do not guarantee anyone permanent employment, and China has significantly rolled back the legal responsibilities of employers.

The acquisition of new and deeper knowledge is a key aspect of the legal mobilization process, building increased feelings of efficacy, competency, and disappointment that the law does not always work as it should. In one plaintiff's interpretation, legal aid provided the "words" that the plaintiff needed to know in order to speak in a legal venue. It provided a new vocabulary. For most respondents, the most important aspects of their newly attained knowledge were in the realm of understanding laws and regulations, understanding legal procedure, and understanding how to attain and use evidence. [...]

[...] A healthy sense of cynicism and disappointment with the law was common among the plaintiffs as they went through the legal process and discovered it to be more complicated than they expected and more advantageous to employers with their wealth of legal experience, their ability to hire skilled lawyers, and their importance as employers and investors in the local economy. The vast majority of plaintiffs reported, however, that they would sue again if they encountered another employment dispute, and for many this extended to other types of disputes as well. Eighty percent of all plaintiffs reported that they would sue again if they encountered another employment dispute. This tendency was not significantly affected by the outcome of the case-those who lost were almost as likely to want to sue again as those who won (88% versus 100%). However, in the cases in which the judgment had not been implemented, only 40% of the plaintiffs reported that they would sue again. This lower figure for cases with unimplemented judgments shows that the plaintiff's rejection of the legal system is far more likely when the process fails than when it produces a judgment that is not in the plaintiff's favor [table omitted].

This ability to distinguish between the legal process and out-come accords with an instrumental approach to the law as a game in which the plaintiff understands that the outcome depends on how the battle is waged, not on the moral positions of the two sides. [...] The high rate of positive response regarding future disputes was unexpected and did not match the tenor of the interviews, in which the plaintiff tended to dwell on the difficulties of and barriers to attaining just outcomes. But this gap between attitudes and response rates regarding present and future behavior is not unusual in a context where legal options are pushed by the state while alternative paths, such as petitioning, are narrowing. As Hendley notes in the Russia case, "[a] sense of resignation about the legal system consistently infused my interviews with managers. This hopelessness did not correlate with litigation behavior. In other words, apathy regarding law and high levels of litigation can co-exist."

*Finding Social Networks of Support*
Workers who sue remain concerned about their social status and their public reputation and often will try to hide the fact of their lawsuit from their neighbors, friends, and even close relatives. This reticence speaks to the continuing belief as reported by Du, an old worker who was left with nothing when his state-owned enterprise was acquired, that "only bad people file suits." Others are embarrassed that they were fired or laid off, believing that it will seem to everyone else that they must have done something wrong. The frequency with which these sentiments are expressed indicates the level of social and psychological barriers to legal mobilization. Most people decide to sue because they have no other choice, having exhausted the other options of negotiation or because their employer has rejected outright any chance at negotiation or reconsideration.

Legal mobilization through legal aid can mitigate plaintiffs' feelings of isolation and embarrassment by providing a social network and a fixed space through which plaintiffs can interact with each other, student volunteers, and legal aid staff. Many plaintiffs reported hearing about a new strategy or a relevant regulation while waiting in line at the legal aid center. Some workers find that their cases are similar, form a relationship, and help each other with their suits. Others realize by listening to the complaints and problems of those around them that their own grievance is part of a broader systematic trend. This reduces feelings of self-blame and embarrassment and can embolden plaintiffs to link their problems to broader political challenges, such as the lack of an effective organization to represent workers and the emphasis that local governments place on the "investment climate," which often trumps the protection of workers' rights. A young worker was struck at how serious the problems were of the older people crowded around him. "I thought if [the director of the center] can help these people, then surely he should be able to win my case."

Inclusion into a space and network such as legal aid can be an empowering experience for people who are otherwise discouraged, angry, and often deeply depressed. Li, the injured engineer, believed he "went from being someone with a future to something that wasn't even human." For people who have been laid off, summarily dismissed, or otherwise pushed out of their workplace, legal aid becomes the "turning point" from an experience in passive humiliation to an aggressive battle for rights and economic security. Ying, a young woman from rural Jiangxi Province who had to sue her employer twice (the second time on her own), reported,

> [a]s an outsider, who didn't know anyone in Shanghai, law was my only choice. I never thought about "letters and visits." Of course no one would have paid the slightest attention to me ... this strengthened my personality; nobody can just take away what is mine. I used to just give up. I sued the second time because I had the time and the experience. [...]

*Post-Dispute Activism: Becoming a Little Expert*
This new sense of empowerment among plaintiffs (even while remaining deeply angry with the results of the process) leads many into post-dispute roles as "little experts." Their newfound expertise in labor law leads many to give advice, copy materials, introduce friends to legal aid, and even serve as witnesses or citizen representatives in the cases of other aggrieved workers. As with the propensity to sue again, post-dispute little experts are the norm, not the exception. more than three-quarters of the plaintiffs re-ported that in the post-dispute period they advised friends and family, introduced others to legal aid, and in some cases served as witnesses for other aggrieved workers. [table omitted] A female forklift operator who reported crying all the time during her lawsuit now assists with her relative's own worker compensation case and coined the phrase I use in this article: "My husband's brother-in-law now has a worker compensation case, I helped him with the case at first and then introduced him to the center ... Now everyone comes to consult me, I've become a little expert." [...]

Old Du, whose case remained up in the air without final implementation, summed up his experience in a way that captures the common path of a plaintiff from passivity, to knowledge, to strategy, and to anger:

> I didn't know a single thing about the labor law [before this]. During Mao's time, everything was handled for us, like children. I used to think that only bad people file suit, now I know every-thing ... arbitration, first appeal, second appeal. I'm famous. People ask me for interviews. [After the TV program] my phone started ringing off the hook, didn't stop ringing for a week, all these old workers wanting to know about my case and to resolve

their own problems. An old worker from Bayer waited outside my door to talk to me. I gave him some advice and then later served as his witness in court on the question of job transfers in SOEs. I am so angry and frustrated. I didn't use to be like this. My poor parents at home. They are over 80 years old!! I'll do anything to help these kinds of cases.

### 5.10 A People's Constitution: The Everyday Life of Law in the Indian Republic, *Rohit De*

Rohit De's study of previously unexplored court records tells the history of constitutional rights litigation in the Indian republic of the 1950s. The following selection comes from the chapter, "The Case of the Honest Prostitute," which details how sex workers filed a series of constitutional challenges against anti-prostitution laws that aimed to mold women into a "moral, productive member of society." Starting first with a Muslim woman, Husna Bai, sex workers asserted their constitutional right to a trade or a profession and to freedom of movement around the country, and questioned the procedural irregularities in such statutes as the Suppression of Immoral Traffic in Women and Girls Act of 1956 (SITA).

The enactment of the Constitution transformed the everyday regulation of prostitution in India. First, by abolishing trafficking through the Constitution, the authors sought to create conditions of freedom for prostitutes (from individual exploiters) while also providing a legitimate basis for the state to regulate the daily lives of these newly freed subjects. This process of abolition and rescue by the bureaucracy of social welfare, in contrast to its colonial predecessor, became marked as an arena where women could play a role in public life. Second, a prostitute who filed a lawsuit in the Indian republic was able to represent herself as an economic actor asserting her rights in a public space. Central to such prostitutes' claims was the redefinition of the idea of the productive citizen, challenging claims made by elite women that prostitution was unproductive work.

How does one evaluate the process of litigation that began with Husna Bai's petition? What insights does it offer into the relationship between women and a postcolonial constitutional republic? If one adopts a doctrinal approach, the process of litigation initiated by Husna Bai stands defeated in the Supreme

Court's decision in Kaushalya Devi's case. The Supreme Court declared SITA to be constitutionally sound and held that the rights of prostitutes could be restricted in the interest of the general public. This reading echoed the views of Indian feminists, who have argued that law is a hegemonic project of patriarchy and modernity that legitimizes only particular ways of being and doing, and that rights lose their transformative potential when institutionalized by law. Such a reading would also find favor with American critics of the rights revolution, who have argued that courts have limited power to create social change and that the costs of litigation are not worth the small judicial victories that can be achieved. Prabha Kottiswaran, a legal ethnographer of the contemporary sex industry in India, argues that sex workers are unlikely to participate in bourgeois civil society mechanisms like litigation, winning greater victories through their participation in political society.

This skepticism toward the law is a valuable corrective to triumphant accounts of legal liberalism. However, viewing the success or failure of legal mobilization purely in terms of a judicial verdict severely limits our understanding of the role of law in society.

Legal practices and rights discourses develop lives outside formal state institutions. It is remarkable that before Husna Bai's petition, there existed in the popular imagination of prostitutes the belief that the right to work in the Constitution meant that the state could not abolish prostitution. This argument was made several times to the ASMH members (Advisory Committee of Social and Moral Hygiene), so they had to recognize the fact at the beginning of their report. Prostitutes talked back to middle-class women's groups in the language of rights. A bemused Rameshwari Nehru recounted that a number of prostitutes marched to her house "to claim the freedom given to them by the Constitution to ply their trade unharrassed by police for earning their livelihood."

Any interpretation of these cases must begin by acknowledging the significance of both the number of prostitutes who became litigants and the confident assertion of their rights. This challenges us to rethink the belief that the courts in India were the exclusive domain of the bourgeoisie. Muslim prostitutes like Husna Bai faced several degrees of marginalization and do not fit easily with other oppressed groups whose presence in the colonial courtroom has recently been studied. Nita Verma Prasad and Mitra Sharafi attribute the legal successes forged by Hindu widows and Muslim wives to "liberal judges" and "chivalric imperialism," respectively. But destitute widows and abandoned wives were easier objects of sympathy than prostitutes, whose disruptive presence was recognized even by judges who gave favorable hearings.

I would argue that the presence of prostitutes in courts and their legal consciousness are both products of their marginalization. Prostitutes became subject of intense state scrutiny and regulation since the mid-nineteenth century. Their lives and movements were often circumscribed by regulations, the breach of which subjected them to harassment from state authorities. Prostitutes had multiple points of contact with state agencies, ranging from policemen and doctors to social workers. Their experience with the criminal justice system would bring them into contact with lawyers. Thus, they would have greater awareness of the laws that affected them than middle-class or elite women, who had little direct contact with the state. [...]

More significantly, prostitutes rarely acted alone. Almost all the cases that appeared before court had multiple petitioners, and even in Husna Bai's case it becomes clear that her petition was being supported by other prostitutes in the city. The role of associations in supporting legal mobilization has also been emphasized. Living in geographically restricted areas and linked to each other with kinship and caste ties, prostitutes began forming organizations in the 1950s. The Allahabad Dancing Girls Union and the Calcutta organizations had already been discussed.

As professional associations, these organizations were distinct from charitable groups that worked with prostitutes. A study of the Bombay red-light district contrasted the Gomantak Maratha Samaj, an organization led by middle-class men who sought to prevent the dedication of girls of the Naik community, and the activities of the Association of Tawaifs and Deredars, a prostitutes' society that ostensibly promoted music and provided facilities for its members to train in music and dance. Although the first organization was praised for its success in providing matrimonial opportunities to Naik girls, the second was described as a "shield to protect the unscrupulous from law-enforcing activities."

The role of caste in this process cannot be overemphasized; it provided a resource for organizing, and the existence of a hereditary group of prostitutes complicated the narrative framed by trafficking. Despite the efforts of colonial law to homogenize all nonconformist sexual practices as prostitution, the courts were able draw upon the cultural memory of categories such as courtesans. It is striking that no other common- law jurisdiction recognized or sustained arguments defending the right to practice prostitution as a profession. It is this recognition of cultural categories that has allowed for the Supreme Courts of India, Pakistan, and Bangladesh to recognize rights of sexual autonomy for *hijras* and *kwajasarahs* (traditional transgender communities) while rejecting claims by gay men and lesbians.

Studies of legal mobilization emphasize that every culture offers only a limited stock of resources and practices from which citizens draw to construct meaning and negotiate social interactions. The enactment of the Constitution created a powerful new resource and added to this stock. The ability of prostitutes to mobilize the resources was limited by the biases the figure of the prostitute evoked in the judicial system. This interplay becomes clear when we notice what arguments have greater legal traction. Husna Bai's claim that SITA restricted her freedom to practice her profession is more easily dismissed than her complaint that the powers of expulsion granted to the magistrate were arbitrary and violated her right of free movement. The prostitutes were successful to the extent that they were able to show that SITA adversely affected society at large, such as by granting unregulated powers to a magistrate. Michael McCann observed, "To take advantage of contradictions, to open up silences, to turn the rules against the rulers, to work for change within existing cultural traditions – these generally are the most effective strategies available to traditionally oppressed and marginal groups."

This recognition by the court was not insignificant, and till the decision in *Kaushalya Devi*, it operated as a precedent in almost all cases. Even after the decision in *Kaushalya Devi*, the judgments for Husna Bai and Begum Kalawat circulated in legal textbooks and commentaries and continue to be used by lawyers.

Litigation was also one of those rare instances in which a subaltern would appear to speak. This remained its most discomfiting feature, particularly for female leaders who had carved a role for themselves within the postcolonial state by speaking on behalf of these marginalized women. This form of speech also manifested itself in petitions of habeas corpus brought by women who were confined to rehabilitation and shelters and were seeking to free themselves from the state's interference. These moves drove one editorial to sarcastically remark that "the primary assumption behind the rescue of fallen women now being systematically undertaken in the country in obedience to SITA is that the fallen women are anxious to be rescued"; however, the escape of women from shelters and their challenges to their confinement should compel sociologists and psychologists to address themselves to the "mystery of certain women's prejudice against respectability." I am not suggesting that this was the authentic voice of the prostitutes, but the Constitution did allow for a voice that represented the prostitute to become visible in a public domain. [...]

Since the early 1990s scholars and activists have increasingly being paying attention to sex-worker mobilization in India and other developing countries for decriminalization and access to welfare. However, this is held to be catalyzed by the rise of transnational NGOs and the concerns over HIV and AIDs, which led to a greater engagement with the needs of sex workers. The argument that sex can be work is a radical position that emerged in the West in the 1980s. Husna Bai's case revealed a long history of sex workers organizing in India and a rights narrative shaped by engagements with the Indian Constitution, contrary to the vision of the Indian women's movement. Despite judicial pronouncements, the belief that the right to work in the Indian Constitution guarantees the right to exchange sex for money continues to be asserted by prostitutes' organizations. In 2012, four decades after *Kaushalya Devi*, the Darbar Mahila Samanwaya Committee, a prostitutes' union in Calcutta, distributed pamphlets to its members that open with Articles 19 and 21 of the Indian Constitution, asserting the right to a trade and a profession, as well as to life and liberty.

REFERENCES

**Featured Readings**

Becker, Margaret. 2015. "Constructing SSLM: Insights from Struggles over Women's Rights in Nepal." *Asian Studies Review* 39 (2): 247–65. doi: 10.1080/10357823.2015.1021754

Cheng, Sealing. 2011. "The Paradox of Vernacularization: Women's Human Rights and the Gendering of Nationhood." *Anthropological Quarterly* 84 (2): 475–505. doi: 10.1353/anq.2011.0021

Chua, Lynette J. 2012. "Pragmatic Resistance, Law, and Social Movements in Authoritarian States: The Case of Gay Collective Action in Singapore." *Law & Society Review* 46 (4): 713–48. doi: 10.1111/j.1540-5893.2012.00515.x

——— 2019. *The Politics of Love in Myanmar: LGBT Mobilization and Human Rights as a Way of Life*. Palo Alto, CA: Stanford University Press.

De, Rohit. 2018. *A People's Constitution: The Everyday Life of Law in the Indian Republic*. Princeton, NJ: Princeton University Press. doi: 10.1017/S073824801900066X

Ela, Nate. 2017. "Litigation Dilemmas: Lessons from the Marcos Human Rights Class Action." *Law & Social Inquiry* 42 (2): 479–508. doi: 10.1111/lsi.12207

Gallagher, Mary E. 2006. "Mobilizing the Law in China: 'Informed Disenchantment' and the Development of Legal Consciousness." *Law & Society Review* 40 (4): 783–816.

Nguyen, Tu Phuong. 2018. "Labour Law and (In)justice in Workers' Letters in Vietnam." *Asian Journal of Law & Society* 5 (1): 25–47. doi: 10.1017/als.2017.29

Parmar, Pooja. 2015. *Indigeneity and Legal Pluralism in India: Claims, Histories, Meanings*. New York: Cambridge University Press. doi: 10.1017/CBO9781139962896

Wang, Di, and Sida Liu. 2020. "Performing Artivism: Feminists, Lawyers, and Online Legal Mobilization in China." *Law & Social Inquiry* 45 (3): 678–705. doi: 10.1017/lsi.2019.64

**Other Works Cited**

Anderson, Ellen Ann. 2006. *Out of the Closets and into the Courts: Legal Opportunity Structure and Gay Rights Litigation*. Ann Arbor: University of Michigan Press. doi: 10.3998/mpub.17550

Arrington, Celeste L. 2021. "Rights Claiming through the Courts: Changing Legal Opportunity Structures in South Korea." In *Rights Claiming in South Korea*, edited by Celeste L. Arrington and Patricia Goedde, 151–71. New York: Cambridge University Press. doi: 10.1017/9781108893947

Chua, Lynette J. 2022. *The Politics of Rights and Southeast Asia*. New York: Cambridge University Press. doi: 10.1017/9781108750783

Engel, David M. 2012. "Vertical and Horizontal Perspectives on Rights Consciousness." *Indiana Journal of Global Legal Studies* 19: 423–55. doi: 10.2979/indjglolegstu.19.2.423

Epp, Charles R. 1998. *The Rights Revolution: Lawyers, Activists, and Supreme Courts in Comparative Perspective*. Chicago: University of Chicago Press.

Geertz, Clifford. 1964. "Ideology as a Cultural System." In *Ideology and Discontent*, edited by David E. Apter, 47–76. New York: Free Press.

Keck, Margaret E., and Kathryn Sikkink. 1998. *Activists beyond Borders: Advocacy Networks in International Politics*. Ithaca, NY: Cornell University Press. doi: 10.7591/9780801471292

McCann, Michael W. 1994. *Rights at Work: Pay Equity Reform and the Politics of Legal Mobilization*. Chicago: University of Chicago Press.

——— 2014. "The Unbearable Lightness of Rights: On Sociolegal Inquiry in the Global Era." *Law & Society Review* 48: 245–73. doi: 10.1111/lasr.12075

Merry, Sally E. 2006. *Human Rights and Gender Violence*. Chicago: University of Chicago Press.

O'Brien, Kevin J., and Lianjiang Li. 2006. *Rightful Resistance in Rural China*. New York: Cambridge University Press. doi: 10.1017/cbo9780511791086.002

Rosenberg, Gerald N. 2008. *The Hollow Hope: Can Courts Bring About Social Change?* Chicago: University of Chicago Press. doi: 10.7208/chicago/9780226726687.001.0001

Scheingold, Stuart A. 1974. *The Politics of Rights: Lawyers, Public Policy, and Political Change*. Ann Arbor: University of Michigan Press.

Scott, James C. 1984. *Weapons of the Weak: Everyday Forms of Peasant Resistance*. New Haven, CT: Yale University Press.

Tsutsui, Kiyoteru. 2017. "Human Rights and Minority Activism in Japan: Transformation of Movement Actorhood and Local-Global Feedback Loop." *American Journal of Sociology* 122: 1050–103. doi: 10.1086/689910

Yeo, Andrew, and Danielle Chubb. 2018. *North Korean Human Rights: Activists and Networks*. New York: Cambridge University Press. doi: 10.1017/9781108589543

Zemans, Frances. 1983. "The Neglected Role of the Law in the Political System." *American Political Science Review* 77: 690–703. doi: 10.2307/1957268

**Suggested Readings**

Arrington, Celeste L., and Patricia Goedde, eds. 2021. *Rights Claiming in South Korea*. New York: Cambridge University Press. doi: 10.1017/9781108893947

Harms, Erik. 2016. *Luxury and Rubble: Civility and Dispossession in the New Saigon*. Oakland: University of California Press. doi: 10.1525/luminos.20

Stern, Rachel E. 2013. *Environmental Litigation in China: A Study in Political Ambivalence*. New York: Cambridge University Press. doi: 10.1017/CBO9781139096614

# 6 Legal Professions

## Contents

| | | |
|---|---|---|
| I | The Plurality of Law Practitioners | 228 |
| II | Lawyers in the Market | 245 |
| III | Lawyers and State Transformations | 257 |

The study of lawyers seems like a natural research topic for law and society scholars. After all, lawyers are among the most populous and accessible actors in the legal system. Most of them are private practitioners and do not face the same institutional constraints from the state as judges or police officers do. There is a theoretical difference, however, between studying lawyers as individual participants in legal cases and studying lawyers as one or more organized professions with distinctive social structures and cultural practices. The rise of sociolegal scholarship on the legal profession in the late twentieth century benefited much from the sociological theories of professions, which make professions rather than individual professionals the primary unit of analysis (Abbott 1988; Abel 1989). Accordingly, law and society scholars have analyzed the social structure of the bar, the legal profession's market monopoly, political mobilization, gender and racial inequalities, globalization, and many other topics.

The legal profession is often assumed to be a unified, high-status, and politically influential profession in Anglo-American contexts. For many Asian countries, however, this assumption is imprecise, to say the least. Judges, prosecutors, and lawyers are separate professional groups in most civil law jurisdictions across Asia. There is also a large plurality of law practitioners in the market for legal services, historically and presently, such as barristers, *vakils*, pleaders, and *mukhtars* in British India (Schmitthener 1968), *bengoshi* and judicial scriveners in Japan (Ota and Rokumoto 1993), or lawyers and basic-level legal workers in China (Liu 2011), complemented by various forms of unauthorized legal practice. Lawyers often play important roles in market transactions, yet many notable economic changes in Asia occurred without a highly developed legal profession.

The relationship between the legal profession and the state is even more complex. Strong, developmental states are prevalent in Asia, and thus many lawyers rely on their "political embeddedness" (Michelson 2007) with government agencies or officials to facilitate their work and serve their clients. However, not all lawyers are pragmatic brokers who are dependent on the state for survival. In the legal and political transformations across Asia, lawyers are often found on the frontlines fighting against arbitrary state power. That is why many studies on the legal professions in Asian cases focus on political mobilization and collective action.

Therefore, it is risky to make any general assumptions about the legal professions in Asia in terms of their social stratification, status, market positions, or political orientations. Instead, this chapter presents a variety of lawyering in different Asian contexts by focusing on three related topics: (1) the plurality of law practitioners; (2) lawyers in the market; and (3) lawyers and state transformations.

## 1 THE PLURALITY OF LAW PRACTITIONERS

Despite all the variations across jurisdictions and cultural context, the legal profession is always highly stratified in its social structure (Heinz and Laumann 1982). Persisting gender, racial, and class inequalities have been meticulously documented in many Western countries, and they arguably also exist in Asia. However, there are many other layers and boundaries by which law practitioners in Asia are differentiated. One key factor is the enduring legacy of colonialism, which permeates the social structures of a large number of Asian countries and regions. Therefore, understanding the colonial origins of Asian legal professions is of great importance. Additionally, the state is an influential actor, perhaps the most important one, in shaping the plurality and social differentiations of lawyers and other legal professionals across Asia. More recently, globalization has become another driving force for change in many countries, especially in the corporate legal sector. The four studies in this section use the cases of Indonesia, India, Japan, and Myanmar to illustrate the roles of colonialism, the state, and globalization in the development of Asian legal professions.

### 6.1 Origins of the Indonesian Advocacy, *Daniel S. Lev*

In his groundbreaking study of lawyers in Indonesia, Daniel S. Lev provides a historical account of the origins of the Indonesian advocacy. The Dutch colonial rule looms large in shaping the history of the Indonesian bar. This case suggests that privileged family and social backgrounds are great assets for indigenous lawyers to thrive in the shadow of colonialism. The struggles of the first generations of ethnic Javanese and Chinese lawyers to gain their places in the Indonesian legal profession also echo the experiences of indigenous lawyers in many other Asian cases.

> In the Netherlands Indies, until the mid-1920s, all advocates and notaries were Dutch. Neither native Indonesians nor ethnic Chinese had yet joined these professions. The small size and influence of the Indonesian advocacy just after independence was due at least in part to its late beginning. This was not true of all colonies. In most English colonies and the American-controlled Philippines, indigenous lawyers were numerous. It is tempting to attribute the differences simply to divergent Anglo-American and Continental legal traditions: English and American colonial officials would see many private lawyers as a basically good thing, while the French, Dutch, and Belgians would not. In reality, however, colonial officials nearly everywhere were reluctant to encourage indigenous private lawyers, and this was equally true on the colonial right and left. Hard-liners regarded native lawyers as a likely source of corruption, litigiousness, misuse of the law, and general trouble-making. Europeans with more sympathy for the societies they dominated perceived private lawyers as a symptom of the breakdown of traditional social intimacy in favor of a less kindly impersonal rule of law, which must spread social and cultural disruption. Each view had its own peculiar validity, though probably for reasons different from those usually argued. In any event, indigenous private lawyers did emerge earlier and in greater numbers in some colonies than in others, depending on a combination of colonial administrative ideology and economic policy. The English and the Americans tended to view the rule of law as an essential ingredient of colonial policy and part of their mission. Encouraging native lawyers therefore had some logic to it, despite European misgivings. But, at the same time, the English and the Americans were also more inclined to encourage local political participation and some entrepreneurial development, from which local private lawyers would tend to sprout if allowed to do so. In French and Dutch colonies, however, ideological conceptions of the imperial mission were quite different, and so were economic policies. A more pervasive administrative conception of colonial governance emphasized the role of European executive will, not law per se. Combined with a rather exclusive European (and minority middle-man) monopoly over commerce, this neither encouraged nor left much room for indigenous private lawyers. [...]

The colonial administration never encouraged Indonesians to take up private legal practice. Fundamental assumptions of colonial pluralism in the Netherlands Indies excluded such a notion from the imagination. The highest levels of commerce were in European hands, and businessmen would naturally rely upon Dutch advocates and notaries. Nor would Chinese entrepreneurs choose an Indonesian over a Dutch lawyer. Social status considerations alone would have made this unlikely, and besides, as the legal system was dominated by Dutch officials, it obviously made sense to use Dutch counsel. (There were no ethnic Chinese private lawyers either until after Indonesians had begun practice in the mid-1920s.) Moreover, the common myths of colonial paternalism no doubt made the idea of Indonesian advocates, if anyone thought of it, seem outlandish. European administrators usually assumed that the colonial bureaucracy was sufficient for the "simple" legal problems of village life. This same view that native legal problems were uncomplicated, along with other considerations, undoubtedly helped to inspire the simpler procedural requirements of the H.I.R., by which it was assumed that Indonesian litigants did not require assistance by counsel. I do not mean to argue that the simpler procedures were without virtue, but that the policy grew out of a colonial world-view that had other institutional consequences. One of them was that Indonesian advocates seemed out of the question.

Indonesian society was not much more receptive than the Dutch to the possibility of Indonesian advocates. Or at least Javanese society was not, and at first it was only Javanese who took up legal studies. When legal training was finally made available to Indonesians, it was confined to Javanese priyayi. Since legal training was seen as preparatory to government service, only the sons of high priyayi – often from bupati families – were encouraged to study law; the traditional elite was to be modernized, not expanded. Once the opportunity for legal education became available, however, some lower priyayi families also took advantage of it. But among both higher and lower strata of this Javanese elite, social status was attached to bureaucratic position. Private occupations of nearly any kind, and certainly occupations related to commerce, were regarded unfavorably as low status and unworthy. Few sons of the priyayi were likely, therefore, to receive much family encouragement to become private lawyers.

Consequently, two kinds of change had to take place in the colony in order for Indonesian private lawyers to appear. One was institutional and obvious: legal education had to be made available to Indonesians. The other was cultural and attitudinal: a few Indonesians with legal training had to become comfortable with the possibility of private practice. [...]

The extent to which law was an aristocratic preserve is indicated by the rank titles of names on the list. Of the 175 Javanese lawyers, 30 used the low title of *mas* and 135 had royal ranks of *raden, raden mas*, or higher. Aristocratic titles among lawyers from Sumatra and other islands were no less common. The colonial government, after all, had originally intended to provide legal education only to the upper-most part of the Javanese (and later Indonesian) elite. Its purpose was not to encourage social mobility, which would have threatened the old aristocracy, and cost more, but to equip this elite with the modern means by which to maintain its place in the civil service. For an aristocracy interested in maintaining its political and bureaucratic status, law became an obvious place to go. [...]

Still, any young Javanese willing to become an advocate then had to be unusual. The difficulties were for the most part professional and social, rather than financial. None of the new advocates was hopelessly poor. Most came from reasonably well-off and well-connected priyayi families. But professionally a new Indonesian advocate had to take his chances in a field dominated by Dutch lawyers linked comfortably with Dutch commerce in a system of legal institutions fully controlled by Dutch officials. The derision of Dutch advocates alone might have put off a less determined candidate. Often he had to be committed enough to put up also with his family's opposition, more or less outspoken, to working outside the bureaucracy. Despite the nationalist movement, it was still government, not private practice or commerce, where the old elite found social status and security. [...]

Ethnic Chinese advocates also began to appear by the late 1920s. Nearly all were from *peranakan* families, born in Indonesia rather than China. Educational facilities for Indonesian Chinese had improved greatly since the nineteenth century, and many young Chinese men and women now attended Dutch-language schools. As ethnic Chinese commerce developed, moreover, the traditional middleman role produced a dynamic and growing middle class, socially and culturally much closer to the Dutch than to Indonesians. Nevertheless, ethnic Chinese came late to the private legal profession. Unlike Javanese priyayi, they received no government encouragement to go into law, and the near monopoly of non-Dutch government service by ethnic Indonesians gave young ethnic Chinese little reason to study law in the first place. But for the same reason, when ethnic Chinese students did take an interest in law, the advocacy was an obvious goal. While a few did eventually take positions in the colonial courts and central administration, most found as advocates that they had a natural economic base in Chinese commerce, which provided them with business contacts, support, and a reasonably permanent clientele.

For both ethnic Indonesian and ethnic Chinese advocates, starting practice was hard. While occasionally they got useful advice from a sympathetic Dutch advocate, by and large they were shunned. Many Dutch advocates evidently perceived them as a competitive threat. It was nearly impossible for the newcomers to find places in established Dutch law firms. [...] It meant that new advocates, unless they could join an Indonesian firm, had to start from scratch without experience or clients. There were also slights. Most Indonesian (and ethnic Chinese) advocates who began practice in the colony can recount instances of real or imagined discrimination. Where there were local advocates' associations, they could not join or found it difficult to do so. Some were burdened with an extraordinary number of pro-deo (pro-bono) indigent cases, often, they suspected, because Dutch advocates refused to take them and advised the local raad van justitie to appoint Indonesian advocates. In the memories of older Indonesian advocates today personal humiliations experienced while getting started are mixed with a more precisely nationalistic animus against colonial treatment of Indonesians.

### 6.2 India's Grand Advocates: A Legal Elite Flourishing in the Era of Globalization, *Marc Galanter and Nick Robinson*

Colonial history has had a lasting influence on the development of the legal professions in many postcolonial societies in Asia. India is a good case in point. Under British rule, the Indian legal professions were divided into two tiers and sociolegal scholars often consider it a consequence of legal pluralism. English-style barristers and solicitors coexisted with indigenous *vakils* and *mukhtars*, serving different clients and practicing law in different courts. Although this bifurcated and fragmented social structure of the legal professions changed profoundly over the twentieth century, as a unified profession emerged after independence, it led to the rise of "grand advocates" who dominate the apex of the contemporary Indian legal profession. Marc Galanter and Nick Robinson examine the privilege of this small and elite group of practitioners in one of the world's largest legal professions.

Pre-British India had learned specialists in law, but nothing that corresponded to the legal professions of the modern world, which are made up of qualified practitioners who earn a living by representing clients before courts and tribunals and designing transactions that are affected by legal rules. Today's Indian legal profession is a product of the complex of British-style legal institutions imposed on India in the eighteenth and nineteenth centuries, but lawyers in India developed along different lines than their counterparts in England or elsewhere in the common law world.

The professional pattern as it crystallized in the late nineteenth century was a composite, drawing upon two main streams: (1) the royal courts in the Presidency towns (Bombay, Madras, and Calcutta) were ruled by the British crown and English law administered by British judges and there was a dual profession, with barristers briefed by solicitors; (2) until 1857 most of India (i.e. the mofussil or interior) was ruled by the East India Company, which operated courts staffed by civil servants and which licensed indigenous vakils (a Persian word that earlier referred generally to an agent or emissary) to represent clients in those courts. The two systems of courts were merged when the British government displaced the East India Company after the 1857 rebellion.

Recruitment to the profession was through multiple sources: British barristers arrived from the UK to enjoy the higher fees that could be earned in India; elite Indians went to the Inns of Court in London to secure qualification; others acquired on-the-job training at the Indian courts; and (after the establishment of universities in India starting in 1857) these were joined by those who had attended law courses in India.[...]

With the passage of the Advocates Act (1961) all the old grades of practitioners (vakils, barristers, pleaders of several grades, and mukhtars) were abolished and consolidated into a single body of advocates who enjoy the right to practice in courts throughout India. ... Most of the old categories and grades of practitioners have been abolished, but new forms of diversity amongst lawyers have emerged. Lawyers may be found in firms, as in-house counsel, and in legal process outsourcing. All of these have proliferated in the last 20 years, but the great bulk of India's lawyers remain attached to the dominant model of professional life – the free-standing advocate who practices mainly, if not exclusively, at a single court. This model, formed in colonial times, was firmly institutionalized by the early twentieth century. In spite of the vast political and social change India has undergone, if we were to go around India in 2013 and observe lawyers, we would find a set of distinctive and characteristic features of professional life that are surprisingly similar to what we would have found in 1913.

We might think of these features as the "basic structure" of the Indian legal profession. A schematic portrait of the modal organization of legal services in India, then or now, would include:

- Individualism: lawyers practice by themselves, usually assisted by clerks, and sometimes by juniors in a casual and temporary apprenticeship arrangement. There are few firms or other enduring units for coordination and sharing among lawyers. Firms are proliferating, but still involve only a tiny fraction of practicing lawyers – perhaps 2 or 3% – and the larger firms are rarely focused on litigation.
- Lawyers are oriented to courts (and other court-like forums) to the virtual exclusion of other legal settings. The orientation to courts is displayed spatially: lawyers spend much of their working day at a particular court. They typically see clients in home offices or in chambers near or attached to the court, or simply at the verandah or a corridor of the court. The identification of the lawyer with a particular court goes back to the earliest days of British rule.
- The performance of the lawyer is overwhelmingly oral rather than written. With occasional exceptions, advocates focus on courtroom advocacy rather than advising, negotiating, or planning. That is, they are *de facto* barristers who operate in a setting in which the 'solicitor' functions of advising are far less developed. Judges frequently cite oral argument in their judgments and advocates feel little constraint in making arguments that were only partially developed in the written submissions, or that were not mentioned at all. The dominance of the barrister model is displayed in, and reinforced by, the structure of remuneration. Lawyers are typically paid by the "appearance" – that is, for court work in a particular case on a given day.
- Lawyers are relatively unspecialized. Although some advocates have a special expertise in tax or criminal matters, few lawyers limit themselves to one area of law. [...]

The pre-eminence of the Grand Advocates is a contemporary expression of a long-standing and pervasive pattern of steep hierarchy at the bar. At every level, the provision of legal services was (and is) dominated by a small number of lawyers with outsized reputations, who have the lion's share of clients, income, prestige, standing, and influence. [...]

We estimate that the number of pre-eminent seniors – those we are calling Grand Advocates – at the Supreme Court today is something on the order of 40–50. If we add those of comparable status at the High Courts, there are at most 100 that make up what one observer refers to as the "giants and legends of the litigation system". This shape – very steep hierarchy, with a concentration of prestige, authority, and prosperity in a narrow group of senior lawyers – has been a constant feature of law practice in India in colonial times and after Independence, in the highest courts and in local courts, when the bar was flourishing and when it went through difficult times. [...]

Top advocates in India enjoy incomes that rival the most highly remunerated lawyers anywhere in the world. Abhishek Manu Singhvi, who along with being a top litigator is also a member of the Rajya Sabha, reported his annual income at 50 crore (about $10 million) in 2010–11. Ram Jethmalani, another leading lawyer who is a member of the Rajya Sabha, reported his at 8.4 crore ($1.7 million). Shanti Bhushan, a leading advocate who was on a public committee to design a new anti-corruption agency, disclosed an annual income of 18 crore ($3.6 million). Both Jethmalani and Bhushan are well over 80 and no longer litigate as much as they once did. One advocate estimated that top Supreme Court lawyers are generally earning between 10 and 50 crore a year (i.e. $2–10 million annually). Leading lawyers that appear before the Bombay and Delhi High Courts have comparable fees, while those elsewhere in the country usually charge considerably less.

Despite their high rates, client demand for these select lawyers is robust. Most of the leading advocates we interviewed conceded that their fees were exorbitant, but justified continuously raising fees as a mechanism to keep their workload manageable. As one Supreme Court lawyer explained, "Lawyers like me charge the sky. It is a way of filtering clients". [...]

Young lawyers often complain about how difficult it is for them to break into the elite world of litigation. Some of these barriers to entry are obvious. For example, the Grand Advocates operate in an English-speaking world, where fluency is a necessity and British diction lauded. Only a minority of lawyers in India grew up in English-speaking households. Others struggled to gain the necessary command over the language to become a Grand Advocate. However, language is not the only filter restricting entry into this high-end world.

Family connections, or being part of certain social stratum, have clear benefits for a young litigator. [...] With a family member in the profession, clients and briefing advocates become aware of you more quickly and one can use the office space and library of one's family member. All of this helps in the early years of litigation when paying briefs are rare and income negligible. Indeed, being able to make it through the early bare bones years as a litigator is perhaps the most formidable screening mechanism for the profession, favoring the survival of those who come with wealth and connections.

Being part of the same social milieu also helps in arranging to junior with a leading senior. Most of today's prominent seniors had themselves juniored for a prominent senior, and older seniors we interviewed spoke proudly of their "alumni" who had gone on to become successful lawyers themselves. There is a feeling that if you don't have an actual father in the profession you at least need a "godfather" (i.e. a prominent senior that you junior with) who can help guide you in the early years and raise your profile, bringing you critical early cases. However, most seniors said they accepted juniors on the request of friends, retired justices, or colleagues – there was no formal selection process. Thus it is beneficial, if not essential, to be located in this social stratum in order to elicit the needed referral to a senior.

The powerful role of social networks in acquiring clients and setting up a practice helps perpetuate the disproportionate presence of certain ethnic and religious groups in the profession. For example, in Madras, elite Brahmins dominate the upper ranks of the bar because of their tight networks and long-standing proficiency in English. In Bombay, the Parsis, Gujratis, and Bohra Muslims were early first movers in the profession and continue to dominate its upper reaches. In the Delhi High Court, post-partition refugees, particularly Sikhs from the Lahore High Court, had an advantage, and their descendants continue to be disproportionately represented in the top ranks of the bar. The Supreme Court bar tends to be an amalgam of these privileged groups from around the country. Despite repeated inquiries we could not identify any Scheduled Caste, Scheduled Tribe, or Other Backward Class advocates who were regarded as part of the elite stratum of lawyers.

Women also have had a difficult time breaking into the small group of Grand Advocates and into the upper ranks of litigation more generally. Of the 81 senior advocates designated by the Bombay High Court in the 20-year period 1991–2010, only three were women. No women have been designated since 2006. Historically, women have faced discrimination from colleagues, judges, and clients, even if there are signs that such barriers may be lessening. ... In 2012, after a woman lawyer was slapped by a male colleague in the Delhi High Court, 63 women lawyers successfully petitioned the Supreme Court to set up a committee to hear complaints of sexual harassment at the Supreme Court and in the lower courts. More women are entering litigation, but clearly discrimination and obstacles still remain. [...]

If Motilal Nehru or Muhammad Ali Jinnah visited the Supreme Court today they would find a Court not altogether different from the Allahabad or Bombay High Courts in which they argued in the early years of the twentieth century. The multiple courtrooms, buzz of lawyers and clients in the hallways, and the structure of the bar would all seem quite familiar. Independence, liberalization, and globalization may have changed some of the clients, key provisions of law, and office technology – briefs are now neatly typed on a computer – but many elements of the culture of the justice system have remained surprisingly constant. In particular, the steeply hierarchical structure of the bar has endured, suggesting that it is an expression of more deeply entrenched features of Indian social life, or at least of Indian legal institutions. The reputational capital of the Grand Advocate remains one of his primary assets in a court system marked by overwhelmed judges with little assistance, the multiplicity and blurriness of precedent, and the centrality of oral presentation. In such a context, being known and trusted by judges is a positional good of which there can only be so much, placing those who have it in both a potentially lucrative and commanding position in relation to the rest of the bar.

### 6.3 Setting the Limits: Who Controls the Size of the Legal Profession in Japan?, *Kay-Wah Chan*

Whereas India has the largest number of law practitioners in the world, Japan adopted a different approach in developing its legal profession. For most of the twentieth century, the Japanese legal profession was a small elite group, with an extremely low number of lawyers *per capita* among developed countries. The pass rate for its bar exam was as low as 2–3 percent, and it was common for law students to take (and fail) it several times before entering the profession. From 2001, however, the Japanese government initiated a massive reform of its system of legal education and legal profession. Kay-Wah Chan's article offers an overview of this reform and its consequences for Japanese lawyers, with an emphasis on the political process behind the reform. It provides an excellent example of how state bureaucracies shape the development of the legal professions in Asia.

As compared with many other advanced economies, Japan is relatively late in seeing substantial growth in the number of lawyers (*bengoshi*). It had a paucity of *bengoshi*, which has only commenced to substantially expand since 2001. A pre-determined quota regulates the number of entrants to the profession. Legal professionals (*hôsô*) in Japan are divided into three branches: *bengoshi*, judges and prosecutors. To qualify as a legal professional, an aspiring candidate needs to pass the National Legal Examination (NLE), and then take a training programme and pass the graduation examination at the Legal Training and Research Institute (LTRI), operated by the Supreme Court. Until recent years, basically nobody failed the graduation examination. The large majority of LTRI graduates become *bengoshi*. Therefore, supply in the form of the quota on the number of NLE passers determines the size of the *bengoshi* profession. This supply, however, may have no connection with social demand.

The development of the NLE can be divided into four periods. First, from the late 1960s to 1990, the number of passers remained stagnant. Then, in the 1990s, with the first round of reforms, the number of passers started to increase. This expedited the increase in the number of *bengoshi* from the mid-1990s. The third period (the late 1990s to 2001) is characterised by the justice system reform movement and deliberations. Reform recommendations made in 2001 included a significant increase in the number of legal professionals. In the fourth period (post-2001), such reform was to be implemented. The number of passers increased substantially but recently the increase has slowed. [...]

Sixty-eight law schools opened in 2004 and were subsequently joined by six additional law schools. A new NLE was introduced for their graduates. The first new NLE was held in 2006. To phase out the old system, the old NLE was basically kept until 2010. From 2011, people who are not law school graduates can take a preliminary examination and, if they pass, can take the new NLE. The number of NLE passers initially sharply increased, but declined after reaching its peak in 2008.

As Miyazawa commented, there was "ample opportunity" for the politicians, bureaucrats and parties with vested interests to "chip away at and minimize" the reform during its implementation. An important factor for maintaining the reform momentum was the prime minister's leadership. The justice system reform received support from the former Prime Minister, Keizo Obuchi, who passed away in the midst of the reform movement in 2000. His successor, Yoshiro Mori, served a relatively short term (until April 2001). The next Prime Minister, Junichiro Koizumi, was a reformist and stayed in the post until September 2006, after law schools were opened. However, subsequently, the prime ministership in Japan became unstable. In the three years after Prime Minister Koizumi completed his terms, the LDP had three prime ministers before its loss of power to the Democratic Party of Japan (DPJ) in 2009. Then, the DPJ also had three prime ministers before its defeat in a lower house election in December 2012. In addition, after 2008, Japan was affected by the global financial crisis, the EU crisis and the strongest earthquake it had suffered in recorded history and tsunami. The natural disaster led to huge financial and human losses as well as a nuclear reactor crisis. These crises, for the government, are more imminent and serious than justice system reform.

The LDP's attitude towards the scale of the NLE reform also seemingly changed. In August 2007, then Justice Minister Kunio Hatoyama commented that it was excessive to have 3,000 NLE passers. On 16 October 2007, LDP's Justice System Research Council decided to examine whether to reconsider the extent of the increase in NLE passers. Justice Minister Hatoyama in January 2008 said that an increase in the number of legal professionals would influence quality, and that the Ministry would consider this issue. Such a change in attitude could also be due to the change in the prime ministership. The LDP Cabinets after Koizumi have revised the approach towards deregulation. As opposed to Koizumi's and his successor, Abe's, reformist direction (structural reform towards a self-responsibility society), the Fukuda administration (September 2007–September 2008) reverted to the traditional model of the government playing the "guardian" role. In March 2008, the Fukuda Cabinet decided to halt the acceleration of the increase in the number of NLE passers. Within the LDP, some members also began to demand a reconsideration of the pace of increase.

Further, as Miyazawa predicted, there was a possibility that the LDP and the business sector would stop their pursuit of justice system reform when their immediate goals were achieved. The business sector's needs indeed have, to some degree, been satisfied. The increase in the number of *bengoshi* in recent years has facilitated the expansion of the commercial legal practice sector. Foreign lawyers' operations in Japan have also been liberalised. Corporate in-house *bengoshi* have increased. The business sector may also have reservations regarding further substantial expansion of the *bengoshi* profession due to the change in the public's attitude towards the role of law (in other words, their legal culture). A survey conducted in 2009 found that, when asked about the action that they would take if an acquaintance failed to repay a large amount of money borrowed after the agreed deadline expired, the second most popular choice (multiple answers possible) picked by the respondents was "consultation with a *bengoshi*" (41.9 per cent). When asked about the action that they would take regarding disputes with siblings over the distribution of a deceased father's estate, the most popular choice (multiple answers possible) was "consultation with a *bengoshi*" (47 per cent). In contrast, in a survey conducted in 1983, when participants who did not think that their rights had been infringed in the past were asked about the type(s) of action that they would take if their rights were infringed, only 6.7 per cent of the respondents picked "consultation with a *bengoshi*" (multiple answers possible). The choices varied between these two surveys but comparison can be made because all these questions permitted multiple answers. This comparison shows a change in society's legal culture. To the large enterprises, a further expansion of the legal profession may be detrimental because it would enhance the general public's access to legal services and to the power to challenge them.

With the gradual implementation of reform and the increase in the number of *bengoshi*, there was growing opposition within the *bengoshi* profession against the increase in NLE passers. On 18 July 2008, the JFBA proposed a slow-down in the pace of expansion of the legal profession. Many local bar associations also demanded a reconsideration of the plan for growth.

Although the then Chief Cabinet Secretary criticised JFBA's proposal/demand, it is obvious that there was a "lack of political leadership at the highest level". This provided an opportunity for the three *hôsô* to be the sole decision-making parties. In reality, it is predominantly in the hands of the Supreme Court and particularly the MOJ.

The justice ministership, like the prime ministership, also keeps changing. In any case, the "main actor in policy-making" in a ministry in Japan is the administrative vice-minister who is the highest-ranking civil servant in that ministry and often "more powerful" than the minister. Persons serving this post in the MOJ almost all come from the PPO. The judiciary and MOJ are apparently not supportive of the substantial increase. They already showed a "cautious" attitude towards "hasty" reform during the justice system reform discussions of the late 1990s. As Kinoshita pointed out, a substantial increase in the number of *bengoshi* would cause an increase in civil and criminal litigation and necessitate a rapid increase in the number of prosecutors and judges, which the PPO and the judiciary do not want. The LTRI has a maximum annual capacity of 3,000 new apprentices. Replacement or abolishment of the LTRI would meet opposition from the Supreme Court, which insisted on maintaining the LTRI. It would not want to lose its involvement in legal training. In fact, the judiciary and the MOJ already took such a stand during the time when the JSRC was holding deliberations on the reform. Through the LTRI, the Supreme Court has a gatekeeper role. The Supreme Court therefore would not support a drastic increase in NLE passers. In its report produced to the JSRC, the Supreme Court stated that it did not agree to reform that began with a substantial increase in the number of legal professionals and left it to the market.

Further, as Okada commented, the government agencies which regulate quasi-legal professions in Japan might have a dislike towards the substantial increase in the number of *bengoshi* because this would result in *bengoshi's* encroachment into these quasi-legal professions' jurisdictions. Quasi-legal professions include judicial scriveners (regulated by the MOJ), tax attorneys (regulated by the National Tax Agency, the Ministry of Finance) and patent attorneys (regulated by the Japan Patent Office, the Ministry of Economy, Trade and Industry). Among these professions, judicial scriveners' practice areas are closest to *bengoshi*'s practices. They handle the work of drafting legal documents for filing with courts, and real estate and corporate registration matters. *Bengoshi* can also conduct such work. Hitherto, they were not interested because they had more lucrative and 'higher-status' matters to handle. A substantial increase in *bengoshi* will pose a serious threat to judicial scriveners and, albeit probably to a lesser extent, the other quasi-legal professions. *Bengoshi* are entitled to register as tax and patent attorneys without the need for passing the relevant certification examinations. Furthermore, the governmental agencies have respective supervisory power over the quasi-legal professions but not the *bengoshi*. Continual expansion of the number of *bengoshi* might cause a decline in these quasi-legal professions and replacement of them by *bengoshi*. This would worry their respective supervisory governmental agencies. The MOJ is one such agency.

The number of NLE passers declined after reaching its peak in 2008 and it remains far below the JSRC's target of 3,000 for 2010. The exact number of NLE passers is decided by the National Legal Examination Committee (NLE Committee) and the MOJ. The Justice Minister chose the NLE Committee members. Kinoshita concluded that the parties which really have an influence on the decision regarding the number of NLE passers were the Justice Minister and the ruling party. However, as discussed above, the bureaucrats inside the Ministry could also exert a strong influence. [...]

With the disappearance of both political leadership and the business sector's pressure on NLE reform due to political changes and seemingly the satisfaction of the business sector's needs, the issue of the number of NLE passers was again in the hands of the three *hôsô*. In reality, this means control is predominantly in the hands of the Supreme Court and particularly the MOJ. Both want to maintain the LTRI and a highly competitive NLE. Reform has been scaled down. The *bengoshi* who oppose an increase in their number are gradually getting what they want. Nevertheless, as shown in the analysis above, the size of the *bengoshi* profession in reality is controlled by the judiciary and the MOJ, due to their gatekeeping roles via the LTRI and the NLE, respectively. Their wishes, however, as shown by the justice system reform movement in the late 1990s, can be overridden by the wishes of the business sector, which is powerful and influential in policy making in Japan.

## 6.4 Practising on the Moon: Globalization and Legal Consciousness of Foreign Corporate Lawyers in Myanmar, Arm Tungnirun

In addition to state intervention, another external force that has strongly influenced the development of Asian legal professions in the early twenty-first century is globalization, especially the rise of the global market for legal services. As Anglo-American law firms entered Asian legal markets and set up offices in regional financial hubs and national business centers, many foreign corporate lawyers also found job opportunities in various Asian cities. Hong Kong, Singapore, Tokyo, Dubai, Shanghai, and Beijing have become popular locations for these expatriates from Britain, the United States, Canada, and other Western countries, but the role of foreign lawyers in shaping the local legal profession and corporate legal market is perhaps more significant in less conspicuous places. Arm Tungnirun's article on foreign corporate lawyers in Myanmar gives a rare glimpse at the work and lives of this unique group of law practitioners in Asia.

> "Whatever contract you are drafting, you have to think that, OK, I am now doing a project on the moon. There is no law." This is how Patrick, a Westerner, described practising corporate law in Myanmar. It is a bit strange then that, throughout my interview with him, he talked a lot about law. What did he mean exactly when he said there is no law in Myanmar? Do other expatriates who are practising corporate law in Myanmar agree with him?
>
> Patrick is now among a large group of expatriates – from both Western countries as well as neighbouring Asian ones – who came into Myanmar after the opening-up of the economy in 2011 and marketed themselves as "local legal advisers" for foreign investors or domestic enterprises doing business with these investors. When Myanmar opened its doors in 2011 after five decades of economic isolation, foreign investors flowed into the country to take advantage of opportunities to build from scratch power plants, roads, railways, telecommunication infrastructures, oil refineries, and a modern financial system. To serve this new business demand, foreign corporate lawyers set up shop and established themselves as legal experts in Myanmar's market. To date, they have been successful in pioneering and dominating Myanmar's corporate legal services market due to the lack of native corporate lawyers and the absence of restrictions that would prevent foreign lawyers and law firms from providing local legal advice. [...]
>
> Strictly speaking, 2011 was not the first time Myanmar had been exposed to the arrival of foreign lawyers and law firms. There had been a brief period when a similar process happened during the early 1990s, albeit to a far lesser

degree compared to the opening-up of the economy in 2011. Because of democratic protests and widespread economic discontent, in July 1988, the military government ended socialist policies. By November 1988, a new investment law was passed. Myanmar's attractive factors for foreign investment were there – rich natural resources and an inexpensive labour force. But, with a failed democratic election in 1990 following by the house arrest of Aung San Suu Kyi, human rights advocates effectively campaigned to shame foreign investors and governments from doing businesses with Myanmar. The US imposed sanctions on all new investments in 1997 and followed with even harsher sanctions in 2003. The EU also imposed major restrictions. There was a brief optimistic period during the early 1990s (prior to the US sanctions in 1997) when foreign investors came in to explore investment opportunities in Myanmar.

There were a handful of foreign law firms at the time. When the sanctions were imposed in 1997, most of these firms and their lawyers left the country. Only three to four foreign law firms remained, each with one or two foreign lawyers and one or two native lawyers assisting them. The foreign lawyers often flew in and out, dividing their time between the Yangon office and another office in a neighbouring country. When I asked whether there was work to do, Dan, a foreign lawyer who was in Myanmar during this period, explained that some foreign companies were grandfathered in. As he explained: "It was a pond with a few fishes. Basically we did all the work for the foreign companies that were still here." Thus, there were still three to four tiny foreign law firms during this closed period. In this study, I have interviewed all the "old hands" from that period who are still practising in the country today.

Since 2011, the number of foreign law firms in Myanmar has grown exponentially – perhaps at a rate unprecedented in world history – from a couple to more than 30 within four years. There is a variety in types of law firms: a small number of global firms with offices worldwide, firms focused solely on Myanmar or the region established by expatriates, and firms from neighbouring countries. Corresponding to this variety of firms, the "newcomers" – foreign lawyers who have come into the country after 2011 – are very diverse, consisting of Western lawyers as well as Asian lawyers from neighbouring countries such as Singapore, Thailand, the Philippines, Japan, China, and India.

Foreign law firms employ both foreign and native lawyers. Whereas native lawyers might play a major role in foreign firms in other countries, at this stage of development in Myanmar, foreign lawyers play the leading and dominant role in the firms I studied. The size of the firms is relatively small – ranging from an average of less than 10 to 30 lawyers in a couple of big firms. [...]

Old hands choose to join and assimilate into the local community of native lawyers while the newcomers choose to create their new, separate community. Social changes associated with economic globalization explain this difference. During the closed period prior to 2011, there were extremely few old hands. They also lacked social and economic capital due to the strict control of the military regime and the closed nature of the economy. Understandably, their best strategy was to join the community of local lawyers and to share the legal consciousness associated with that community, which placed an emphasis on local law and practices. In other words, they tried to assimilate themselves into the local community and the local legal system. In this sense, they became more passive, remaining as mere translators and communicators of local law and practices for foreign clients. They did not seek to actively change the legal consciousness or the legal system of the local community.

By contrast, since the country's exposure to the global economy in 2011, the number of foreign law firms and lawyers has grown exponentially within a short period, forming a critical mass sufficient to create their own separate community. They have also gained more prestige and power as they are connected to global capital that is in high demand from the new reformist government. Hence, they have formed their own community with a shared sense of legal superiority, representing what they perceive as more advanced legal systems and international business norms. They have also connected their identity with a larger community of international corporate lawyers outside of Myanmar. With their own community and legal consciousness, they have also begun to contest and shape the legal consciousness of the emerging community of corporate lawyers in Myanmar, which includes both themselves and native lawyers working in their firms.

In addition to the changes associated with the exposure to the global economy, another factor that might help explain the difference between the two groups is that their narratives correspond to the ways they wish to market themselves to clients. The old hands emphasize local law and practices because doing so fits with their comparative advantage of having practised in the country for a long period of time. In contrast, the newcomers lack experience and knowledge of local law. By portraying Myanmar as a country in which there is not much law and insisting that native lawyers do not know much law anyway, they justify their value. In turn, they also embark on a project of advocating for legal changes to transform Myanmar's legal system to adhere more to international standards that will benefit them and their clients in the long run. From this perspective, each community has its own underlying interests that explain their formulation and dissemination of certain legal narratives.

However, it is important to emphasize that the legal consciousness of the old hands in Myanmar is a product of their having practised in the closed period, rather than merely a product of the length of time of their practice. The finding of this study is not only that the old hands emphasize local law and practices, but also that they are more passive compared to the newcomers who actively promote the importation of foreign business law and norms. Newcomers are able to assume this more active role because the changes associated with Myanmar's economic globalization enable them to form their own separate community and legal consciousness. One might very well find that the old hands in any country, with their years of experience, will similarly emphasize localized expertise. For example, in his paper on China, Sida Liu also found that corporate lawyers with extensive experience there tend to emphasize expertise that is highly adaptive to the local Chinese context. It is true that perhaps the newcomers in Myanmar, after accumulating years of experience, may slowly shift to a greater engagement with the Myanmar's legal context. However, it is important to keep in mind that this very context will increasingly converge more with international norms. This will take place because of the newcomers' disdain for traditional norms and practices in this early stage of the country's development.

## II LAWYERS IN THE MARKET

The plurality of law practitioners in many Asian contexts leads to complex and vibrant ecologies of legal services markets, in which multiple types of legal professionals coexist and compete with one another in everyday work. This section uses three selections from the cases of China, India, and Vietnam to illustrate the different logics of market relations among law firms and their practitioners. While Sida Liu's article examines the market competition among ordinary law practitioners, Swethaa Ballakrishnen's study focuses on lawyers in corporate law firms. John Gillespie's article, by contrast, examines cause advocacy by successful commercial lawyers. Taken together, they present three different sites in which lawyers navigate or resist the forces of the legal services market.

## 6.5 Lawyers, State Officials, and Significant Others: Symbiotic Exchange in the Chinese Legal Services Market, Sida Liu

What drives the dynamics of competition in the market for legal services? In addition to the "turf battles" within a profession and between different professions, the relationship between legal professions and the state is also significant. As Sida Liu demonstrates, in the case of China, the "symbiotic exchange" between law practitioners in the market and judges and other officials in the state is a key social process that determines the outcomes of interprofessional competition between lawyers and basic-level legal workers. Drawing on in-depth interviews with over two hundred law practitioners across twelve provinces of China, Liu suggests the great importance of understanding the social positions of law practitioners between market and state and the interactions among them.

The Chinese legal profession has a recent yet broken history. The first group of Chinese lawyers in the modern sense appeared in the Republican era (1912–49), but most of them were concentrated in a few major cities. Although the Republican legal profession was initially denied by the Communist government, in July 1954 the MOJ appointed a number of major cities to establish "legal advisory divisions" (falü guwenchu) following the Soviet model. By June 1957, 820 such divisions had been established in 19 provinces, with a total of 2,572 full-time and 350 part-time lawyers. However, during the Anti-Rightist Campaign in 1957, lawyers were classified as a type of "rightist" and therefore disappeared from the Chinese legal system in the following two decades.

It was not until the late 1970s that lawyers were formally revived in China. The 1980 Interim Regulation on Lawyers defines them as "state legal workers" (article 1). At the time, all lawyers were employed by the state and worked in legal advisory divisions affiliated with different levels of state agencies or work units. Criminal defence, divorce and inheritance constituted much of lawyers' work during the 1980s. By 1988, when "co-operative law firms" (hezuo suo) were first permitted, there were just 21,051 full-time and 10,359 part-time lawyers in 3,473 law firms. Meanwhile, with the beginning of the "law dissemination" (pufa) campaigns in the mid-1980s, demands for legal services rapidly increased all over the country. This huge imbalance of the supply and demand of legal services generated a large vacant space in the market. In particular, the vast area of individual legal services at the street and township (jiedao xiangzhen) level was almost an unexplored territory.

It is into this vacant territory that alternative legal service providers began to emerge. As early as 1980, some street and township level justice agencies (*sifa suo*) in Beijing and a few provinces (such as Liaoning, Guangdong and Fujian) had already started to provide legal services to the local community, and in 1984 the Liaoning experience was adopted by the MOJ as the model to be spread to the whole country (IN04106). The 1987 Interim Regulation on Township Legal Service Firms formalized this type of grassroots legal service and named it "township legal service" (*xiangzhen falü fuwu*). In practice, like law firms' affiliation with different levels of the justice bureaus, all township legal service firms in the 1980s were affiliated with the grassroots justice agencies at the street and township level.

Compared to lawyers, the qualification standard of township legal workers was very low, requiring only a high school diploma and "certain legal knowledge." Even today, the educational and licensing requirements are still much lower for basic-level legal workers than for lawyers. Despite this, the work scope of the township legal service and lawyers has striking similarities. Except for criminal defence, township legal service firms were permitted to handle almost all areas of legal work, and because of their affiliation with streets and townships, they also assumed some administrative functions in local communities. In fact, most legal service firms and local justice agencies were merely "one team, two titles" (*yitao renma, liangkuai paizi*). [...]

An examination of the competition between lawyers and their emulators – mostly notably basic-level legal workers – requires an analysis of their symbiotic exchange with judicial and administrative agencies. It is necessary to start from a classification of all the major species in the Chinese legal services market according to their structural positions between market and state. In general, lawyers, basic-level legal workers, legal advisory agencies and various kinds of "black lawyers" are outsiders of the state apparatus, while judges, procurators, police officers, justice bureau officials and other state officials are insiders. This insider-outsider distinction is crucial for the market-state exchange because it differentiates actors' power and resources: the outsiders are rich in economic and social resources but lack political power; the insiders have firm control over political power and the allocation of resources but are often insufficiently remunerated by the state for their work. This sharp imbalance in resource distribution provides a hotbed for the symbiotic exchange between insiders and outsiders.

However, not every actor in the legal services market can be classified as an insider or an outsider. There are some law practitioners who are brokers between market and state, that is, they worked in the state apparatus and then moved out to practise in the market. A good example is the retired high-ranking officials who practise in law firms or legal service firms, or as individual "black lawyers." Another is the large number of law practitioners who used to work in the state sector or are close relatives of judges or state officials. These brokers are the "amphibians" in the legal services market because they have access to both state power and market resources. This structural position gives brokers enormous advantages in the resource flow between the two systems.

The closest symbiotic exchange in the Chinese legal services market is probably that between basic-level legal service firms and local justice bureaus. The justice bureaus set up legal service firms and transfer their retired officials and extra personnel to them. They also give the firms advantages for their practice. For instance, the housing of many legal services firms is provided free by the local justice bureaus or the street/township government, and when people come to the local justice bureau for legal help, they refer them to the legal service firms. On the other hand, legal service firms pay an annual "management fee" to the justice bureaus, use their revenue to support the operation of local justice agencies, and assist the justice agencies in their daily work. As a former district justice bureau chief in Ningxia vividly comments: "These legal workers are all my soldiers". Not incidentally, a lawyer on the All-China Lawyers Association forum also describes basic-level legal workers as the biological "sons and daughters" of the justice bureaus, whereas lawyers are only the "stepchildren".

Besides justice bureaus, basic-level legal workers also have frequent exchanges with local courts. Because legal service firms accommodate many retired or transferred judges and court staff, they often get case referrals from local courts, including a large number of legal aid cases. In extreme instances, the offices of some legal service firms are even located inside the court or its tribunals, and some basic-level legal workers occasionally work as judicial clerks during court trials or even draft judicial opinions for the judges. More frequently, basic-level legal workers would give judges a certain amount of "kickback" for every case referral, usually 20–30 per cent of the billings.

In fact, giving inducements to judges is not the prerogative of basic-level legal workers, but a general survival rule that most law practitioners in ordinary litigation must follow, regardless of their formal identities. Lawyers with no previous work experience or connection to the judicial agencies also have to use a variety of means to nurture their relationship with judges. Sometimes this takes the form of negotiated exchange, such as giving "kickbacks" to the judge on a case-by-case basis. More frequently, however, lawyers and other practitioners use reciprocal exchange to maintain and consolidate their symbiosis with judges. A successful lawyer in Taiyuan gives a great lecture on the subtle techniques of reciprocal exchange:

> To maintain these relations, even if [you have] no money and cannot give gifts, [you] still have to accumulate emotions in a piecemeal way, to penetrate step by step. Even if nothing is urgent, make some phone calls for greetings, ask whether he needs help in the family, and keep in touch, when cases come up give it to me your buddy. Remember his birthday and his child's birthday, because some people may not support their parents, some people may not love their wives, but everybody cares about his children. Send a small cake when the time comes, some emotional credits are established, and let him refer cases to me. These kinds of things are not about the amount of money, because the greediness of human beings could never be filled, but about striking him with emotions. If I give cigarettes to the judge, no matter how many judges are in the office, I always give each person a pack, five packs of cigarettes are only a little more than 100 yuan. Just like the commercial says, "Input one drop of water every day, when difficulties come up, you will have the pacific ocean."

This quotation clearly shows the incremental nature of reciprocal exchange. To build a solid bridge from market to state, case-by-case monetary transactions are necessary but often not sufficient. Emotional attachment and mutual trust are at least equally important. Moreover, as receiving money or gifts for specific cases is considered to be corruption, reciprocal exchange is a safer choice in order to evade external sanction. Other techniques that law practitioners adopt in symbiotic exchange with judges include hosting dinners and entertainments, playing "business mah-jongg" with judges and intentionally losing money, or even renting apartments in the court's residential community and becoming neighbours with judges. In a nutshell, the symbiosis between market and state actors often rests on emotions and trust rather than pure economic benefits.

### 6.6 Just Like Global Firms: Unintended Gender Parity and Speculative Isomorphism in India's Elite Professions, *Swethaa Ballakrishnen*

As discussed earlier, the state and globalization are two major social forces that shape the development of Asian legal professions. While the state intervenes in the legal services market by setting up professional groups and mediate their competition, globalization penetrates the legal profession by influencing its most prestigious and profitable sector – namely, corporate law firms that serve large, multinational corporations. Swethaa Ballakrishnen's study of India's new corporate law firms, which emerged in the 1990s, connects the sociolegal scholarships on gender equity and the globalization of law firms and provides an account of the unintended consequences of globalization on gender in the legal profession.

> Recent comparative demographic research on the legal profession reveals that while most countries have followed a trend of positive feminization over the last half a century, two countries – India and China – still offer strong resistance to this norm. Of these, India, despite having one of the world's largest legal professions with over a million lawyers, still remains the least feminized with women comprising less than 10% of the profession overall. This unequal representation becomes even starker at senior levels. And the patterns described in historical accounts continue today, with many successful professional women still facing inhospitable work environments. India's new corporate law firms, however, offer a sharp contrast to this pattern, with women attorneys in these firms experiencing a vastly more encouraging professional environment. Among these new and prestigious firms, women constitute slightly more than half of the entering cohort and a similarly significant representation at partnership. This kind of gender parity is unusual for prestigious workplaces in general but especially stark given the broader evidence about gender and professional work in India. What enables women professionals to so successfully navigate their environments? In particular, what about these new kinds of organizations afford women within them a differential experience? This is the empirical point of departure that motivates this research. [...]
>
> While lawyers with successful pre-liberalization practices started many of these firms, it was only post-1991 that the organization of elite law firm practice began to mimic the institutional prototype of the Anglo-American corporate mega-law firm. The context of these firms' emergence were essential because it set up why these firms were in a uniquely vulnerable position, both vis-à-vis their peers within the profession as well as their global audiences.
>
> As I describe above, before 1991, private investment in domestic industries was not allowed and trade was heavily regulated. This meant that domestic lawyers were involved in mainly domestic transactions. However, with liberalization, domestic law firms had to reinvent themselves to deal with a range of

international cross-border transactional work (e.g., mergers and acquisition, private equity, and international finance transactions). [...]

Together, these emergence conditions created a fragile position for elite Indian law firms. These firms were organizing themselves in new ways, doing new work, facing sophisticated international clients, *and* they were doing all of this without the direct structural intervention of foreign firms. And as firms that were boisterously opposing the entry of foreign law firms, Indian law firms seemed to be in a particularly vulnerable position for maintaining and signaling a competitive global image to their competitors and clients alike. To strategically position themselves, firms adopted two dominant mechanisms, each of which was meant to signal a certain identity of modernity and meritocracy both to external audiences (i.e., clients, international peers) and to their own associates. First, they differentiated themselves from the rest of their peers and made clear that they were unique professional spaces not tainted by the old-school logic of their predecessors. And second, they started aggressively signaling that they were capable of being global firms. Both these approaches, especially the latter, required them to mimic norms of global firms, which they did in a variety of ways. However, crucially, as firms without any real connections to these Western firms, this knowledge was asymmetric and the mimicking, as a result, speculative. [...]

But it was not just that these associates and partners *felt* like their firm was different from traditional litigation practice. Top law firms in the country recruited in local law schools almost exclusively on the basis of merit and invited their new associates to an environment that was both visibly and organizationally different from traditional legal practice. While litigation practices and smaller firms operated in decrepit old buildings, offices of large elite law firms in Mumbai looked and felt like any international law firm. Located in prime real estate, and designed to impress, these air-conditioned, fine-art-studded offices felt distinctly different from the pigeon-nest lined buildings, with their old elevators, that housed older litigation offices. But it was not just how these spaces were experienced by associates that was telling of how deeply ingrained this logic of differentiation was. Partners, many of whom had been central to the creation of these firms, were keen to highlight the ways in which their firms were unlike traditional legal practice in the country, especially when it came to how the firm treated its associates. Kamal, a senior partner who had seen the firm grow over the last two decades, made the comparison this way:

> In the courts, in litigation practice, nobody is treated equally – the judiciary still hasn't reached that level of maturity. The thinking used to be "Ah, the

women will come, get married" or, even, "If they make a point (during court arguments) then it will be more emotional than substance." But all other things being equal, in a place like this [an elite law firm] women score over men ... Things like gender discrimination, gender harassment, that just isn't there ... look, we have equal number of male and female partners. A thought like this doesn't even arise... The culture is just different here.

The "culture" Kamal mentioned is important because it set the tone for the kind of merit-based workspace that Niyant and Nina spoke about. This projection of being more gender sensitive than litigation practice was central to the identity of these firms – as was the ideology that gender would not be the yardstick used to discriminate. Instead, by maintaining high standards of merit-based entry, they saw themselves as being above the clutches of discrimination that plagued their more traditional peers. And this commitment was well received. Like many of her peers, Lata, a senior associate in one of these firms who saw her path to partnership clearly before her, told me "if I had been in litigation, it would have been different... But not here [in an elite law firm]." [...]

I use the phrase "assumed similarity" here because this perception of international firms as capstones of meritocracy and gender parity was closer to an ideal-type assumption than it was to reality. And this senior partner's statement was not an isolated reference – some version of the phrase "merit is everything" came up in other conversations about gender in these firms, confirming that even if they did not have structural access to global firms, there was a central assumption that the ideology of merit and equal opportunity was important to those global firms. The pressure to "keep up with the times" demanded an aggressive reorientation that brought these Indian firms' own image in line with this prominent ideology, to show that they were serious global players. At the same time, as local firms without strong connections to the global firms they were trying to mimic, their knowledge and response to these macrocultural scripts was both speculative and, incidentally, more adherent. I use the term "speculative" here because there is no indication that firms thought gender equity was the only or even a central way to signal this global isomorphism. They were trying to do everything they could to gain legitimacy by being "modern" and "meritocratic": being gender-agnostic happened to be one way of accomplishing this. But importantly, many of the ways in which they were trying to be "just like global firms" arose out of conjecture rather than actual knowledge. In fact, as the case of consulting firms revealed, actual knowledge was counterproductive to the gender project because, among other things, actual knowledge could reveal that women were ill represented in most elite global workforces. [...]

In other words, lawyers did not necessarily think that Western firms had equal number of women; instead they saw meritocracy and equal opportunity as core ideals on which these firms were built – or at least saw meritocracy, independent of outcome, as an important ideology that these firms subscribed to. And in their need to aggressively signal both competence and competitive advantage in a global environment, meritocracy became a predominant ideal norm that Indian firms paid ceremonial deference to. In turn, their offices looked like the firms in whose image they emerged: they structured their partnerships with lockstep compensation, they hired from prestigious law schools in the country with recruitment and internship cycles that resembled those of their foreign peers, and they promoted their women partners without attention to gender. This lack of attention to gender did not mean these firms were being gender friendly, and this nondiscrimination on the basis of gender did not mean that firms were substantively egalitarian. As I show in other work, these conditions privileged different kinds of inequalities and reproduced a range of other hierarchies. But in being nondiscriminatory on the axis of gender within a professional sector where this was highly unusual, these firms, almost inadvertently, superseded the gendered outcomes of the Western firms they were attempting to ideologically mimic. As the senior partner above put it, these development occurred "sometimes not consciously...it's just happened that way."

### 6.7 The Juridification of Cause Advocacy in Socialist Asia: Vietnam as a Case Study, *John Gillespie*

Although commercial lawyers are often assumed to be apolitical, some of them also fight for legal and political reforms. This is especially the case for developing countries in which there is not a high degree of specialization in the legal professions. In such cases, prominent lawyers often wear multiple hats – they are key actors in commercial cases but also advocate for reforms of the legal system. It is also not uncommon for commercial lawyers to shift their practice toward public interest law or human rights at a later stage of their careers. John Gillespie's case study of cause advocacy in Vietnam tells the story of Le Cong Dinh, one of Vietnam's most successful commercial lawyers who was later charged and sentenced because of his criminal defense work on constitutional issues. It is a telling example of the political side of lawyers' commercial practice.

In many post-colonial Asian societies law is the language of the state, and lawyers actively construct this language and police its boundaries. Socialist Asia has a different legal history. Engineers, rather than lawyers built the state. There were no lawyer revolutionaries like Gandhi to inspire future generations of cause advocates and no memory of courts protecting civil rights to guide them. Socialist revolutionaries not only expelled the colonial regime, but also colonial legalism. They discredited colonial notions such as private rights and independent courts to clear space for Leninist organizational structures that subordinated the legal system to the Communist Party. This article argues that despite decades of legal reform, the socialist legacy continues to mediate the way cause advocates use the law in Socialist Asia. [. . .]

Given the tight state management of lawyers, it is surprising that public interest litigation occasionally surfaces in Vietnamese courts. Interviews reveal a complex range of reasons why lawyers take on social causes. Although all the lawyers interviewed believed that the law should protect the poor and vulnerable, they expressed wildly different views about who are the poor and vulnerable and how to use courts to protect them.

A. *Classifying Cause Lawyers*
It is possible to position cause lawyers along a continuum with those advocating *hoan thien* (improving) the legal system at one end and those promoting *cai cach* (reforming) the legal system at the other. *Hoan thien* implies small incremental and technical changes to the legal system while *cai cach* presents a more radical challenge, especially to socialist legality. Naturally, there is considerable overlap between these approaches.

*Hoan thien* entails some form of engagement with state officials to make the existing system, including socialist legality, work more efficiently. In an economy dominated by state-owned and -controlled firms, many prominent commercial lawyers owe their success to personal relationships with the party and state officials. Not only are they reluctant to promote causes that might embarrass the party, they do not want to promote rights-based discourse that might disrupt lucrative personal networks by shedding light on the porous legal boundaries between state and society. Lawyers from this group occasionally accept politically sensitive criminal cases, but are careful to base their arguments on procedural issues that avoid challenging party narratives. In short, they advocate incremental improvements to procedural justice rather than state protection of civil rights-substantive justice.

Support for *cai cach* (reforms) comes primarily from foreign law firms and a handful of domestic law firms that work with international donors on law reform programs. Foreign law firms want private legal rights to disrupt the state-supported relational networks that regulate domestic commerce, but they are more interested in property rights than civil rights.

What unifies the domestic lawyers who promote *cai cach* reforms is a desire for the law and legal institutions to check party-state prerogative powers. They push the boundaries of party-state narratives by arguing that *nha nuoc phap quyen* doctrines should entirely displace socialist legality. Although sceptical about the willingness of party leaders to move in this direction, some members of the group work with reform-minded state officials to secure a law-based state.

A much smaller subgroup of *cai cach* lawyers believe that the party-state has no intention of abandoning socialist legality and placing the party and state under legal rule. For them, confrontation and protest are the only ways to highlight shortcomings in the legal system and pressure the party-state to protect civil rights. It is estimated that there are fewer than twenty lawyers comprising this subgroup at any one time.

B. *Le Cong Dinh: Case Study*

Le Cong Dinh exemplifies the confrontational cause lawyers. For a time, he was considered one of Vietnam's most successful commercial lawyers. Dinh rose to national prominence by defending Vietnamese catfish exporters in 2002 against anti-dumping actions brought by United States producers. His commercial law firm represented prestigious foreign companies such as Yahoo!, Sun Wah International, Nestle, and Toyota.

Dinh fulfilled the state ideal that lawyers should work to build the economy and promote state socio-economic policies. He cooperated closely with the Ministry of Justice in preparing an industry plan to develop a globally competitive legal profession in Vietnam and worked to protect Vietnamese commercial interests against foreign competitors. Eventually, the government rewarded Dinh by appointing him as the Vice Chairman of the Ho Chi Minh City Bar Association.

Dinh's commercial practice brought him into contact with foreign lawyers and academics, and through these connections he gradually developed an interest in civil rights and defending Vietnamese dissidents. Most significantly, while he continued to think of himself as a patriot working for the national interest, he became convinced that a just society needed radical *cai cach* reforms. Without a local tradition of cause lawyering to guide him, Dinh looked first to France and then to the United States for inspiration. A Fulbright scholarship to study at Tulane University completed the transformation in his thinking.

Most of Dinh's clients were charged with violating article 88 of the Criminal Code, which forbids "raising propaganda against the state." The state branded his clients dissidents, not only for sponsoring fundamental constitutional change, but also for joining banned pro-democracy parties, such as Bloc 8406. None of his clients were accused of using or advocating the use of violence against the state. Some clients attacked the government for allowing environmental damage, others for colluding with China over border disputes, and still others for corruptly benefiting from land dealings. These issues are routinely discussed in the state-controlled media. According to Dinh, their real crime was advocating multi-party democracy and freedom of speech as the remedy to Vietnam's social and economic problems.

Dinh defended his clients by arguing that article 69 of the Constitution 1992 protects free speech, as do international covenants signed by the Vietnamese government. He maintained that the Constitution 1992 affords citizens "freedom of opinion and speech" to propose unorthodox and controversial views about the state. This right was meaningless, he argued, if state agencies could use criminal sedition laws to arbitrarily suppress critical thought. He emphasized the role legal rights play in defining boundaries between the state and society in commerce, land tenure, and family disputes. He also challenged judges to extend legal protection to civil rights. During a trial in 2007, Dinh informed the court: "Talking about democracy and human rights cannot be seen as anti-government unless the government itself is against democracy."

Dinh knew that his arguments were entirely rhetorical and that, even if the courts were willing, they lacked the discretionary powers to assess the constitutionality of legislation and administrative action. He wrote that the courts functioned like "civil authority machines rather than as adjudicative agencies which [have] a role to uphold one justice in a community with a plurality of interests." He urged the courts to become more active in protecting constitutional rights; a process he thought might "blow a stream of vitality into the dry and motionless body of legislation ... ."

Dinh relied on arguments developed by academic lawyers who for decades had called for *bao hien* (literally, constitutional protection). *Bao hien* can mean anything from promoting the Constitution as the supreme legislative instrument to a Western liberal form of constitutionalism. What unites the different threads of this discourse is a shared belief in the need for a constitutional court (or tribunal) with powers to bring the Constitution Vietnam 1992 into daily life.

Police charged Dinh on June 13, 2009 with the same sedition offense used to silence his clients. They claimed that Dinh used court cases to "propagandize against the regime and distort Vietnam's Constitution and laws." To identify the boundaries of permissible discourse, it is instructive to examine why the state moved to silence Dinh. Lawyers familiar with his case claim that his crime was not advocating constitutional change, but rather disloyalty to the party. Most of what Dinh said about state protection of civil rights had already been published by the mainstream media and academic journals. In the lawyers' opinions, the authorities were offended because Dinh continued to challenge party orthodoxies after security police had warned him to stop.

What complicates Dinh's case is the charge that he joined with banned foreign organizations in Thailand to overthrow the state. To the surprise of many who knew him well, Dinh admitted in a televised confession that he collaborated with "foreign agents." He also confessed to acquiring subversive ideas about civil rights while studying in the United States. This link between civil rights and foreigners resonates with the "peaceful evolution" (*dien bien hoa binh*) campaign mounted by conservative party cadres. According to this narrative, foreigners – especially overseas Vietnamese living in America – use civil rights and democracy to discredit the party and engineer regime change in Vietnam. Perhaps due to his public affirmation of loyalty to the party, Dinh was given a comparatively light sentence of five years imprisonment for a crime that carries a twenty year maximum sentence.

## III LAWYERS AND STATE TRANSFORMATIONS

From the readings in Sections I and II of this chapter, it is evident that the fate of Asian lawyers is closely tied to state transformations. These political changes include not only revolutions, military coups, and other types of regime changes, but also incremental and recursive changes in a country's political culture and state institutions. Situated between legal rules and political power, lawyers are frequently found in the frontline of state transformations. The legal professions in many Asian states were created and transformed in the shadows of colonialism and authoritarianism, as well as lawyers' struggles for legal and political ideals such as proceduralism, judicial independence, human rights, and rule of law. This section focuses on this political aspect of the lawyer-state relationship and provides three cases of political mobilization in which lawyers, judges, prosecutors, and other legal actors seek to transform the nature of their states. Some of these struggles led to the democratization of an authoritarian state, as in the case of Taiwan, whereas others retreated or suffered setbacks, as in the cases of Pakistan and Hong Kong.

## 6.8 The Political Origins of Professional Identity: Lawyers, Judges, and Prosecutors in Taiwan's State Transformation, *Ching-fang Hsu*

In most civil law jurisdictions, judges, prosecutors, and lawyers are the three pillars of the legal professions. However, these three professional groups do not always share similar norms, political ideologies, or causes for collective action. As Ching-fang Hsu demonstrates in her historical study, all the three legal professions in Taiwan contributed to the process of democratization since the 1980s, which transformed Taiwan from an authoritarian one-party state to a vibrant democracy. Nevertheless, lawyers, judges, and prosecutors pursued different political ideals and, in this process, formed distinct professional identities.

The three Taiwanese legal professions pledge to different professional norms in accordance with their political positions and experiences with the party-state. The timing of ideational transformation also reflects this political relationship: Taiwanese lawyers, incorporating most social momentum afar from direct party-state manipulation, made a major breakthrough early in 1989–90; judges, with a strong constitutional mandate and political concession, started a series of norm-building in the mid-1990s; and prosecutors, facing the most persistent (attempts at) political control, aligned the latest, in 1998.

Taiwanese lawyers experienced a modest degree of control, as the state contained the bar from upstream by a differentiated admission policy. As the following section shows, the government mainly admits legal practitioners with a prior relationship to the state to ensure their deference before entering the profession, yet has limited direct control of the overall lawyer population. Being a relatively autonomous and embedded actor in the Taiwanese society, liberal-minded lawyers first reclaimed their own bar association and quickly joined the societal momentum at the height of democratization to become the Taiwanese people's advocate. Taiwanese judges, on the other hand, were systematically restrained through multiple channels to institutionalize their conformity, which, in turn, allows political influence to trickle down. Pushing back against this party-state manipulation, judicial independence became the highest priority and focus for action. Co-optation serves the main strategy of judges during democratic transition: skillfully utilizing various institutional platforms available to them, reformist judges collaborated with politicians and judicial bureaucrats to consolidate the normative pledge, despite the fact some of them were agents of the authoritarian party-state. Prosecutors, however, witnessed the strongest degree of political control. Institutionally inseparable from the state, prosecutors faced top-down and persistent attempts to instrumentalize them, even after Taiwan's first party turnover in 2000. Combating such abuse of power, Taiwanese prosecutors developed an identity of justice. The reformist prosecutors consistently resist policy or political actions aiming to compromise them; they focus on investigating corruption and only selectively co-operate with the administration to secure conditions facilitating such pursuit of their ideals. [...]

In Taiwan, a strong tradition of "people's advocate" is shared by many politically active lawyers. Originally initiated in the 1990s, the identity as "the legal profession in opposition" denotes the mission that lawyers should scrutinize those in power and advocate for those who are not. This professional norm was developed as opposed to the KMT party-state by a minority of locally educated lawyers in the 1980s. Most evidently observed in their contestation in the Taipei Bar leadership elections, the final success in 1990 marked the end of not only state control over their profession, but also the baseline principle representative of Taiwanese lawyers' collective pursuit. [...]

The dissemination of the reformist ideal that lawyers *should* advocate for the people goes beyond bar associations. Catching the wave of democratization, many who carried reformist ideals entered, even created, diverse types of leadership positions in the rapidly transforming Taiwanese society. On the one hand, a number of active members of the Taipei Bar entered politics to run the newly democratized government. In the 1990s, the electoral system began to open up, and lawyers associated with the ACL network logically transferred their expertise as advocates and their identity as local elites into representative politics. In the civil society, on the other hand, the liberal lawyers connected to a wide range of civic movements as they shared the same momentum challenging the party-state. Directly funded and lobbied by the ACL network, the Judicial Reform Foundation (JRF) was established in 1995 as a NGO, while the Legal Aid Foundation was legislated for in 2003, fully funded by the national budget but run by an executive team of lawyers. Despite three party turnovers in the twenty-first century, both organizations expanded exponentially in budget scale and stood as key players shaping the agenda of judicial policy and practice of access to justice in Taiwan. Loosely connected to the network are the Taiwan Association for Human Rights, the Humanistic Education Foundation, the Taiwan Alliance to End the Death Penalty, and a feminist lawyer Yu Mei-nu, who successfully led gender-equality movements in both constitutional litigations and legislative lobbying by the mid-2000s. Admittedly, the ACL and the related networks do not represent all causes of all Taiwanese lawyers. There are a number of key organizations supported by lawyers (such as the Consumers Foundation) and other lines of legal mobilization (such as the environmentalist attorneys connected to the Wild at Heart Legal Defence Association) contributing to the vibrant and diversified "rights revolution" in Taiwan. Nevertheless, the ideal that the ACL signifies – lawyers as "the legal profession in opposition" – is still representative of Taiwanese lawyers that marked the beginning of such ideational turn.

Simply put, the impact of such an ideal is twofold. First, the embodiment in the early 1990s directly and radically changed the character and self-perception of the profession, from a contained subordinate of the party-state apparatus to an autonomous and vocal representative of Taiwanese citizens. Those who carry these ideals sustained their influence in the profession and mobilized societal and political capital to institutionalize and expand this line of pursuit. Second, the rhetorical and symbolic legitimacy of "people's advocate" has been elevated to become the default in the community, which in turn prepares a space to facilitate other lines of advocacy. After all, a functional democracy allows a wide variety of causes, and it is only natural for this professional ideal in the name of the people to be so prevalent that it is hardly discernible from the general public-interest practice of lawyers as Taiwan democratizes. [...]

Taiwanese judges, by contrast, strive for *independence*. The Taiwanese experience nicely demonstrates that judges *act* to defend judicial independence not out of pure self-interest or strategic concern, but for normative reasons. That is, judges act because they believe they *should* be independent, as opposed to the institutionalized control they witnessed in the party-state era. Similarly to the pattern of formation and dissemination of their lawyer counterparts, small groups of young and reformist-minded judges first aligned in the early 1990s, and collectively mobilized to challenge the top-down administrative control and lobbied for constitutional protection of judicial independence. The network later entered management positions in the judicial bureaucracy, first under KMT, and continued working with the administration after the first party turnover in 2000. [...]

It would be inaccurate, however, to say that the reformist network succeeded in all their reform attempts. Some reformist judges did enter authority positions (whereas others simply remained on the bench), but they encountered various pushbacks when putting their reformist ideals into practice. For example, when one of the key figures, Judge Lu Tai-lang, was promoted to directorship of the personnel department in the Judicial Yuan to carry out organizational reform, his promotion was criticized so heatedly that the Control Yuan, the ombudsman agency, issued a report targeting him: "Ever since Judge Lu assumed office, his work on personnel business ... no positive outcome is observed, but negative impact has occurred." His intended reform policy to set a term limit on chief judges of the trial panel, delinking seniority and professional capacity to prevent case meddling, also experienced strong counter-mobilization from senior judges in the High Courts. Following Lu Tai-lang, another reformist judge, Chou Jan-chuen, succeeded the directorship to continue personnel reform, but similarly experienced great pressure. The pressure even went up to the president of the Judicial Yuan, who intended to support Chou but faced extensive opposition. An anecdote shows the degree of pressure: one day, the president was literally "cornered" in his office by some senior judges before leaving work, to make him promise to let go of the internal reform guideline. Indeed, the reformist network's attempt to transform the personnel structure was compromised considerably. Their experience after entering the judicial administration accurately shows not all ideals were elevated, but judicial independence is *the* normative commitment, among others, that survived and was institutionalized in the Taiwanese judicial community. [...]

For Taiwanese prosecutors, *justice* is an indispensable professional norm. Particularly, checking the abuse of power is at the core of this ideational pursuit. While the pattern of formation, mobilization, and dissemination is similar to their judicial counterparts, Taiwanese prosecutors' normative commitments come *through* interest-based requests, including securing resources for investigation and status protection as "judicial officer." Targeting the KMT's clientalist party-state in the 1990s, a small group of reformist-minded prosecutors successfully aligned in 1998 and mobilized to break the top-down administrative control and lobbied for institutional support to prosecute abuse of political power. The network of the Prosecutor Reform Association (PRA) plays a critical role in setting the agenda and lobbying for legislations reforming the procuracy, while many key figures in the PRA network lead a number of prominent, if not legendary, corruption investigations in post-transition Taiwan, including the charges of three democratically elected presidents. [...]

Commentators familiar with Taiwanese politics may argue against the advancement of the prosecutors' pursuit of the ideal of justice, especially between 2008 and 2016, when the KMT was back in power, when the political instrumentality of the SIU was discernible. However, attempts to instrumentalize the prosecution for the interest of individual politicians are, and will always be, present in politics; in fact, the attempts precisely constitute the structural constraints from which prosecutors demonstrate their agentic pursuit. It is hence imperative, first, to seek empirical evidence if, and where, Taiwanese prosecutors show consistent logic of action to resist such instrumentalization under different political containment. It is the *presence* of resistance, not the *success* of resistance, that indicates prosecutors' normative commitment. Second, how such action, allegedly out of the pursuit of an ideal, is received by the prosecutors' community is another important piece of evidence. As the following analysis aims to argue, a second, even third, generation of "reformist prosecutors" clearly passes on the ideal that prosecutors *should* pursue justice to check power, and there is also evidence suggesting the collective support of such an ideal. [...]

It is empirically challenging to verify the impact of ideas, especially when actors face great external constraints. For those politically active prosecutors in Taiwan, they *do* experience political containment, and their attempts to establish, disseminate, and consolidate their normative commitments are shadowed, if not covered, by continuous instrumentalization from the incumbent political power. However, evidence still reveals the consistent presence of ideationally driven pursuits within the system and with numerous case investigations, both as individual cases and as a lock-in institutional effect by different generations of reformists who are linked intellectually through a particular network.

### 6.9 Civil Society and the Lawyers' Movement of Pakistan, *Sahar Shafqat*

Taiwan's state transformation was a long, incremental process that involved all the three legal professions of judges, prosecutors, and lawyers. By contrast, in the case of Pakistan, the lawyers' movement was a shorter, more conspicuous event, but it also involved a coalition of lawyers, judges, and civil society activists. As Sahar Shafqat argues, Pakistani lawyers and their allies positioned the movement as a prodemocracy movement rather than a movement for professional interests, which enabled them to broaden its public appeals in order to challenge the authoritarian regime.

This article examines the 2007–2009 lawyers' movement in Pakistan in order to explore the conditions under which judiciaries become politicized under authoritarian regimes. The conventional wisdom on judicial politics has tended to exclude judicial actors as agents of democratization, but there is a growing body of work that recognizes that courts and lawyers can play a democracy-affirming role even in authoritarian regimes. The lawyers' movement arose in March 2007 in response to General Pervez Musharraf's unconstitutional sacking of the Pakistan Supreme Court Chief Justice Iftikhar Chaudhry. Remarkably, the movement, which was led by lawyers but also included citizen groups, students, women's rights activists, religious groups, and political parties, was able to challenge the Musharraf dictatorship successfully. Although it is referred to as the "lawyers' movement," it was a prodemocracy movement that came to represent the multiple and sometimes competing goals of judicial independence, antimilitary dictatorship, and civilian electoral democracy. It played a crucial role in the return of democratic politics, the eventual ouster of Musharraf, and the reinstatement of the Chief Justice in 2009. Pakistan's case provides an opportunity to examine the ways in which judiciaries become politicized in authoritarian regimes, and the role that lawyers and judges can play in assisting the democratization process. As Ginsburg notes, such cases are rare because "there are many reasons that we should not expect courts to be at the very forefront of democratization" – and in the case of Pakistan, it was the bench that led the way by being the first to resist the dictatorship before the bar followed. The mobilization of lawyers and judges against the Musharraf dictatorship is even more remarkable given that the Pakistani judiciary has historically provided judicial cover to military dictators.

This article argues that under the right conditions judicial actors can play an important role in the democratization process. In the case of the Pakistani lawyers' movement, several conditions helped embolden an erstwhile proestablishment judiciary under the authoritarian regime. When the regime attacked the judiciary, the lawyers' community organized to defend the interests of the legal community, but it was not until the regime imposed an Emergency that the legal community joined forces with other civil society actors to push for democratization. Civil society, defined here as nonlawyer citizen activist groups, played a vital role in helping the judiciary become politicized, and in linking the lawyers' movement to the larger political cause of democratization. By helping to position the movement as a broad national prodemocracy movement rather than a movement narrowly focused on the professional interests of the legal community, civil society played a crucial role in helping the Pakistani lawyers' movement succeed. I argue that without this important factor, the lawyers' movement would have been unable to act as the vanguard of the movement to oust the dictatorial regime of General Pervez Musharraf, which eventually led to the restoration of democracy. [...]

The Pakistan lawyers' movement can be divided into five phases: mobilization, confrontation, resistance, reorientation, and revival.

*Phase I: Initial Mobilization (March–July 2007)*
The first phase of the movement took place after General Musharraf placed Chief Justice Iftikhar Chaudhry under suspension (against procedural norms), following a legal reference against him. Both the act itself and the imagery of the moment served to inflame the legal community and arouse public opinion against the Musharraf regime. Although Musharraf's intention was clearly to remove Chaudhry from the bench altogether, the Chief Justice and the legal community joined forces and insisted on following due process. Consequently, the bench was successful in constituting a Supreme Judicial Council to investigate the charges against Chaudhry. This period saw the beginning of the legal community's popular mobilization, with the advent of the Chief Justice's tour to various bar associations around the country and a regular strike by lawyers; both were highly successful modes of protest that helped unify the legal community and would continue throughout the movement. The Supreme Judicial Council eventually restored Chaudhry to his office in July 2007.

*Phase II: Confrontation (July–November 2007)*
The period after Chaudhry's initial restoration was a period of increasing confrontation between the Musharraf regime and the judiciary. The fulcrum of this tension was Musharraf's decision to contest the election for the presidency. The Pakistani Constitution places limits on military personnel holding public office. Since 2002, Musharraf had held the dual offices of Chief of the Army Staff (a military post) and president (constitutionally, a civilian political post). Musharraf had managed to do this by passing amendments to the Constitution, and the Supreme Court, consistent with its historically proestablishment role, upheld these changes, but now, Musharraf indicated that he would run for another five-year term when his term was up in October 2007. Lawyers, civil society groups, and opposition political parties filed legal petitions against Musharraf's eligibility to run for office. The court was about to rule against Musharraf on November 3 when he imposed the Emergency, sacked all the members of the higher judiciary, and demanded that they take a fresh oath of office under a new Provisional

Constitutional Order (PCO). Two-thirds of the judges refused, and were placed under arrest and replaced with new, compliant judges.

*Phase III: Emergency and Active Resistance (November 2007–February 2008)*
The Emergency measures Musharraf imposed targeted more than just members of the judiciary; the regime also began arresting thousands of lawyers and issued a crackdown on the media, especially the electronic media, which he had found so nettlesome. This presented an opportunity for civil society activists to mobilize against the regime, and this renewed attack also convinced the lawyers' leadership that independence of the judiciary was now possible only with the removal of Musharraf and a return to civilian rule: in other words, democratization. For example, Munir Malik, one of the main lawyers leading the movement, noted that:

> After the 20th of July, when the Chief was restored, there was a section [of lawyers] which said OK, [Chaudhry] has been restored, the movement is over. But we said no. We should look at what has caused this in the first place. That was the lack of constitutionalism, the lack of civilian supremacy.

Thus, the mobilization of lawyers and civil society activists intensified. The main political parties became louder in their opposition to Musharraf. Protest activity, tentative at first, became bolder, especially as it became clearer that even Musharraf's external patron, the United States, was alarmed at his actions and his seeming inability to transition smoothly to a "guided democracy." Bar associations began mobilizing, organizing protests and rallies, and lawyers refused to appear before the PCO judges, viewing them as illegitimate. Meanwhile, the Chief Justice and his advisors tested the regime by continuing his tours at local bar associations. These tours quickly turned into opportunities for protest activity, as both lawyers and civil society activists would march with the Chief Justice's caravan for miles as it made its journey around the country. Other judges made similar tours and were often showered with rose petals by admirers.

A few events during this period helped catalyze important political shifts. First, there was the assassination of former Prime Minister Benazir Bhutto in December 2007, which shocked the nation and also threw previous political deals into turmoil. Second, Musharraf was pressured not just by movement activists, but also by his supporters in the army as well as in the United States, to step down as Chief of the Army in order to remain president, to retain at least some semblance of constitutionality. Musharraf resigned his military post in late November 2007, which was a great victory for the movement.

*Phase IV: Pivot and Reorientation (February–August 2008)*
Elections were held in February 2008, and the Pakistan People's Party (PPP), which was now chaired by Bhutto's widower Asif Ali Zardari, was swept into power on a sympathy wave. Zardari was not held in high esteem by some in the party and in the country, and people focused their anger on a deal between Bhutto and Musharraf, which had been formalized in the National Reconciliation Order (NRO). The NRO was deeply unpopular among Pakistanis and was being challenged in the courts. A truly independent judiciary that might challenge the NRO on constitutional grounds posed a danger to Zardari as well as to some other PPP leaders, so the PPP government resisted taking action on this matter.

The postelection situation was confusing at best for movement leaders, and cracks began to show within the lawyers' community, as well as between lawyers and their civil society compatriot. The movement had directly helped force Musharraf to resign as army chief and enabled democratic elections to go forward; however, it was one thing to oppose a military dictator; but another entirely to go against an elected civilian government.

In June 2008, as the PPP government continued to resist restoring the judiciary, the lawyers leading the movement decided to hold a Long March culminating in a dharna (sit-in) in Islamabad to demand the restoration of the high court judges to their positions, and the removal of the PCO judges. As a logistical matter, the Long March was a much more ambitious project than anything the movement had planned before, and was a remarkable feat made possible by the infrastructure of the bar. As many as 100,000 demonstrators converged onto Islamabad, intent on staging a sit-in until their demands were met. The dharna began with great enthusiasm but after only a few hours, the lawyers' leadership called off the dharna. This proved to be a highly unpopular and controversial decision, and it destabilized the movement by taking the wind out of its sails. The leadership insisted that it had the safety of the protesters in mind, but movement activists had taken the call of a dharna till restoration seriously, and were angry at having to go back home empty-handed. The PPP government agreed in principle to restore the judges, but it continued to stall on delivering on its promise.

*Phase V: Retreat and Revival (August 2008–March 2009)*
After the failure of the 2008 Long March, many movement activists privately believed that restoration was a lost cause. Meanwhile, the main political parties continued to press for Musharraf's resignation, and in August 2008, he did so. In a transition heavy with symbolism, Zardari replaced Musharraf as president.

> The movement might well have died there, save for some serious miscalculations by the PPP government. In February 2009, Zardari dismissed the elected government in Punjab using his powers as president, providing the catalyst that the PMLN needed to oppose the PPP openly and to throw its weight behind the lawyers' movement. Movement leaders, emboldened by this fresh infusion of energy into the movement, scheduled another Long March in March 2009 to make a new demand for restoration. This time, the politics of the moment put the PPP government squarely in the cross-hairs of the movement, and although Zardari made furious attempts to prevent the march from taking place, he was eventually forced to accept the demands of the movement and restored all the judges who had been sacked under the Emergency, although in a compromise they had to serve truncated terms.

## 6.10 The Political Origins of Cause Lawyering in Hong Kong, *Waikeung Tam*

Compared to the cases of Taiwan and Pakistan, the mobilization of Hong Kong lawyers against authoritarian rule was not as successful. After two decades of political struggles since Hong Kong's sovereignty was handed over from Britain to China in 1997, the imposition of the 2020 National Security Law and the detention of a number of high-profile activist lawyers afterward marked an end to the Hong Kong lawyers' prodemocracy movement. But how did this movement arise, and how did its core members gain their status in the legal profession? Waikung Tam's book chapter offers an overview of the emergence of this critical mass of lawyers who later became central figures in Hong Kong's democratic struggles. It examines the political origins of the rise of cause lawyering in Hong Kong and what cause lawyers have done to advance legal mobilization.

> I argue [here] that the process of the sovereignty transition led to the rise of cause lawyering in three important ways. First, the process opened up a favorable legal opportunity structure: the implementation of the Hong Kong Bill of Rights Ordinance (HKBORO) and the Basic Law and the establishment of a final appellate court (the Court of Final Appeal [CFA]) located in Hong Kong. The new legal opportunities have provided lawyers with the

necessary legal basis to engage in cause lawyering. Second, concern over civil liberties prompted a few international human rights lawyers to move their practice to Hong Kong. Third, Beijing's tightening of political opportunities in the post-1997 legislature prompted several prominent liberal lawyers-cum-politicians to use their legal expertise to promote democratic changes through the courts. In addition to the aforementioned three factors, a rights-receptive judiciary has facilitated cause lawyering as well. [...]

These cause lawyers share a number of characteristic features. First, although many of them were admitted to practice in Hong Kong between the mid 1960s and the 1980s, they did not actively engage in cause lawyering during that period of time. This fact indicates that other favorable conditions are required for these lawyers to take up cause lawyering. The section below discusses these conditions. Second, the majority of cause lawyers are active in promoting civil liberties, democracy, and social justice through other non-court settings. For example, about half are the core members of either the Civic Party or the Democratic Party: Paul Harris, Philip Dykes, Johannes Chan, and John Clancy founded the Hong Kong Human Rights Monitor; and Michael Vidler and Hectar Pun have been actively involved in social movements. The long-standing political activism of all of these lawyers has expanded their social capital in areas such as social networks, reputation, and political power. They have frequently used this social capital to further their work, for example, in mobilizing their political influence to help disadvantaged clients.

Third, Hong Kong cause lawyers practice in different settings. Audrey Eu, Margaret Ng, Denis Chang, Philip Dykes, Hectar Pun, and Jocelyn Leung practice in large chambers, while a number of cause lawyers practice in small law firms. Barnes and Daly, where Mark Daly is a partner, has three employees: the two partners and a trainee lawyer. Ho, Tse, Wai and Partners, where Ho Chun-yan and John Clancey practice, has seven lawyers. Cause lawyer B practices in a small firm that employs three lawyers. Compared with large law firms, small firms allow cause lawyers to enjoy more freedom to choose their causes, colleagues, and strategies. As an example, before starting his own law firm in 1995, Ho Chun-yan was a partner elsewhere (which he requested be unnamed). At that time Ho found it difficult to engage in cause lawyering for two reasons. First, law firms in Hong Kong tend to avoid politics; and, second, Ho's support for democratic movements in China since the 1989 Tiananmen crackdown angered Beijing, and therefore his partners felt intense political pressure from the Chinese government. By establishing his own law firm and hiring colleagues with similar political and ideological beliefs, Ho has a more supportive setting to practice his cause lawyering work. Finally, apart from practicing in law firms, cause lawyers in Hong Kong are also found working as law professors. Johannes Chan, for example, teaches constitutional and public law at the University of Hong Kong. [...]

The majority of Hong Kong cause lawyers are active in promoting democracy, civil liberties, and rights of marginalized groups through other non-court settings. Their long-standing political activism has expanded their social capital in areas such as social networks, credibility, and political power. They have frequently used this social capital to further their work.

First, the social networks of these cause lawyers provide more opportunities for them to contact and interact with the marginalized groups so that they can explore the possibilities of litigation. The two cases below illustrate the important roles of these social networks. The first case concerns gay rights litigation. After exhausting all means to press the Broadcasting Authority to change its decision to censure a TV program on the love affairs of gay and lesbian couples in 2006, a gay rights activist (Joseph Cho) contacted his friend at Amnesty International Hong Kong and enquired about the feasibility of litigating against the Authority's decision. More important, Cho asked his friend to recommend lawyers for help. Cho's friend introduced him to Michael Vidler, who is a member of Amnesty International's Lawyers' Network. Vidler became Cho's lawyer and they established a cordial lawyer–client relationship.

The second case concerns a housing rights case launched by the Evangelical Lutheran Church in 1999 on behalf of emigrant families from China. The Church retained Ho Chun-yan as its lawyer. Two social workers of the Church explained how and why they retained Ho to litigate for them, as they noted:

> When we lobbied the legislature against the government's discriminatory housing allocation policy, Ho Chun-yan was one of the legislators we met. During various meetings, Ho showed his sympathy with our cause. After deciding to sue the government, we turned to Ho for legal advice because we had already established contact and knew that he was supportive to our cause.

In short, the extensive social networks of cause lawyers have facilitated their interactions with marginalized groups who want to use the law to advance their interests.

Second, the political influence attached to the networks of cause lawyers has facilitated their work as well. They can mobilize their political influence to help their clients. In the litigation against the government's public housing rental policy in 2003–04, for example, the rights advocacy groups retained Ho Chun-yan because they sought to use Ho's expansive political networks to further the movement of affordable public housing. As an activist said, "We instructed Ho Chun-yan as our legal representation because he, as a core member of the Democratic Party, could help us to persuade the Party to support our movement."

Finally, the track record of cause lawyers in promoting democracy and defending the rights of marginalized groups has helped them to establish trust and credibility within civil society. Human rights and public policy litigation is generally politically charged and thereby demands greater trust and cooperation between the litigants and their lawyers. As a cause lawyer remarked:

> In high-profile judicial reviews, litigants often have their strategies in mind. Thus, they need trustworthy lawyers who understand and are willing to litigate from their perspectives. Moreover, public policy litigation requires substantial information about the policy such as the policy-making process and government's standpoint. In that regard, litigants (who are often social activists) are more resourceful.

The following comments by three political activists illustrate the importance of a trusting relationship between litigants and their lawyers in politically sensitive litigation. In their litigation against the government's decision to privatize shopping and car park facilities within public housing estates in 2004–05, the rights advocacy groups retained Philip Dykes and Hectar Pun because of their trust in them. As an activist explained their decision:

> We chose Philip Dykes and Hectar Pun to be our lawyers because, apart from their legal expertise, we had a cordial working relationship before. Dykes was famous for representing civil society organizations in human rights litigation; and Pun and I knew each other when we were student activists in the late 1980s and early 1990s.

Leung Kwok-hung, who has filed a number of high-profile lawsuits against the government after the sovereignty handover, also emphasized the significance of having trustworthy lawyers in litigation. As he noted, "It is crucial that my lawyers are able to sympathize with my political viewpoints. Otherwise, they can hardly advocate my case enthusiastically." Fernando Cheung Chiu-hung, who organized a judicial review defending disabled students' rights to special education in 2009, mentioned that he chose Martin Lee, Hectar Pun, and Dennis Kwok as his lawyers because of both their expertise in human rights cases and their credibility in championing human rights.

> In brief, my interviews find that human rights and public policy litigants require a higher level of trust in their lawyers because of the political salience of their cases. The track record of cause lawyers in promoting democracy and civil rights helps them to gain the confidence of potential litigants.

REFERENCES

**Featured Readings**

Ballakrishnen, Swethaa S. 2019. "Just Like Global Firms: Unintended Gender Parity and Speculative Isomorphism in India's Elite Professions." *Law & Society Review* 53 (1): 108–40. doi: 10.1111/lasr.12381

Chan, Kay-Wah. 2012. "Setting the Limits: Who Controls the Size of the Legal Profession in Japan?" *International Journal of the Legal Profession* 19 (2–3): 321–37. doi: 10.1080/09695958.2012.783990

Galanter, Marc, and Nick Robinson. 2013. "India's Grand Advocates: A Legal Elite Flourishing in the Era of Globalization." *International Journal of the Legal Profession* 20(3): 241–65. doi: 10.1080/09695958.2014.912359

Gillespie, John. 2013. "The Juridification of Cause Advocacy in Socialist Asia: Vietnam as a Case Study." *Wisconsin International Law Journal* 31: 672–701.

Hsu, Ching-fang. 2019. "The Political Origins of Professional Identity: Lawyers, Judges, and Prosecutors in Taiwan's State Transformation." *Asian Journal of Law and Society* 6 (2): 321–46. doi: 10.1017/als.2018.35

Lev, Daniel S. 1976. "Origins of the Indonesian Advocacy." *Indonesia* 21: 135–69. doi: 10.2307/3350960

Liu, Sida. 2011. "Lawyers, State Officials and Significant Others: Symbiotic Exchange in the Chinese Legal Services Market." *The China Quarterly* 206: 276–93. doi: 10.1017/S0305741011000269

Shafqat, Sahar. 2018. "Civil Society and the Lawyers' Movement of Pakistan." *Law & Social Inquiry* 43 (3): 889–914. doi: 10.1111/lsi.12283

Tam, Waikung. 2013. *Legal Mobilization under Authoritarianism: The Case of Post-Colonial Hong Kong*. Cambridge: Cambridge University Press. doi:10.1017/CBO9781139424394.009

Tungnirun, Arm. 2018. "Practising on the Moon: Globalization and Legal Consciousness of Foreign Corporate Lawyers in Myanmar." *Asian Journal of Law and Society* 5 (1): 49–67. doi: 10.1017/als.2017.30

## Other Works Cited

Abbott, Andrew. 1988. *The System of Professions: An Essay on the Division of Expert Labor*. Chicago: University of Chicago Press. doi: 10.7208/chicago/9780226189666.001.0001

Abel, Richard L. 1989. *American Lawyers*. New York and Oxford: Oxford University Press.

Heinz, John P. and Edward O. Laumann. 1982. *Chicago Lawyers: The Social Structure of the Bar*. New York: Russell Sage Foundation. doi: 10.2307/2578996

Michelson, Ethan. 2007. "Lawyers, Political Embeddedness, and Institutional Continuity in China's Transition from Socialism." *American Journal of Sociology* 113 (2): 352–414. doi: 10.1086/518907

Ota, Shozo, and Kahei Rokumoto. 1993. "Issues of the Lawyer Population: Japan." *Case Western Reserve Journal of International Law* 25: 315–32.

Schmitthener, Samuel. 1968. "A Sketch of the Development of the Legal Profession in India." *Law & Society Review* 3: 337–82. doi: 10.2307/3053007

## Suggested Readings

Fu, Hualing, and Richard Cullen. 2011. "Climbing the Weiquan Ladder: A Radicalizing Process for Rights-Protection Lawyers." *The China Quarterly* 205: 40–59. doi:10.1017/S0305741010001384

Ishida, Kyoko. 2017. "Deterioration or Refinement? Impacts of an Increasing Number of Lawyers on the Lawyer Discipline System in Japan." *International Journal of the Legal Profession* 24: 243–57. doi: 10.1080/09695958.2017.1324557

Rajah, Jothie, and Arun K. Thiruvengadam. 2013. "Of Absences, Masks, and Exceptions: Cause Lawyering in Singapore." *Wisconsin International Law Journal* 31: 646–71.

# 7 Courts

## Contents

| | | |
|---|---|---|
| I | Courts as Cultural Symbols | 274 |
| II | Courts as Social Organizations | 282 |
| III | Courts as Political Battlegrounds | 296 |

Courts are arguably one of the most important sites of a formal legal system. They are probably the most studied sites in law and society research, despite a theoretical orientation to move away from formal legal institutions among sociolegal scholars (see, for example, Chapters 3 and 4). However, what is a court for law and society research? And how do courts vary in Asian contexts? The answers to those two questions are not as straightforward as they seem to be. From the law and society perspective, a court can be studied as a physical or social space, a cultural symbol of justice or religious beliefs, a social organization or political institution, a formal or informal channel of dispute resolution, a site of legal, moral, or other discourses, or as a vehicle for authoritarian rule or political change.

In addition to those theoretical variations, courts in Asia also follow different legal traditions and bureaucratic structures, and some judicial systems are more secretive or corrupt than others. As a result, there is no single best sociolegal approach to the study of courts, and Asian law and society researchers have offered a large body of scholarship on the social structure, culture, personnel, and politics of courts. Some use participant observation in courtrooms or interviews with judges, while others collect archival data from judicial documents or media sources. There is an additional literature on the judicialization of politics, mainly using quantitative methods and publicly available data sources. In recent years, the impact of digitalization on Asian courts has also become a burgeoning research topic. This chapter aims to present a snapshot of this diverse range of scholarship with a selection of readings from seven different countries and jurisdictions.

I COURTS AS CULTURAL SYMBOLS

The legal system is a myth, and courts are symbols of that myth. As we see from Chapter 4 (Legal Consciousness), ordinary citizens often stand "before the law" (Ewick and Silbey 1998), believing in law's majestic power without knowing what to expect in the judicial process if they ever participate in litigation. This mythical character of law is symbolized in many aspects of courts, ranging from the physical structures of court buildings to the robes and gavels that judges use, from ceremonies in religious courts to political slogans in authoritarian courts. Symbols are not merely formalities. They have deep historical roots and cultural meanings. Justice, fairness, equality, consistency, transparency, social stability – all those values and ideologies, and their distorted manifestations in practice, are embodied in the social structure and daily operation of courts. This section uses three excerpts on court judicial iconography, Buddhist courts, and *shari'a* courts to explore the symbolic aspects of the judicial system.

7.1 Legal Consciousness as Viewed through the Judicial Iconography of the Madras High Court, *Rahela Khorakiwala*

The Madras High Court was constructed in India during the British colonial era, and the court building has been used until the present day. As Rahela Khorakiwala describes, the court was built on consecrated grounds that used to host two temples, which were destroyed in a fire. This symbolic meaning of the court as a "temple of justice" was carried on from the colonial era to contemporary India, and, as the author argues, it continues to shape the legal consciousness of Indian society (see Chapter 4). When doing the research for this article, Khorakiwala adopted a novel method of "judicial iconography," which combines traditional sociolegal methods of interviews and participant observation with the mapping of the court architecture and the analysis of judges' portraits. This enabled the author to present a fascinating account of the Madras High Court as a cultural symbol of justice.

To understand how the Madras High Court reflects the recurring historical tension between British and Indian ideas of justice, it is imperative to recall the origin of the legal system itself in colonial India and how in particular the architecture and iconography of the high court building thus established reinforce the ambivalent legal consciousness of the court personnel that utilize this space.

Beginning in the 1600s, colonial courts of law were established in Madras. Over the centuries, the system of law and courts evolved, culminating in the establishment of the Madras High Court as a separate entity in 1862. Tracing the history of law courts from the 1600s reveals the creation of judicial systems through the East India Company. While the East India Company's original motivations were related to trade, its emergence as a political power soon made the administration of justice central to their concerns. They did this by establishing judicial institutions in a centralized manner across all their territories. By 1862, the year when the Madras High Court was established, the British had become a world power and it was during this period that they granted a Letters Patent that created the high court in the presidency town of Madras.

Political events of 1857 triggered changes in the functioning and power structure of the East India Company, and the government of England assumed direct rule over the territory of British India. One of the major changes was the introduction of The Indian High Courts Act, 1861 that was passed on 6 August 1861. This act empowered the Queen of England to issue a Letters Patent that established the Madras High Court, along with high courts in Calcutta and Bombay. Once the Letters Patent was brought into effect, the existing courts in the presidency town of Madras were abolished. All the existing powers and jurisdiction of these courts were transferred to the high court thus established.

With India's independence in August 1947 and the adoption of the Constitution of India on 26 January 1950, the Supreme Court of India was established, which superseded the authority of all the high courts, including the Madras High Court. The jurisdiction of the Madras High Court was also redefined at this time. This jurisdiction has evolved and changed over time, with the regional, political, and administrative boundaries being altered in independent India since 1950.

While the Madras High Court officially commenced its work on 15 August 1862, it moved to its present building only in 1892. The construction of a separate building specifically for the high court was authorized after the issuance of the Letters Patent. The new building was opened with much pomp and grandeur, and a majestic ceremony was held to establish the high court as the epitome of justice in the Madras area. This occurred on 12 July

1892, almost 30 years after the commencement of work in the Madras High Court.

Before construction of the present building of the Madras High Court commenced, it was necessary first to find an appropriate location. The area selected used to be an enclosure of two temples. As folklore goes, the temples were destroyed in a "mysterious" fire, making the location available for construction of the high court. During my fieldwork, several court personnel I spoke with recounted the mysterious fire. They suggested that the fire was caused intentionally in order to make the space for the court available. However, there is conflicting information on this point. Some records note that, in 1762, for the purposes of expanding their army, the East India Company had the temples razed and offered an area of equal space for the temples to be rebuilt elsewhere. The two temples stand at this new location on China Bazaar Road even today. Therefore, while the high court still stands on the ground that used to host the temples, it is not confirmed that the temples were actually destroyed for the purpose of accommodating the high court.

However, the high court is still associated with being built on consecrated grounds. As Justice V. Ramasubramanian writes in his article on the history of the high court, "The destruction of the temple of God paved way for the construction of the temple of justice." Many authors, judges, and advocates of the Madras High Court are of the opinion that "The edifice of justice thus rests on consecrated ground." Senior advocate T.R. Mani recollects that, up until 50 years ago, *prasadams* from these temples would be brought to the Madras High Court to "facilitate the witnesses who took the solemn oath in the name of God." He further notes that this practice has since been discontinued. Senior advocate N.L. Rajah also narrated the story of priests from these temples who would use the water from the River Ganga and *tulsi* leaves to facilitate the oath-taking in court. He also pointed out that this practice was stopped once the Gita and Quran were accepted for oath-taking. While this practice was in place, Rajah stated, there was still a connection between the high court and the temples. Rajah's narrative suggests a strong relation between law and sacrality, and history and memory in everyday forms of memorialization. The example of this memory of history reflects on how legal culture is developed within a set of individuals in particular localities, in this case, the personnel of the Madras High Court. The relationship between legal consciousness and society is constituted by the persistence of a narrative that deifies the court and gives it reason to be referred to as a "temple of justice."

The belief that the court was built on holy ground led to the practice of using artefacts from the temples within the court precincts. The mix of the secular court, as designated by the Constitution of India, with these religious traditions then becomes a reproduction of the legal consciousness of the court personnel in transferring their ideas of the court into their everyday practices.

### 7.2 Judging in the Buddha's Court: A Buddhist Judicial System in Contemporary Asia, *Benjamin Schonthal*

The influence of religion on Asian courts is far greater and deeper than locations or buildings (see Chapter 1). In many countries, religious courts coexist with state courts, and even official courts often extend deference to religious laws and norms in judicial decision-making. Schonthal's study of Buddhist courts in Sri Lanka presents a detailed account of the hierarchical and sophisticated monastic judicial systems that widely exist in South and Southeast Asia. These Buddhist courts not only are officially sanctioned but also have developed complex legal rules and texts. They are autonomous from the state but also linked with the state judicial system through the migration of disputes. It is a telling example of how formal and informal channels of dispute resolution are intertwined in Asian contexts.

Like other systems of religious law in the contemporary world, the judicial systems of Buddhist monks in Asia interact with state law in varying ways. In some contexts – Myanmar, Thailand, and Bhutan, in particular – Buddhist monks have access to monastic judicial systems that are officially recognized and/or administered by the state. While these official Buddhist courts do not displace completely more traditional procedures of dispute resolution that take place within monasteries, they do provide a decisive venue for addressing significant disputes among monks that cannot be resolved by their immediate community of peers. These tend to include: disputes over the use and distribution of *saṅgha* properties (such as paddy land and temples); quarrels over which monks ought to be given prestigious and powerful positions; controversies over the proper interpretation of Buddhist doctrine; and arguments about whether a monk has or has not violated the *saṅgha*'s stringent behavioural code. For example, when serious disputes arise over Buddhist doctrine in Myanmar that cannot be resolved within the monastery, those disputes can be referred to a government-appointed monastic tribunal, at either the regional or the national level. Where major accusations of heresy or "monastic malpractice" are involved, Myanmar's State Sanghamahanayaka Committee (which is appointed by the government to oversee the monastic community) will convene a special national "Vinicchaya Court" to hear the matter. Similarly, in Thailand, disputes between monks that cannot be handled at the local level may be dealt with in monastic tribunals that come under the jurisdiction of the state's official monastic body: the Supreme Sangha Council. A comparable system can also be found in contemporary Bhutan.

These systems of officially sanctioned monastic courts represent the exception rather than the rule. In most Asian countries, as well as most countries outside the region, governments do not officially recognize or sponsor Buddhist monastic judicial systems, meaning that the determinations made by monastic judges cannot be enforced by the police or other state authorities. Although Sri Lanka is a Buddhist-majority country with a national Constitution that obligates the government to "protect and foster" Buddhism, Sri Lanka's legal environment follows this second system. While Sri Lanka's state-court judges acknowledge the existence of a monastic judicial system as a factual reality, they do not treat the decisions given by Buddhist monastic judges as authoritative sources of law nor as legally binding precedents that state courts are obliged to follow. At the same time, long-standing doctrines in Sri Lankan case-law prohibit state-court judges from intervening in disputes over specifically "ecclesiastical" matters such as Buddhist teachings or monastic discipline, which are deemed to be entirely "spiritual" in nature and therefore beyond the competence of state judges.

This is not to say that state and monastic courts are completely isolated from each other. Some state-court judges treat monastic-court decisions as important evidence or advisory opinions when ruling on a dispute. Moreover, state courts admit routinely cases where "spiritual matters" mingle with "temporal" ones, as in the frequent cases of disputes concerning the guardianship, use, and transfer of property that has been entrusted to monastic groups. Today, Sri Lanka's civil courts regularly hear property disputes, often between two monks, concerning the guardianship or use of monastery-owned rental lands, buildings, or even sacred relics. So common and complex are these disputes that an important statute (called the Buddhist Temporalities Ordinance) and entire body of case-law (referred to as Buddhist Ecclesiastical Law) have evolved to address them. In almost all cases of this type, the disputes are first heard by monastic judges in the Buddhist judicial system and then appealed to the civil courts by a disputant who receives an unfavourable judgment.

This means that, in Sri Lanka, as in other places, Buddhist monastic fraternities must design and oversee their own in-house rules of conduct, procedures of adjudication, and conventions of punishment through which they can effectively manage disputes concerning not just property, but also Buddhist teachings, discipline, monastic comportment, membership, and a variety of other matters. Moreover, because the state courts do not recognize most of these issues as falling within the jurisdiction of lay judges (being purely "spiritual" in nature), this legal system must also be able to deliver judgments that appear acceptable and legitimate to the monastic litigants in the absence of any threat of enforcement by police. Therefore, the design of contemporary monastic judicial systems in Sri Lanka (and in other countries where there is no state-backed monastic system) should not only align with principles of fairness and truthfulness taken from Buddhist texts, but also be structured so as to discourage monastic parties who receive unfavourable decisions from ignoring those decisions or, more disruptively, relitigating the "temporal" aspects of the issue in state courts whose judgments *are* backed by coercion.

These concerns are not hypothetical. Monastic disputes migrate frequently from monastic tribunals to state courts in Sri Lanka, with disputants translating Buddhist legal arguments into the language of public and private law in order to make their case justiciable by state courts. In one widely publicized case, for example, a monk rejected directives given by senior monastic officials declaring that driving automobiles was forbidden according to monastic law; he then filed petitions in the Court of Appeals (and eventually the Supreme Court) arguing, among other things, that forbidding monks from driving violated their constitutional rights to equality under the law. There are many other cases in which monks go to civil courts when they feel that the monastic judge (or other senior monastic official) has unfairly awarded the abbotship of a monastery to an undeserving monk. One lawyer who litigates these cases regularly estimates that approximately 30–40 cases like this may be pending in the island's civil courts in any one year. These sorts of legal affairs – which seem to be occurring with increasing frequency – underscore the importance for monastic fraternities of making sure that their in-house legal structures, and particularly their procedures and norms for making judgments, are perceived as legitimate by the monks who adhere to those fraternities. [...]

As can be seen above, Buddhist judging connotes more than a set of pious principles or mindsets that decision-makers ought to adopt in interpreting law and resolving disputes, more than the cultivation of Buddhist moral values (equanimity, compassion, patience, etc.) in the minds of judges. Viewed through the lens of legal texts written by and for Buddhist monks – particularly those produced by the Rāmañña Nikāya – Buddhist judging also implies a set of procedural elements: fair, consistent, and systematic methods for managing disputants, running trials, airing grievances, considering evidence, ordering authority, and processing appeals. Buddhist judging, in this view, connotes not simply a form of virtue jurisprudence, but a broader set of institutional arrangements as well.

Those who are interested in judging and judgment in Asia ought to pay attention to these Buddhist conceptions of judging (in this broader sense of combined jurisprudential and procedural features) and take seriously the contemporary examples of Buddhist judicial systems that appear in the region. They should do so not only because these systems form a key part of the plurilegal landscapes in virtually every Asian country, but because they also reveal a (perhaps unexpected) coherence between the legal imaginaries of religious virtuosi and those of state legal actors. The concerns of Rāmañña Nikāya monks with developing clear and systematic protocols for making plaints, organizing trials, assessing evidence, or processing appeals align closely with the concerns of Sri Lanka's law-makers and jurists in reforming the state legal system. One can see similar kinds of alignments in the judicial apparatus associated with Thailand's official *saṅgha* organization, which condenses decision-making authority in a small coterie of senior monks who reign over a large group of middling monastic officials – a monastic legal structure that shows striking similarities to the elite-led and bureaucracy-heavy universe of state legal power that one finds in contemporary Thailand.

These alignments between Buddhist and state legal cultures are not simply the result of political interference in religious law or the deliberate imitation of state law by Buddhist monastic law-makers. Even when monastic judicial systems come into being as a result of state-led legislation or administrative reform, as in the cases of Thailand or Myanmar, the legal and institutional imaginaries that form the basis of those reforms circulate widely among cultural elites, both political and religious. Rather than simply exporting legal prototypes from one domain (politics) to another (Buddhism), the institutions of monastic judging and those state judiciaries – or at least the idealized presentation of those systems in normative texts – draw concurrently from a shared reservoir of cultural assumptions about who should interpret rules and resolve disputes and how they should do so. Official Buddhist judicial institutions, such as those in Myanmar and Thailand, are the product of explicit and implicit co-ordination between the legal imaginaries of high-ranking monks and those of high-ranking legislators, not the displacing of one imaginary by the other. A similar argument may be made about the Buddhist judicial systems created by monastic groups in Sri Lanka. As one can see in the long quote from the monastic judge in the section above, as well as in the many parables of wise judges taken from the Buddhist-story literature mentioned in the introduction, the same qualities and procedures that contribute to a perfect act of judgment by the Buddha also make for a perfect act of judgment by the magistrate. Utopias of judicial action circulate freely among populations, ignoring the imagined boundary between religious and secular law.

### 7.3 Are Women Getting (More) Justice? Malaysia's *Sharia* Courts in Ethnographic and Historical Perspective, *Michael G. Peletz*

Buddhist courts are only one of many types of religious judicial institutions in Asia. *Shari'a* courts in the Islamic tradition are another major type of religious court and are important cultural symbols of Islam (see Chapter 1). Traditionally, *Shari'a* courts are considered unfavorable to women as they strictly follow the Quran and other sources of Islamic jurisprudence. In this ethnographic and historical study, however, Michael G. Peletz shows that female plaintiffs in *Shari'a* courts are not always worse off than male plaintiffs or defendants. Although there is still no level playing field for women and men, *Shari'a* courts are timelier and more flexible in responding to women's claims today than in the past, and women also have more access to resources in the judicial process. Peletz challenges the conventional wisdom of describing Islamic law and Islamic courts as repressive institutions for women.

As in times past, the vast majority of plaintiffs in the nation's Islamic courts are women of modest or meager means, just as most defendants are men, from generally comparable socioeconomic backgrounds, typically plaintiffs' husbands or former husbands. Noteworthy as well are continuities in the types of cases that women (and to a lesser extent men) bring to the courts, the lion's share of which concern civil rather than criminal matters. As in previous decades, female plaintiffs typically petition the courts to help them resolve problems associated with their husbands' failure to provide spousal or child maintenance (*nafkah*); to clarify the status of their marriages; or to seek a termination of marriage via *fasakh* or *taklik* (due to violation of a stipulation in the marriage contract). The first two sets of issues are often inextricably linked insofar as women who have not received support from husbands who have left home to seek a living do not always know if their husbands have been delinquent in providing them with money or news of their whereabouts, or have divorced them via the talak/repudiation clause. Women seeking *fasakh* or *taklik* divorce are often in the courts for the same general kinds of reasons.

Male plaintiffs, in contrast, usually approach these courts to obtain formal approval of their divorces or to seek permission for polygynous unions but not for clarification of ambiguity or because of financial hardship. In this too we see considerable congruence with times past and important changes that require men to secure the court's consent to effect a divorce or a polygynous marriage that is legal in the eyes of the state's religious bureaucracy. A more general continuity involves the complex entanglement of Islamic law with state directives, whose formal authority and clout, like those of the Islamic judiciary in its entirety, derive ultimately from the secular constitution. There is no "firewall separation" between the religious and the secular. [...]

First, women's legal petitions are dealt with by the courts in a more timely and substantive fashion than in the past. Second, compared to the previous decades under consideration here, the courts are more likely to impose punitive sanctions on men who contravene *sharia* family-law enactments. A third, more general point, also related to sentencing, is that most harsh punishments are meted out to men, not women. Fourth, women currently have at their disposal much more information concerning their formal legal entitlements and obligations with regard to conjugal ties and their dissolution and can rather easily tap into densely configured networks of support to aid them in negotiating marriage, the shoals of divorce/annulment, and the precarities that may ensue. The fifth component of the answer is that, despite these generally encouraging developments, women and men do not experience marriage, divorce, or the *sharia* court-system on a level playing field. This too is changing in ways beneficial to women, however, albeit primarily for those who heed increasingly pronounced and restrictive expectations regarding obedience and heteronormativity.

## II COURTS AS SOCIAL ORGANIZATIONS

Judicial independence is a universal notion enshrined in many nations' constitutions and other legal texts, yet its meaning is often contested empirically. When it comes to everyday operations, courts are social organizations constantly influenced by a variety of political and social forces. Local governments, political parties, the military, large corporations, wealthy or powerful individuals, or social activists can all exercise notable influence on judicial decision-making and the social structure of courts. The "haves" not only come out ahead in litigation as Marc Galanter (1974) famously argues; they also shape the social organization of courts. This can be observed from the administration of justice in grassroots courts to the appointment and promotion practices of higher courts, from the internal hierarchy of the judicial bureaucracy to the external political control exercised upon the judiciary. The three articles in this section present three different aspects of courts as social organizations – namely, everyday judging in lower courts, political and bureaucratic control, and the (gendered) career trajectories of judges.

### 7.4 Punitive Processes? Judging in Thai Lower Criminal Courts, Duncan McCargo

Although traditional legal scholars tend to focus on the activities of higher courts, lower court justice has been a paradigmatic topic in law and society scholarship. The Anglo-American literature on lower courts, however, often focuses on the unpredictable nature of judicial decision-making or the power dynamics between judges and other participants of litigation (e.g., Silbey 1981; Merry 1990). The everyday activities of judges, especially outside trials, are less studied. By contrast, courts in many Asian countries are more bureaucratic and open to external influence. Judicial behavior can only be fully understood by observing the daily work of judges and how they interact with each other and with other legal actors, such as lawyers and prosecutors. In this article, Duncan McCargo provides a detailed ethnographic account of the mundane work of Thai judges in lower criminal courts.

Unlike judges in the Anglo-American common-law mode, who typically serve as lawyers or prosecutors for many years before being elevated to the judiciary, most judges in Thailand's nominally civil system are recruited at an early age through a highly competitive examination process. Their exam performance when they enter the profession determines the arc of their subsequent careers. In effect, the examinations distinguish between Bangkok-centred high-fliers destined to end up in the Supreme Court or the upper echelons of the Courts of Appeal and regular judges who will spend more of their working lives in courts of the first instance and in the provinces. In previous decades, judges maintained a strong sense of detachment and tried to avoid socializing that might bring them into contact with politicians or businesspeople who could embroil them in conflicts of interest. More recently, these restrictions have loosened, but many Thai judges still prefer to limit their social entanglements. In principle, judges are not supposed to be posted to their home provinces – though exceptions can be made – and junior judges are regularly rotated to different courts, often in different parts of the country. [...]

Thai trials for relatively minor crimes in the provinces are often quite cursory affairs, in which there is limited witness testimony. The shape of the trial is largely determined by the decision of the defendant concerning their plea. If a defendant confesses to the crime and pleads guilty (*rap sarapap*), proceedings are generally extremely rapid. In theory, since 2008, defendants cannot be convicted solely on the basis of their own confessions. But, in practice, the Thai police have limited expertise in investigating crimes; the primary *modus operandi* is to identify a suspect and persuade the suspect to confess. Confession is more than a legal or bureaucratic procedure; it involves an acknowledgement of the sovereignty of the state and a surrender of the rights of the individual. According to Article 78 of the Penal Code, confession and repentance can reduce a sentence by up to half. Defendants place themselves at the mercy of the judges. In doing so, they are effectively throwing themselves upon the mercy of the king. Confession is an act of loyalty. By contrast, a refusal to confess may be construed as an act of disloyalty, a failure to accept the legitimacy of the legal proceedings, which masks a failure of loyalty to the state and indeed an implicit rejection of the authority of the monarchy.

Inside the courtroom, judges have a great deal of power. Everyone rises when a judge enters the courtroom, from a special door at the rear used only by judges. Defendants and even those attending the trial are not only forbidden from speaking; they are also not permitted to cross their legs, are supposed to sit up straight, and are not allowed to take any notes. While not all judges enforce these rules strictly, some judges seemed to enjoy exercising their authority. Large gold-framed pictures of the king hang behind the bench in all Thai courtrooms: many judges see themselves as the literal embodiment of royal authority and dignity, rather than as arbiters of justice working on behalf of a neutral state apparatus. Judges can punish anyone who demonstrates contempt for court proceedings with a jail sentence of up to six months.

One explanation for the empty power plays performed by some provincial judges is that most of their work is terribly dull: they spend many hundreds of hours each year listening to testimony that often makes very little sense, much of it delivered by semi-competent or monosyllabic police officers, or by "professional" witnesses who appear implausibly articulate and well rehearsed. Most defendants are sad characters whose lives are in a mess: a significant proportion of them have obvious mental-health problems. Only by imposing an arbitrarily harsh discipline on courtroom conduct can some judges feel in control of the often muddled and even futile cases before them.

The format of Thai trials is highly predictable. Prosecutors and lawyers are not given structured opportunities to present oral opening and closing statements, though some judges invite them to explain the basis on which they plan to argue their cases. The defendant has no specific right to speak, unless called as a witness. Typically, prosecution witnesses greatly outnumber those for the defence. Many provincial defendants have court-appointed lawyers who are badly paid and put little effort into lining up witnesses on behalf of their clients. Many Thai feel reluctant to appear in court and contradict testimony by police officers and other prosecution witnesses. Witnesses from both sides frequently fail to show up for hearings, as do defendants. All this results in repeated rescheduling and constant delays. As a result, it is quite unusual for even a very simple criminal trial to be conducted and completed on two or three consecutive days.

The sheer volume of cases in Thailand is astounding: almost 1.4 million new court cases were filed in 2015 – the equivalent of 316 cases per judge. No wonder there were such strenuous attempts to divert as many cases as possible to non-judge mediators, while prosecutors routinely dropped charges if they thought there was a strong chance of acquittal. While a number of Thai judges approvingly cited to me Blackstone's famous ratio that it is better to let ten guilty men go free than to convict one innocent man, none of them mentioned that conviction rates in Thailand are above 95%. Accordingly, most parties to any given court case probably regard conviction – often meaning jail time – as a foregone conclusion. Thailand also has one of the world's largest prison populations.

Unlike virtually all other courts around the world, Thai courts do not produce verbatim transcripts of proceedings: while hearing witness testimony or statements from lawyers, judges regularly pause the proceedings to dictate summaries of what they hear into a small tape recorder. Tapes are then passed to a clerk, who types up not what was said in court, but what the judge has summarized. After a witness has testified, the summary is typed up and witnesses are asked to sign the summary. However, there is no explicit opportunity for the witness, or even a lawyer, to ask that the summary be amended or edited – though I saw this happen occasionally. On the very rare occasions on which a witness does not wish to sign – one former judge said he could not remember a single such instance in his ten years on the bench – the refusal of the witness to do so is noted. In theory, the witness signs the summary in the presence of court officials. However, in practice, the statements are often signed after judges have left the room. In one case, I saw a court security officer ask a Malay-Muslim defendant who was unable to read Thai to sign the summary of his testimony, even before it had been translated to him. The defendant signed without hesitation. Co-operating with the court procedures is a requirement in Thailand, not an option: to assert your rights as a defendant is to question the integrity of the proceedings and to brand yourself as a troublemaker.

A significant minority of judges I talked to favoured changes to the system of note-taking (*banthuk*). The current system means that judges have to focus on note-taking, rather than concentrating on the facts of the case; it also means that, when cases are appealed to higher courts, those courts cannot establish exactly what was or was not said during the trial. One senior judge said he would support a full-transcript system in the interests of consistency and fairness; there were considerable variations in practice between individual judges, which could affect the interests of defendants. Another judge had actually tried to use a full-transcription system for some cases, but the clerk assigned to him could not type fast enough and he was forced to abandon the experiment. A more junior judge said he was extremely meticulous about the *banthuk* process, not wanting to leave open grounds for appeal. Paper records were used for the transcripts: there were no digital files, other than scans of hard-copy summaries, so it was impossible to search quickly through summaries of testimony.

The 200 or so courts in Thailand are literally ranked in descending order of desirability, in a list that closely correlates with their distance from Bangkok. The more senior the judge, the stronger was her or his claim on a higher-ranked assignment. Judges with more seniority are rarely posted to provinces that are very distant from Bangkok so, in more remote parts of the country – such as in the deep South – there is a preponderance of inexperienced judges who often find themselves dealing with very important cases. One of the first Thai trials I attended was in Narathiwat, for the notorious "Khru Juling" case in 2006. A group of Malay-Muslim women from the village of Kuching Rupa were accused of involvement in the kidnapping of two teachers, one of whom later died. The case of an idealistic young Buddhist woman teacher who was brutally murdered in an insurgency-related episode captured national media attention and inspired a major documentary film. On the opening day of the trial, before charges had been formally filed, the prosecutor tried to call the village headman and a young woman as witnesses, on the grounds that they might be going away to work in Malaysia. Normally, no witness testimony would be heard at such an early stage in the proceedings. The request was purely opportunistic – an attempt to wrong-foot the defence and gain the upper hand. But, instead of simply dismissing it, two very young-looking judges agonized for several minutes before adjourning the court and going off to consult the chief judge. They returned about 45 minutes later to declare that the prosecution was not allowed to call the witness. The apparent inability of junior judges to handle slightly unusual requests was a theme of my trial observations; judges seemed to be in constant fear of making mistakes and so hardly dared to decide anything. Problems were compounded whenever the chief judge was not around or could not be reached; subordinates often seemed at a complete loss concerning what to do.

Accessing court cases in the provinces can be a challenge. In theory, virtually all legal cases other than those involving juveniles are open to observers and anyone can show up. This worked pretty well at the main criminal courts in Bangkok, where people were quite used to seeing foreigners. However, random Westerners almost never wander into provincial courtrooms and my presence there clearly unsettled some of the judges and court officials I encountered. Before I started fieldwork at one court, a local justice ministry official helped me draft a letter to the chief judge, asking permission to observe some trials. The chief judge seemed rather flummoxed, but eventually I found a senior judge from another province who could vouch for me, and he reluctantly agreed. I tried to be on my best behaviour, making myself as inconspicuous as possible. But, after about three weeks, I got a call informing me that I was no longer welcome at the court building. Nobody would tell me why, but this particular stint of fieldwork came to an abrupt end.

For my next attempt, embarking on a spell of observations at a court in a different part of the country, I was able to meet the chief judge in advance and sound him out. He seemed completely open to my doing some observations. Nevertheless, on my first day of fieldwork, I decided it was best to submit an official letter in Thai, requesting permission to attend cases. I went to the appropriate office on the ground floor to do so. A woman clerk took the letter and stamped it, ready for signing off by various officials before it could be sent to the office of the chief judge. She asked me to wait upstairs.

Meanwhile, though, I promptly bumped into the chief judge on the second floor. He was running around the building popping into different rooms. He had no jacket on and, unless I had recognized him, I would never have guessed he was the boss. He was very friendly and took me up to his office, asking his secretary to bring us both coffee. He told me that "our house has been closed for too long" and he wanted to open it up. Judges needed to have a chance to talk to people and exchange ideas, he said. During the month that followed, I ran into the chief judge a few times and he was always ready to chat. He did not mention the official letter I sent him requesting permission: in fact, I never heard anything more about the letter. Perhaps the invitation from the chief judge to have coffee with him in his office was already such an obvious green light that the official request became an irrelevance. Or perhaps the letter was simply mislaid. I will never know.

Getting permission to access trials was one matter, but working out what cases were going on was another. At one court building, the list appeared on a single dot-matrix-printed sheet, which was pinned up on a noticeboard. There were no computer screens. Outside each of the courtrooms was a small board, but the different clerks put up information there using varying formats. The main noticeboard tended to list the law under which the person was being charged, instead of the actual charge itself. I sometimes resorted to asking lawyers I encountered in the hallways whether they were conducting any interesting cases. Sometimes, I just followed a friendly looking group of people into a courtroom, with no idea what sort of case was underway. My fieldwork involved a great deal of serendipity.

### 7.5 Chinese Courts as Embedded Institutions, *Kwai Hang Ng and Xin He*

Underneath the legal ideal of judicial independence or autonomy, what does it mean to say courts are embedded institutions? In their book *Embedded Courts*, Kwai Hang Ng and Xin He propose an analytical framework consisting of four types of institutional embeddedness for Chinese courts, namely, administrative, political, social, and economic. Arguably, Chinese courts are an exceptional case in the sense that the party-state, especially its administrative bureaucracy, dominates both the formal structure and the daily operation of courts. Nevertheless, these four types of embeddedness also widely exist in other Asian countries, sometimes in less explicit forms. Among them, administrative embeddedness is perhaps the most prevalent, especially in civil law jurisdictions. The dual identity of court leaders that Ng and He describe in this chapter is also at the heart of an empirical, sociolegal understanding of judicial autonomy.

Courts deal with multiple external constraints. These constraints set limits to when their judges can use the law and when they have to do away with the law. The constraints come from different sources. A reference group includes her colleagues and seniors, judges in higher courts, local political leaders, mass media, and "trouble-making" litigants. Together, these different strands of constraints constitute a court's *institutional environment of judging*. This environment is the context through which judges make their everyday decisions. To use law as a means to resolve social disputes in China is always contingent upon the courts' interactions and shifting relations with other state actors, the public and the mass media, and the litigants.

The institutional environment of judging in China is highly fluid and ever evolving. To put it in sociological parlance, the development of the *juridical field* of China remains at a nascent stage. A field, according to sociologist Pierre Bourdieu, is a well-demarcated social space whose logic of practices is shaped by its own field-specific interests. Accordingly, a juridical field is one that converts direct conflicts between parties into regulated debates between (legal) professionals who accept the rules of the field. A strong field is one in which players can operate in a relatively stable institutional environment – actors have to adjust to the rules of the game, rather than the game having to change its rules on an *ad hoc* basis to adjust to the interests of powerful actors. Powerful actors dominate by playing by the rules, i.e., holding a monopoly over legitimate practices. The legal field of China, however, is limited in its ability to translate social, political and economic conflicts into legal disputes. This limitedness means that legal disputes are often not resolved by legal rules, but have to be dealt with by other rules – for example, as social or political conflicts as well.

It is in this sense that we suggest that the Chinese courts are deeply embedded institutions. We use the term "embeddedness" to describe the open-ended and indefinite character of the institutional environment of judging within which the courts operate. The contingent character of judicial actions is particularly pronounced in the case of China. [...]

We emphasize the *immediacy* and *directness* of external influences in China. The Chinese system differs most markedly in that the influences of other social realms are deeply embedded within the bureaucratic process of resolving problem cases. By and large, Chinese courts now follow standard procedures to deal with new, incoming cases at the grassroots level. But Chinese judges are not persistent in applying the law. It helps if one understands how Chinese judges think. For them, when the law fails to satisfy all parties, it becomes the judges' "problem." The case at stake becomes a "problem case" that requires further actions from the judiciary. What these further actions entail all is too-often guided by mixed and complicated considerations, including public reactions, social stability, control over resources, and personal connections. This enigma is well captured by a comment made by a head judge from Zhejiang. The judge said to us during his interview, "Do you know what's really surprising about our laws? China is not a democracy. The Communist Party can pass whatever laws it wants to make. Who could've thought that carrying them out is so darn difficult?" But if the law is just one among many forms of central policies, it should not be so surprising after all. As Xueguang Zhou points out, "The more uniform the state policy and/or the greater the separation between policy making and implementation, the less the fit between the policy and local conditions, therefore the greater flexibility allowed in the implementation process." The law is the most uniform of all state policies; as a result, courts are flexible in not just carrying it out, but also deciding when to use it. [...]

The judiciary is supposed to be a *different* government branch. In a liberal democracy, the court is supposed to be independent, though, as [Martin] Shapiro points out, this ideal of judicial independence is often unrealized. At a minimum, the court aspires to follow a relative clear set of rules (the law) in every step of the judicial decision process. This rule-based nature distinguishes judicial decisions from political decisions. Disagreements or blatant mistakes are addressed by referring to the same set of rules through an iterative mechanism of appeal. Administrative embeddedness refers to the high degree of selfsameness between the court and other government bureaus in its decision-making process. Important judicial decisions in China are at least partly based upon some assessment of non-legal factors. Administrative embeddedness can be analytically differentiated into two subtypes: internal and external. By internal administrative embeddedness, we refer to the manner in which the decisions of the Chinese courts are subject to the supervision and collective consensus-creating process of senior judges. The superiors have strong decisional control over their subordinates. [...][T]he "administrative" review process of a problem case is structurally porous to such an extent that it becomes almost amorphous at the very top end. A Chinese court follows a decision-making structure that operates like an inverted sieve – as a case is kicked up, the context of consideration expands from one that is predominately (and narrowly) legal to one that is increasingly (and broadeningly) social and political. As it goes up the administrative hierarchy, legal issues become embedded within a larger and larger social and political context of consideration. This "spiraling-over" tendency, as cases move up the hierarchy, is the most emblematic trait of Chinese-style judicial decision-making. Often, a judge cannot decide on her own but must coordinate both internally with senior judges in the court *and* externally with other local party organs and government bureaus, through various formal and informal mechanisms.

This decisional hierarchy is an administrative bureaucracy. It certainly is different from the Anglo-American model of the professional court. It also deviates significantly from the judicial bureaucracy in the continental

European systems. In a judicial bureaucracy, the law and the rules governing the application of the law are followed as to what has to be done, regardless of who makes the decision. In an administrative bureaucracy, however, rules are only applied as to who should be in charge of making the decision. In other words, rules decide *who* makes the decision, but not so much *how* the decision should be made or *what* the decision should be. Instead, the designated decision-maker often, as in the case of China, actively refers to extra-legal reasons in arriving at her rulings.

While a judicial bureaucracy is designed to defend a juridical space within which officials with specialized legal knowledge can operate, an administrative bureaucracy emphasizes supervision and oversight. This structure is vertically organized in a nested way to make sure that "problems" can be spotted and dealt with as early as possible. Chinese courts, from the very top (SPC) to the bottom (grassroots), from the biggest urban court to the smallest rural one, all share a similar basic organizational structure. Such a baseline structure made up of roughly three layers of supervision – with the collegial panel as the first layer, division meeting as the second, and the adjudication committee as the third. Each layer oversees a bigger pool of cases and holds veto power over the immediate layer below it. Power is distributed according to administrative rank instead of judicial expertise. At each layer, those who occupy senior administrative roles (the president, and to a much lesser extent, the vice presidents, division heads and deputy division heads) have broad powers over their subordinates. These power actors play a dominant rule in the vertical process of supervision. Hence, the degree of professional division of labor in fact descends as one ascends the hierarchy. Those at the top oversee everything.

Chinese courts have not cultivated a rule-centered institutional culture (even though this is changing in some courts). Consistency and predictability, the qualities that define modern legal systems, are not entrenched as core values. Chinese judges in many grassroots courts are at their innovative best for finding ways to resolve "problem cases" without using the law, either by bargaining in the shadow of the law or by getting around the law and resorting to other means. In interviews, some Chinese judges acknowledge that it is challenging for them to follow the law if following the law will produce bad social consequences. They cannot just "go with the law" this time and wait for the law to change next time. Judges would not say: "Let's rule by the law even if we do not like the result. Our government will change the law and get the right result next time." Judges are so involved in everyday governance that they would rather find ways to get around the law if following the law would jeopardize governance. Because the courts are expected to achieve immediate responsiveness, they are not inclined to treat like cases alike (and when immediate responses are difficult to give, they tend to stall rather than to rule).

This brings us to the second dimension of administrative embeddedness: the external dimension. External administrative embeddedness refers to the manner in which the Chinese courts and their judicial decisions are shaped by the sometimes converging, sometimes diverging interests among members of local party-state coalition. China's state bureaucracies, including the courts, coexist in a highly complex system of interdependency and competition. Courts, particularly those located in the inland region, work for other, more powerful government branches. The image of a professional court quietly and passively resolving cases fails to convey the sensitive and precarious atmosphere in which many of the courts operate. Courts are expected to provide support to local policies. This is shown, at a superficial level, by judges who are asked to show up in various local political campaigns, from anti-corruption to promotion of public hygiene. More important, courts are expected to support local governance by being "friendly" in judgments involving local government and state-owned enterprises. This has led to the persistent charge of local favoritism among Chinese courts. [...]

As an institution, the court has a dual nature. This dual nature is reflective of the character of the Chinese state as a party-state. The court is both an organ of the local party-state and a unit of the judicial hierarchy. Local party and government officials can influence a grassroots court through the Chinese Communist Party (CCP)'s Political-Legal Committee (PLC). The PLC is composed of senior officials from the local party committee, relevant government branches, the procuratorate, and people's congress. The court president is also a member of the PLC. She is also a member of the local governance coalition. But the committee is usually headed and convened by a senior party member who often serves in the government, such as the head of the police.

By the same token, the court president plays a dual role. On the one hand, she is the head of the court. She and her judges are the officials who apply the law locally. On the other hand, she serves as the vessel to facilitate the flow of information between the court and other members of the local party-state. She is involved in formulating key policies. When the president discusses matters with other core members of the governance coalition, she thinks as a senior bureaucrat. The context of consideration is not merely whether a decision is legal or not. The president has to persuade (and be persuaded) and bargain with other bureau heads. The coalition as a whole must balance the bureaucratic interests of different departments. The outcome of their consideration will depend on their respective political weight and on their ability to demonstrate that a certain course of action that benefits the court is most desirable, in the bigger interests of the party-state and the public.

The necessity of political consideration means that court leaders are chosen from a pool of pragmatic bureaucrats. Certainly, court presidents come in different shades. Some are tigers and some are tabbies. Nevertheless, scholarly intellectuals rarely make Chinese senior judges. These judges are deft, worldly administrators. They play the role of "politician" for their courts. They assess not just the legal, but also the political merits and risks of a certain pending decision. Their risk assessments are crucial for determining the court's decisions on "problem" cases.

Often, the two halves of her dual identity collide. She must therefore tread a fine line between carrying out the law and working with local government officials, who have considerable control over the courts' personnel and budget, and, increasingly, responding to the media and public opinion. Senior judges know the importance of not appearing too subservient to local governments. Sometimes judges have no choice but to apply imposed solutions, but at other times they exploit the power fragmentation of local government in order to allow themselves to exercise innovation at the margins. For example, while weak local courts must restrain themselves from using the law *positively* to defy the will of the local party-state, some are able to *innovatively* decline the use of law to promote the interests of powerful local political players.

### 7.6 The Elastic Ceiling: Gender and Professional Career in Chinese Courts, *Chunyan Zheng, Jiahui Ai, and Sida Liu*

As social organizations, courts are not only constituted by their internal hierarchy or interdependency with other organizations, but also by the career mobility of their judges. In common law jurisdictions, judges are often appointed to the bench later in their legal career and thus career mobility is mostly an internal movement within the judiciary. By contrast, judges in civil law jurisdictions have more diverse mobility patterns in their careers. In this article, Chunyan Zheng, Jiahui Ai, and Sida Liu use the case of Chinese women judges to demonstrate how the promotion tracks in courts and the outbound mobility to the government and legal services sectors shape the gendered dynamics of judges' professional careers, resulting in an "elastic ceiling" for women in courts.

Chinese courts are no exception to the global trend of feminization, though it is still at an early stage. Since the 1990s, the numbers of women in law school classrooms and on the bench, as well as in law firms, have been increasing steadily. In 2010, there were approximately 45,000 female judges in China, accounting for about a quarter of all judges in the country. By 2013, the number of female judges had increased to about 57,200, or 28.8 percent of all Chinese judges. In younger cohorts of judges, the proportion of women is even higher, exceeding half of assistant judges in many courts. More importantly, many women judges have risen to mid-level leadership positions in Chinese courts, such as division chiefs and vice-chiefs, who are in charge of specialized divisions in the judicial bureaucracy. However, it remains difficult for women to be promoted to top leadership positions, such as vice-presidents and presidents. In other words, despite the structural barriers and workplace challenges that they face, women have at least weakened the glass ceiling in the Chinese judicial system. [...]

We argue that the elastic ceiling for women is not simply a consequence of human capital investment or gender stratification, but the result of two social processes that structure the patterns of gender inequality. The first social process is *dual-track promotion*, which concerns the vertical mobility of judges in the judicial and civil service bureaucracies. In Chinese courts, two tracks of promotion coexist. In the *professional track*, promotion primarily is based on the evaluation of a judge's professional expertise and work performance. In the *political track*, promotion primarily is based on a judge's social and cultural capital and political connections with higher level Party or administrative leaders. We argue that women are more disadvantaged in the political track of promotion than in the professional track. As [Fiona M.] Kay and [John] Hagan demonstrate, women are often deficient in their social and cultural capital in the masculine culture of the legal profession (and, in our case, the bureaucracy), which makes them less competitive than men in the political track. The prevalence of patronage and corruption in the Chinese judiciary further increases women's disadvantages in high-level leadership promotion. However, when female judges are evaluated by the same technical standards about their work performance as their male colleagues, they are not significantly disadvantaged in the professional track. The elastic ceiling in the careers of Chinese women judges, therefore, is structured by the different effects of the two coexisting tracks in mid-level and high-level leadership contests.

The second social process is *reverse attrition*, which concerns the horizontal mobility of judges from courts to other law-related jobs. The potential destinations of judges' horizontal mobility can be divided into two routes: the money route and the power route. In the *money route*, judges quit their public-service jobs to become lawyers in law firms, in-house counsel in enterprises or financial institutions, or take lucrative positions in other market sectors. In the *power route*, judges transfer from courts to government offices, the people's congress, the Political-Legal Committee, or other Party-state agencies. We argue that, in both routes, men aspiring for more money or power are more likely to leave the judiciary than women, who tend to stay behind due to lack of opportunities, family obligations, or personal considerations. Women often assume lower positions in the labor queue than men and, in the Chinese case, a judge generally is considered less profitable than a lawyer and less prestigious than a government official. In other words, the corresponding lower positions of women and judges in legal and political careers contribute to the emerging feminization in Chinese courts, and it helps explain the elastic ceiling in female judges' careers because male judges often abandon their posts at mid-level leadership positions, but not high-level ones. This pattern of horizontal mobility is the reversal of the mobility patterns often observed in Anglo-American law firms, in which women usually are the subjects of attrition. [...]

Why are these "connections or backgrounds" so important in high-level leadership promotion? It is because, as the Anhui judge explained in the quote above, once a judge's administrative rank reaches the deputy division head level or above, which is usually the case for vice-presidents and presidents in basic-level courts or division chiefs in intermediate courts, the appointment decision must be confirmed by the Party Organizational Department. The cadre selection process of the Chinese Communist Party is heavily based on clientelism and thus political ties with local Party and administrative leaders are extremely important for a judge to be promoted to the high-level leadership in his or her court. Nevertheless, women face significant barriers in developing such connections in the workplace. [...]

Cultural capital presents another barrier for women in Chinese courts. When asked about the essential qualities for high-level leadership, masculine words such as "piloting abilities", "macro perspective", "determinant", "authoritative", "bold", and "autocratic" were mentioned frequently by our interviewees. A judge in Zhejiang even told us that "silly girls like us are not interested in questions like whether or not to become leaders". And when asked what type of women could become high-level leaders in courts, two female judges in different provinces answered with the same popular term "tough girl" and then explained that female court leaders must have "masculine qualities" and "gender-neutral qualities". Indeed, like female partners in law firms, female court leaders also face serious role conflicts between their identities as women and as leaders in the judicial bureaucracy. [...]

When is the optimal career stage for a judge to take the money route and become a lawyer? Although brain drain occurs at almost every level of the judicial hierarchy, mid-ranking judges younger than 40 years old are the most likely targets for law firms. This is because these judges usually have reached a plateau in their judicial career, but the legal expertise and social networks that they have accumulated over the years are highly desirable for law firms and in-house legal departments. If a judge was promoted to vice-president or president in the court, his or her chances of leaving the post would significantly decrease. The loss of many mid-ranking male judges leaves plenty of vacancies at the division chief and vice-chief levels, which usually are filled by women. The horizontal mobility of mid-ranking judges partially explains why so many women have been promoted to mid-level leadership positions, but not high-level ones.

Why did many female division chiefs and vice-chiefs choose to stay in the court despite the low income, declining prestige, and heavy workload? Some of our interviewees referred to their age, personality, desire for stability, or the weaker breadwinning pressure for women. Another frequently mentioned reason is that the legal services market is less friendly for women than the judiciary and "getting clients and developing connections feel too burdensome". Similarly, it is also easier for men to pursue a political career in the Party-state bureaucracy than for women. In other words, women's decisions of staying in the court are not only their individual choices but also the results of the structural constraints that they face in both the market and the bureaucracy. The reverse attrition of men, accordingly, is a social process driven by their advantageous positions in the job market and it reproduces gender inequality in both the judiciary and its adjacent social spaces.

### III COURTS AS POLITICAL BATTLEGROUNDS

Law is inherently political, and courts are one of the best manifestations of the political dimension of a legal system. Across the world, many political battles are fought and settled in the judicial process, including both high-level and grassroots politics. In exceptional circumstances, even the results of presidential elections and other "palace wars" can be decided by judges. When studying courts, political scientists often focus on the judicialization of politics, treating the judiciary as an arena for various political battles to settle. However, this view of courts as a legal safeguard of democracy only captures one aspect of the complex relationship between courts and politics. As political battlegrounds, courts require legitimacy from both the state and the public. Yet, such legitimacy is not always given to the judiciary, particularly not in authoritarian contexts. Therefore, it is not surprising that many socio-legal studies on judicial politics in Asia are situated in the context of democratization. The two studies on Cambodia and Taiwan in this section offer good examples of how democratization gives rise to political struggles in Asian courts.

### 7.7 The Judicialization of Politics in Taiwan, *Chien-Chih Lin*

Taiwan is perhaps one of the leading examples of the judicialization of politics in Asia in the context of democratization. As Chien-Chih Lin demonstrates in this article, the democratization of Taiwan since the 1980s has greatly empowered the Constitutional Court in relation to other political institutions, especially the legislative and executive branches of the state. As political parties fight for dominance in the political arena, the judiciary becomes a cornerstone for safeguarding Taiwan's newly established democracy. In particular, the deference extended by the other political branches enables the Constitutional Court to use a series of judicial decisions to consolidate the democratic system and the legal rights of its citizens.

Specifically, this paper analyzes the judicialization of politics in Taiwan – a process which has never been elaborated comprehensively, focusing mainly but not exclusively on Taiwan's Constitutional Court (hereinafter "the Court"). Structurally, Taiwan transformed itself from an autocracy into a democracy in the late 1980s. Before democratization, political power in Taiwan was highly monopolized, and judges were generally deferential to dictators. Even after democratization, judicial independence has not been completely entrenched, and the Court is still subject to political attack from time to time. Nonetheless, due to the need to legitimate its reign in Taiwan, the Kuomintang (KMT) regime relied on the Court even during the authoritarian periods, let alone after political liberation. Politically, ideological conflicts have become increasingly intense, especially during the period from 2000 to 2008 when the executive and the legislative powers were held by different parties. Because of the political dynamic, the Court was asked to solve issues regarding constitutional politics frequently. Furthermore, the change of personnel and procedural rules also rendered the justices more willing to step in the political thicket. After 2008, the KMT took back both the presidency and the legislature. Understood against this background, the development of the judicialization of politics in Taiwan may shed new light on the research of judicial politics. [...]

During the authoritarian period, the Court was quite obedient to the executive. Despite its impotence, however, the Court did render three cardinal decisions that demarcated the boundaries between the executive, the legislature, and the judiciary. The first one was Interpretation No. 31, in which the issue was whether the national representatives elected in mainland China should remain in office after the expiration of their terms when re-elections were thwarted by national calamity, namely the Chinese Civil War. The KMT could have just unilaterally prolonged the terms of these representatives, but it chose to resort to the Court. In its opinion, the Court transformed such political expediency into a constitutional necessity, emphasizing the necessity of the prolongation. The second decision was Interpretation No. 76, in which the Court was asked which department counted as the congress in Taiwan. Up to that point, legislative powers in Taiwan had been divided into three parts and exercised, respectively, by the Legislative Yuan, the Control Yuan, and the National Assembly. The Court found that all three institutions en masse constituted the congress. The third was Interpretation No. 86. During the party-state period, all high courts and district courts were subordinate to the Executive Yuan, instead of the Judicial Yuan. Located at the apex of the judiciary, the Court ruled in Interpretation No. 86 that all courts, without exception, should be subordinate to the judiciary. This is the most important decision with respect to judicial independence. In ruling against the executive, the judiciary tried to take back control of the lower courts. Nevertheless, this interpretation was not implemented for decades, and judicial intervention in politics did not effectively constrain the executive at that time.

Since democratization, the expansion of judicial power has gradually shifted the balance between the judiciary and its co-ordinate branches, in that both the legislature and the executive have been more obedient to the judiciary. In terms of executive deference to the judiciary, this change can be observed in three respects: judicial control over political conflicts, heightened scrutiny of executive discretion, and judicial intervention in policy-making and mega politics. Specifically, with the expansion of judicial power, politicians now rush to the Court for judicial decisions whenever there is a political conflict, despite the existence of other constitutional solutions. Even though they may not be completely satisfied with the outcomes, few challenge the authority of judicial decisions. The paradigmatic example is

Interpretation No. 520, in which the Court was engulfed in an energy policy issue, namely whether the executive could refuse to implement the budget of the Fourth Nuclear Power Plant without notifying the congress beforehand. This was politically controversial, since the Fourth Nuclear Power Plant was one of the most high-profile disputes in the presidential campaign of 2000. Instead of issuing a clear-cut opinion, the Court asked both parties to negotiate further and, if that failed, to look for other resolutions. Both parties were dissatisfied with the decision, but it successfully unravelled the political gridlock. In addition, in both Interpretation Nos. 613 and 645, one common issue was whether positions of independent Commissions could be awarded in proportion to the percentages of seats in the congress. This was controversial, since the KMT wanted to maintain its control over personnel of the executive even after it lost the presidency. In Interpretation No. 627, in which the president and his wife were accused of venality, embezzlement, and other misconduct, the president refused to testify and invoked the presidential criminal immunity and state secret privileges. In Interpretation No. 632, the KMT congress refused to consent to the appointment of Control Yuan commissioners nominated by the DPP [Democratic Progressive Party] president. In vertical separation-of-powers cases, conflicts mostly occur between the central government and Taipei City. In Interpretation No. 550, for instance, the Taipei City and the central government disagreed over who should pay for implementing certain national health insurance programmes, while, in Interpretation No. 553, the central government revoked a decision made by the Taipei City government to postpone a local election.

For the purpose of this article, the holdings in these cases are not that important. What is more noteworthy is that these cases show that political conflicts are now often solved not in the congressional hall, but in the courtroom. This was especially true from 2000 to 2008, since the executive and the legislature were controlled by different parties. Due to mutual distrust, almost every political fight between the ruling party and the opposition party was eventually addressed by the Court. By solving these political conflicts, the Court became the *de facto* policy-maker. What is more, politicians now take potential judicial reactions into account during the formation of national policies, since they know opponents may try to use the judiciary to undo these policies.

This shift in political equilibrium is also reflected in heightened judicial control over executive discretion. Politically, the executive could do no wrong during the authoritarian period. Economically, Taiwan was a developing state that "favor[ed] technocrats for public governance and [found] the legal regime and its main players – lawyers – hostile or at least unfriendly." Because of this, the executive enjoyed vast discretionary power beyond the reach of judicial scrutiny, and its regulations were binding upon judges. After 1987, Taiwan transformed itself not only from an autocracy to a democracy, but also from a developmental state to a regulatory state. Since then, executive regulations are no longer binding upon judges; the ruling of special-power-relations cases further constrains the executive; and the enactment of two Administrative Acts has not only greatly reduced the room for executive discretion, but has also made the executive more accountable to the rule of law. All of these developments are reflected in the docket records of the Administrative Courts, which have begun to invalidate administrative regulations and rule against the government more aggressively in recent years.

Finally, the Court has gone one step further and started to make policy through abstract judicial review. In Interpretation No. 400, an eminent domain case, the appellants asked for just compensation. Instead of delivering a minimalist opinion that focused only on the concrete facts of the case, the Court made a general policy decision which suggested that the government should compensate owners of expropriated land in all similar situations. This decision imposes an untenable financial burden on the government, and has not been fully implemented to date. Interpretation No. 603 is another example in which the Court had the final say over national policy. In this case, the DPP government had tried to collect the fingerprints of every citizen, claiming that the policy was consistent with several public interests and endorsed by most people. The Court first suspended the implementation of the policy by issuing a preliminary injunction; three months later, it prohibited the government from implementing this policy. The executive submitted to this decision, and the fingerprint collection project was aborted. Although the Court based its decision on privacy concern, it does not change the fact that it was the Court, rather than the executive, that determined the fate of this policy.

Moreover, the reach of judicial policy-making encompasses the mega politics – "questions concerning the very definition of the polity" – that relates to the nationhood and national identity of Taiwan. As described earlier, Taiwan for much of the latter half of the twentieth century was a party-state in which the KMT, a Leninist party, controlled the military, the media, and all government apparatuses. The influence of this authoritarian legacy manifested in Taiwan's post-democratization mega politics in the form of both institutional and ideological problems. The issue in terms of the former was the separation of the party (KMT) from the state, while the latter issue was seen in the fantasy of recovering mainland China. As to the entanglement of the party and the state, the Court had delivered several decisions about whether concurrent occupation of different offices is constitutional. These decisions occupied the lion's share of the Court's docket in its early days. The ideological problem relates to the legitimacy of the KMT government in Taiwan. After the KMT retreated to Taiwan in 1949, it still claimed to be the only legitimate government in China. Hence, Taiwan was regarded not as a sovereign state, but as one province of China. To maintain the formal distinction between the Republic of China and Taiwan province, there was, in addition to the central government, a Taiwan provincial government before 2000, even though the population and territory of both governments overlapped significantly.

After democratization, the Court issued several decisions that aimed to dismantle this ideology. In Interpretation No. 261, the Court required that "national" elections should be held in Taiwan, thus implicitly recognizing that mainland China was no longer part of the Republic of China. In Interpretation No. 467, the Court ruled that the aforementioned Taiwan provincial government "shall not be recognised as a legal public legal person of local self-government." In Interpretation No. 479, the Court struck down related regulations that prohibited the China Society of Comparative Law from registering its name as "Taiwan Law Society." In Interpretation No. 618, the law at issue prohibited Chinese people who have moved to and registered their household in Taiwan for less than ten years from serving as government employees. The issue is essentially a question of national identity: who counts as Taiwanese? Even though this statute is in effect discrimination based on national origin, the Court upheld the law, arguing that "it is not unreasonable to give discriminatory treatment to such a person [with Chinese national origin] ... with respect to the qualifications to serve as a governmental employee." In making this ruling, the Court took the position that some of the most suspicious discriminations can be justified because Chinese people per se are not regarded as Taiwanese people. Other decisions dealing with the relationship between Taiwan and China include Interpretation Nos. 497, 558, 710, and 712. None of these decisions clearly articulates the relationship between China and Taiwan, but all implicitly recognize that these two jurisdictions are separate and are controlled by different sovereign governments.

Finally, with respect to the issue of restorative justice, the legislature enacted the Act Governing the Recovery of Damage of Individual Rights during the Period of Martial Law to deal with the so-called torturer problem. Despite the act's lofty name, progress in implementing restorative justice in Taiwan has been quite slow. The KMT government had been reluctant to face this issue, since it was the ruling party that committed these crimes; the

DPP government had been unable to tackle this issue because it was paralyzed by political stalemate. Perhaps due to the political atmosphere, the ruling of the Court in this matter was conservative as well. In general, the Court struck a balance between seeking restorative justice and tolerating the crimes committed during what it deemed the "exceptional circumstances." In Interpretation No. 272, for example, the Court, in order to maintain social stability, ruled that "those who are not in active military service may not appeal the final court decisions with respect to criminal cases adjudicated in the military tribunals during the period of the Martial Law."

Not only the executive, but also the legislature has become more submissive to the judiciary. Regarding the change of the legislature–judiciary relationship, the heightened scrutiny in judicial review is the first step to contain legislative power. Second, the Court also gradually expanded the scope of judicial review by examining issues that formerly pertained to legislative self-governance. Finally, the Court began to replace laws that it ruled unconstitutional with its own ruling without waiting for further statutory amendments.

To begin with, the increase in the percentage of constitutional decisions against the government clearly shows that judicial control over the legislature has strengthened. Given this fact, whether a law can survive the gauntlet of judicial review has become one important concern that legislators take into account. This is particularly evident after the revision of the Constitutional Interpretation Procedure Act, which allows congressional minority to challenge the constitutionality of laws passed by the majority. The significance of this sort of challenge may be best seen in the case of the Shooting Act cases, in which the Court decisively ruled against the KMT. When President Chen was running for re-election in 2004, he and Vice President Annette Lu were shot the day before the election. Since Chen and Lu won by a razor-thin margin of 0.2%, the KMT congress enacted the Shooting Act to investigate the shooting. Outvoted by the KMT, the DPP legislators petitioned the Court, trying to "veto" the act; the Court struck down the act twice on constitutional grounds in Interpretation Nos. 585 and 633. It is worth noting that the infuriated KMT congress curtailed the judicial budget unconstitutionally between the promulgation of the two decisions as revenge. Still, the Court declared the revised Shooting Act unconstitutional and void.

Moreover, the judiciary has gone one step further, examining whether legislators have followed specific rules when legislating – an area putatively within the self-governance domain of the legislature. At the beginning, the Court was deferential to the congress in this regard. In Interpretation No. 342, for example, the Court cited a US Supreme Court decision, arguing that whether the congress was in compliance with its procedural rule falls into the realm of parliamentary autonomy that lies beyond judicial scrutiny. In Interpretation No. 381, the Court once again emphasized that the National Assembly had ultimate discretion in determining what procedures were needed to effect a resolution of a constitutional amendment. These two decisions held that procedural requirements fall into the domain of congressional self-governance and do not generate constitutional concerns. Notwithstanding the two precedents, the Court was considerably bolder in Interpretation No. 499, wherein it argued that "not all parliamentary proceedings that are clearly and grossly flawed may take the pretext of being internal, self-regulatory matters and evade their legal consequences." The Court thus declared the 1999 Constitutional Amendment unconstitutional partly because of procedural deficiencies.

Finally, legislative deference to the judiciary is most evident when the Court expressly usurps the power to legislate after striking laws down. In the past, the Court would simply ask the legislators or related governmental agencies to promptly revise the annulled laws in accordance with its constitutional decisions. This state of affairs has changed recently – the Court now tends in its decisions to prescribe solutions to replace the laws it has nullified. To name a few, in Interpretation No. 624, the Court designated an alternative mechanism for petitioners to file suits against the government even before allowing time for any statutory revision. In Interpretation No. 627, the Court unilaterally expanded the scope of the Criminal Procedure Code, and designated a five-judge special tribunal. In Interpretation No. 677, the Court decisively prescribed when prisoners should be released without any legislative response. In each of these instances, the legislature simply accepted the ruling without any dissent, and no one seriously questioned the legitimacy of judicial law-making.

Another category of judicial (con)law-making is the creation of new rights through constitutional decisions. Formally, the participation of the congress as well as the public was required to amend the ROC Constitution. Nevertheless, the Court has created many new rights by interpreting broadly Article 22 of the Constitution, which is similar to Article 9 of the US Constitution. To name a few, the Court has recognized the right to marry, the right to choose one's own name, freedom of sexual behaviour, freedom of contract, information privacy, and the right to reputation. Likewise, no one has seriously challenged the Court's right to grant such rights.

## 7.8 The Judicial System and Democratization in Post-Conflict Cambodia, Kheang Un

Judicial corruption is a widespread problem in Asian courts (e.g., Li 2012; Cheesman 2015). Democratization can bring checks and balances of power to a political system, yet it may not be sufficient to prevent corruption in courts. In this chapter, Kheang Un traces the establishment of the contemporary judicial system in Cambodia after 1979 and examines in detail the reasons for and dynamics of judicial corruption in Cambodian courts. As the analysis shows, judges' low income is not the sole reason for judicial corruption. The lack of institutional constraint is also a significant factor for the prevalence of bribery and other rent-seeking behavior.

[W]hen the People's Republic of Kampuchea (PRK) came to power in 1979, there was no legal system in place. The PRK, following the Vietnamese and Soviet models, re-established a judicial system to give Cambodia at least the pretense of legality. Because of staff shortages, the PRK set up short-term training courses for would-be judges and prosecutors. However, because the regime considered the legal system an integral part of the ruling party's apparatus, the training emphasized Marxist-Leninist doctrines over legal subjects. Prosecutors and judges were usually former school teachers and literate Cambodians with "good biography", meaning that they had no political connection to the previous regime.

The PRK was slowly able to create a formal court system. However, as in other communist states, the PRK judicial system was subservient to the party and the government. The official party line was that the court could not be entirely trusted, and this distrust opened a space for frequent interference in the judicial process by government officials at both the central and provincial level. The party or powerful individuals, but not law, determined the course of the proceedings and the verdicts of trials. A former Minister of Justice complained during a meeting at the council of Ministers in 1986: "Sentencing depends on the influence of persons offering an opinion, not on the law". [...]

Court officials also suggest that impunity is a product of patronage, corruption and the abuse of power. Despite the existence of internationally endorsed "free and fair" elections, the state is not being ruled by democratic political institutions. The mechanism through which the state is governed has changed little since the late 1980s. The Cambodian state is structured by interlocking pyramids of patron-client networks that serve as a means of exclusion and inclusion in a multi-network competition. In other words, like many developing countries, the Cambodian state is built not on rational institutions but on patronage, a political pattern in which a leader's power comes from his ability to capture and maintain loyalty of key sections of political elite by fulfilling their material aspirations through the distribution of perquisites. [...]

Court officials including judges and prosecutors publicly stated that low salaries are a factor contributing to judicial corruption. Up until 2002, the average monthly salary for judges, prosecutors and other court officials was around US$24. A monthly salary of US$24 was never anywhere near sufficient to support individual court officials, let alone their families. According to a judge, the living conditions of court officials under the current regime are poorer than those during the PRK/SOC. During that period, the government at least offered state employees, including court officials, supplementary rations including rice, gasoline and soap. Therefore, poverty causes corruption. As one judge acknowledges, "The court is corrupt and that I am not denying. But there are some good people. There are some bad people but these people are the product of poverty. Poverty generates illegal acts."

Corruption is not attributed as much to poverty as it is to rent seeking behaviour, a common practice of present day Cambodia. Through decades of war and social upheaval, Cambodians experienced constant uncertainties in their lives. Such uncertainties forced many of them to maximize their personal gains whenever opportunities permitted, with little concern for societal consequences. However, because of an absence of institutional constraints, rent seeking behaviour has become excessive, permeating all state institutions. The propensity of corruption is enforced by the belief that their posts are temporary, therefore prompting them to take advantage of their position whether through legal or illegal acts. 'Corruption among judges in the court does exist', says a prosecutor. "Some judges think that they will not occupy their posts forever, so they engage in bribery. It is dreadful that way."

The absence of institutional constraint coupled with a wider sociopolitical environment dominated by patronage and corruption blurs even judges' perceptions of what constitutes legality and illegality, and morality verses immorality. Judges whom the author interviewed did not reject the allegation that the courts were corrupt. However, they defended their actions forcefully arguing that some acts of receiving money from litigants do not constitute corruption. Rather, they argued that these monetary transactions can rightfully be called "fees". Accepting such a fee is not wrong – if not legally, at least morally. Defending their act of accepting money from litigants, a judge explained: "We [judges] help those who are right. [When] they win their cases, they repay their gratitude to us [*pel ke chneah ke song sarkun yoeng*]. This is Khmer culture."

Another judge admitted that she accepted money from people. However, she emphasized that "What should be asked is what service did I provide those people? The money that they offered was for the service that I offered them and this service is not at all illegal. If accepting money for doing things is illegal, then it can be called corruption. If accepting money for doing things is legal, then it cannot be called corruption." Tith Sothy, chief judge at Kampong Cham provincial court, was reported to have admitted: "I cannot tell a lie. Even I take money from time to time. But after the case is decided, and sometimes I do not know they are giving me money. Sometimes, they are giving me a box, and I think it is a gift."

Despite the judges' claim of moral conduct, this author's interviews and conversations with clerks, lawyers and litigants reveal that very often judges manipulated those who came into contact with the judiciary to ensure the maximum bribe. According to a lawyer, on some occasions judges employed delaying tactics in their rulings in order to extract more bribe money from litigants. The office of the former governor of Phnom Penh alleged that seven PPMC judges accepted US$310,000 in bribery in exchange for releasing 20 criminals.

Corruption within the judicial system is intertwined with the overarching system of patronage; they are two aspects of a single way of thinking of power. As in other branches of the government, merit counts for little within the judiciary. On the contrary, appointments and promotions are based on patronage and bribery. "Within the court system," a prosecutor said, "if someone wants to be promoted he/she has to make a request and the request involves paying a bribe. I could not understand. I knew some people who requested to be promoted and they did just that [paid a bribe]." Transferring to PPMC or to the court in a prosperous province also requires paying a bribe. A judge who was able to get transferred from a remote province to a more populous and relatively prosperous one said she could not afford the price to transfer to the Phnom Penh Municipal Court.

# REFERENCES

## Featured Readings

Khorakiwala, Rahela. 2018. "Legal Consciousness as Viewed through the Judicial Iconography of the Madras High Court." *Asian Journal of Law and Society* 5 (1): 111–33. doi: 10.1017/als.2017.33

Lin, Chien-Chih. 2016. "The Judicialization of Politics in Taiwan." *Asian Journal of Law and Society* 3 (2): 299–326. doi: 10.1017/als.2016.10

McCargo, Duncan. 2021. "Punitive Processes? Judging in Thai Lower Criminal Courts." *Asian Journal of Law and Society* 8 (2) : 324–47. doi: 10.1017/als.2020.22

Ng, Kwai Hang, and Xin He. 2017. *Embedded Courts: Judicial Decision-Making in China*. Cambridge: Cambridge University Press. Chapter 1. doi: 10.1017/9781108339117.002

Peletz, Michael G. 2018. "Are Women Getting (More) Justice? Malaysia's Sharia Courts in Ethnographic and Historical Perspective." *Law & Society Review* 52 (3): 652–84. doi: 10.2307/j.ctvw1d56p.13

Schonthal, Benjamin. 2020. "Judging in the Buddha's Court: A Buddhist Judicial System in Contemporary Asia." *Asian Journal of Law and Society* 8 (2): 1–22. doi: 10.1017/als.2020.13

Un, Kheang. 2009. "The Judicial System and Democratization in Post-Conflict Cambodia." In *Beyond Democracy in Cambodia: Political Reconstruction in a Post-Conflict Society*, edited by Joakim Öjendal and Mona Lilja, 70–100. Copenhagen: Nordic Institute of Asian Studies Press. doi: 10.1355/cs33-1i

Zheng, Chunyan, Jiahui Ai, and Sida Liu. 2017. "The Elastic Ceiling: Gender and Professional Career in Chinese Courts." *Law & Society Review* 51 (1): 168–99. doi: 10.1111/lasr.12249

## Other Works Cited

Cheesman, Nick. 2015. *Opposing the Rule of Law: How Myanmar's Courts Make Law and Order*. Cambridge: Cambridge University Press. doi: 10.1017/cbo9781316014936

Ewick, Patricia, and Susan S. Silbey. 1998. *The Common Place of Law: Stories from Everyday Life*. Chicago: University of Chicago Press. doi: 10.7208/chicago/9780226212708.001.0001

Galanter, Marc. 1974. "Why the 'Haves' Come Out Ahead: Speculations on the Limits of Legal Change." *Law & Society Review* 9: 95–160. doi: 10.2307/3053023

Li, Ling. 2012. "The 'Production' of Corruption in China's Courts: Judicial Politics and Decision Making in a One-Party State." *Law & Social Inquiry* 37 (4): 848–77. doi: 10.1111/j.1747-4469.2012.01285.x

Merry, Sally Engle. 1990. *Getting Justice and Getting Even: Legal Consciousness among Working-Class Americans*. Chicago: University of Chicago Press. doi: 10.2307/2073733

Silbey, Susan S. 1981. "Making Sense of the Lower Courts." *Justice System Journal* 6: 13–27.

**Suggested Readings**

Dressel, Björn, and Tomoo Inoue. 2022. "Politics and the Federal Court of Malaysia, 1960–2018: An Empirical Investigation." *Asian Journal of Law and Society* 9 (1): 26–58. doi: 10.1017/als.2020.18

Li, Ling. 2019. "Political-Legal Order and the Curious Double Character of China's Courts." *Asian Journal of Law and Society* 6 (1): 19–39. doi: 10.1017/als.2018.42

Ng, Kwai Hang, and Peter C. H. Chan. 2021. "'What Gets Measured Gets Done': Metric Fixation and China's Experiment in Quantified Judging." *Asian Journal of Law and Society* 8 (2): 255–81. doi: 10.1017/als.2020.28

# 8  Crime and Justice

**Contents**

| | | |
|---|---|---|
| I | Punishment | 310 |
| II | Justice | 323 |
| III | The Criminal Process | 334 |

Crime and punishment are enduring themes in law and society research, as is justice. In the empirical study of these topics, law and society studies and criminology overlap. The emergence of the "punishment and society" literature in recent decades further blurs the boundary between the two fields. However, law and society researchers often approach the criminal justice system differently from criminologists. They care less about crime rates, crime prevention, or severity of punishment and more about the social processes by which crime is constituted and punishment is carried out. Furthermore, law and society scholars consider justice a culturally sensitive concept, something socially constructed and politically embedded. This is especially the case for Asia, where no uniform patterns of crime and punishment or notions of justice can be found.

Studying the criminal justice system, however, presents daunting challenges for empirical researchers. Much of police practice is not open to the public. Police officers and prosecutors usually are reluctant to accept requests for interviews or participant observation. Even for criminal trials, which are publicly accessible in some countries (but not in others), the view offered to sociolegal researchers is often limited to the performative aspects. What goes on between judges and other actors beyond the public trial is a large black box. Whereas criminologists draw on surveys and other statistical methods to compensate for the lack of fieldwork access, sociolegal researchers, especially ethnographers, must find innovative ways to approach their research subjects and issues (see Chapter 9 for more in-depth discussions on methodology).

The selected readings in this chapter present a variety of ways to study crime and justice in the law and society tradition. They range from historical overviews and archival research to experiments, in-depth interviews, and participant observation. None of these studies are perfect, as they only reveal small parts of the black box of criminal justice. However, each of them penetrates the hard surface of this box and shows how things work inside of it. The theoretical interests of the researchers are quite diverse, ranging from ideologies of punishment and justice to concrete procedures and practices on the ground. To some extent, this intellectual diversity reflects the characteristics of criminal justice as a field for law and society research. It is largely driven by empirical issues rather than theoretical debates. As different Asian countries face distinct practical challenges in their criminal justice systems, scholars' interests and concerns are also quite different, even under the same research topic (e.g., punishment).

I PUNISHMENT

Punishment is often measured by its severity or examined by its instruments. For postmodern theorists like Michel Foucault ([1975] 1977), punishment involves complex technologies that produce docile bodies and pervasive forms of social control. Yet even this Foucauldian perspective cannot fully capture the wide range of punishment practices across Asia. There is no linear progressive trend toward a particular mode of punishment, nor is there any fixed pattern of harsher or more lenient sanctions over time. This section offers three vastly different examples of punishment in Asian contexts, including benevolent paternalism in Japan, governing through killing in the Philippines, and quantified capital punishment in China.

## 8.1 The Benevolent Paternalism of Japanese Criminal Justice, Daniel H. Foote

The criminal process is always harsh for those subjected to it, yet the styles of the process can be either lenient or punitive. The Japanese criminal justice system, as Daniel H. Foote demonstrates, is characterized by a "benevolent paternalism," which solves most reported crimes but only sends a small percentage of adult suspects to prison. In comparison with other criminal justice systems that rely on mass incarceration or torture to control crimes and render punishment, Japan's system is based on a close relationship between the police and local communities. The stigma of arrest and the high confession rate also help make the system work.

> Japan's criminal-justice system has been widely praised both within Japan and abroad as both highly efficient and generally lenient. There is much truth to these characterizations. Japan's clearance rate – the percentage of reported crimes that are solved – is among the highest in the world, and its conviction rate stands at over 99.8%. Yet fewer than 5% of the adult suspects considered by police to have committed Penal Code offenses are sentenced to prison; those who are sentenced to prison serve a median sentence of under two years. In the United States, by contrast, over 30% of arrestees are sentenced to prison where they spend an average of nearly four and one-half years. [...]
> 
> The organization of the police force and its manner of patrolling bring the Japanese police into much closer contact with individuals and the community than is currently the case in the United States. Although this might in part be an inevitable result of the fact that Japan has far less land than the United States, Japan also has considerably fewer police per capita than does the United States. What brings the police into closer contact with the community is the stationing of police in local police boxes (*koban* and *chuzaisho*) within each neighborhood or town, coupled with regular patrolling through neighborhoods on either foot or bicycle. A considerably higher level of contact also arises from twice-yearly residential surveys, in which police are supposed to visit every residential unit and inquire about such matters as the name and age of each resident, employment or other activities, automobile ownership, and the like. This information is kept on file at the police box, and may be used for criminal investigations (and, presumably, other purposes as well). Furthermore, at least in certain areas in Japan, fixed cameras not only regulate traffic but also provide routine surveillance. In various ways, therefore, the authorities keep close watch on individuals.[...]
> 
> Notwithstanding the elaborate postwar reforms in the area of interrogation and confessions, Japanese police and prosecutors possess broad powers for preindictment interrogation. Police may request individuals to cooperate voluntarily in questioning and to "voluntarily accompany" them to the police station for such questioning. As interpreted by the Japanese courts, this police power to suggest voluntary accompaniment may be quite broad indeed. In the most extreme reported case to date, the so-called *Takanawa Green Mansion Case*, four police officers met a murder suspect at his company dormitory one morning and, without arresting him, asked him to accompany them to the police station in their police car. At the station, officers questioned the suspect throughout that day and late into the evening. The questioning continued for

three more days; on each of the intervening nights, officers placed the suspect in a nearby hotel room where he could be kept under observation. Finally, the suspect's mother came to Tokyo and signed a form asking the police to release her son into her custody. [...]

Of course investigators do not have time to question each suspect throughout all that time, but they do consider obtaining a confession to be a vital part of each case. And they usually succeed: approximately 90% of Japanese cases involve full confessions, and in most of the remainder the defendant confesses to all but certain elements of the crime (such as intent).

For Japanese investigators, however, obtaining a confession signifies more than just getting the suspect to admit to having committed the crime. It entails obtaining a thorough account of all relevant details of the crime and the personal background and circumstances of the suspect, including possible involvement in other crimes. Obtaining a confession also means getting the suspect to accept moral responsibility. Yet despite the importance of confessions, the confession statement itself need not include a verbatim account of the suspect's words. To the contrary, it is a standard and court-approved practice for investigators to prepare summarized confession statements following – sometimes long after – the conclusion of one or even several interrogation sessions. These summarized confession statements typically form the heart of the evidence introduced at trial. Furthermore, the constitutional and statutory prohibitions on use of involuntary confessions have been construed narrowly. As a practical matter courts almost always focus their attention on questions concerning the reliability, rather than the voluntariness, of confessions.[...]

Japanese police boast one of the highest rates for clearing reported crimes of any system in the world. Even excluding cases involving professional or gross negligence causing death or bodily injury by traffic accident (all of which were reported as cleared), the 1988 official overall clearance rate for Penal Code offenses was 59.8%. Yet police arrested fewer than 20% of the adult Penal Code suspects they themselves identified. Does this mean that the police were wrong over 80% of the time? That there was no more than minimal intrusion on the personal autonomy of the unarrested 80%? Apparently neither.

In Japan, a crime may be treated as cleared even if police have not arrested a suspect for it. Only a relatively small percentage of those identified as suspects are later deemed to have had nothing to do with the crime in question, and 80% of all identified suspects are not arrested. Yet the substantial majority of those not arrested are nevertheless subject to prosecution on what is frequently referred to as an "at-home basis." In other words, these suspects are not arrested and legally have no duty to present themselves to the authorities for questioning, but their cases are sent on to the prosecutors for further proceedings.

Even before referral, however, a substantial minority of the cases – nearly 40% of adult Penal Code offenders in recent years – are closed by the police as petty offenses. In principle, this option, known as *bizai shobun* (disposition of trivial crimes), is reserved for a specified list of minor offenses, including assault, theft, fraud, embezzlement, and gambling. Given the breadth of several of these offenses, police have considerable discretion over what to treat as minor. Suspects in this category are not punished in a formal sense. Yet neither are they cleared from the system free from any consequences whatsoever. On the contrary, pursuant to official investigation standards, if police release a suspect on the basis of *bizai shobun* they must take certain steps. Police are required to counsel the suspect sternly and admonish him or her not to commit crimes in the future. Accordingly, suspects can expect to be questioned carefully and given a lecture by police. They may also be required to sign an apology and pledge not to engage in inappropriate behavior again. The investigation standards also instruct police to call in a member of the suspect's family, the suspect's employer, or some other such responsible individual, counsel that person to keep close watch over the suspect in the future, and even have that person undertake in writing to provide such ongoing supervision. Finally, police are required to persuade the suspect to provide restitution, to make an apology, or to take other appropriate measures for the victim. In addition, a record of the *bizai shobun* will be kept, which presumably will affect decisions on leniency in the event of future wrongdoing.

Thus, for relatively minor crimes in the category of *bizai shobun*, police have discretion to withhold formal sanctions and avoid substantially disrupting the life of the suspect. In an effort to deter any future misbehavior, police nonetheless seek to impress upon the suspect the gravity of the situation and its potential consequences as a means of deterring any future misbehavior. As a group, police are undoubtedly the most deterrence-minded among criminal-justice authorities in Japan. Yet in handling cases of this sort and in recommending that the prosecutors deal leniently with suspects who have "shown sincere repentance," police give considerable weight to interests of rehabilitation and specific prevention.

There are at least two broad categories of cases in which police decline to arrest a suspect but still refer him to the prosecutors on an at-home basis. If police have received a formal complaint of crime from a victim or other person, the Code of Criminal Procedure requires the police to refer the matter to the prosecutors. Thus, even if the police feel that a complaint is groundless or that the matter is insignificant they must refer the case to the prosecutors, but in such cases they are unlikely to arrest anyone. Many other at-home referrals fall into a second category, however. These involve relatively serious offenses, with substantial evidence that a particular suspect is guilty. In such cases, even if there has been a formal complaint, the police may nonetheless conclude that there is no need for a formal arrest if factors such as the nature of the crime and the suspect's personal circumstances so indicate. Again, this does not mean that the suspect is not questioned by the police. On the contrary, this latter category of cases is composed almost entirely of suspects who voluntarily cooperate in the investigation, and such "voluntary" questioning can be lengthy and intense. But in cases in which they refer suspects to the prosecutors without arresting the suspect, the police are implicitly determining that the interest in maintaining order does not necessitate arrest and that the interest in reforming the suspect would best be served by minimizing disruption in the suspect's life. At least in the case of moderately serious crime, police almost certainly will take this approach only if the suspect provides a full and apparently sincere confession and displays true remorse.

The absence of a formal arrest requires further comment. Although there are other, more severe types of stigma in the Japanese criminal-justice system, I am convinced that arrest is in practice the most important. In part, this reflects the practical consequences: an arrest carries with it the prospect of physical confinement for at least forty-eight hours and potentially much longer. The first such confinement, presumably, has the greatest psychological and symbolic impact on the individual. More importantly, despite the existence of a presumption of innocence under Japanese law, upon arrest a suspect is widely regarded by the media and the public as guilty. The arrest record can also have a significant effect on employment, community attitudes, and other social relations.

The powerful stigma of arrest, I believe, helps to explain in part why Japanese courts have been willing to relax greatly the standards for voluntary accompaniment. The courts seem inclined to let police use considerable "persuasion" to convince suspects to consent to accompaniment and questioning, rather than force the police to take the formal and stigmatizing step of arrest. Other factors, however, provide the primary rationale for the broad license that courts have recognized in the area of voluntary accompaniment. These include great deference to the perceived needs of investigators and, apparently, a feeling that such police intrusions are not unreasonable. In the *Takanawa Green Mansion Case*, for example, the Supreme Court explicitly referred to "the need [for investigators] to obtain detailed facts and explanations from the [suspect] promptly" as a major reason for permitting the four-day "voluntary" accompaniment of the suspect. In many cases where the voluntary accompaniment does not look altogether consensual, however, the police appear to have possessed probable cause sufficient to justify an immediate arrest. If the courts declared that questioning in those borderline cases was illegal, the police presumably would make more arrests.

### 8.2 Governing through Killing: The War on Drugs in the Philippines, David T. Johnson and Jon Fernquest

In contrast to the benevolent paternalism in traditional Japanese criminal justice, punishment in other Asian contexts can be much harsher. The death penalty remains legal in many countries, including Japan, and public support for capital punishment is generally high across Asia as it is still widely perceived as an effective means to deter crimes. Accordingly, how capital punishment is enforced in practice is a more important empirical question than the normative debate on its validity. Focusing on Rodrigo Duterte's war on drugs in the Philippines and drawing on media and archival sources, Johnson and Fernquest present a paradoxical case in which extra-judicial killings were widely supported by the public in a country plagued by both drug abuse and crimes as well as a corrupt and ineffective criminal justice system.

> Please feel free to call us, the police, or do it yourself if you have the gun – you have my support. Shoot [the drug dealer] and I'll give you a medal (President elect Rodrigo Duterte, 6 June 2016).
>
> Hitler massacred three million Jews ... There's three million drug addicts. There are. I'd be happy to slaughter them (President Rodrigo Duterte, 30 September 2016).
>
> In the name of eliminating drug crime, President Rodrigo Duterte has plunged the Philippines into a nightmare of brutal slaughter. The police say that since July 1 [2016], they have killed more than 2,000 people suspected of drug-related crimes. In addition, more than 3,500 homicides remain unsolved, many at the hands of unknown vigilantes.
>
> (New York Times, 11 December 2016)

Labels such as "state killing" and "the killing state" are often used to describe the legally permitted judicial killing that occurs in systems of capital punishment. But states kill extra-judicially too, and sometimes the scale so far exceeds the number of judicial executions that death-penalty reductions and abolitions seem like small potatoes. [...]

[Our focus here is] on extra-judicial killing in the Philippines during the first year and a half of President Rodrigo Duterte's war on drugs (June 2016–January 2018), for three reasons. First, the Philippines is a large country whose systems of punishment have seldom been studied. With more than 100 million people, it is the thirteenth most populous country in the world, and it has more people than any country in Europe. Second, extra-judicial killing in the Philippines has attracted much attention because of its large scale and the impunity enjoyed by its perpetrators. In January 2018, Philippine police acknowledged that approximately 4,000 suspected drug users or sellers had been killed in the war on drugs, while Human Rights Watch put the number at 12,000 and Philippine human rights advocates claimed it was more than 16,000. Despite thousands of slayings, only a handful of investigations have occurred, and not a single government official has been convicted. Third, we aim to focus attention on extra-judicial killing because it [is] a neglected subject in scholarship on punishment. By our count, the journal *Punishment & Society* published 35 articles and 20 book reviews about capital punishment in its first 19 years, but only two articles on extra-judicial killing. There has been a huge increase in the range and depth of scholarly work on the punishment of offenders who violate the criminal law. There is also a growing literature on the so-called "justice cascade" – how offenders against human rights norms are increasingly punished and called to account. But these two bodies of work "barely overlap" and both of them neglect the ways in which politicians, police, and members of the military frequently construe their own violence as morally justified acts of punishment and social control. For these reasons, we want to encourage research that will "expand criminology's domain" to include a subject that is interesting, important, and marginalized. In studies of law and society, too, extra-judicial killing has largely flown under the radar.

Some analysts argue that the "abolition of capital punishment in all countries of the world will ensure that the killing of citizens by the state will no longer have any legitimacy and so even more marginalize and stigmatize extra-judicial executions." Others claim that the abolition of capital punishment is "one of the great, albeit unfinished, triumphs of the post-Second World War human rights movement" and that "abolition is a prerequisite for any regime aspiring to dissociate itself from those dark forces known for their hostility to democracy, equality and human dignity." This article suggests that these views are too sanguine. What is happening in the Philippines – thousands of executions in a country without capital punishment – represents a pattern that has been seen before and that will be seen again in polities with weak law, strong executives, and fearful and frustrated citizens. State killing often survives and sometimes thrives after capital punishment is abolished (see Mexico, Brazil, Nepal, and Cambodia). And in countries where capital punishment has not been abolished, extra-judicial executions have frequently been carried out after the number of judicial executions fell to near zero (as in Bangladesh, India, and Indonesia). [...]

For decades before the slaughter that started in the summer of 2016, the Philippines had one of the highest rates of homicide in the world. In 2014, it had the highest homicide rate among 51 countries in "Asia." With 9.8 homicides per 100,000 population, its homicide rate was twice as high as the rate for the US, three times higher than the average rate in Europe, and four times higher than the average rate for ten other countries in Southeast Asia. Because of underreporting and other data difficulties, it is hard to tell whether the Philippines has high rates for crimes such as theft, robbery, and rape but, in the years leading up to Duterte's election in 2016, official crime rates soared, at least partly because of increased reporting by police.

The Philippines may also have higher rates of drug use and abuse than other countries in East and Southeast Asia, especially for methamphetamines (*shabu*). In 2014, 89% of drug seizures in the country involved methamphetamines, 8.9% involved marijuana, and 2.1% involved other drugs. In 2011, the US State Department reported that 2.1% of Filipinos aged 16–64 abused methamphetamines. It is hard to tell because the data are of poor quality, but there may be more than 1 million methamphetamine users in the country, and Duterte and others have claimed there are more than 3 million. Some methamphetamine users exhibit signs of addiction and acknowledge committing crimes in order to support their habit, but the best ethnographic work on this subject finds that most users remain functional and that the only crime many commit is taking drugs.

But, for some Filipinos, methamphetamine is personally destructive and criminogenic. Trafficking is organized and financed mainly by ethnic Chinese gangs. Because the Philippines is located near large nations such as China, Indonesia, and Japan, it is a major hub for methamphetamines in the region. The Catholic Bishops Conference of the Philippines released a pastoral letter calling methamphetamine the "poor man's cocaine" and warning that the drug is "dangerously ubiquitous" and "peddled openly in parks, bars, and street corners." Years earlier, Filipino bishops described drug users as "mental and physical wrecks" who were the "worst saboteurs" and who deserved "the highest punishments" – views that are shared by many

Filipinos. There are few rehabilitation facilities in the country, and treatment is all but impossible to obtain for the vast majority of drug users and addicts. To most Filipinos and many outside observers, the failure of Philippine drug policy is obvious.

Although methamphetamine often harms individuals, families, and communities, it also performs positive functions, especially for the poor. It empowers manual labourers to work for long hours. It alleviates hunger. It provides emotional escape from the grinding conditions of daily life that millions of Filipinos endure. And, as Clarke Jones of Australian National University observes, "A lot of the people involved in the [methamphetamine] drug market have no other opportunity for income, so a lot of [the drug] money [they earn] also goes to support families in communities." In a country that has failed to address the circumstances that generate demand for methamphetamine, Duterte's war on drugs is considered a necessary evil by many Filipinos – including many who live in locations that are being targeted by this campaign. Unless the social and human sources of the country's drug problems are addressed, reduced drug use seems unlikely. The Philippines may well need a "war on drugs," but the war it has been fighting under Duterte seems to be the wrong war, fought with the wrong weapons, and against the wrong enemies. The root causes of the country's drug problem are poverty and corruption. If it does not reckon with the social and economic deficits that push people into drug use and trafficking, it will not be able to discourage demand for a substance that so many find appealing.

In addition to high rates of lethal violence, strong public demand for drugs, and deep public concern about drug-related problems, support for extrajudicial killing in the Philippines is fostered by the dysfunctions of its criminal justice system. Countries such as the US and Japan have serious criminal justice problems but, in many respects, they pale in comparison to those found in the Philippines. Most Filipinos believe there is little justice to be had from its "injustice system." Its criminal process proceeds at a glacial pace. Its judiciary has a backlog of 600,000 cases and at least 20% of the country's trial courts lack judges. The average prosecutor handles 500 cases per year and the average public defender 5,000. The police are understaffed by about 50,000 officers and some analysts believe they are "the biggest criminal institution in the Philippines." Many persons accused of crime languish in jail for years, only to be released when police fail to testify or the evidence against them proves unreliable. Under Duterte's predecessor as president, Benigno Aquino III, only about 25% of criminal cases in the country ended in conviction – and that was an improvement over the previous administration of Gloria Macapagal Arroyo. During Duterte's war on drugs, Philippine courts –

including the Supreme Court – have proved "incapable of asserting their independence and doing their work in a credible way," which motivated prosecutors in the International Criminal Court (ICC) to initiate their own investigations.

In short, criminal justice in the Philippines is ineffective, inefficient, and corrupt. It is also toothless. According to Mexico's Center for Studies on Impunity and Justice, the Philippines has the highest Global Impunity Index of any country in the world – just above Mexico, where the drug trade and extra-judicial killing also flourish. These failures of criminal justice seem to be "at the root of broad acceptance of Duterte's draconian drug war." They also help explain why millions of Filipinos cheer extra-judicial killing or passively acquiesce to it, even though there is little evidence that it actually deters drug use.

### 8.3 Body Count Politics: Quantification, Secrecy, and Capital Punishment in China, *Tobias Smith*

Punishment can be discretionary and unpredictable, but it can also be counted and measured with technology and, in Foucault's term, governmentality. The frequency of capital punishment, for instance, is a sensitive matter in China, which executes a higher number of convicted criminals than any other country on earth. Amid international criticisms, China centralized its death penalty review from the provincial high courts to the Supreme People's Court (SPC) in 2007. Drawing on seventy-three interviews with insiders of China's death penalty system and the analysis of capital cases, Tobias Smith shows how the shallow secrecy of capital punishment data is maintained in the judicial bureaucracy.

China's continued resistance to international calls for disclosure of death penalty data stands in tension with its domestic policy of rapid capital punishment reform in the twenty-first century. The biggest reform took place in 2007, when the SPC reestablished central review of all death penalty decisions. The central review process provides that every death sentence handed down at trial by a provincial High Court undergoes a final, independent, substantive review in Beijing that can take months or years to complete. Each case is assigned to one of five criminal divisions of the court based on a combination of geography and case type. A collegial panel of three judges from the assigned division manages each case. A presiding judge on the panel reviews the full case record, conducts a final interview with the condemned, collects supplementary evidence, and, reportedly, sometimes even travels to the scene of the crime to clear up gaps in the record. The panel provides a recommendation to the head of the court division, who in turn submits a decision to the head of the SPC, who issues the final death warrant.

Death penalty reform has had a significant impact on capital punishment in China. In a rare formal admission, the SPC reported that, in the year that it reinstituted central review, death sentences declined by 30 percent. Despite a lack of aggregated indicator data, recent estimates by both international and Chinese experts suggest that, while China remains the world's leading executioner state in absolute numbers, executions have dropped precipitously since 2007. The estimated decline in executions accompanies a raft of qualitative changes to death penalty law and procedure, including reduction in the number of capital-eligible offenses, heightened due process in capital cases, increased legal representation for capital-eligible defendants, and expanded guiding jurisprudence on capital sentencing.

The reasons for the reform are overdetermined. Certainly, international condemnation may have played a role directly (by raising pressure on central leadership) and indirectly (by increasing awareness about the issue among judicial elites). But China's leaders also faced domestic pressures. China's "strike hard" state crime control policy expedited conviction and execution and removed SPC oversight of provincial court verdicts in capital cases. By the 2000s, national leaders became concerned that they lacked control over the lower courts, while Chinese citizens were shocked by the revelations of wrongful conviction and even wrongful execution. While China's central leadership can weather protracted international criticism, domestic challenges to state legitimacy and stability – such as mistrust of court power or a lack of central oversight over local court actors – represent a more significant existential threat.

In the midst of claims that China has made a "turn against the law," death penalty reform is not an exceptional instance of a pivot to legal liberalism. Rather, death penalty reform fits with the flexible repertoire of seemingly democratic initiatives that authoritarian regimes have deployed to maintain a hold on political power in the twenty-first century. Authoritarian regimes such as China have been particularly adept at harnessing the power of courts. Empowered courts in authoritarian regimes can increase state legitimacy, attract foreign investment, deflect criticism of human rights abuses, promote dispute resolution, and channel local information to leaders. These benefits may incentivize authoritarian states to increase domestic transparency, accountability, and indicator culture through law and courts as means to an end of continual rule. Death penalty reform has served as a vehicle for many of these domestic governance goals by increasing central control over local courts and boosting court legitimacy and consistency.

But the domestic governance advantages that the Chinese state enjoys through death penalty reform and the wider principles that animate reform pose a challenge to the imperative of secrecy over death penalty indicator data. Prior to 2007, the central government could plausibly argue that because death penalty review was decentralized – handled by the provincial courts – Beijing did not possess precise national data on capital punishment. In other words, China could claim it did not keep count. Now that death penalty review is consolidated under the SPC in Beijing, this claim no longer holds; annual data is nothing more than the record of the SPC death penalty review rulings. [...]

Not only has central review made the excuse of unavailable data untenable, it has also surely made the logistics of actual data secrecy harder to maintain. To facilitate death penalty reform, the SPC drastically expanded and centralized its legal infrastructure. The SPC moved its criminal court operations to a separate high-rise office building in downtown Beijing to accommodate this new work. Between 2005 and 2007, the court hired large cohorts of new judges to oversee death penalty review. Hundreds of judges and administrators now staff the death penalty review division. Since condemned defendants may also hire counsel to represent them on review as part of this new process, thousands of lawyers potentially visit the building every year. The SPC established a single site in order to consolidate death penalty review. In the process, the SPC also consolidated national-level data as a work product.

Centralization has thus produced a court environment of extreme contradiction. Since all cases up for review carry capital sentences, the most basic descriptive statistic from this court – total caseload – is an indicator that China has designated as a top secret. Straightforward work products such as court dockets and decision logs are now repositories of national secrets. On the one hand, death penalty review promotes centralization and indicator culture and increases opportunities for transparency. On the other hand, death penalty review increases the amount of aggregate data that must therefore be kept under wraps. And without aggregate data – most importantly, a denominator – a whole host of other rates, proportions, and disparities are incalculable. Conversely, any rate, proportion, or disparity that might be used in conjunction with a tally to derive a total denominator must also become a secret. [...]

States maintain plenty of secrets, but not all state secrets are alike. In this article, I have shown that China's annual execution figure is a secret with certain particular characteristics: most notably, it is a shallow secret – one whose existence and rough dimensions are widely known to all parties. Despite international criticism, the Chinese government reaps multiple political benefits from maintaining shallow secrecy over its death penalty data. It can engage in strategic doublespeak, sending different messages about its reliance on capital punishment to domestic and international listeners and crafting mixed signals through strategic opacity. And it can maintain policy flexibility, leaving open the possibility of quietly increasing executions without facing immediate global censure over a rising indicator. These benefits may encourage state leaders to continue a policy of shallow secrecy, even if maintaining secrecy produces tensions with other domestic policy objectives related to law.

China's death penalty statistics are not only shallow secrets; they are also legal secrets. And as China's leaders increasingly turn to legal reforms as strategies to improve social stability, government accountability, and state efficiency, maintaining shallow secrets in the legal domain becomes increasingly difficult. Unlike shallow secrets in other political areas – such as economic production, natural resources, or military capacity – shallow secrets in law stand in direct conflict with the values of legal transparency and judicial responsibility that China's state leaders want to deploy in domestic governance. While scholars of authoritarian legality traditionally dwell on the theoretical contradictions of illiberal legalism, the body count politics of death penalty secrecy pose a practical, rather than a conceptual, limit on China's ability to harness indicator culture and quantification for instrumental goals in the domestic legal sphere.

Death penalty secrecy poses a unique challenge to legal reform because it is an instance of secrecy about total court outputs. While secrets about individual cases are easy to keep, the example of China's capital punishment data makes clear that it is extremely difficult to maintain secrets about institutional statistics in a highly centralized, integrated bureaucratic legal system. Now that the SPC reviews all death penalty cases, national death penalty figures have become aggregated as a matter of course. Simple descriptive data – such as the number of cases on the docket for the death penalty review divisions of the Court – effectively become a top national secret. While death penalty secrecy is a national directive, the burden of implementing opacity falls on the courts, frontline institutions that must operationalize competing policy priorities.

> Tracing the contours of secrecy shows the impossibility of disentangling the qualitative from the quantitative dimensions, as well as the politically meaningful aspects, of legal acts. Publishing a court case, retaining legal counsel, and notifying an individual that an execution has taken place do not appear to be numeric activities. But, in a centralized and uniform legal system, each of these actions is transformed into a data point that may be tallied to arrive at a total. So long as that total is a secret, any new uniform procedure becomes a threat to data secrecy, producing the potential to derive a denominator and, thus, a statistic of social and state significance.

## II JUSTICE

"Justice," like rights, is an elusive term. Conflicting notions such as revenge and restoration are embodied in it. Justice can be substantive or symbolic. It can be politicized, performed, or transgressed. In the realm of criminal law, the pursuit of justice is of even greater importance than in civil or administrative law, because the very definitions of crime and punishment cannot be maintained without some basic notions of justice in society. Yet criminal justice is not merely what Durkheim ([1895] 1984) calls "repressive law" – in Asia, as elsewhere, the expression and implementation of justice has gone far beyond the traditional repressive orientation to include many other elements of politics, culture, and legal institutions. The two selections in this section present two distinct ways to study the issue of justice. Sapio, Trevaskes, Biddulph, and Nesossi offer a political and performative approach to criminal justice in China. By contrast, Won Kyung Chang adopts a pragmatic and experimental approach to examine the introduction of the notion of restorative justice in Korean courts.

### 8.4 The Expression of Justice in China, *Flora Sapio, Susan Trevaskes, Sarah Biddulph, and Elisa Nesossi*

China has arguably one of the oldest justice systems in the world, but its concept of justice has undergone significant changes since the rise of Communism in the twentieth century. The Communist ideology requires a criminal justice system close to the masses and harsh to the people's enemies, yet this system is also an ideological instrument of the party-state. The edited volume *Justice: The China Experience* provides a set of studies on the discourses of justice in China using legislative and judicial texts, government documents, as well as other media and archival sources. Adopting the concept of "expressive justice" in this introductory chapter, Sapio, Trevaskes, Biddulph, and Nesossi trace the historical evolution and contemporary manifestations of justice in China's legal system, with the emphasis on its performative nature and political purposes.

> Claims about a strident pursuit of justice weave through all of China's modern history. The intellectual, political and social ferment that exploded on to China's political stage on 4 May 1919 was motivated by a common will among the intellectual and political class to find a proper place for China among the family of nations. Pursuit of justice underpinned this movement, as it did the establishment of the Republic of China (ROC) eight years earlier. Communism was cultivated in China in the 1920s replete with a political vocabulary that was indebted to liberal and democratic political philosophies as much as it was to communist ideology. Here too, it was the ideal of attaining justice for the populace that prompted popular reaction to the inequalities, corruption and violence endemic in the ROC from the 1920s to the 1940s. This quest drove the civil war and the foundation of the People's Republic of China (PRC) in 1949. Over the course of the revolutionary era in the 1930s and 1940s, ideas put forward by some leading theorists and activists of the Chinese Communist Party advocating for a more democratic-liberal socialism were suppressed and eventually wiped out, while Maoist discourse became progressively privileged.
>
> The launch of successive waves of ideological reform during the years before establishment of the PRC obeyed a certain political logic that forced some notions of justice out of the political picture while privileging others. And after the PRC's establishment in 1949, efforts to achieve what Party leaders articulated as a just society drove the mass campaigns that were launched in the 1950s and 1960s with varying fortunes. From 1949 to 1976, Maoist ideology imposed itself as the alternative to an indigenous and traditional moral code. But the demise of Maoism in the late 1970s unveiled a moral abyss that threatened to swallow the nation. The promises of the Four Modernisations, the adoption of repressive social control strategies to contain crime and spiritual pollution, and the formulation of twenty-first-century political agendas such as Harmonious Society and the China Dream have done very little to fill this moral void, or to offer a credible explanation for the idea of justice in modern China.

With this underlay of historical antecedents, how are dominant notions of justice conceived and sustained in China today? Here, we are not seeking to address a philosophical issue. The main question pursued in this book is not *what* constitutes justice in relation to contemporary Chinese moral philosophy or political philosophy *strictu sensu*, but *how* certain ideas about justice have come to be dominant in Chinese society and rendered more powerful and legitimate than others. This focus on the interrogative "how" also incorporates a second and equally important question about how even the most powerful political ideas about justice can be challenged in an environment that does not favour, indeed actively rejects, political pluralism. In short, our aim in this book is to investigate the *processes* and *frameworks* through which certain ideas about justice have come to the political and social forefront in China today, and to explain how these ideas are articulated through spoken performances and written expressions.[...]

Operations and processes to administer justice in China are highly instrumental in both nature and purpose. To ensure the party-state achieves its desired outcomes, the instrumental concept of justice that it sponsors pervades every dimension of the PRC legal system. Activities such as law-making, law-enforcement, and adjudication and sentencing are the three most obvious dimensions of the PRC legal system, but another dimension that is extremely important is not easily visible. It is the dynamics within and across these three dimensions that the wider socio-legal field calls expressive or performative justice. This is where and how politico-legal concepts, not just the concept of justice, embed solidly in all other areas of the legal system.

Justice practices and operations perform an expressive function that can – and usually do – shape social attitudes and acceptance of certain political or social agendas. With this recognition, the idea of expressive justice has been studied in the fields of law and criminology outside China for decades. Yet little has been written about the utility of this conception for exploring Chinese justice. Socio-legal and justice scholars focusing on Western jurisdictions have long argued that legal and judicial institutions create and sustain images of power and authority through the dissemination of ideas and principles that they announce and perform in routine everyday practice. In the criminal justice field, for instance, leading scholars have long recognised the expressive capacity of justice practices as conduits that organise, classify, and construct images and messages about law and authority. David Garland, for instance, argued more than two decades ago that the penal system "acts as a regulatory social mechanism in two distinct respects: it regulates conduct through the physical medium of social action, but it also regulates meaning, thought, attitude – and hence conduct – through the rather different medium of signification". Studies in the field of law such as Sarat and Kearns[1] and Ericson[2] also argue that law and justice practices have both a routine instrumental role and a performative role. These practices are at once instrumental and expressive; while they function to secure the overall objectives of maintaining social order and regulating social relations in a society, they also perform an expressive function because they operate as mechanisms that shape understandings and values at the popular level. As the authors in this book identify, the expressive dimension of law and justice practices pervade the entire Chinese legal system. Performance of these practices in settings where decisions are made transports justice from the realm of legal concepts to the cogs and wheels of the legal system, and through symbolism, to popular understanding beyond. Juridical performances are the pillars that sustain the politico-legal (*zhengfa*) culture of the PRC. They not only serve as the cement that binds law with politics, they literally *enact*, manifest and convey justice, enabling it to be visible to and ultimately accepted by Chinese society.

But it is not only party-state functionaries who perform justice. Those who challenge the party-state's claims to dominance over creation and maintenance of concepts of justice are also performers here through their social action. Some engage in the performance of justice through scholarly argument or social media commentary. Others engage in public protest, usually collectively pursuing in public what they perceive is lacking in Chinese society or is owed to them by society or state. People who protest against what they perceive to be injustice often draw from traditional ideas and concepts such as petitioning and other actions to demand that injustice is ceased and remedied. They reference traditional Chinese notions of "injustice" (*yuan*) that are well-known across Chinese society. Performing acts that draw attention to *yuan* is a way to increase the cogency or legitimacy of their protests. Images of protestors kneeling and begging for justice, or carrying placards adorned with the Chinese character *yuan* are obvious examples.

Since 1979, the party-state has advanced the goals of raising the people out of poverty; building a more inclusive society; achieving social harmony, sustainable economic growth and national development centred on the person; as well as achieving and maintaining regional and global hegemony. Each of these goals has been articulated and popularised through a corresponding political programme ranging from late twentieth-century agendas

---

[1] Austin Sarat and Thomas R. Kearns (1993), *Law in Everyday Life* (Ann Arbor: The University of Michigan Press). [Editors' note]
[2] Ricard V. Ericson (1996), "Why Law Is Like News," in *Law as Communication*, edited by David Nelken, 195–230 (Aldershot: Dartmouth). [Editors' note]

such as the "Four Modernisations" and Deng Xiaoping's "Rule of Law", to early twenty-first-century agendas such as "Harmonious Society", "Stability Maintenance" and the "China Dream", and Xi Jinping's more recent "Rule of Law" agenda. These agendas may differ in focus, but a singular "red" thread underlies them all: the idea that individuals, society and the nation *ought to be given what they are* due. The thread is "red" because the party-state is recognised as responsible for arranging this giving.

At different points in the history of the PRC, "what they are due" has been variously understood in relation to what the Chinese polity and society has lacked: material security, political representation, an unpolluted environment or the respect of other nations. In this context, justice is expressed at its most basic level as a way of giving to each what they are due or giving to each what they deserve. This notion holds not only in Chinese tradition but also in ancient and modern Western thought. Its silence on agency – who/what should identify what/how much is due or deserved – is highly problematic and politically convenient. In China, as a minimum common denominator, this notion lies at the heart of party-state policy agendas, slogans and buzzwords. The party-state uses the popular understanding of "what is due" in articulating its role as provider of justice and protector of society from injustice and inequality in order to give the populace what is perceived as their due. It has sought to fulfil its protective role by striving for the goals of raising the people out of poverty; building a more inclusive society; achieving social harmony and a sustainable economic growth.

The party-state also has other roles in the enactment of "what is due", beyond providing what (it considers) is due to the people. It is instrumental in identifying and determining this "due" for the people and in both determining and seeking to obtain its *own* due. What is determined as the party-state's own due – what its leaders identify as party-state prerogative – is the authority to define the scope and means to effectively realise its protective role over society and to create its own narratives to justify the choices it makes in performing this role. For instance, Article 33 of China's Constitution sets out the principle of mutuality of rights and duties, which inscribes the inseparability of the people's rights from their duties prescribed by the Constitution and other laws. As a condition of bestowing rights to citizens, the party-state is due certain duties and obligations from citizens. In this political logic, the party-state is due the right to govern in a socially stable environment. It can therefore justify withholding the rights of people, such as their freedom of expression, when they do not give the party-state its due. That is, the party-state has the faculty to bestow rights on citizens in the first place. The rights around leading a good life are promised by the party-state, and the ability to keep to this promise forms the basis of political legitimacy. The ability to bestow rights entails the possibility to withdraw the rights of citizens when they do not provide the state a socially stable environment in which to govern, such as by creating social disorder or failing to respect the authority of the party-state to dictate who is due what in society. The granting of civil and political rights was never part of the party-state's promise, therefore any accommodation made to allow individuals to express their voice should not be considered as a 'natural' exercise of their rights.

The party-state dominates and jealously guards the political space around which this dominant political logic about justice is based. One way that it does so is by establishing and supporting certain notions of justice through discursive frameworks that help to shape and sustain particular political and legal values. Discourses are an enabling device, giving capacity for state functionaries to govern and respond to economic and social change in different ways for different purposes: from responding to threats to state and society, to providing legal frameworks for political oversight of power. Across the three decades of post-Mao China, the rise and fall of key justice operations and processes ranging through diverse practices from anti-crime campaigns to civil mediation have been maintained by legitimating discourses based on political agendas that have their foundations in a number of philosophical traditions, the most dominant being socialism.

Institutions involved in administering justice articulate their roles and responsibilities through key narratives that rationalise political choices in terms of not only the party-state's protective role over society but also what individuals within society deserve as their due. The party-state's current leading criminal justice discourse exemplifies this well. "Balancing Leniency and Severity" (*kuanyan xiangji*) was introduced into the prevailing Harmonious Society discourse in the mid-2000s and remains dominant today in the Xi Jinping period. It has since been elevated to the status of China's leading and "foundational" criminal justice policy. Balancing Leniency and Severity encompasses a myriad of criminal justice practice and nowadays is even a practising discourse in prison organisation. Its premise is: "When leniency is due, let leniency be given; when severity is called for, let severity be used" (*dangkuan zekuan gaiyan zeyan*). This is a commonplace saying with origins in the classics and in imperial codes. The saying recurs in legal documents enacted throughout the last six decades, albeit until recently, under the rhetorical auspices of the policy of "Combining Punishment and Leniency". This is also the meaning coded in contemporary political speeches by Xi Jinping. We see that the opening of this saying reaches straight for the familiar legitimising concept of "what is due" (here latched to the notion of leniency).

Entire political programmes in China seek to legitimise the understanding that the party-state has the authority to determine who in society is to be given their due, what is owed to each person, and how what is owed to them differs according to an individual's status, conduct and other variables. For instance, the Stability Maintenance programme in the Hu Jintao era had as its underlying logic the idea that members of society have an obligation to the state to behave in ways that do not create social instability. Citizens "owe" the party-state this due since the party-state needs a high degree of stability to successfully fulfil its protective role over society and provide a basis for the success of economic reform and development. Discursive frameworks like Stability Maintenance, especially those that seek to legitimise state-sponsored justice practices, enable authorities to rationalise the choices functionaries make about law and order. We see this in the policing practices of the Stability Maintenance period in the Hu Jintao era and in Xi Jinping's party-led rule of law today.

These frameworks derive their vocabulary from socialist ideology as well as from areas outside the discursive boundaries of socialism. It is not controversial to suggest that the legitimacy of the PRC and its legal system today rest largely upon the success of the nation's economic marketisation programme. Therefore, the language of the market is a crucial legitimising tool for state actions across the full spectrum of governance including the organs of justice administration. For instance, studies such as Michael Dutton's work on policing and contractualisation point to the prevalence of managerialism in the contemporary policing lexicon in the 1990s and early 2000s. More recently, marketisation trends have induced an even stronger emphasis on social management. The party-state, not unlike other state entities, has favoured adopting key performance indicators in justice administration, which portray a notion of justice administration as a product of bureaucratic efficiency.

## 8.5 Old Wine in New Wineskins? A Trial of Restorative Justice in a Korean Criminal Court, Won Kyung Chang

Restorative justice is a relatively new and foreign concept in most parts of Asia. In contrast to the traditional emphasis on punishment and retribution in criminal cases, restorative justice seeks to repair harm caused by the criminal behavior by facilitating communications and restoring trust between the victims and offenders of a crime. In the context of South Korea, this concept is appropriated to strengthen the protection of victims' rights in the criminal process. In this article, Won Kyung Chang examines a pilot project of restorative justice implemented at a Korean lower criminal court and shows the cultural and practical difficulties of transplanting such a novel idea and procedure of justice to the local context.

> The idea of restorative justice was first introduced into the fields of criminal law and justice policy studies in Korea in the early 2000s. It was initially discussed largely in the context of "victim protection." As the inquisitorial system gradually transitioned to a trial-centred adversarial system with the 1954 enactment of the Criminal Procedure Act of Korea and its subsequent amendments, several steps were institutionalized to ensure the rights of suspects and defendants under criminal justice processes. Until the 1990s, however, the protection of victims' rights had hardly come into the purview of criminal justice policy. As the concept of restorative justice was first introduced to Korea, at a time when the necessity of victim protection was just beginning to be discussed in academia, restorative justice was mainly recognized in terms of victims' security and compensation for damages.
>
> Along with such theoretical discussions, since the mid-2000s, criminal justice policy-makers have extensively redirected existing diversion programmes by adding some elements of restorative justice – such as apology or compensation to victims and the participation of community members. At the same time, several institutionalization schemes were presented to introduce restorative justice programmes into criminal and/or juvenile justice procedures. For instance, various pilot programmes labelled "restorative justice" were launched by criminal and juvenile justice agencies – such as the Seoul Metropolitan Police Agency, Changwon District Public Prosecutor's Office, the Supreme Prosecutor's Office, the Seoul Family Court, the Juvenile Protection Education Institute, the Seoul Probation Office, and the Seoul District Correctional Facility.
>
> Most of these programmes, however, contained only minimal elements of addressing the harm caused by crime or allowing participation of victims and/ or community members. Only three reflected the essential elements of restorative justice – namely an informal process of face-to-face discussion among parties most directly involved in a particular offence: (1) the family group conference applied to juvenile cases during the investigation phase, (2) the compromise recommendation introduced in juvenile courts at trial, and (3) the criminal mediation conducted in criminal cases before a prosecutor's decision to indict. [...]

The pilot project implemented at the Bucheon Branch Court of Incheon District Court was an attempt to overcome such limitations of existing restorative justice programmes and to conceive how to harmonize the present retributive and adversarial process into restorative justice principles. Several judges, including the chief judge of Bucheon Branch Court, shared recognition that the current criminal justice procedure is optimized for investigating evidence through legitimate steps and punishing the accused based on the principle of responsibility, but fails to respect victims and offenders in the process and to help the recovery of trust between parties. These judges presented the future direction of the criminal justice system as moving from judgment towards healing, and suggested that restorative justice could help to construct a better society by addressing individual needs and respecting individuals on their own terms.

In order to test the suitability of restorative justice practice in Korean criminal trials and to unearth any practical obstacles against such implementation, the Bucheon Branch Court carried out this pilot project from August to December 2013. The principles of restorative justice were applied to serious adult violence and/or property cases during criminal trials for the first time in Korea.[...]

This pilot project, which was originally designed to measure the institutional feasibility of implementing restorative justice within the Korean criminal justice system, was instead confronted with the fundamental question of restorative justice – whether people truly prefer face-to-face meetings to the impersonal and structured process of criminal justice procedure. The parties in this pilot project might have previously learned concepts of crime and punishment based on individual responsibility and proportional deservedness through formal or informal legal education and relevant experience. Thus, to them, except for the parties in one case (Case #3 [Car accident]), it was an impossible mission to understand this strange idea of restorative justice and to follow an unfamiliar way of communicating with other parties, as this process requires.

The judge in charge of this pilot project illustrated the general characteristics of victims after they were informed about the restorative justice option at trial:

> In the case of most victims, they wanted damage recovery, but the only way they were familiar with was submitting petitions in criminal trials and receiving compensation through a separate civil suit. Since they had never seen or heard of any further damage recovery other than monetary

compensation, it was quite difficult for them to understand that more practical and sincere damage recovery would be possible through conversation with the defendants, with help from professionals. In particular, victims who suffered severely because their damage became compounded for as long as they failed to receive any damage recovery from the defendants were hurt by or feared the idea of confronting the defendant with optimistic expectations.

The cases in this pilot project show how rigid the parties', especially the victims', ideas of crime, retribution, and punishment are, and how challenging it can be to encourage the parties to transition their reactions to restorative justice. In some cases, parties agreed to the referral to restorative justice, in order to avoid any disadvantage that they feared might be caused by their refusal. In others, the victims participated with doubts and distrust towards the judicial system, suspecting that the restorative justice process only serves the interests of the defendant. In yet others, the victims tried to control the whole process by using their higher structural position as a "victim" to demand excessive requests compared to other similar cases. In others, the victims revealed their overall tendency to desire the formal criminal process and its outcomes. As such, the parties in this pilot project did not act in accordance with the manner predicted by restorative justice theory.

This result is itself unsurprising, because it would be almost impossible for the parties to change their response to the crime after listening to a brief introduction of restorative justice for the first time in their lives, even though guided through it by restorative justice professionals. Despite the Bucheon Branch Court's efforts to promote social consensus on restorative justice in the local community – necessary in order to successfully run this pilot project and achieve its goals – it seemed unable to reach the actual targets of the project, namely victims and defendants of pending criminal cases. Furthermore, from the perspective of victims, the process of requesting their participation to an additional procedure of restorative justice happened abruptly, without any prior notification, in a court hearing where the victims were summoned as *ex efficio* sentencing witnesses. If time had been taken to distribute information about this restorative justice project to parties during the criminal justice procedure before asking their intent to participate, or if an educational session about restorative justice had been provided to parties after their decision to participate, the parties' understanding of restorative justice would likely have been enhanced and their attitudes somewhat changed.

On the other hand, even if they had been fully informed over a considerable period of time, it is still uncertain whether they would rather choose this ancient solution to crime rather than the institutionalized system of modern criminal process. In Korea, from the beginning of the 1990s, it has been seen that people depend on the judicial system heavily to resolve their everyday trivial disputes and even misuse the system as a tool to threaten other parties. This tendency that pervades all of society has even spurred the coining of new words like "judicialism" or "judicial omnipotence." Furthermore, in this project, the parties' reliance on the judicial system appeared in most cases by comparing the clear offer suggested by the other party in restorative justice to the unclear outcome that could be obtained through the formal judicial process. In addition, the representative of Nonviolence Peaceforce Corea who led the restorative justice process of Case #9 [Rob thy neighbour] complained that "the defendants kept asking the restorative justice facilitator for legal advice," even though he told them in advance that the facilitator is a neutral coordinator who does not give any such advice.

Illuminating this current situation in Korea, it becomes apparent that an official adoption of restorative justice in adult criminal cases in the trial-and-sentencing phase merely on the basis of its laudable humanist promises runs the real risk of producing yet another restorative justice programme in name only. The introduction of this government-oriented programme will become just one additional pathway for processing a defendant based on a judge's suggestion, or it will simply institutionalize the existing informal practice of reflecting the agreement between victim and defendant in a judge's sentencing decision. In addition, most of the parties participating in the restorative justice practices will apply the same communication methods and litigation strategies as they used in the conventional criminal procedure, including condemning, criticizing, manipulating, and retaliating against their legal adversaries, as well as maximizing their own interests. Consequently, it could end up pouring old wine into the new wineskins of restorative justice, contrary to Daniel W. Van Ness's vision of new wine in old wineskins.

In order to defend a future restorative justice programme from similar criticisms of being far from the original idea of restorative justice, it must be preceded by changes in people's reactions to and feelings about crime, the criminal justice system, and punishment. Judging from the mixed results of this pilot programme, a hasty introduction of restorative justice at trial will produce a situation where the success of restorative justice in cases will be determined by chance – each party's individual characteristics, psychological status, and realistic circumstances, their attorneys' assessment of legal matters and attitudes toward the other parties, and the restorative justice professionals' style of leading the conversation, etc. Thus, the introduction of restorative justice at trial should not be understood as merely a new kind of diversion programme, but should be viewed as an entire shift of people's values vis-à-vis their own lives, human relations, and community.

III THE CRIMINAL PROCESS

Criminal justice involves not only substantive sanctions but also elaborate procedures. Legal scholars often emphasize procedural justice as an inherent element of criminal justice and a counterbalance to the abuse of power in the criminal process. From the sociolegal perspective, however, the criminal process is not just about procedure. As Malcolm Feeley (1979) famously put it, "The process is the punishment." In his case study of the criminal justice system in New Haven, Feeley shows that many human and social factors are key to understanding the criminal process in addition to procedural rules on the books, such as corruption, compromises, political connections, and the interactions between judges, lawyers, prosecutors, defendants, and other actors in the process. The same observation holds true for understanding criminal processes in Asia. The three selections in this section use the cases of Vietnam, Myanmar, and India to illustrate how those nonlegal elements are at work in the criminal process.

## 8.6 In Search of Judicial Legitimacy: Criminal Sentencing in Vietnamese Courts, *Trang (Mae) Nguyen*

The criminal process is hierarchical in the sense that a criminal case sometimes goes through multiple levels of courts and involves complex communications and negotiations among judges and legal professionals. Higher-level courts are often responsible for correcting the mistakes made by lower-level courts. In civil law jurisdictions where courts are a bureaucratic hierarchy, higher-level courts also assume the task of curbing corruption by lower-level judges. Based on her analysis of 242 criminal judgments issued by the Supreme People's Court (SPC) in Vietnam and interviews with judges, court officials, lawyers, and academics, Trang (Mae) Nguyen's article discusses how the SPC fights the entrenched judicial corruption in the criminal justice system, focusing on the use of the suspended sentence.

> Lower courts' undisciplined use of suspended sentencing has long plagued the SPC. The Criminal Code allows judges discretion to impose a suspended sentence in lieu of imprisonment for defendants convicted of non-serious offenses – a measure akin to probation in the U.S. Seen as a leniency measure to promote reentry and rehabilitation, suspended sentencing has become a red flag for corruption. As one attorney explained,
>
>> The judge called me and asked me to "cooperate." It is not just him, he said, but also the people assessors and other people in the process who need to be taken care of. He asked for 20 million Vietnamese *dong* [about $1000] per year of reduction in imprisonment, or a lump sum of 100 million for a suspended sentence. A bad judge would insist on a fixed price; a 'good' judge would consider their [the defendants'] household situation and income levels in determining the price . . . .
>
> Another defense attorney described the systematic entrenchment of corruption:
>
>> Judges are people too. Look at their salary scale ... how do you think they live and put their children through school? There are good and bad corruption. Bad corruption is extortion; 'good' corruption is to get the people in the process to do their jobs.
>
> Another attorney elaborated:
>
>> To obtain a lighter sentence or a suspended sentence is an investment. To obtain an acquittal is a lifetime investment. I morally oppose [bribery], I am vehemently against it, but I have to do it in order to do my job. I try to not think about it as justice for sale [*chạy án*] but as an investment for my clients' future. While others put cash into envelopes to do the exchange, I instead use a nice card, to show that it is not just a transaction.
>
> The rampant abuse of suspended sentencing caused damages to the judiciary's reputation, as an article in a popular news outlet chided, "Even a judge who received bribery for abusing suspended sentencing received a suspended sentence." [. . .]
>
> Legal practitioners interviewed also cautioned that the use of suspended sentencing could signify another issue: a plea bargaining-like mechanism. Though data on the conviction rate in criminal cases is scarce, a consensus exists that it is near 100%, and judges and prosecutors are generally under pressure to secure convictions. A promise for a suspended sentence is an easy

way to bargain with criminal defendants, especially in cases with weak evidence. As one lawyer puts it:

> I told my client that I have negotiated a suspended sentence for him if he would express remorse in court and offer to compensate the victim [in a battery case]. The chance for acquittal is basically zero, so it is better to accept this deal.

Cases analyses support a portrait of Vietnamese courts as a forum to determine sentencing, rather than to contest guilt. As one lawyer explains,

> Getting clients a good sentence is the game here. As a lawyer, I'd consider it a lifetime achievement if I get even one client acquitted. It rarely happens.

Of over 200 cases in the database, the Judicial Council returned a non-guilty verdict in only two instances – a contract dispute it deemed belonging in civil courts, and a corruption case in which the procuracy indicted several lowly employees but failed to prosecute the responsible leadership. In two other instances where defendants obtained non-guilty verdicts in lower courts, the Council reversed those determinations, noted the holes in the evidence collected, and remanded the cases to the procuracy offices for re-investigation. Remanding a non-guilty verdict so the prosecution can build a better case may seem perverse, but is an accepted practice in Vietnam's inquisitorial tradition. One lawyer noted that judges rarely, in her experience, went beyond the sentence that the procurator recommended, likely because they had come to an agreement at pre-trial "interbranch coordination" meetings [họp liên ngành] to which lawyers no access. Given such an uneven footing in trial practice and the rarity of acquittals, a plea bargain in the form of a suspended sentence might be the most strategic choice to defendants.

The SPC's tightening of lower courts' sentencing discretion directly tied to several facets of the Court's legitimacy. Seen as a remedy for judicial corruption and providing clarification for vague laws, it boosts moral and legal legitimacy. It also reinforces the SPC's interbranch legitimacy as the Court was able to coordinate with and support the government's overarching crackdown campaign on corruptions. However, as acquittal remains rare and suspended sentencing continues to be used as proxy for plea bargaining in undeserving cases, citizens are unlikely to trust that they would get a fair day in court, detracting from measures of sociological legitimacy.

## 8.7 Performing Order, Making Money, Nick Cheesman

The previous article on the Supreme People's Court in Vietnam gives a top-down snapshot of how judicial corruption works in routine criminal cases. In this book chapter on Myanmar, Nick Cheesman offers a fascinating grassroots, ethnographic account of how police officers, lawyers, and judges engage in overt and subtle monetary transactions in everyday criminal practice. These transactions run through the entire process of a criminal case, from police custody all the way to court trial and sentencing. The prevalence of such practices in Myanmar leads Cheesman to term it "the business of criminal justice."

Every official involved in a criminal case has at least a small amount of control that he can use to get a payment. Control is of different types. In this section, I will discuss just two: one over the physical body of the accused, and another over the material evidence of a crime. The first is a type of control that I looked at in the last chapter with reference to the use of confession and torture, and here will extend to the practices of the marketplace. The second is a type of control over the production of evidence "whenever and however the law as procedural code demands, rather than as a reality preceding" it.

The most effective means to get control over a person in a criminal case is through control over the body: through confinement or the prospect of confinement. Any government office in Myanmar is a place of latent confinement, a place for the ordinary person to avoid, a place from which one has to struggle to get free. The longer one stays inside, the harder it becomes to leave. As more officials and agencies get involved, everybody wants something to let you go, and the transactions become more complicated and expensive.

Here is one example of a successful effort to get a person out of custody quickly, which also illustrates how practices of control and coordination, or negotiation, start from the moment the police appear on someone's doorstep. The story is from 2005, in a northern town on the border of China, where narcotics are rife and criminal cases for possession of narcotics are common, not just because of the quantities of drugs but also because of the need for high numbers of convictions and exemplary sentencing – as discussed in Chapter 4. According to the brother-in-law of the person arrested, policemen came to a shop where a young man was working and accused him of having illicit drugs. At the time, the brother-in-law asked the police if the accused man would be released. The police inspector leading the arrest replied, "We'll give you an answer at the station. We'll let you know what needs to be done for our side to settle the case." The quick-thinking brother-in-law went to get a local official to play the role of broker. The official went to the station with the brother-in-law, and took the inspector to an eatery nearby. After the official went home and the detainee's family came to see him, he reassured them that everything would work out, as retold here in a signed written narrative of the sequence of events:

> "I have negotiated it. Inspector Myint Kyi asked for twelve lakhs [1.2 million, around USD1,200]. I negotiated for six. So, you look for six. He will come get it in the evening." Around 3 p.m., my sister-in-law and I took five lakhs to U Maung Maung's house. Inspector Myint Kyi was sitting in the kitchen. "Will he take five?" my sister-in-law said. U Maung Maung took the money to Myint Kyi in the kitchen. He came back and said, "He won't take five." "My sister-in-law needs to find another lakh. Set a time for it," I said. "Give it now," Myint Kyi said. "We'll go find it," we said, and departed. We left the five lakhs. We borrowed a lakh from a neighbour, and went back to U Maung Maung's house. We gave the whole amount, exactly six lakhs. When we gave it, Inspector Myint Kyi threatened us that, "Make sure news about this doesn't get out. If it gets out, I'll have you in jail."

The policeman released the detainee from the lockup that day. Having surrendered his control over the body, he had only the threat of impending action to keep the young man and his family from making complaints about the negotiation, or 'coordination' of the release – the word being the same for both, hnyi-hnaing. Sometimes, the police are just looking for opportunities to let a body go, and the coordinating involved is relatively effortless, even if the amounts demanded are not trivial. In a written complaint of mid-2013 to the national human rights commission, for instance, one detainee who alleged that he had already been assaulted at a police station in Mandalay described being railroaded with a co-accused into a transaction for a quick reduction of sentence inside the courthouse:

> The next day [after arrest] the two of us were sent for inquiry at the Chan-aye-thazan Township Court. They did not say anything about what we had been arrested for, or with what section we were charged. A plump policeman came and negotiated [hnyi-hnaing] with us that, "If you want the case lightened, pay 170,000 Kyat" [at the time, around USD200]. So I begged my friend for help to pay that policeman. My friend on the very same day paid the amount of money to a uniformed policeman at the

Chan-aye-thazan Township Court. After paying the money, other police told us that when the judge asked if I was guilty to admit it.

The defendant learned that his payment had bought him a seven-day prison term for a misdemeanour that could otherwise have carried up to three months in jail. The relatively high amount he was prepared to pay might in part have been due to his confusion and fear of what the police would do if he did not cooperate, and in part due to the location – a lucrative, business-oriented city where the premiums are high. Notably, the police did not offer him an opportunity to get out of the case completely, perhaps from concern to balance the needs of the marketplace with the need for fast and easy convictions to maintain the semblance of orderliness in processing of criminal cases, as discussed further below.

The threat of control over the body is also a source of power for court staff negotiating prices for case outcomes. In a similar scenario to the one above, a judge and court clerk in Yangon allegedly advised a man accused of running an unlicensed bodyworks that if he paid them and pled guilty to a charge then he would get off with a fine, but if he fought the case and lost he would go to jail. He said he watched court personnel divvy up an initial payment, which bought him two weeks to come up with the remaining money. After the time was up and he could produce only one-fifth of the amount, the clerk gave an extension, whereupon he gave most of the amount requested and begged the judge to accept it since he could not find any more.

Control over the body gives its custodians opportunities to earn money, large amounts and small. Wherever people encounter junior custodians, they have to pay little amounts of money for delivery of food and medicines to detainees, and for opportunities to meet with them. Some families also pay superior officers not to torture or mistreat the detainee. They may also pay the crime-reporting officer to put the case to the top of the list that the police will submit to court, and thereby jump the queue for bail.

Wealthy and influential detainees can have a different custodial experience from everyone else. A lawyer recounted one case to me about the son of an army officer and a friend in northern Shan State who in 2008 faced charges for the attempted rape of a classmate. As the victim was from a well-known family in her locality, she pressed a complaint with the backing of some officials. The police had little choice but to arrest and open cases against the alleged perpetrators. But once in custody, the two young men did not stay in the cells with other detainees. The station commander put them in a room next to his office normally reserved for playing cards and drinking. Both of the accused reportedly had access to whatever food and alcohol they wanted, as well as to visitors. A court quickly let the officer's son out on remand, due to a supposed medical condition. It later acquitted both men.

Research conducted during 2012 at the main court complexes and township courts in five states revealed patterns in the practices of moneymaking through control over the body. Like the VIP detainees in the abovementioned case, remanded detainees in Loikaw, the capital of Kayah State on the border of Thailand, could avoid being sent to prison by paying from fifty to a hundred thousand Kyat to be kept at a room set aside for the purpose in the police station. The room was not luxurious, but it was better than prison, where remanded detainees feared becoming prey of seasoned inmates.

At many places, police and court officials have a lively trade going for the granting of bail. The Criminal Procedure Code distinguishes between two types of offences, one for which bail should be given automatically and another for which a court order is required under section 497(1). Defendants commonly have to pay for bail in the latter type of case. Complainants can also pay to prevent defendants from going free. During 1996 in a town near Yangon, for instance, a woman whose daughter had eloped with her lover got revenge by paying for the arrest and detention of the young man involved and his four brothers. Foolishly, the judge neglected to shift the charge and denied them bail under a section of the Penal Code for which he should automatically have granted it, giving the detained men strong grounds for complaints against him after they got out.

Going rates for people who want to pay to get out on bail fluctuate from place to place. In Loikaw during 2012 lawyers advised that typically two to three hundred thousand Kyat would do it, with two-thirds of this amount for the judge and a third for the public prosecutor. The bench clerk, who can change the sequence of cases posted for hearing and speed up or delay processing of paperwork, would receive ten to twenty thousand Kyat; the police, thirty to fifty thousand.

In Mudon, a town in Mon State further to the south, the bail rates for offences like causing hurt by dangerous weapons under section 326 of the Penal Code or assault on a woman 'with intent to outrage her modesty' under section 354 were about 50 percent more than in Loikaw, although the subsidiary fees of the police and court clerk were roughly the same. The prices in Sittwe, capital of Rakhine State, on the western seaboard, were at least as much as in Mudon; however, lawyers indicated that in cases where an accused was patently innocent or unable to pay, judges and public prosecutors would sometimes settle for less than the standard amount. In Hpa-an, the capital of Karen State, the prices were lower: a minimum of a hundred thousand Kyat for the judge, and around eighty thousand Kyat for the prosecutor, with five to ten thousand Kyat paid to the court clerks and prosecutor's clerk.

Cases are managed and coordinated in similar ways across much of the country, but differ regionally. At a township in Chin State, on the border of India, professionals in 2012 reported that most cases were sorted out through payments in the police station, with relatively few matters going to court. The amounts that the police demanded were also modest – around fifty thousand Kyat to close a vehicle accident case, a bit more if the vehicles involved were unregistered; roughly the same for cattle smuggling; and, twenty to thirty thousand Kyat for minor assault. Professionals attributed the low amounts and tendency of police to keep matters out of court to local customs and fraternal feelings among members of ethnic minority groups there; however, the fact that the region is relatively poor and the money economy still relatively small may be contributing factors.

In certain types of cases where material evidence is unusually important, the control and coordination dynamics differ somewhat from other cases. Narcotics cases may involve chemical analysis of seized drugs or, in the case of users, urine. Under section 15 of the 1993 Narcotic Drugs and Psychotropic Substances Law, a drug user who fails to register voluntarily for rehabilitation can go to jail for three to five years. Police officers collect urine from accused users and send it for chemical analysis. A lab tests the urine and sends a result to the court where the case is posted. Depending on the positive or negative finding, the judge convicts or acquits the accused. In effect, a finding of guilt or innocence in these cases is made at the lab. The judge has limited discretion to decide on the sentence. So in cases lodged against alleged drug users, unlike many others where confession is the best evidence, control over the outcome of the case is contingent on control over the material evidence.

Professionals working on narcotics cases in the late 2000s said that the chemical analysis labs interpreted government policy on deterrence to mean that the default result for urine analysis should be positive. Labs offered negative results in exchange for payment. The 2009–10 starting figure in Kyat for a negative result was around one hundred thousand per urine sample, and a million per sample in the case of seized drugs: at roughly a hundred U.S. dollars and a thousand U.S. dollars respectively, small change for those accused who can afford to pay, including people actually trading in drugs. They are not affordable amounts for anyone with no money, contacts, and knowhow, like an alleged user brought to one station in the north during 2007. A court sentenced him to five years' imprisonment for a positive test result somehow taken from a sample of dirty water that he had provided the police from the toilet bowl at the station, where he was unable to urinate due to an infection.

Chemical analysis plays a part in other types of cases, such as murder, grievous hurt, and rape cases. Lab results are relevant, but trial outcomes do not hinge on them. Judges can also call for expert witnesses, as provided in sections 45 to 49 of the Evidence Act, such as in cases where persons are accused of trafficking items other than narcotics. Some parties pay expert witnesses to provide false evidence, such as to testify that tiger bones found in baggage on a train and apparently being taken to be sold for medicines were bones of another animal; and jade being smuggled illegally was some other, non-valuable, stone. The police also can switch real evidence for fake evidence, either with the complicity of the expert witness or without her knowledge. Township courts generally lack secure arrangements for keeping evidence during trial. Material evidence may be held at the bailiff's quarters on the court premises or at the police station. At either location, police officers and court staff have ample opportunities to damage, misplace, or sell stored items.

When bringing charges of possession, trafficking, and cultivation of narcotics, chemical labs' findings are also relevant, but unlike in users' cases, courts can admit and interpret a range of evidence to reach a verdict. For instance, if a group of people stand accused, a judge can arrange to acquit the ringleaders or real dealers and convict the minor offenders or substitutes. However, in cases where dealers have been caught red-handed with large quantities of narcotics and equipment for its manufacture, like one case in the capital of Shan State in 1994, this method might not be enough to insulate the judge from criticism.

One professional who handles narcotics cases in 2010 said prices vary for acquittal under different offences in the Narcotic Drugs and Psychotropic Substances Law. Many factors affect outcomes, including the severity of the crime, the number of persons involved in the case, and the police units investigating. For example, a township or district judge in the north of the country might be paid anywhere from one to three million for acquittal in cases where the defendant is charged with possession of prohibited materials or implements under section 16(b) of the law, which carries a sentence of five to ten years in jail. In 2009–10 prices, for a charge of possession with intent to sell under section 19(a), which carries a minimum sentence of ten years, an acquittal can cost up to twenty million in payments to judges alone. Thus, narcotics cases contain many meeting points between the semblance of orderliness required of courts and their moneymaking imperative. One does not simply give way to the other. The two intersect and complement one another, communicate with one another, and reinforce each other throughout the business of criminal justice.

### 8.8 Justice Is a Secret: *Compromise* in Rape Trials, *Pratiksha Baxi*

The criminal process is not only subject to corruption but also influenced by social norms and practices outside the legal system, such as out-of-court settlements. Not all settlements are legal, yet many are influential in communities as well as in court. Pratiksha Baxi's study of rape trials in India provides a telling example of how the patriarchal practice of "compromise" in rape cases, which is not a legal procedure, nevertheless becomes a tool of defense lawyers and an influential element in trials. As a result, justice is distorted, and the rape victims are injured again with the excuse of keeping secrets and restoring social relations.

This article is based on an extended case study of a trial of rape, abduction and kidnapping which I documented in a trial court in Ahmedabad, Gujarat, in 1996–98. In the court, I was repeatedly told that rape cases are routinely compromised. Intrigued by this practice, which the law books clearly state as against the intent of law, I decided to pursue the story of "compromise cases". In this article, I argue that the sociolegal process encapsulated in the word "compromise" (or *samadhan*, the coexisting Gujarati usage) is an exposition of how secrecy may be thought of as "indispensable to the operation of power rather than as an abuse of power". Unlike other forms of out-of-court settlements described as mechanisms of alternate dispute resolution, plea-bargaining or mediation in courts of law, compromise is not legal in rape cases in India. In such cases, witnesses turn hostile routinely after an out-of-court settlement and yet, the processes of compromise are effaced from the judgement.

I suggest that the specific manifestation of the rape trial as a "compromise case" allows us to examine the courtroom as a site of public secrecy. Michael Taussig persuades us to query how "so easily we join truth and secret" and how "with rapture we skid between them, envelop the one in the other: truth = secret". He asks, "what if the truth is not much a secret as a public secret, as in the case with most important social knowledge, knowing what not to know?" If public secrecy is one of the "most interesting, the most powerful, the most mischievous and ubiquitous form of socially active knowledge", then Taussig argues that "...it is the task and the life force of the public secret to maintain that verge where the secret is not destroyed through exposure, but subject to a quite a different sort of revelation that does justice to it".

Drawing from this insight, I argue that compromise as a form of public secret is not destroyed by its utterance before the judge, but rather, is subjected to a specific revelation in court. This specific revelation in a courtroom is actualised through the law of evidence, where we find that the prosecution witnesses turn hostile to the prosecution case. Trial transcripts or trial court judgements do not record these as "compromise cases" except as a residue via the category of hostility. The ethnographic account of the way testimony is structured in a "compromise" case demonstrates how this effacement in law produces a specific revelation, which is perceived somehow to perform "social justice". [...]

During the trial, compromise acts as a tool in the hands of defence lawyers and the accused to pressurise complainants and victims to change their testimonies in a courtroom. Let us turn to a recent case from Agra wherein a young Dalit woman was gang-raped and the rapist let off on bail. The accused threatened to rape the victim again if she did not compromise. Nearly a year after she was raped, she committed suicide. While we find that the judgement records that the victim committed suicide following the pressure to compromise, the judgement does not criminalise the pressure to compromise as criminal intimidation of the victim and her family. The normalising function of the socio-legal category of compromise converts terror into a bargain in a context where there is no witness protection programme. This often accounts for why prosecution witnesses routinely turn hostile by the time the case comes on trial, if the victim does not lose the will to live.

Compromise also moves across another set of cases where it is difficult to read the distinction between consent and coercion from the legal records. In this article, I focus on such cases where compromise acts to signal the dissonance between what is legally constituted as rape and the social uses the rape law is put to. This set of cases operates under the sign of seduction, love and illicit sex. Police complaints on the charge of kidnapping, abduction, rape and theft are routinely filed against couples who elope. In such cases, when the couple is found, the woman may be forced to support the version of the complainant, usually a parent, and return to her lawful guardian. The family then get her married to someone else and compromise is seen as the only way of preserving her marriage. Or, if the woman continues to hold her ground and deny the charge of rape and abduction, she may face violence from the police and/or her family. Such cases are often registered when the man is from another community or from a lower caste. Thereby the distinction between elopement and abduction, or rape and consensual sex is blurred by this criminalisation of love and seduction.

The construction of rape as a sexual offence, which is concerned with offences against codes of alliance rather than concerned with the bodily integrity of all women, allows for this criminalisation of love. The severity of caste violence is most stark in hypogamous unions, that is, unions between upper caste women and lower caste men. In such relationships, the distinction between love and consensual sex on the one hand and rape, on the other hand, is not socially intelligible. [...]

By pointing out that the court is a site where public secrets are negotiated, I aimed to show how different actors during a trial agree to hide the very meaning of rape such that these meanings remain unacknowledged in the legal record. The operations of public secrecy are detailed by following the socio-legal processes that make the legal record. I have drawn attention to the culture of compromise that underwrites rape prosecutions, an aspect of rape prosecutions that has not been sufficiently discussed either within the women's movement, the judiciary or the contemporary discourse on judicial reform. The term "culture of compromise" emphasises how a criminal trial becomes a site for the contestation over the monopoly of an out-of-court settlement between the accused, the complainant and the prosecuting agencies. Through this case study, I have shown how the struggle to monopolise the compromise is staged between the father–complainant and the accused, but the subjectivity of the woman whose violation is prosecuted is difficult to read from the court records. The court records detail a politics of ambivalence where two versions of what may have happened are recorded simultaneously as a potential for the father–complainant to use in the future. The laws on rape, kidnapping and abduction then situate violation in the realm of the collective rather than represent individual women's experiences of coercion or consent.

In other words, I have shown how legality is actually perceived as disruptive of sociality; in this instance, a sociality that is marked by caste-based patriarchies, such that compromise is actively perceived, to put it in the words of a woman judge of a district court, as a mechanism for "restoring social relations in society".

## REFERENCES

### Featured Readings

Baxi, Pratiksha. 2010. "Justice Is a Secret: *Compromise* in Rape Trials." *Contributions to Indian Sociology* 44 (3): 207–33. doi: 10.1177/006996671004400301

Chang, Won Kyung. 2018. "Old Wine in New Wineskins? A Trial of Restorative Justice in a Korean Criminal Court." *Asian Journal of Law and Society* 5 (2): 391–411. doi: 10.10117/als.2017.34

Cheesman, Nick. 2015. *Opposing the Rule of Law: How Myanmar's Courts Make Law and Order*. Cambridge: Cambridge University Press. Chapter 6. doi: 10.1017/cbo9781316014936.008

Foote, Daniel H. 1992. "The Benevolent Paternalism of Japanese Criminal Justice." *California Law Review* 80: 317–90. doi: 10.2307/3480769

Johnson, David T., and Jon Fernquest. 2018. "Governing through Killing: The War on Drugs in the Philippines." *Asian Journal of Law and Society* 5 (2): 359–90. doi: 10.1017/als.2018.12

Nguyen, Trang Mae. 2019. "In Search of Judicial Legitimacy: Criminal Sentencing in Vietnamese Courts." *Harvard Human Rights Journal* 32: 147–88.

Sapio, Flora, Susan Trevaskes, Sarah Biddulph, and Elisa Nesossi. 2017. *Justice: The China Experience*. Cambridge: Cambridge University Press. Chapter 1. doi: 10.1017/9781108115919.001

Smith, Tobias. 2020. "Body Count Politics: Quantification, Secrecy, and Capital Punishment in China." *Law & Social Inquiry* 45 (3): 706–27. doi: 10.1017/lsi.2020.10

### Other Works Cited

Durkheim, Emile. [1895] 1984. *The Division of Labor in Society*, trans. W. D. Halls. New York: The Free Press. doi: 10.4324/9780203405338-13

Feeley, Malcolm M. 1979. *The Process Is the Punishment: Handling Cases in a Lower Criminal Court*. New York: Russell Sage Foundation. doi: 10.2307/1288075

Foucault, Michel. [1975] 1977. *Discipline and Punish: The Birth of the Prison*, trans. A. Sheridan. New York: Vintage Books. doi: 10.2307/2077073

### Suggested Readings

Ciocchini, Pablo, and George Radics (eds.). 2019. *Criminal Legalities in the Global South: Cultural Dynamics, Political Tensions, and Institutional Practices*. London: Routledge. doi: 10.4324/9780429459764

Johnson, David T. 2002. *The Japanese Way of Justice: Prosecuting Crime in Japan*. Oxford: Oxford University Press. doi: 10.1017/als.2018.12

Trevaskes, Susan. 2012. *Policing Serious Crime in China: From "Strike Hard" to "Kill Fewer."* London: Routledge. doi: 10.1007/s11417-012-9131-5

## 9 Practicing Law and Society Scholarship in Asia

Contents

| | | |
|---|---|---|
| I | Gaining Access and Getting Data | 350 |
| II | Navigating Identities | 367 |
| III | Practicing Law and Society Research in the Digital Age | 376 |

We have introduced an array of Asian law and society research in the previous chapters and shown what is distinctive about this field of study – in particular, how it differs from the doctrinal scholarship of Asian legal academies. One hallmark of law and society scholarship is that it is empirically grounded. The researcher conducts empirical research on the places and people in question to find answers to a research puzzle that has presented itself in the research process. Often, scholars design their research to gather data in imaginative yet rigorous ways. In some cases, even when they do not conduct empirical research firsthand, their arguments and viewpoints originate from deep understandings of the context, in which they have been previously immersed or about which they have learned from the empirical insights of other scholars. The answers that law and society scholars produce for their research puzzles is thus informed by what they have learned from the data. Crucially, they do not begin their research with a fixed answer in mind or simply seek out data that support their preconceived arguments. They are open to being surprised by what they learn from the empirical research.

Parmar (2015), whose legal ethnography was featured in Legal Mobilization (Chapter 5), studied the dispute over a Coca-Cola bottling facility on Adivasi lands in India by conducting in-depth interviews, participant observation, and textual analysis. She wanted to find out how different parties experienced the dispute and made their claims, but she encountered a situation that exemplifies the distinctiveness of law and society scholarship:

# Practicing Law and Society Scholarship in Asia     349

> One question that I have been asked several times during the course of this research and at conferences and other places by lawyers, officers of courts, law students, concerned friends, and others is about what specific "law" I meant to study or propose. Two social activists I interviewed were clearly disappointed that despite my legal training, I did not plan to use this opportunity to propose a new law. Although proposals for newer and better laws serve extremely useful purposes, questions such as the ones posed to me are often based on a narrow positivistic understanding of law and its separateness from other fields of knowledge [...] One conversation that I was most troubled and inspired by took place after I had presented my work in a law school. Three bright students [...] were confident that "we" know what the dispute is about. In order to ensure justice for those who have suffered, we need to look at "the law," and how it can be made better. That is undoubtedly a very important exercise. I failed, however, to convince them of the importance of a prior question that I was pursuing: Do we know what the dispute is about? I hope the stories I present here show the importance of paying attention to how we know, and in what ways in failing to doubt our knowledge we limit our abilities to listen and respond. These insights are essential for understanding both the potential and limits of law and formal legal processes.
>
> (21–2, original emphasis by author)

This chapter is not a conventional how-to introduction to methods and methodology, whereby the student learns how to formulate a research question, design the project, carry out the data collection, and analyze the data. Many other books serve those purposes.* Instead, we illustrate how Asian law and society scholars go about designing and executing their research projects, what type of challenges they commonly encounter, and how they address those challenges. Along the way, we highlight classic, tried and tested methods, and newer, creative ways of conducting grounded research as Asian law and society scholars respond to ever-changing political repression, legal restrictions, and technological developments.

Most of the readings in this chapter come from the same publications that were extracted in the earlier chapters or from the same research project. We strive for continuity because the substantive content of law and society research is inseparable from the research process. How do the authors we have read in earlier chapters arrive at their findings and conclusions? How do they know what they know? We hope that this chapter's behind-the-scenes look will offer further insights into Asian law and society scholarship.

---

\* See "Suggested Additional Readings" at the end of this chapter.

## I GAINING ACCESS AND GETTING DATA

Asian law and society scholars, like their peers conducting research in other parts of the world, do not limit themselves to case law, legal codes, or statute books. They adopt approaches widely accepted in sociolegal studies, as well as the social sciences at large.

These include quantitative and qualitative approaches, and data collection methods such as semi-structured interviews, ethnography, archival work, surveys, experiments, and discourse analysis. Their data are wide-ranging, originating from such sources as interviews, field observations, legal proceedings, government records, professional journals, letters and petitions, news reports, videos, photographs, and social media.

The readings in this section illustrate how Asian law and society scholars chose their methods and data sources, formulated strategies to gain access and collect the data, and responded to difficulties in the field. The readings also capture the common feature of multi-methods in law and society research projects, the combining of different methodologies or methods, such as qualitative with quantitative analyses, or interviews with observations and archives. A researcher may undertake mixed methods to triangulate, supplement, or complement data derived from different sources and methods. To be sure, the methodological choice flows from the research question and the researcher's intellectual background and training, but it is also shaped by the feasibility of getting access to data. For example, government agencies or corporations may be unwilling to grant permission to use their databases or to speak with their personnel, and may treat with suspicion researchers whose findings might cast them in a negative light. As a result, the choice of research method is not purely an academic matter but additionally grounded in the research context.

### 9.1 Tort, Custom, and Karma: Globalization and Legal Consciousness in Thailand, *David M. Engel and Jaruwan Engel*

In Chapter 1, we read an extract of the Engels' book discussing the relationship between state injury law and Buddhist practices in northern Thailand, and, in Chapter 4, we considered David Engel's article on the legal consciousness of northern Thai villagers. Both the book and the article are based on the Engels' research spanning the 1970s through to the early 2000s. Their long-term fieldwork and multi-method design enabled them to connect macro changes across time to the experiences of individual injury victims at the micro level.

Our fieldwork had two major components: (1) extended ethnographic interviews with more than a hundred individuals in Chiangmai, Thailand, thirty-five of whom had been hospitalized for treatment of serious injuries; and (2) a survey of personal injury and other tort cases litigated in the local trial court over a thirty-five-year period. [...]

The design of the study reflects a pyramid model of litigation and dispute processing that is familiar to and widely used by sociolegal scholars. As applied to the personal injury field, the pyramid is said to rest on a broad base consisting of all the harms that might potentially be perceived as wrongful and, in some cases, as having legal significance. The middle layers of the injury pyramid involve unilateral or bilateral claims and negotiations, intervention by unofficial third party intermediaries or lawyers, and other extrajudicial settlement procedures. The tip of the pyramid involves tort cases that are actually litigated, adjudicated, and – even more rarely – appealed. Our study of injuries in Thailand concentrates on two layers of the pyramid: the base and the tip.

[...][T]he characteristics of the pyramid's base must be understood before meaningful inferences can be drawn about any other aspect of the handling of tort cases in society. Analysis of "lumping," negotiation, settlement, or the decision to litigate depends on information about the pyramid's base: the number and kinds of injuries that occur in society and the ways in which individuals interpret them – the raw materials from which claims, disputes, or lawsuits might be fashioned.

Understanding the base of the injury pyramid is thus essential to the analysis of all the other layers, including the litigation of tort cases. The perception and interpretation of injury determines all that follows – whether the injured person holds another party responsible, whether compensation is expected or demanded, what mechanisms for obtaining compensation are considered, and whether legal or other normative systems are invoked to assess the responsibilities of the parties. At the base of the pyramid, cultural factors are extraordinarily important. Here the analysis of legal consciousness can shed considerable light.

Our methodology for exploring the legal consciousness of ordinary people at the base of the injury pyramid in Chiangmai builds on research that examines how individuals tell stories about their lives, their experiences, their social relationships and interactions, and their sense of self. Such narratives are used primarily to understand the subjectivity of the narrators – how they interpret events, how they explain their own behavior and that of others, and how they view themselves in relation to the world around them and in relation to legal norms, procedures, and institutions. We encouraged interviewees to provide an extended narrative covering a broad sweep of time, in which they described their lives from childhood to present and the changes that had occurred in their social environment over a period of many years. Within the broader narrative of their personal history, they located the specific incident that caused them to seek treatment in a hospital for physical harm.

To obtain the injury narratives of ordinary people in Chiangmai, we identified a large hospital that treated patients from the entire province of Chiangmai and thus drew cases from a "jurisdiction" comparable to that of the provincial court. With the help of the staff at Suan Dok Hospital, we obtained the names of ninety-three current or recently discharged patients who had volunteered to participate in interviews. All had suffered physical injuries involving the conduct of another party. After recording baseline data for all ninety-three volunteers, we selected thirty-five for extensive, in-depth interviews, which we conducted in Thai at the hospital or at the interviewee's home or place of work in 1999. Participants were chosen to provide a range of perspectives, based primarily on rural versus urban background, gender, circumstances of the injury, and age. Despite its diversity, this group was not a random sample of Chiangmai's population. The thirty-five interviewees were not selected to make quantitative predictions about a broader universe, but they do illustrate in considerable depth some of the ways in which globalization has affected the legal consciousness of differently situated individuals in Chiangmai.

This study focuses on the subjective and interpretive processes that occur in the pyramid's base, but the findings have implications for each succeeding level of the pyramid, including the use of courts and lawyers. While a systematic study of the entire injury pyramid in Thailand was beyond the scope of this study – and unfortunately there are few other studies of the injury pyramid in Thailand – we sought to shed additional light on the injury narratives by interviewing a number of other persons who had knowledge of injuries, village life, insurance, negotiations, legal practice, and other matters relevant to our study. Our study therefore included more than sixty-five additional interviews with a broad spectrum of persons ranging from village leaders to insurance adjusters, monks, spirit mediums, attorneys, judges, Thai scholars, doctors, government officials, and others. These interviews supplemented the thirty-five interviews with injury victims.

The second major component of the study, in addition to the interviews described above, consisted of an exploration of the tip of the injury pyramid – the Chiangmai Provincial Court. We had the great advantage of having researched tort litigation in the same court twenty-five years earlier. From 1974 to 1978, we had surveyed all the case files in the Chiangmai Provincial Court for cases litigated from 1965 through 1974. In particular, we obtained detailed information taken from the pleadings, witness testimony, and judicial opinions of every tort case that appeared in the court during four of those years: 1965, 1968, 1971, and 1974. Further, we had conducted interviews in 1975 with litigants, lawyers, judges, police officers, village leaders, and others. Our study in the late 1990s was, in some respects, a "restudy" that involved a return to a familiar setting and provided an opportunity to trace changes and continuities over a relatively long period of time.

From 1997 to 2000 we once again surveyed the docket of the Chiangmai Provincial Court, this time selecting cases litigated from 1992 through 1997. Using the court registers, we identified every injury case filed by a private party. Most took the form of civil actions, but some were litigated as private criminal cases. We retrieved and photocopied the entire case file of each of these civil and criminal cases, analyzed their contents, and compared them to the ten years of cases we had studied during our previous fieldwork in 1975. As we shall discuss in later chapters of this book, we found to our surprise that tort litigation rates at the tip of the injury pyramid had actually decreased over the past quarter-century, and this finding proved to be consistent with the alienation from law we discovered at the base of the injury pyramid. These parallel developments at different levels of the pyramid invite more general theorizing about the relationships among globalization, legal consciousness, and tort law in Thailand. Therefore, although much of this book focuses on the injury narratives, we analyze them with one eye on the diminished rate of litigation in the formal legal system, and we suggest that both the base and the tip of the pyramid reflect and contribute to the social transformations Chiangmai has experienced during the past twenty-five years.

The Engels' book spanned four decades of research, from initial fieldwork in the 1970s to publication in 2010, a length of time that seems rather unattainable for younger scholars. The next two readings demonstrate feasible strategies to conduct law and society research without having to spend decades in the field. Nevertheless, both of these research projects share the common characteristics of still requiring considerable time in the field and employing a mix of methods.

## 9.2 Constituting Religion: Islam, Liberal Rights, and the Malaysian State, *Tamir Moustafa*

We read Moustafa's article on legal consciousness (Chapter 4), which is an earlier publication based on the same project as his book. In the article and the book, Moustafa studied court decisions, but his research went far beyond the verdicts of Malaysia's apex courts. As we can see from his description of the fieldwork, Moustafa collected and analyzed newspaper reports, as well as conducted one-on-one interviews, focus groups, and a nationwide survey.

> Fieldwork for the project was conducted in the summer and fall of 2009, in the fall of 2010, and over several subsequent stretches between 2012 and 2015. A total of 170 semi-structured interviews were conducted, seventy with lawyers, judges, activists, politicians, and journalists, and an additional 100 with "everyday Malaysians." Findings also rest on an extensive textual analysis of court decisions and press coverage of prominent cases. I examined the full universe of cases where there was a question of jurisdiction between the civil courts and the shariah courts. A context-rich, process-tracing method was adopted to map the development of legal institutions over time, as well as the flow of individual cases through the courts. This two-level (institutional and case-specific) process-tracing approach facilitated careful consideration of the continuities and critical junctures where legal/institutional change produced new patterns of contention inside and outside the courts. I examined the full life cycle of each case, from its first appearance in court through to the public spectacle that emerged around certain of those cases. I considered the origin of each case and the legal logics invoked, as civil court judges navigated complex entanglements and contending claims concerning shariah court jurisdiction. Next, I noted whether cases became subjects of popular debate. For those cases that did gain political salience, I examined how they came into the public spotlight. I then studied the contending frames of understanding that were crafted for consumption in the court of public opinion. Here, I examined the public statements issued by non-governmental organizations, political parties, and various state officials (including the religious establishment) to understand the role of different actors in the construction of a rights-versus-rites binary. With the assistance of a research team, I also compared press coverage of select court cases across Malaysia's diverse media landscape, from the Malay-language newspapers *Utusan Malaysia*, *Berita Harian*, and *Harakah*, to the Tamil-language papers *Makkal Osai* and *Malaysia Nanban*, to the Chinese-language *Sin Chew*, and the English-language press. This comparison suggested the extent to which Malaysia's segmented

ethnolinguistic media environment further refracts competing frames of understanding across variously situated communities. Finally, I circled back to examine the extent to which these frames differed from the logics that were at work in court. Studying the full life cycle of these disputes provided an empirically grounded examination of how the rights-versus-rites binary is continually inscribed in the Malaysian public imagination.

Elite-level interviews enabled a deeper understanding of the various positions and strategies of civil society organizations, which had mobilized around controversial cases, both inside and outside formal legal intuitions. I was mindful of the need to seek out views from across the political and ideological spectrum to consider the full range of thinking about the cases and the controversies they produced. I therefore interviewed lawyers litigating on opposite sides of the same cases, as well as activists from the most prominent liberal rights and conservative NGOs who had staked out opposite sides of public lobbying efforts. (The absence of a middle ground was striking, and it speaks to the ways that judicial institutions frame a binary logic that is hard to escape.) I found it relatively easy to empathize with the views and positions of liberal rights lawyers and activists, as their frames of understanding aligned closely with my own. Yet I was cognizant that a better understanding of the concerns, anxieties, and aims of conservative groups and their audiences is essential for a deeper appreciation of the legal entanglements and their polarizing effects on popular legal consciousness. Many of the lawyers, activists, and journalists whom I interviewed became key sources of information. The lawyers among them provided access to case files and legal briefs. Repeated discussions with all key actors helped to round out my understanding of important cases and controversies beyond what was available through official court records and press archives.

To assess the radiating effect of courts on popular legal consciousness, I organized a multiethnic research team to conduct semi-structured interviews with "everyday Malaysians." The aim of these informal interviews was to study popular understandings of court cases and legal controversies. I was interested in assessing whether popular understandings of prominent cases matched the legal logics that are deployed in court, or if they matched the frames that political activists constructed for media consumption. I supplemented these semi-structured interviews with several structured focus groups and a nationwide, stratified survey of popular understandings of the Islamic legal tradition. [...]

The national telephone survey was nationwide in scope. It used appropriate sampling techniques to ensure that respondents represented the composition of the Muslim community in Malaysia across relevant demographic variables including region, sex, and urban–rural cleavages. Execution of the telephone survey, including the sampling of respondents, was conducted by the Merdeka Center for Opinion Research, the leading public survey research group in Malaysia. The sampling population was drawn from the national telephone directory, which comprises all households with fixed-line telephones. In stage one of the sampling, a random number generator was used to produce a sample of three million fixed-line phone numbers from the national directory. The resulting list was then checked to ensure that it was proportional to the number of Muslim residents in each state per 2006 Malaysian census figures. In stage two, a randomly generated respondent telephone list was prepared, comprising five times the desired sample size of one thousand respondents. In step three, interval sampling was applied to the respondent telephone list. One respondent was contacted in each household on December 9–13, 2009. Respondents were balanced to ensure an equal number of males and females. The random stratified sample of 1,043 Malaysian Muslims ensures a maximum error margin of 3.03 percent at a 95 percent confidence level. [...]

Four focus group sessions were organized on July 14, 20, and 21, 2013 in Petaling Jaya. Each focus group lasted approximately 1.5 hours and drew participants from across metropolitan Kuala Lumpur. The first focus group was composed of Malay participants with a Malay facilitator; the second group was made up of ethnic Indian Malaysians with an ethnic Indian facilitator; the third group had ethnic Chinese Malaysians with an ethnic Chinese moderator; the final focus group was ethnically mixed, with both ethnic Malay and ethnic Chinese facilitators. The focus group questions were designed by the author and executed with the assistance of the Merdeka Center for Opinion Research, which provided organization and assistance.

## 9.3 China and Islam: The Prophet, the Party, and Law, *Matthew S. Erie*

The Engels and Moustafa did not say much about whether they had encountered hostility or rejection when they were contacting potential interviewees or obtaining written records. For other researchers, gaining access may be more plainly difficult, due to the nature of the subject matter or the identity of the researcher. In Chapter 2 (Legal Pluralism), we read an article by Erie on the Hui people, Muslim minorities in Northwest China. The excerpt below comes from his book, in which he recounts his experiences in the field as he tried to learn about the practices, norms, and institutions that inform Hui religious belief, what he calls *"minjian"* (literally "among the people"), by gathering interviews with local religious leaders, officials, and ordinary residents, observing Hui religious and social life, and collecting archival materials.

> To understand the dynamics of the localization and revitalization of Islamic law, in 2004 I began examining potential field sites during preliminary fieldwork. From 2009 to 2011 I conducted eighteen months of fieldwork in Northwest China, with follow-up fieldtrips in 2012 and 2015, for a total of twenty months in the field. Against the backdrop of heightened disquiet in the region after the July 2009 riots in Urumqi, a foreign researcher was a liability to any potential local sponsor. The competitive advantage of anthropology is "being there." Yet being there can also be the worst of things – for one's interlocutors and for oneself. As a matter of pragmatics, one learns in China that there is the official way and the unofficial way to do things. I spent a great amount of time, effort, and funds trying the former. Eventually, I realized that not only was the latter preferred by most Chinese (Han or minority), but it would also allow me a window into those practices that occur beyond the pale of formal law.
>
> Given the extreme difficulty of conducting field research in the shadow of the Urumqi riots, my fate was determined by a gathering of three individuals – a police officer, a local legislator, and a scholar (all Hui) – during a meeting in Linxia to which I was not invited. Because two of the three people in the room were my allies, I was allowed to stay. I developed a complex relationship of mutual irritation/tolerance with the third participant at the meeting, a police officer I will name Officer Zeng. After the meeting, we became beeping red dots on each other's radars. When passing me on the street, Officer Zeng would pretend to ignore me as he wrestled control over the involuntary snarl that would appear on his face. When ignoring each other became untenable and we engaged in conversation, for instance in a public park, we would inevitably start arguing through forced smiles as we found ourselves defending our respective countries' views on social justice. He would stop by unannounced at my place of residence to "check in" with me as he casually fingered through the books on my desk. We eventually settled into a kind of uneasy equilibrium. I became both his daughter's English tutor and convenient dinner table scapegoat for US foreign policy gaffes, as we participated in the exchange of favors and verbal barbs. He advised me that "Linxia is not like other places" and "I should be careful." I initially dismissed such warnings as Chinese paternalism, but after experiencing subtle shades of hostility that

once flared up into face-to-face confrontation, I can reflect that Officer Zeng was correct.

In short, our relationship was confounding and yet, over time, became familiar. Although my status was never clearly defined in legal terms, it was only because of our relationship (however ambivalent it was) that I was allowed to conduct my research. Thus, my fieldwork was directed by some of the same forces that shape the *minjian* in China as experienced by Hui: on the one hand, constraints, if not blockages, imposed by state law and policy and, on the other hand, the obligations of personal and communal (in my case, anthropologists') ethical and professional commitments. The friction between these impositions and drives forced me to reflect empathetically on being Muslim in postsocialist China.

I established myself in the old Muslim quarter of the city known as Bafang. I realized that given the importance of the teaching schools to the localization of Islamic law in China, I would have to conduct visits to other field sites in the Northwest. I visited additional areas in Gansu, including Dongxiang Autonomous County, home of the Dongxiang, and the Hui-Han-Tibetan town of Lintan (formerly Taozhou), the base of the Xidaotang. In Qinghai I traveled to Xunhua Salar Autonomous County, the seat of the Salars, and also to the great Hui center of Xining. I took overnight trains with Hui students to Ningxia, visiting Guyuan and Haiyuan, places of extremely low socioeconomic levels but centers of Hui, particularly Khufiyya Sufi, communities. I also took several trips to Yinchuan, the capital of the autonomous region and the city that is perhaps the most flourishing in the contemporary Islamic revival. Since 2004 I have taken half a dozen trips to Xinjiang, ranging from two to four weeks in length. These research trips entailed data collection in Hami (Kumul), Urumqi, and oasis cities around the Taklamakan Desert, including Kashgar and Shache (Yarkand). My approach was thus a modified multi-sited ethnographic study.

Though my study was heavily focused on Linxia, my collection of data gathering radiated outward, following missionaries, circulating texts, and Sufi pilgrimage routes. Such an approach enabled me to obtain a depth of knowledge in the "intensively-focused-upon single site of ethnographic observation and participation" while recognizing that China's Little Mecca is located in larger "wholes." Plural sites enabled me to compare a number of variables across the Northwest, including the effects of the Islamic law revival and the impacts of Communist policy on Hui communities.

The bulk of the data analyzed in this book comes from more than two hundred interviews. Over half of these were with Muslim authorities, including clerics, Sufi shaykhs, madrasa teachers, and other administrative personnel in mosques and Sufi tomb complexes. A smaller proportion were conducted with officials and Party cadres in legal, judicial, and public safety bureaus as well as with entrepreneurs, teachers in state-run schools, students, and merchants. I collected interviews by use of "snowball sampling," which enabled me to extend my network of interlocutors through the social connections of individuals I had previously interviewed.

The core data set of my study comes from time spent at thirty-four mosques and the twenty-three main Sufi tomb complexes in Linxia. Mosques (and also schools, Islamic banks, and sheep hide markets) are arenas in which Hui make sense of their adherence to state law and Islamic law, the site where the Hui social field is most visible. Interviews were conducted principally in Mandarin. The local dialect is called Bafanghua, "the language of Bafang." Bafanghua incorporates Arabic, Persian, Urdu, Tibetan, Mongolian, and various other local dialects of Muslim ethnicities, including Dongxiangyu and Salarhua. I studied Arabic, one of the main foreign languages in Bafanghua, in Linxia and, in between field trips, in Amman, Jordan, so as my ability in the dialect increased, I was able to introduce more Bafanghua into my conversations. Interviews were semistructured, and wherever possible, more informal interviews were conducted as follow-up. To develop extended case studies, I selected several influential clerics, as defined by their leadership at "administrative mosques" (*hanyi dasi*, or *hanyisi*) or at Sufi tombs where founders of orders are buried. Given the sensitivity of the topic of Islamic law in China, I did not record conversations but took copious notes during interviews, which I immediately afterward transcribed in full. I kept these transcripts in a double-password-protected laptop that I carried with me wherever I went. (Several times, Hui prevented me from entering their mosque suspecting I carried a bomb in my backpack.) Contrary to ethnographic approaches to Islamic law in the Middle East and North Africa, without recourse to courts and case filings, written petitions, collections of fatwas (legal opinions), or law-related archives, my fieldwork was shaped by the Hui experience, which is off-the-official-record. Consequently, I have elected not to disclose identifying information about my interlocutors.

In addition to interviews, I observed and, where permitted by Hui, participated in all aspects of devotional and social life. These included prayer, ritual feasting and holidays, charitable giving, and attendance at weddings and funerals. I also collected case studies of dispute resolution in a variety of forums, such as informal mediation by clerics in mosque offices and more formalized mediation jointly conducted by clerics and police. On-site data collection was supplemented by participation in Chinese Muslim online networks, blogs, and virtual communities that produce and consume matters of Islamic law.

In compliance with professional ethics, I safeguarded information entrusted to me. Furthermore, even if I was not entering into lawyer-client relationships with related privileges, my training as a lawyer instructed me to protect information. This was not always easy, given that Hui learned of my research through their networks (and on social media platforms where Hui discussed me and my intentions often quite erroneously) and sometimes knew to whom I had been speaking. In addition, I collected local histories of teaching schools, and I sometimes participated in their writing when asked to do so.

In addition to fieldwork, I conducted research in governmental archives in Linxia and Urumqi as well as the Gansu Provincial Archives in Lanzhou, which also contain material for Ningxia and Qinghai. I also conducted archival research at the Northwest Minority Research Center Materials Room at Lanzhou University, the National Library in Beijing, and the University Services Center at the City University of Hong Kong – as well as the Harvard-Yenching Library at Harvard University, which has the finest collection of Christian missionary material from those families who visited Linxia in the tumultuous 1920s and 1930s.

While Erie, Moustafa, and the Engels were interested in court decisions (though these were scarcer in Erie's case), they did not devote their attention entirely to the judiciary. However, as we saw in Chapter 7, court-related studies are a significant aspect of Asian law and society research. Some Asian law and society scholars go to courthouses and courtrooms to study the activities and norms related to judges and other people associated with the judiciary, with the aim of illuminating the workings of legal power or state power more broadly.

Rahela Khorakiwala's ethnography of the High Court of Madras (Courts, Chapter 7) is an innovative example. Her Madras article comes from her larger study of the High Courts of Bombay, Calcutta, and Madras (Khorakiwala 2020) in which she treats "law as visual field" to examine law's ocular representations to understand how formal legal actors of these Indian courts practiced the law and how they imagined what the law was and should be: "The avenues of analysis are not restricted only to the outwardly visual, but also to the visual that is controlled in forms of restrictions on photography and video-recording in and of courts that speaks of, to borrow from Robert Cover, the 'jurispathic' tendency of the law to violently control competing images that challenge its legitimacy" (Khorakiwala 2020:3). To that end, Khorakiwala observed court proceedings in the three High Courts; interviewed judges, solicitors, lawyers, court clerks and other court staff, secretaries, peons, journalists, professors, and gown-makers for judges; and gathered records on court architecture and procedure, manuals of the High Courts, autobiographies, judgments, and newspaper articles.

Even though courthouses are usually open to the public, Khorakiwala and other researchers ran into obstacles when they tried to enter these buildings without being on any official court business. Sometimes they were not allowed to observe proceedings in what was supposedly an open court. When carrying out their fieldwork on grassroots courts in China, Ng and He (2017:206) (Courts, Chapter 7) were given access to courtrooms only because of their personal connections:

> Even with collegial introductions, there were visible differences in the degree of easiness that judges displayed toward us. There were occasions where we were, for example, told not to take any notes inside the courtroom. [...] In all cases, we were mindful of the possibility that our observations of the judges and their trials could possibly be affected by our connections [...] To address the problem of the intervening effects of our presence, we did two things. We stayed for as long as we could in courts to which we were given access. After the first few days, we found that the judges we observed became more relaxed as they became accustomed to our presence. They reverted back to their routine practices and habits. We also deliberately walked into courtrooms presided over by judges to whom we were not introduced. We observed those trials as strangers. This served as a kind of "control" for us. Observations of this type offered a good way to corroborate our observations. Obviously, without a collegial introduction, our showing up at some trials became a more precarious event. In some cases, we were asked to identify who we were and then we were asked to leave ... [O]ne trick of avoiding being kicked out by a judge was to slip into the courtroom only after a trial had commenced. Once a trial had commenced, the judge would be busy dealing with litigants. This minimized the possibility that a judge would ask us (sitting at the back) questions.

## 9.4 A People's Constitution: The Everyday Life of Law in the Indian Republic, *Rohit De*

When law and society scholars do focus on court decisions, they do not simply resort to published court opinions, especially the final judgments of apex courts on which conventional legal scholars typically place the most weight. Instead, as we saw with the Engels and Moustafa, they examine entire case histories and the social processes connected to those cases. In the selection below, De describes using previously unexplored archives to track "how the Indian Constitution, a document with alien antecedents that was a product of elite consensus, became part of the experience of ordinary Indians in the first decade of independence" (De 2018:4).

The Supreme Court of India is located on seventeen acres in the heart of New Delhi. Built in 1958 and designed by Ganesh Bhikaji Deolalikar, the first Indian to head the Public Works Department, the white and red sandstone complex closely mimics the architectural style of the colonial public buildings in New Delhi. The complex itself is shaped to symbolize the scales of justice. A majestic red sandstone staircase directs visitors and the public gaze toward a high colonnaded gallery that wraps around the building.

Much of the public business of the court is carried out at this level. The colonnade leads to multiple wood-paneled courtrooms hung with portraits of legal luminaries. Litigants, visitors, clerks, and interns mill around the courtroom. Bored policemen desultorily pat down visitors and confiscate the occasional mobile phone. The judges, preceded by magnificently turbaned ushers in gilded uniforms, move through their own private red-carpeted corridors, where conversation is carried out in hushed tones. Stoic court officials in black jackets fill up the offices in both wings, slowly moving reams of paperwork. Cutting through all the spaces are hundreds of black-robed lawyers, arguing, gossiping, and occasionally sprinting between courtrooms with their robes billowing around them. This is the public view of the court, emphasized by the dozen odd OB vans and television crews that are almost permanently parked in the lawn across the main staircase. The Supreme Court is a designated court of record and is required to preserve its records for all eternity. Its final judgments are public and are scrutinized extensively by lawyers and reported in newspapers. A recent study showed that more articles in leading English newspapers discussed the Supreme Court than the parliament or the prime minister.

However, underneath the public archive, buried in the basement, is the Supreme Court Record Room, which stores the entire proceedings of the cases: the arguments made by the lawyers, the affidavits and evidence produced before the court, transcripts of witness statements, maps of crime scenes, the occasional bloodstained physical evidence, and so on. In 2010 I became the first scholar to work with materials in this "secret" archive.

The aura of secrecy around the Supreme Court Record Room (and the record rooms of the lower courts) is partly physical, in terms of difficulty of access, and partly methodological, in terms of its value as a source. No formal procedure exists for researchers to consult Supreme Court records; access is granted at the discretion of the registrar. Furthermore, legal scholars emphasize the final reported judgment because it is the only document with future consequences and precedent value. The chief justice of India, who very generously gave me permission to consult the records and work in the court, was bemused by my goal. "The judgments are available online," he reminded me twice, emphasizing that I need not spend several months in the musky interior of the record room. Court officials, while personally welcoming me, were unsure where to place me. The usual visitors to the record room were Advocates-on-Record who wanted to consult a specific file on a case that was usually subject to a continuing litigation, and these individuals left within a few minutes after cross-checking details. In the absence of a designated space for research, it was decided that I would be allotted the workspace of whichever official was on leave that particular day. Over the course of six months, I, along with cloth bundles of files, moved through a series of offices in the court complex. This book is grounded in the exploration of this archive, both as a physical space and a discursive one.

In order to understand the process of constitutional change, I sought early challenges to the new regulatory authorities and legislation that were set up as part of the state project to transform society and the economy, which emerged as critical cases. These cases became important as legal precedents and also resonated outside the legal sphere, in the form of discussions within the government or in the public sphere. Thus some, like the cow slaughter case, were repeatedly and frequently cited by early law textbooks and commentators; others, like the prostitution case, generated anxious correspondence between bureaucrats in state archives; still others, like the Prohibition case, were extensively discussed in newspapers and cartoons. The constitutional archive, while centered in the record room, is much larger than the records it contains.

Another important feature of this archive that became apparent to me was that the challenges to particular regulatory laws were dominated by individuals who belonged to the same caste or community. Since South Asian names mark both religion and caste, I first noticed this phenomenon when looking at the registers of case names, but a close examination of the case file showed that litigants almost always identified themselves by the community they belonged to. Minority communities (of caste and religion) appeared to be overrepresented in the courts, which shows that they took the state's obligations to protect them seriously. This book provides evidence that electoral minorities – that is, members of communities that were unlikely to represent themselves through electoral democracy because of class, sex, or race – were overrepresented before the courts in constitutional cases. Central to the construction of the constitutional order is a distinctive form of subalternity generated with the installation of electoral democracy through the tension between legislation and judicial review.

Although such a study cannot be exhaustive, this book attempts to capture the broadest range possible of regulatory measures and geographical distribution, ranging from Bombay to Bengal and covering large cities, small towns, and rural settings. Much of the existing scholarship on the Constitution is organized on the evolution of particular rights, largely property, free speech, and religious liberty, and is written to explain the evolution of that particular right to the present moment. This book's analytic frame is the new regulatory state that emerged in the 1950s, and it pays considerable attention to the underexplored areas of civil liberties (e.g., freedom of profession) as well as the field of administrative law. Questions over the right to property, religion, equality and free speech are also explored.

## 9.5 Labour Law and (In)justice in Workers' Letters in Vietnam, *Tu Phuong Nguyen*

Many other types of written records on disputes and claims exist outside of the courts and offer alternative sources of data for law and society research. Nguyen, for instance, examines a unique dataset of complaint letters, one of which was featured in her article extracted in Chapter 5. The analysis of these letters formed an integral part of her multi-method study on the legal mobilization of Vietnamese factory workers.

The main source of data for this article is a set of workers' collective complaint letters sent to the provincial Labour Federation and three upper-level unions in Đồng Nai Province, an industrial hub in the south of Vietnam. At those offices, I read through all letters, lodged in 2013 and 2014, and I selected for analysis those letters concerned with collective grievances – grievances related to workplace relations that affect a group of workers. This selection is due to my initial interest in studying how consciousness manifests in workers' binding with each other in their collective acts of resistance. Among the 21 selected letters, 16 letters only contain workers' self ascription as "workers in the company/section X" without any signature. In two out of those 16 letters, the writers stated clearly that they refrained from revealing their names and staff members for fear of losing their jobs. Three letters were written and signed by one person on behalf of a group. Only two letters contained multiple signatures of ten and 18; one of them also contains a list of complainants' names. The analysis also includes one letter published in full in *Lao Động* (The Labour), the national labour newspaper, in 2010 and headlined as "a worker's letter full of grief." Addressed to the VGCL Chairman, the writer clearly identified her name, work position, and the name of her company.

The letters vary in their titles and writing styles. The majority of them, exactly eight letters, are entitled "request letter" (*đơn đề nghị / kiến nghị*). All of them contain the writers' request for the union's and/or management's consideration of the issues they raise. Another eight letters are entitled "complaint letter" (*đơn khiếu nại*). Among them, only three writers state their intent of "suing" (*kiện*) and "complaining" (*khiếu nại*) the supervisors/managers, while the rest talk at length about the issues of concern and request some intervention from the state and union. The third group, four out of 21 letters, are entitled "letter requesting resolution/ assistance" (*đơn xin xem xét giải quyết / trợ giúp*) and only one is presented as a "report letter" (*đơn trình*). The styles and structures of letters in all the groups are relatively the same. As can be seen from their titles, not all the letters are explicitly of a resistance nature; nevertheless, the language that appears throughout the texts suffices to speak of workers' complaints or demands and their wish to rectify existing problems. Even though some of the request letters do not put forth any blame or make any accusations, they are presented in a manner that shows workers' disagreement and dissatisfaction with the businesses' decision.

All letters were lodged by workers across 16 companies, with three companies each having two letters raising similar issues. From the dates in those letters, I find that, in two company cases, the letters were written in two consecutive dates; in the other case, they were written six months apart. All these companies belong to the footwear, garment, electronics, and wood-processing industries, and plastic, metal, and chemical production. The numbers of employees in these companies range from 170 to more 18,000.

Most of the letters appeal to the union and state officials, whom workers address in a respectful manner. Fifteen letters provide detailed stories and impassioned accounts of the situation of the complainants and their affected fellow workers. The rest merely make brief summaries of their problems and requests. About two-thirds of those 15 letters contain comprehensive depictions and stories of workers' experiences on the shop floor. On a close reading, I also find that three letters, entitled "request letter," were initially directed to the company management and were about workers' demands for a higher wage rise. They made their way to the union offices to serve as evidence that workers had previously appealed to the management in vain.

The translation of the letters to English is a fascinating but challenging experience to me as a native Vietnamese speaker. Many of them contain long sentences, sometimes without breaks or commas, spoken language, and shorthand, and at times vague references to the actors or subjects of particular actions, which are all understandable, since most letters were presumably written by the authors in a tense and distressful situation. In my translation, I have refined the grammar of long sentences to make them easy to follow, but I have kept intact the writers' rhetorical devices such as rhetorical question or exclamation. Some ambiguous references can be surmised from reading the surrounding texts. I have tried to literally translate the lay language and common expressions when I could not find the English equivalent. While all efforts have been made to preserve the writers' original meaning, my translation may not have done justice to the feelings and emotions conveyed within the letters, especially through exclamatory and emphatic words.

Besides court records and petition letters, law and society scholars locate and examine a variety of other written materials. Cheesman (Crime and Justice, Chapter 8), for example, assembled a diverse collection of texts and documents for his study on rule of law in Myanmar, *Opposing the Rule of Law* (2015). They included criminal case records, law reports, statutes, rules and official notifications, government gazettes and periodicals, news reports in and outside Myanmar, official and semi-official histories, Burmese reference books on criminal codes, a police manual that sets out the police forces' official structure and routine operations, handbooks and manuals for courts, civil servants and lawyers, records of seminars and congress of the Burma Socialist Programme Party, the ruling party from 1962 to 1988 and the only legal party from 1964 to 1988, articles on party ideology and policy, university textbooks and syllabi, judicial officers' promotion exam papers, and biographies:

> Clearly, the book relies heavily on written sources. This emphasis is deliberate. Writing is not merely a by-product of state activity. Modern bureaucratic states

are constituted through writing. Even more than edifices of stone, accumulations of paper assert the know-how of rule. And perhaps to a greater degree than in any other areas of state activity, juridical practices bind their subjects, and one another, through written record keeping. Each moment in a juridical or administrative process brings forward a document or form for someone to complete and place on file. These forms are the materials of procedure, the records of sequential events. But they are also expressions of power. Mastery of the written text enables control of its subjects. When an official removes a document for completion from his cardboard folder, when a policeman pulls a notebook and click-pen from his shirt pocket, he opens up another world: a world of documentation that the object of record keeping may understand little, and can control even less. Out of these commonplace events come the materials with which Myanmar's courts make law and order.

(13–14)

## II NAVIGATING IDENTITIES

Social science research, especially qualitative research, is reflexive. The process of understanding our research subjects is also a process of understanding ourselves as a researcher. During the course of fieldwork, Asian law and society scholars often have to navigate their own identities, who they are in relation to the research site and the people whom they set out to study. Are they insiders or outsiders? What are the challenges of being an insider or outsider?

### 9.6 Indigeneity and Legal Pluralism in India: Claims, Histories, Meanings, *Pooja Parmar*

One challenge for outsiders is the ability to communicate with research subjects or to understand their language(s) in writing or in conversation. Parmar was an outsider in the Indian region where the Coca-Cola plant dispute was located (Legal Mobilization, Chapter 5). The challenge of language communication arose as she was contemplating a project that would involve not only textual analysis of court records and media reports, but also interviews and participant observations. In the excerpt below, she shares her insights on this common challenge and how she compensated for her shortcomings by making herself more relatable to the interviewees.

From the time I first conceived of this project as one involving long interviews with protestors and others connected to the dispute, I was concerned about issues that might arise in translation of Adivasi accounts that are central to this project. I do not speak any of the languages of the Adivasis and other residents of the area, and they do not speak any of mine. The interviews in the village had to be (and were) conducted through an interpreter. What added to my concern was that most ethnographic accounts I studied to prepare for this research did not offer any advice in this regard. In fact for a long time I believed that researchers, especially anthropologists, never went into "the field" without learning local languages. I was convinced about the importance of speaking with the protestors in order to better understand the dispute, but I agonized over my inability to converse with them directly. I may have given up had it not been for some very helpful conversations with other more experienced researchers.

In Kerala I learned about interpreters who had assisted other researchers during visits to Plachimada, but I had some concerns about working with them given the different focus and approach of the other projects. I also wanted to avoid working with anyone who had a fixed idea about what the dispute in Plachimada is about. That, I realized quickly, was not going to be easy, as most people I met in Kerala "knew" what "Plachimada" was all about, even though opinions varied. As I considered my options, I met Shiny while visiting a friend. Even before I knew she was fluent in both Malayalam and Tamil, loved to travel, and would never complain about long bone-rattling bus rides, I knew I wanted to work with her because she had many questions about my project and about Plachimada. I was thrilled when she agreed to work with me. Like me, Shiny too brought to our conversations her prior knowledge, beliefs, ways of thinking about the world, and about people and events. But she was also open to listening, being questioned, and revising her opinions. That was most helpful as we constantly discussed our conversations and experiences in the hamlets, and transcribed the interviews together. Although the transcription took much longer because of this, it allowed me to understand not only what was said but also why she translated certain words and phrases differently at different times.

It was during one of these conversations that I learned that she translated the word "samaram" as "struggle" during our first few conversations in the village because I had been using the word. She had believed that was how my research required it to be translated. Had she not heard me use the English word repeatedly, she would have also translated the word as "strike" or "protest," which was a more suitable translation in some contexts. This and other such insights into the practices of translation thus became an unexpected reward for the many long hours we spent transcribing the interviews.

In order to further minimize the loss of meaning and attain a deeper understanding, I have also tried to combine care in translation and transcription of narratives with attention to particular stories people choose to tell, the words they use to narrate their experiences and articulate their claims, the willingness to share certain fears and hopes, and decisions to not speak about certain things.

Translation of unfamiliar stories narrated in unfamiliar languages into a familiar language does not, however, automatically lead to comprehension of lifeworlds. As Piya, a character in Amitav Ghosh's novel *The Hungry Tide*, observes, speech "was only a bag of tricks that fooled you into believing that you could see through the eyes of another being." Humans, Ghosh tells us through his characters, have to make an effort to communicate in "our translated world." Here Ghosh's reference is not simply to barriers posed by the existence of multiple languages in the human world, but our inability to see and experience the world as does another human being, living a different life. Ghosh's story is however, not merely about barriers to communication but also about communications that are possible between humans, and between humans and nonhumans, despite the limitations of language, translation, and understanding.

Acutely aware of my linguistic limitations, I also tried to be attentive to nonverbal modes of communication – a smile, a twinkle in the eyes, a shrug, a straightening of the back, a frown, a cautious glance in a particular direction, lowering of voices, and the silences. When understood in the context of all these, translated words can convey a lot more. But sometimes, we do not actually need words to communicate. I had an opportunity to reflect on this on a quiet afternoon in the samara pandal (protest hut) when Maya, a young Adivasi woman, suddenly asked me if I had spoken to my daughter the night before. She asked if my daughter cries when I call. On another afternoon, as I watched some toddlers playing nearby, she asked to see again a picture of my daughter she had seen before. It was passed around to other women present and many remarks were made and questions asked.

Both times I had in fact been thinking about my daughter when Maya mentioned her. I was stunned because I had not said anything. How could Maya have known that I was missing my child at that moment? Her response to the question in my eyes was a smile. I could have spoken out the question, but I did not. At the time that communication had seemed enough to me. I have often wondered if she knew because perhaps she too thought about her two little children on quiet afternoons when they were away at school.

It may not always be possible to "see" the world as the other does or to represent accurately what one does manage to see. But it is always possible to

> try. Sometimes communication across difference is also made possible by honest commitments to translate. According to Spivak, an ethical translation is an "act of hearing-to-respond." It involves "listening with care and patience." What we need therefore are "thick translations," attentive to reasons, motives, and histories of speakers and translators, and to the contexts of translation. It is in this spirit of "trying to be faithful to the original" that I listened intently to all that was shared with me. I have also reminded myself repeatedly of my own role as a translator even as I wrote about similar roles of others.

Parmar's relationship with her translators resonates with Chua (2019), who also worked closely with research assistants in Myanmar and had to try out a few before settling on two assistants who were not biased against sexual or gender minorities. The experience led Chua to consider the position of insider and outsider:

> [M]y experiences in the field eventually made me realize the blurry lines between so-called insider and outsider. One can be an insider and outsider, or shades of them at the same time perhaps echoing the study's findings on the plurality of personhood. An encounter early in my fieldwork was particularly poignant. The first assistant, whom I let go after the first week of research in September 2012, was a Burmese person, but when I asked her to interpret the conversations at the workshop, she kept insisting to me that she could not understand what they were saying. When I asked her to simply give me the literal translation of the words, she told me they were talking about going to the monastery to "eat oranges" (queer slang for having sex with monks). She was either truly ignorant of queer slang, which is rather unique, or she was using naivete to shield her discomfort. However, when I heard the literal translation, I understood the meaning right away, and I was not uncomfortable about the subject matter. Perhaps it is because I had conducted research on LGBT activism in other contexts and was used to the cultural subversions of queer slang. Looking back, I often wondered: In that moment, who was more of the outsider – the Burmese translator or me?

The insider-outsider status is blurry for my assistants too. Moora and Khine Khine, the two assistants whom I eventually hired, are Burmese, but they are outsiders in relation to the movement by several counts. Moora is Karen Christian, and Khine Khine is Burmese Chinese (recall that the movement is predominantly Burman). Both are heterosexual, cisgender women. In addition, they are university educated, speak English fluently, and originate from urban Yangon, unlike many of the LGBT activists.

(147)

### 9.7 Public Secrets of Law: Rape Trials in India, *Pratiksha Baxi*

When Baxi was conducting courtroom ethnography on rape trials in India, she was treated as an outsider on multiple counts – she is a woman, a non-lawyer, and somebody who did not understand the "language of rape." Interested in rape trial cases, Baxi observed routine cases that did not capture media attention and interviewed lawyers, people who were raped, and their families. In her book that was based on the same project as the article featured in Chapter 8 (Crime and Justice), she wrote:

> [H]ow does the legal norm, as a shifting norm, constitute the legal subject? The over-determination of analysis by appellate law has shifted attention from the way in which written records efface those operations of power that make it difficult to read the agency of women other than as victims or manipulators of the law. Such operations of power are far more complex than the usual framing of a legal subject as victim, prosecutrix, witness, or complainant suggests, since a single legal subject may occupy different juridical identities simultaneously. Nor is the category of victim or complainant a stable category in the life of a trial. By focusing on the making of the rape trial, I wish to suggest how the culture of a courtroom alters the very meaning of rape from the point of view of the woman or child.
>
> (xxviii–xxix)

Baxi's fieldwork encounters show that the law and society research process cannot be disentangled from its substantive findings.

After the first few days of sitting in the court, a middle-aged male lawyer who knew about my work gestured to me to follow him. Hesitantly I followed him to his chamber, not knowing who he was. Hirabhai, one of the five additional public prosecutors (hereafter, APP) then began to interview me. Soon I was incorporated as a researcher amongst his juniors, mostly women. One of his junior lawyers, Beenaben, became a confidante and defended the validity of my research, which was keenly contested by lawyers in the court. In the chamber, my research was supported and defended. Hirabhai's journalist friend wanted to do a story on my 'courage'. When a woman clerk gossiped that I was shameless to do research like this, Beenaben stoutly defended me and refused to talk to her. Later she added, 'Do not be discouraged. These people are very narrow-minded. They do not know how courageous you are. Women like you and me are very few. We are different.' Hirabhai was appointed as my 'guide' by one of the judges whose courts I used to observe. [...]

Although the district and sessions judge had granted me permission to document *in camera* trials, I also secured consent from the complainant in each case to follow the case. Consent for me did not mean the routine ways of securing informed consent but was based on full disclosure of my location and my work. The interviews were difficult in the absence of support services for victims or their families. In the case of statutory rape, the anxiety generated by the legal proceedings, my inability to develop a relationship with young children in the space of the court, and above all the fear of harm to the children precluded the possibility of ethnographic interviews. I also found that the parents perceived that talking to a stranger was therapeutic, while revealing what happened to the extended family was perceived as a source of stigma with long-term, deleterious consequences for the child's future. Rapport, then, was not a measure of the amount of time spent with the person interviewed, nor did it remain a given as the case unfolded over time. I was present in the courtroom during their testimonies, yet we would never meet again or keep in touch.

Most interviews with the complainants and their families happened in court corridors. The lack of privacy posed a problem as time went by. I was nicknamed 376 by some male lawyers, after the section on rape, posing an indexical relationship between my presence and the topic of my research. Once when I was interviewing Dhirubhai – whose ten-year-old daughter had been raped – four male lawyers who were passing by stopped, pointed to his daughter, and said, 'This is the one, look at her, so small and she has been raped.' I asked the men to leave and stopped the interview. The fact that I was seen in their presence directed a gendered gaze on the child – an identification I struggled with. Where I felt that it was unethical to interview rape survivors, I refused the help of lawyers or the police to set up such interviews. I have included in the analyses of these cases fragmentary conversations in between the court proceedings with child survivors of rape. [...]

Initially, no one was willing to speak to me about ongoing rape trials. I had yet to learn the vocabulary of how to speak about rape in the court. Just as I had begun to despair, Hirabhai introduced me to a young woman in a statutory rape and kidnapping case he was to prosecute. He then took me to the courtroom, where he asked the bench clerk for the case papers. We sat at the far end of the lawyers' table, and he turned to the medico-legal aspects of the case. Turning to the accused's medical certificate, in his usual booming voice which echoed in the half-empty courtroom, Hirabhai said, 'You know what a man's primary sexual organs are, don't you?' A little taken aback, I nodded. Then he turned to the victim's medical certificate. After going over the other details about bodily development and superficial injuries, he asked me, 'Do you know what a hymen is?' I responded in the affirmative. Rather theatrically, he drew a vagina on small piece of paper to explain the technical terms for injury on the labia minora or labia majora. The discussion continued on in the chamber where he instructed Beenaben to explain 'it' to me. After he had left she said, 'Pratiksha, do you know that a man cannot rape a woman by simply touching her, or kissing her.' I nodded, even more puzzled and curious now. She carried on, 'Well, how do I explain how a man rapes?' I replied, 'Beenaben, do you mean partial or complete penetration?' She nodded in relief.

In performing a specific revelation of the public secrets of rape, Hirabhai directed my attention to the vocabulary by which I could research rape. Insisting that medical jurisprudence separates the social from the clinical, Hirabhai maintained that a 'decent' legal practice could coexist with frank discussions on the topic of rape. The route to generating this 'frank' space initiating the research, as he put it, enabled him to teach his woman juniors how the prosecution could successfully fight rape cases more freely. This linguistic route became his way of teaching me facts of anatomy, sexuality, and the rape law.

Hirabhai and his junior Beenaben made it possible for me to undertake this research in many ways. Hirabhai – whom I called 'sir', unlike other women juniors, who addressed him by fictive kin terms – was like a teacher instructing me in the ways of the court. He did not hesitate to reprimand me on many occasions. I was instructed on whom to speak to and whom to avoid. I stopped wearing bright colours to the court. I was taught what constituted decent modes of dress, appearance, gait, posture, and speech. While I was schooled to 'fit into' the scenes of the court, I remained an outsider. It was this status as an outsider that allowed me access, although on the verge of experiencing alterity. As if aware of this, Hirabhai would reassure me without any obvious cause for it: 'Baxi, you are safe here.' When I was leaving the field, almost reflexively, Hirabhai said to me, 'I don't know why, Baxi, but I never looked at you with that kind of gaze [*nazaar*]. I liked you because you work so hard. Do invite me to your marriage.'

The complicity with adopting medico-legal vocabulary as the modality of talking about rape was deeply problematic. I was tutored not to ask direct questions about rape. For instance, I could not ask direct questions about what lawyers and prosecutors meant when they said that women are habituated to sex. I knew that the determination of whether or not a woman is a habitué is on the basis of a clinical test, which doctors conduct routinely. This test, popularly known as the two-finger test, is used to determine the absence or presence of the hymen, and whether it is distensible or not. If the doctor finds that the hymen is broken and there are old hymeneal tears, they may write that the rape survivor was habituated or used to sexual intercourse in the medico-legal certificate. When a prosecutor or defence lawyers reads a medico-legal certificate that declares a woman to be a habitué, more often than not, they conclude that she has lied about being raped. A defence lawyer routinely uses such medical findings to establish past sexual history. I wanted to know why prosecutors who purportedly represent the victim exploit the category of the habitué.

Towards the last phase of the research (fifteen months after the preceding conversation), I decided to ask direct questions which may have been thought of as talking about secrets men do not share with women as equals in a professional setting. These secrets 'appear in ethnographic texts as signs of alterity'. I cite here a discussion with Mr Rajput, who argued that women could not be raped unless there is grievous violence, and women who were habituated to sex without marks of injury frequently lied about rape. This was not an uncommon view in the court. He pursued this question in the privacy of his chamber to explain to me why he thought that 'habituated' women were liars. He asked me to sit in a chair beside him and lowered his voice so that his colleagues could not overhear him through the wooden partitions that separated the chambers of the public prosecutors. He spoke in English.

> R: That day you were saying about habituated. I did not say anything because other people were around. A woman cannot really be raped.
> PB: Why?
> R: It becomes quite large. The opening in a habituated woman therefore becomes quite large therefore habituated.
> PB: You mean the vaginal canal?
> R: Yes, that's why two fingers go in quite easily.
> PB: But that's what I was discussing with Dr B [a forensic expert] – that is, the finger test is quite unreliable. What about masturbation?
> R: That is there. But see if two fingers go in easily (mimicking such penetration with his fingers) it means that she is habituated, the entire hole, that's why I say a woman cannot really be raped.
> PB: But that was not my point of view. I was trying to say that why must her past sexual history be linked to her credibility?

R: But it must.
PB: Why? Why should it be considered against morality?
R: Because it is. Because with married women rape is not possible, and in our society sex before marriage is not allowed.
PB: Why do women have to experience rape as worse than death or shameful that they will kill themselves? I am arguing for another point of view.
R: But a woman cannot be raped unless ... how do I explain? Do you know what secondary sexual organs are? Do you know why doctors write secondary sex organs are well developed?
PB: You mean...?
R: The organ develops after a woman has an erection, that's why they are well developed, that's how they find out she is habituated. How do I explain this to you?
R: The woman becomes wet. The penis cannot go in unless the woman is not willing. She cannot be willing unless she is wet – like a machine – a rod cannot go in without lubrication. (gestures)
PB: But what about cases in which there is partial penetration?
R: I have not found such cases, they all claim complete penetration; that is why I am saying that a woman cannot be raped.

Mr Rajput stopped speaking when a colleague walked in and I was hugely relieved to put an end to this conversation. He added, 'You see I am an MSc in Biochemistry. We were taught all of this. I have worked in a hospital for one year. Come again we will discuss this.'

Parmar, Chua, and Baxi observed the activities of their research subjects, but they did not partake in them. Other law and society scholars may choose to engage in participant observation and join in the activities of their research subjects. They may do so in order to build trust or cultivate a deeper understanding of their research subjects' experiences. Engaging in participant observation can cause ethical dilemmas and worries about personal safety, especially when illegal or downright dangerous activities are involved. Whatever the choice, it should involve a constellation of considerations, including the research site, the researcher's identity, and their local connections and sense of safety. Moreover, scholars like Hoang (2015) caution against cowboy ethnography, that is, portraying the field site as exotically dangerous so as to cast oneself, the scholar, in an admirably courageous light. In her study of sex workers in Ho Chi Minh City – though not a piece of law and society research – Hoang further deliberated over the dilemmas of whether to disclose her decision to participate or not participate in sex work as part of her immersive fieldwork, and she decided not to say either way.

## III PRACTICING LAW AND SOCIETY RESEARCH IN THE DIGITAL AGE

Increasingly, Asian law and society scholars are looking to the Internet and social media to gain access to research sites, communicate with research subjects, and study social interactions and norms. With the advent of social media and other advancements in communication technologies, the practices of law and society research and, consequently, their challenges may change and assume new forms.

### 9.8 Doing Ethnography on Social Media: A Methodological Reflection on the Study of Online Groups in China, *Di Wang and Sida Liu*

Wang and Liu reflect on online ethnography, which formed the core of their data for the related article on Chinese feminists' and activist lawyers' artivism (Legal Mobilization, Chapter 5). Wang and Liu maintain that the rise of social media has not changed the basic principles of doing ethnography, such as immersion and reflexivity, but has generated new problems and opportunities in terms of access, data analysis, and research ethics. Contrary to the bird's-eye view sketches of Big Data, they argue that the use of qualitative methods to study social media can provide thick descriptions and deep, localized knowledge of social processes that have always been and remain a vital part of social science research.

> In the increasingly digitalized world of the early 21st century, online groups and cyberspace are co-constituted with multiple mediums and complex interconnectivity among users and groups. This makes it even harder for researchers to set a spatial and/or a temporal boundary on her research subjects. In addition, ethnographers sometimes raise concerns of the reliability and validity of social media data. As social media change the nature of people's communication, how sustainable is a researcher–informant relationship built online and how reliable is a person's online profile for predicting her offline actions? How should a researcher crosscheck and analyze an online discussion with a face-to-face discussion? Finally, how would digitalized communication brought by social media affect the researcher–informant power dynamics, as now informants have greater capability to access and respond to a researcher's findings through the internet? Methodological reflections on the challenges

and opportunities of online ethnography remain scarce, particularly in authoritarian contexts. It remains an open question how qualitative inquiry can resist the lure of Big Data and provide alternative approaches to make effective use of social media in social science. [...]

*Living Online, Living Onsite: Access and Ethics of Online Ethnography*
Online ethnography is qualitatively different from aimless online browsing, but its beginning is often similar to accessing any website or social media platform. Ethnographic immersion for social scientists involves observing other people as they respond to social interaction, as well as experiencing the events and interactions oneself. Thus, the researcher must spend a substantial amount of time on the site on a regular (often daily) basis and familiarize herself with its users and discourses. This process of online ethnographic immersion is crucial for developing the researcher's identity in the online group and getting access to potential informants. It resembles traditional ethnographic immersion in many ways, yet there are also notable differences. In this section, we use our own fieldwork experiences to discuss the issues of access and ethics in "living online."

The first author started to observe feminist online actions in China since 2012 and then to participate in some actions since 2013. Through active daily interactions on different social media platforms, her participation as a commenter led her to a chatroom of @FeministVoices (*nüquan zhi sheng*), a Weibo account established by the Media Monitor for Women Network (MMWN) in 2010. @FeministVoices was the largest grassroots feminist media outlet in China with 181,019 followers when it was forcibly shut down on March 8, 2018, the International Women's Day. Because of the time difference between China and the United States (where the first author was based), she altered her daily schedule to maximize interactions with Chinese feminists in the chatroom, from staying up late at night to checking hundreds of messages every morning. As a result, she was able to form close connections with many activists in chatrooms before her first field trip in China in 2014. The following is her story of how an online chatroom became a network of informants:

In the summer of 2013, a Chinese feminist activist I met on Weibo added me to a QQ chatroom for @FeministVoices readers, right around the time when the U.S. Supreme Court ruled the Defense of Marriage Act unconstitutional. Back in 2013, @FeministVoices only had about 16,000 Weibo followers and its reader chatroom had fewer than 300 people, but the account was at the frontline of reporting on feminist activist actions and leading debates on gender issues in China. When I joined, they were having an enthusiastic discussion over law and marriage drawing on personal stories and political campaigns from all around the world. Several prominent feminist activists whom I only knew through reading news and their Weibo posts shared their experiences of campaigning for the anti-domestic violence law in China, as well as their individual politics on marriage and family. To my (joyous) surprise as a young queer woman, many of them were also LGBTQ identified. Over the past five years, my participation in activist chatrooms changed from QQ to WeChat and later to encrypted messenger apps like Telegram. On numberless nights, I fell asleep during a heated debate, waking up still holding my phone and immediately checking the hundreds of messages that I missed. Chatrooms like this became my "neighborhood" where I ran into young Chinese feminists of different genders, sexualities, and geographic locations.

The second author's first encounter with online lawyer activism echoes the first author's account above. As a graduate student interested in studying the Chinese legal profession, he began to regularly visit the All-China Lawyers Association's (ACLA) online forum in 2003, shortly after the forum opened on the ACLA's official website. After actively participating in the forum discussions using a pseudonym for about a year, he became the board manager of one of its discussion boards, "Jurisprudence and Constitutionalism" (*fali xianzheng*). This new role gave him access to not only regular discussions but also the forum's recycle bin, which contained the deleted messages, including many politically sensitive ones. [...]

As our early field experiences suggest, social media, be it a chatroom or a forum, can provide a researcher instant access to the social networks of potential informants, as well as details about their demographic information and political views. This information is critical, especially for researching on under-studied or sensitive topics, for which the population parameters and issue areas have not yet been clearly defined. Through the instant access of a network of potential informants rather than "snowballing" from only one or two informants, the researcher can make more informed decisions on which issue areas to focus on and whether to emphasize certain characteristics of research subjects in sampling and case selection. Even so, information from online chatrooms or forums is often incomplete or even scattered. Sometimes basic demographic information such as gender, age, or geographic location can be ambiguous or missing. In comparison with traditional ethnography, access in online ethnography presents a trade-off between widening research population and deepening information for each informant in that population. Only after a long period of immersion can the researcher gradually assemble the basic profiles of her research subjects.

Although Big Data scientists are usually invisible to their research subjects, online ethnographers are visible and accessible to their informants once they are connected on social media platforms. Consequently, when studying feminist or lawyer activists, social connections and networks are leverages for both researchers and activists. On one hand, researchers can observe more complex dynamics and narratives of the movement through accessing activists' social networks. Snowballing often gets easier through online social networks than in traditional offline fieldwork. On the other hand, when activists mobilize their social connections for collective action, they can also access the researchers' networks for resource mobilization. This reciprocal nature of their interaction complicates another classic question for ethnographers – to what extent should you "go native" and become one of them? Both authors faced this question repeatedly in their online fieldwork over the years, which is further complicated by the risky and unpredictable nature of political mobilization in the authoritarian context of China. [...]

In traditional ethnography, the in-group and outgroup boundaries are relatively clear. On the contrary, online ethnography can often give the researcher instant access to group membership, but it can also generate an identity crisis. Once a member of a social media group, it is no longer possible to completely retreat to the seemingly objective standpoint of a social science researcher, at least on the frontstage of online interaction. Even after the fieldwork is completed, group membership and solidarity remain, unless the researcher withdraws herself from the social media platform. Some researchers use multiple Facebook or WeChat accounts to separate the identity in the field and the identity in the ivory tower, but this is not always convenient or even feasible. More often, online ethnographers struggle with this question in the whole research process and make decisions on a case-by-case basis. [...]

The second author's encounter with this reflexive question has an additional layer of complexity. Although he is not a licensed lawyer and thus cannot directly participate in legal cases as the first author did in feminist actions, over the years he has accumulated a reputation as a scholar who studies and writes about the Chinese legal profession. Consequently, his lawyer informants sometimes would approach him to seek his voice as a public intellectual in support of their activism. He gave the following account of how he dealt with such requests:

Scholars like me who study politically sensitive topics in China like lawyers and human rights have to walk a fine line between an objective social scientist and a visible public intellectual. For example, in 2012 or 2013, a notable human rights activist in Beijing (who was detained later during the 709 Crackdown on activist lawyers in July 2015) sent me a private message on Weibo and asked if I would be interested in meeting with him and discussing possible collaboration. It put me in a real dilemma because, while I very much would like to help him, an in-person meeting with him might put both of us in trouble with the state security agents. So I decided to give him a polite reply online but declined the meeting. I was also often asked by activist lawyers to make public statements on Weibo or WeChat to help their ongoing cases, and I did actively make such online statements in a few critical cases like the Li Zhuang case in 2009–2011 or after the 709 Crackdown in 2015. But if I made my voices heard in public in every case they were doing, not only would my personal safety be at risk in China, I would also lose my objectivity as a social science researcher. This is a constant struggle for me all these years in studying lawyers and political mobilization.

What the second author described above is not only an issue of self-censorship in an authoritarian context, but also the difficult personal struggle of a social scientist who deeply cares about his research subjects yet constantly feels the limit of his own capacity in supporting them in their everyday practice. This leads to a second question: "What would you do if you could not become one of them?" Arguably, researchers can use their scholarly writings to expose the problems and risks that activists face from the authoritarian state. For instance, the second author's book on Chinese criminal defense lawyers (Liu and Halliday, 2016) is considered "an act of solidarity" for activist lawyers by one of its reviewers, though as a piece of scholarly work it still maintains a disciplined distance required by the objectivity of social science writing.

But researchers can certainly do more than scholarly writing and publishing, especially in the age of social media. Posting on public platforms like Twitter and Weibo or semi-private platforms like Instagram and WeChat is often an effective means to assist activists in their collective action. In the authoritarian context of China, such posts require a combination of courage and delicacy, and it is ultimately the personal choice of every researcher on the best way to handle it. Both authors have written many online posts and essays to support their research subjects over the years, but they have also refrained from doing so in many challenging situations. [...]

Nevertheless, having personal experiences as an insider does not guarantee that a researcher would produce the best theory about the community of interest or beyond. The art of doing social science requires the researcher to find her best position to observe and participate in the online community as well as a particular writing style to tell the story. The fragmented and often unbounded nature of social media interactions raises ethical questions of confidentiality and accuracy in representing each informant's stories. On one hand, the pain and pleasure of sharing personal details characterizes social media interactions, which can help ethnographers understand their informants from multiple aspects and through crisscrossing boundaries. For example, a researcher may share membership with an informant in one chatroom for a rescue campaign for a detained activist lawyer, as well as another chatroom for lesbian parents of rescued cats. On the other hand, when online activities over time are intentionally collected and documented, a researcher can have a detailed profile of an informant's life, which can be consequential for this informant's privacy and safety. To be sure, one of the most compelling components of qualitative research is telling stories, especially ones with vivid details and characters. Although it is tempting to do so, a researcher should always consider the social and political consequences of her writings and strictly protect the informant's personal information according to the ethical requirements of social science research.

To deal with such ethical challenges, in the process of his data analysis and writing on activist lawyers, the second author often adopts an analytical way of storytelling, which integrates interviews, online observation, and other empirical evidence from multiple informants in different geographic locations to make one analytical point. This writing style allows him to fully protect the identities of informants while presenting a relatively comprehensive picture of their experiences. The following is an example that he gave on how to weave the online and offline data into a web of anonymized yet analytically interconnected accounts:

When I interview lawyers, I always try to ask their biographies in detail, because I find the early life history of a lawyer not only fascinating in itself but also very helpful for understanding her law practice. A lawyer once told me, the reason he became a human rights activist was that his parents were persecuted during the Cultural Revolution. When others helped their family in that difficult time, as a child his heart felt warm. So now he hopes to use his activism to warm the hearts of others. This kind of in-depth personal stories are hard to get from the fragmented interactions on social media. Some activist lawyers have a tough and courageous image online but, if you get to know them offline, you see a totally different side of them. They would play soccer with their children or make dumplings with their spouses. When I was writing my book, I seriously thought about presenting a few lawyers' life stories in a holistic fashion as case studies, because the stories were so powerful and the lawyers could speak for themselves, but then I quickly realized that it would not be possible to do that without revealing their identities. Finally, I decided to put their biographical accounts from interviews and the ethnography of their online interactions into different sections and chapters. Within each section, I used the similar or comparable experiences of several lawyers anonymously to make the same analytical point, say, how they were harassed by the state security or disbarred by the justice bureau. As a result, readers do not get the coherent life history of any of the lawyers I discussed in the book, but adding the analytical points together, they can still get a pretty good picture of what happened to them as a group. All the bits and pieces were reassembled in writing.

There are disadvantages of "reassembling the social" in this manner, however. The beauty and liveliness of narratives are often lost in the pursuit of analytical rigor. To mitigate this problem, the second author uses extended quotes from interviews and online ethnography in his writings to give readers more original discourses from the informants. This method worked effectively in the earlier periods of online ethnography in China. This was because the most popular online platforms back then were online forums and Weibo, which were considered as in the public domain. However, the situation changed as WeChat replaced Weibo as the dominant form of online interactions in China in recent years and it has become more challenging to collect and make use of online ethnographic data. WeChat requires its users to register with a cellphone number, which is linked to one's national identity card number. Furthermore, WeChat also restricts its users from publicly searching posts outside one's existing contacts. This leads to the non-anonymous and semi-private nature of WeChat-based online interactions. Consequently, researching online groups at the WeChat era has increased not only the ethical burden of researchers but also the risks of surveillance from the state authorities. Although Weibo posts can be deleted, their public nature enables some evidence to be preserved in the public domain not only through any individual user's actions of screenshots and reposts but also through organized efforts such as FreeWeibo.com, which actively monitors and makes available censored Weibo content. In contrast, a WeChat discussion or even an entire WeChat group can be removed by the state censorship without generating much public awareness, because the semi-private interactions within the group had never entered the public domain.

Therefore, as state censorship forces social media interactions out of public spaces in China in recent years, it is even more important for a researcher to immerse in online groups and become a reflexive agent of memory of their "disappeared" stories. It also makes the combination of online and in-person interviews and observation a more effective and desirable methodology for collecting and preserving data. Otherwise, without taking into account "disappeared" information, using a Big Data algorithm or a set of keywords for data collection and analysis would be like typing a story on a keyboard with "an unknown set of keys disabled."

REFERENCES

**Featured Readings**

Baxi, Pratiksha. 2014. *Public Secrets of Law: Rape Trials in India.* New Delhi: Oxford University Press. doi: 10.1093/acprof:oso/9780198089568.001.0001

De, Rohit. 2018. *A People's Constitution: The Everyday Life of Law in the Indian Republic.* Princeton, NJ: Princeton University Press.

Engel, David M., and Jaruwan Engel. 2010. *Tort, Custom, and Karma: Globalization and Legal Consciousness in Thailand.* Palo Alto, CA: Stanford University Press.

Erie, Matthew S. 2016. *China and Islam: The Prophet, the Party, and Law.* New York: Cambridge University Press. doi: 10.1017/9781107282063

Moustafa, Tamir. 2018. *Constituting Religion: Islam, Liberal Rights, and the Malaysian State.* New York: Cambridge University Press. doi: 10.1017/9781108339117

Nguyen, Tu Phuong. 2018. "Labour Law and (In)justice in Workers' Letters in Vietnam." *Asian Journal of Law & Society* 5 (1): 25–47. doi: 10.1017/als.2017.29

Parmar, Pooja. 2015. *Indigeneity and Legal Pluralism in India: Claims, Histories, Meanings.* New York: Cambridge University Press. doi: 10.1017/CBO9781139962896

Wang, Di, and Sida Liu. 2021. "Doing Ethnography on Social Media: A Methodological Reflection on the Study of Online Groups in China." *Qualitative Inquiry* 27 (8/9): 977–87. doi: 10.1177/10778004211014610

**Other Works Cited**

Cheesman, Nick. 2015. *Opposing the Rule of Law: How Myanmar's Courts Make Law and Order.* New York: Cambridge University Press. doi: 10.1017/cbo9781316014936.003

Chua, Lynette J. 2019. *The Politics of Love in Myanmar: LGBT Mobilization and Human Rights as a Way of Life.* Palo Alto, CA: Stanford University Press.

Hoang, Kimberly Kay. 2015. *Dealing in Desire: Asian Ascendancy, Western Decline, and the Hidden Currencies of Global Sex Work*. Berkeley: University of California Press. doi: 10.1525/9780520960688

Khorakiwala, Rahela. 2020. *From the Colonial to the Contemporary: Images, Iconography, Memories, and Performances of Law in India's High Courts*. Oxford: Hart. doi: 10.5040/9781509930685

Ng, Kwai Hang, and Xin He. 2017. *Embedded Courts: Judicial Decision-Making in China*. New York: Cambridge University Press. doi: 10.1017/9781108339117

**Suggested Readings**

Gerring, John. 2011. *Social Science Methodology: A Unified Framework*. New York: Cambridge University Press. doi: 10.1017/cbo9781139022224.002

Halliday, Simon, and Patrick Schmidt. 2009. *Conducting Law and Society Research: Reflections on Methods and Practices*. New York: Cambridge University Press. doi: 10.1017/cbo9780511609770

Luker, Kristin. 2008. *Salsa-Dancing into the Social Sciences: Research in an Age of Info-glut*. Cambridge, MA: Harvard University Press.

# Index

Abe, Masaki, 145, 239
Abel, Richard, 115–16
Abu-Lughod, Lila, 110–11
ACL Network, 259–60
Act Governing the Recovery of Damage of Individual Rights, Taiwan, 301–2
activism
    Adivasis activists, in India, 210–12
    in China, as post-dispute activism, 219–20
    feminist, 201–3
    LGBT activism, in Myanmar, 192–6
        as human rights issue, 193–6
        negative feeling rules and, 195–6
    performance artivism as, 201–3
    in theory of subversive disruption, 201–2
Adat School
    in Indonesia, 7, 84–5
    of Islamic law, 54
    legal pluralism and, 77, 80
    in Malaysia, 51, 84–5
Adivasis activists, in India, 210–12
Administration of Islamic Law Act, 55–7
ADR processes. See alternative dispute resolution processes
Advocates Act, India (1961), 233
Africa
    alternative dispute resolution processes in, 129
    legal pluralism in, colonial influences on, 80
alternative dispute resolution processes (ADR processes), 129–36
    in Africa, 129
    in Asia, 129
    community mediation, in Sri Lanka, 130–6
        Conciliation Boards, 131–2
        gender inequality in, 133–4
        history of, 131–2
    as hybrid practice, 135
    mediation boards, 130–5
        under Mediation Boards Act No. 72, 132
    conceptual development of, 129–30
    modern versions of, 130
American Sociological Association, 6
analogical reasoning, in Islamic law, 52–3
Anglo-Muslim law
    Islamic law and, 54–6
    in Malaysia, 51
anti-clericalism, 48–9
Anti-Rightist Campaign, 246
Anwar, Zainah, 170–1
Aquino, Benigno, 318–19
Armenia, communal clashes in, 23–64
Asia. See also specific countries
    alternative dispute resolution processes in, 129
    religious conflict in, 59–60
Asian Journal of Law and Society, 8
Asian Law and Society Association, in China, 8
Asian legal systems. See also specific countries
    black letter law in, 2
    colonialism as influence on, 1
    norms and practices as distinct from, 1–2
Aung Aung, 193
Aung San Suu Kyi, 193, 243
Azerbaijan, communal clashes in, 23–64

Bai, Husna, 220–4
Baxi, Upendra, 8–9
Bedner, Adrian, 7
belonging and acceptance as proper child/parent. See zìjǐrén
von Benda-Beckmann, Franz, 7

von Benda-Beckmann, Keebet, 7, 76, 81–2, 120
*bengoshi* (lawyers, in Japan), 237–41
Bhushan, Shanti, 235
black letter law, 3–4
Bourdieu, Pierre, 4
Boxer Rebellion, 48–9
Brunei, state religion in, interpretation of, 59–60
Bucheon Branch Court, in South Korea, 331–2
Buddha. *See* Gautama, Siddhārtha
Buddhism, 19. *See also* Gautama, Siddhārtha; *Vinayas*
  causality and, 24
  contributory negligence in, 41
  dharma and, 23–4
    cause and effect in, 25
    as law, 25–6
  in Europe, 25
  guardian spirits, 36–8
  identity, 38–9
    injury and, 39–40
    *khwan*, 38–9
    *winyan*, 39
  injuries
    delocalized causes of, 41–3
    identity and, 39–40
    *phi tai hong*, 40
  karma and, 24
    negligence and, 41–2
  law of sacred centers, 35–43
    household as sacred center, 36–8
    temples as sacred center, 37–8
  legal pluralism in, 83
  as legal tradition, 23–8
    *cakravartin* kings, 25–6
    dharma as law, 25–6
    *Vinayas* and, 24–5
  monasticism in, 26–7
    *sangha* and, 26
  negligence and, 41–3
    karma and, 41–2
  Sasana, in Sri Lanka, 64–9
  *sati*, 41
  in Thailand, 35–43, 152
    household as sacred center, 36–8
    temples as sacred center, 37–8
  Villagers' Buddhism, 35, 39
Buddhist Constitutionalism, 64–9
  protections for Buddhism under, 65–8
  under supreme law, 65

Buddhist law codes. *See Vinayas*
Burma. *See* Myanmar
Burnouf, Eugène, 25
Butler, Judith, 201–2

*cakravartin* kings (wheel-turning kings), 25–6
Casanova, Jose, 47
caste *panchayats*, 106–8
causality, 24
cause and effect, in Buddhism, 25
CCP. *See* Chinese Communist Party
Centre for the Study of Law and Governance, in India, 8–9
de Certeau, Michel, 4
Chan, Johannes, 268
Chang, Denis, 268
Chang Tao-ling, 31
Chaudhry, Iftikhar, 263–4. *See also* Lawyers' Movement
Chen Yingning, 48
Chen Yinque, 48
Cheung, Fernando Chiu-hung, 270
Chi Susheng, 204
Chiangmai Provincial Court, in Thailand, 147–9, 352–3
Chiba, Masaji, 7, 77
child custody, in People's Republic of China, 122–5
China, law and society in. *See also* Buddhism; Confucianism; People's Republic of China; *qing*; Taoism
  Asian Law and Society Association, 8
  Boxer Rebellion, 48–9
  after Communist takeover, 48
  courts in, as embedded institutions, 288–93
    administrative review as part of, 290–1
    cultural capital for women and, 295–6
    external influences on, 289–90
    female judges in, 293–6
    feminization of, global influences on, 293–6
    institutional environment of judging, 288–9
    judicial bureaucracy, 290–1
    juridical field and, 289
    as state organ, 292–3
  evolution of, 8
  informal law in, 100–1
    Islamic law as, 98–101
    legal pluralism and, 98–101

# Index

Islamic law in, 93
  as informal law, 98–101
judges in, 248–9
  female judges, 293–6
  promotion of women, 294
  reverse attrition for, 294–5
"leftover women" in, 155
legal consciousness in, development of,
    139–41, 153–61
  through acquisition of strategic
    knowledge, 216–18
  informed disenchantment and, 216–20
  post-dispute activism and, 219–20
  through social support networks, 218–19
legal pluralism in, 92–101
  governance structures for, 93–4
  informal law and, 98–101
legal professions
  Anti-Rightist Campaign and, 246
  judges, 248–9
  justice bureaus, 248
  lawyers in, reappearance of, 246
  legal services markets, 246–9
lianggu practice in, 153
  *qing* and, 155–8
Maoism and, 50
Marxism and, 49
Muslim mandarins and, 92–3
neo-Kantianism and, 49
one-child policy, 156–7
performance artivism in, 201–5
scholarship on
  ethnographic studies on social media
    users, 376–83
  Islamic law in, 356–61
secularism in, 47–51
  as anti-clericalism, 48–9
  rationalism and, 49–50
  scientism and, 49–50
  "smash temples, build schools," 48
social Darwinism and, 49
Chinese Communist Party (CCP), 48, 97–8
Cho, John, 269
Cho Young-sook, 213–14
Chou Jan-chuen, 261
Christianity, 19
  in Sri Lanka, 67–8
Chu, Tung-Tsu, 8
Chua, Lynette, 176, 192–3
citizenship rights, in Nepal, as women's rights,
    189–92

Civil Justice Research Project, 145–6
civil law, in Java, 84–5
Civil Procedure Law, PRC, 96–7
Clancy, John, 268
Classical Taoism, 29–31
collective order, in dispute-based law, 119
colonialism
  Asian legal systems influenced by, 1
  law and society influenced by, 10, 12
  legal pluralism and, 78–80
    in Africa, 80
    customary law and, 80–1
    modern law and, 78
    primitive law and, 78
  legal professions influenced by, in India,
    232–3
Communist Party, in China, 48, 97–8
community mediation, in Sri Lanka, 130–6
  Conciliation Boards, 131–2
  gender inequality in, 133–4
  history of, 131–2
  as hybrid practice, 135
  mediation boards, 130–5
  under Mediation Boards Act No. 72, 132
comparative law scholarship, dispute
    resolution processes in, 114–15
Conciliation Boards, in Sri Lanka, 131–2
Confucianism
  humanistic elements of, 29
  Taoism and, 28–9
  *T'ien*, 29
  *wu-wei*, 29
Constitution of 1947, India, 361–4
Constitutional Court, in Taiwan, 297–303
constitutional law
  in Java, 84–5
  in Thailand, as legal pluralism, 86
Constitutionalism. *See* Buddhist
    Constitutionalism
corruption, in People's Republic of
    Kampuchea, 305–6
courts. *See also* China; judges; lawyers; Taiwan
  in People's Republic of Kampuchea, 304–6
    judicial corruption, 305–6
  as political battleground, 296–306
  shari'a courts, women's treatment in, 281–2
  as social organizations, 282–96
  in Thailand, 283–8
    judges' role in, 283–8
    *Khru juling* case, 286–7
    trials in, increase in, 285

crime and punishment, as social concept
  criminal processes in, 334–45
    in India, rape trials in, 343–5
    in Japan, benevolent paternalism of criminal justice system in, 310–15
      police forces, 311–15
  justice dynamics in, 323–34
    repressive law, 323
  in Philippines, war on drugs in, 315–19
    drug use rates, 317–19
    homicide rates, 317
    state killings, 315–16
  punishment dynamic, 310–23
  in South Korea, restorative justice in, 329–34
    Bucheon Branch Court, 331–2
    under Criminal Procedure Act, 330
    justice agencies, 330
    victim protection, 330
  theoretical approach to, 309–10
  in Vietnam
    criminal sentencing in Vietnamese courts, 334–6
    judicial corruption in, 337–43
    lab results issues, 342
    Narcotic Drug and Psychotropic Substances Law, 341–3
    narcotics cases, 341–2
Criminal Procedure Act, South Korea (1954), 330
critical legal studies (Crits), law and society as distinct from, 4
customary law, colonialism and, 80–1

Daly, Mark, 268
daṇḍa (punishments), 22–3
democracy, in Timor-Leste, establishment of, 88–92
Deng Xiaoping, 326–7
Deolalikar, Ganesh Bhikaji, 362
Derrett, J. Duncan M., 8–9
descriptive view, of legal pluralism, 75
Devi, Kaushalya, 220–1
dharma
  Buddhism and, 23–4
    cause and effect in, 25
    as law, 25–6
  in Hindu legal tradition, 22–3
dharmaśāstras, 20–2, 44–7
Diamond, Shari, 3

digital age, law and society scholarship during, 376–83
  ethics in online groups, 377–82
  ethnographic studies on social media users, in China, 376–83
Dinh, Le Cong, 255–7
dispute resolution forums. *See panchayats*
dispute resolution processes. *See also* alternative dispute resolution processes; People's Republic of China
  in comparative law scholarship, 114–15
  conceptual approach to, 114–16
  in dispute-based law, 115
  litigation and, 120–9
  *panchayats*, 45–6
    in Rajasthan, India, 106–11
  in semi-autonomous social fields, 116
dispute-based law
  dispute resolution processes in, 115
  harmony ideology, 117
  in Ladakh, India, 116–19
    collective order as focus of, individual rights compared to, 119
    mediators in, role of, 118–19
    public nature of conflicts, 117–18
Disputing Behaviour Survey, 146
divorce, in People's Republic of China, 121–9
domestic violence, in People's Republic of China, 126–9
Durkheim, Emile, 323
Duterte, Rodrigo, 315–19
Dutton, Michael, 329
Dykes, Philip, 268, 270

Egypt, women's rights in, 170–1
Ehrlich, Eugen, 7, 142
Engel, David, 176
entitlements, rights consciousness and, 161–2
Epp, Charles, 186
Eu, Audrey, 268

factual legal pluralism, 82
Feeley, Malcolm, 334
feminist activism, performance artivism and, 201–3
Fiji, communal clashes in, 23–64
*fiqh* (Islamic jurisprudence)
  definition of, 32
  Islamic law and, 53–4, 58–9
    *usul al-fiqh*, 58–9
  legal consciousness and, in Malaysia, 171–5

# Index

in Malaysia, 52
shari'a and, 33
Fitzpatrick, Peter, 43
flighty spiritual essence. *See khwan*
Foucault, Michel, 4

Galanter, Marc, 8, 115–16
Garland, David, 325–6
Gautama, Siddhārtha (Buddha)
   early life of, 24
   in *saṅgha*, 24–5
   teaching career of, 24–5
Geertz, Clifford, 20
gender inequality
   community mediation and, 133–4
   in Indian legal professions, 249–53
   in People's Republic of China, 121–9
gender roles, reinforcement of, in South Korea, 214–15
Ghosh, Amitav, 369
ghosts. *See phi tai hong*
globalization
   legal consciousness influenced by, 152–81
   legal professions influenced by, in Myanmar, 244–5
Gluckman, Max, 80
Goffman, Erving, 97, 201–2
Goh Chok Tong, 63
Gomantak Maratha Samaj organization, 222
Grand Advocates, in India, 234–5
guardian spirits, in Buddhism, 36–8
Gutschow, Kim, 119
Gyo Kyar, 196

Haley, John, 142, 146
Han Fei, 30–1
Hanafi school, of Islamic law, 52–3
Hanbali school, of Islamic law, 52–3
harmony. *See* religious harmony
harmony ideology, 117
Harris, Paul, 268
Hatoyama, Kunio, 239
Hatoyama Yukio, 71
hegemony school, of legal consciousness, 140–1
Herriman, Nick, 90
hierarchies, in law and society, 11
   of living law, 11
   of social class, 11

Hinduism, 19
   daṇḍa in, 22–3
   law and society in India and, 8
   legal pluralism in, 83
   as legal tradition, 20–3
   dharma in, 22–3
   dharmaśāstras, 20–2, 44–7
   prāyaścitta, 22–3
HKBORO. *See* Hong Kong Bill of Rights Ordinance
Ho Chun-yan, 268–70
Hobsbawm, Erik, 56
Hodgson, Brian, 25
Hong Kong, legal professions in, cause lawyering and, 267–71
Hong Kong Bill of Rights Ordinance (HKBORO), 267–8
Hooker, M. B., 75
household of sacred center, 36–8
Hu Jintao, 329
Hui customary law, 94
   in autonomous regions, 94
   informalization of, 95–8
human rights
   LGBT activism and, in Myanmar, 193–6
   vernacularization of, in South Korea, 212–15
   criminalization of sex workers, 212–15
   reinforcement of gender roles, 214–15
   victimhood and, of prostitution, 212–14
   Women for Human Rights, in Nepal, 186–9
*Human Rights and Gender Violence* (Merry), 192–3
humanism, Confucianism and, 29
*The Hungry Tide* (Ghosh), 369

identities, construction of, 12
   in Buddhism, 38–9
   injury and, 39–40
   *khwan*, 38–9
   *winyan*, 39
   law and society scholarship and, 367–76
   legal consciousness and, 180
   rural, 12
   urban, 12
identity school, of legal consciousness, 140
iemoto laws, in Japan, 77
Ihromi, Tapi Omas, 7

India, law and society in. *See also* Rajasthan, India
  Centre for the Study of Law and Governance, 8–9
  communal clashes in, 23–64
  dispute-based law, in Ladakh, 116–19
    collective order as focus of, individual rights compared to, 119
    mediators in, role of, 118–19
    public nature of conflicts, 117–18
  evolution of, 8–9
  Gomantak Maratha Samaj organization, 222
  Hinduism and, 8
  Indian Council of Social Science Research, 8
  indigenous law in, restoration of, 44–7
    nationalist movement and, 45–6
    *panchayats*, 45–6
  legal mobilization in
    Adivasis activists in, 210–12
    for constitutional rights litigation, 220–4
    for indigeneity, 210–12
    for legal pluralism, 210–12
  legal pluralism in, 102–11, 367–71
  legal professions, 232–7
    under Advocates Act, 233
    basic structure of, 233–4
    colonial influences on, 232–3
    English-style barristers, 232
    gender inequality in, 249–53
    Grand Advocates, 234–5
    indigenous practitioners, 232–3
    meritocracy in, 251–3
    women in, 236, 249–53
  rape trials in, 343–5
    scholarship on, 371–6
  scholarship on
    Constitution of 1947, 361–4
    indigeneity and, 367–71
    legal pluralism and, 367–71
    for rape trials, 371–6
    Supreme Court of India, 362–3
  secularism in, 47–51
  Suppression of Immoral Traffic in Women and Girls Act of 1956, 220
Indian Council of Social Science Research, 8
indigenous law, in India, restoration of, 44–7
  nationalist movement and, 45–6
  *panchayats*, 45–6

Indonesia, law and society in
  Adat School, 7, 84–5
  Dutch role in, 7
  evolution of, 7
  legal professions, 228–32
    colonial influences on, 229–31
    ethnic Chinese in, 231–2
    native lawyers, 229
    the Netherlands and, 229–31
    social status and, in Java, 230–1
inequality, in law and society, 11
informal law, in China, 100–1
  Islamic law as, 98–101
  legal pluralism and, 98–101
informalization of adjudication, in People's Republic of China, 95–101
  Chinese Communist Party Oversight of, 97–8
informed disenchantment, in China, 216–20
injuries, Buddhism and
  delocalized causes of, 41–3
  identity and, 39–40
  *phi tai hong*, 40
injury narratives, in Thailand, 148–52
International Sociological Association, 6
Iran
  communal clashes in, 23–64
  women's rights in, 170–1
Iraq, communal clashes in, 23–64
Islam, 19
  legal pluralism in, 83
  Islamic Family Law Act, 55–6
  Islamic jurisprudence. *See fiqh*
  Islamic law, 52–9. *See also usul al-fiqh*
    Adat School, 54
    Administration of Islamic Law Act, 55–7
    analogical reasoning in, 52–3
    in China, 93
    as informal law, 98–101
    law and society scholarship on, 356–61
    consensus in, 52–3
    consideration of public interest in, 52–3
    in Egypt, 170–1
    *fiqh* and, 53–4, 58–9
    *usul al-fiqh*, 58–9
    Hanafi school, 52–3
    Hanbali school, 52–3
    in Iran, 170–1
    Islamic Family Law Act, 55–6

# Index

legal consciousness and, in Malaysia, 172
  as legal code, 173–5
  as legal method, 173–5
  plurality of, 174
  shari'a and, *fiqh* compared to, 171–5
  Shari'a Criminal Offenses Act, 172–3
  for women's rights, 169–76
legal pluralism and, 85
in Malaysia, 51–9
  law and society scholarship on, 354–6
  secularism in, 57–9
  shari'a law in, 56
  under state law, 57–9
Maliki school, 52–3
in Morocco, 170–1
in People's Republic of China, 93–4
  Muslim mandarins, 95–8
politics of, 57–9
in Qur'an, 54–5
secularism and, 57–9
Shafi'i school, 52–3
shari'a as, 31–4, 53–4
  as legal rules, 33–4
  in Malaysia, 56
  sources of, 32
in Southeast Asian legal systems, 85
in Sunna, 54–5
Syariah Criminal Offenses Act, 55–6
Syariah Criminal Procedure Act, 55–6
transformation of, 54–9
  Anglo-Muslim law, 54–6
  through codification of law, 54–5
  through naming, 55–6
  pluralism and, 54–5
  through state monopoly on religious law, 56–7
  women's rights as part of, 55
Islamic legal theory. *See usul al-fiqh*

Japan, law and society in
  benevolent paternalism of criminal justice system in, 310–15
  Civil Justice Research Project in, 145–6
  conventional wisdom in, in postwar era, 69–72
  Disputing Behaviour Survey, 146
  evolution of, 7
  iemoto laws, 77
  legal consciousness in, 142–7
    dynamic state of, 147
    Kawashima on, 142–4, 146
    Rokumoto on, 144–5

legal professions
  control of, 237–41
  corporations in, 239–40
  National Legal Examination, 237–8, 241
  reform movement for, 239–40
legal professions, control of, *bengoshi*, 237–41
Litigation Behaviour Survey, 146
myth of reluctant litigant, 142
Shintoism, 69–72
  Yasukuni shrine, 69–72
  shrine communities in, 77
Japanese Association of Sociology of Law (JASL), 6–7
Java
  civil and constitutional law in, 84–5
  legal professions in, social status and, 230–1
Jethmalani, Ram, 235
Ji, Weidong, 8
Jinnah, Muhammad Ali, 236–7
JRF. *See* Judicial Reform Foundation
Judaism, 19
judges
  in China, 248–9
    female judges, 293–6
    institutional environment of judging, 288–9
    promotion of women, 294
    reverse attrition for, 294–5
  in Taiwan, 260–1
  in Thailand, 283–8
Judicial Reform Foundation (JRF), 259–60
justice bureaus, in China, 248

Kang Youwei, 48
karma, 24
  negligence and, 41–2
Kashgar Islamic Association, 98
Kato, Masanobu, 145
Kawashima, Takeyoshi, 7, 142, 146
Khawaja Sira community, in Pakistan, 162–9
Khorakiwala, Rahela, 360–1
*Khru juling* case, in Thailand, 286–7
*khwan* (flighty spiritual essence), 38–9
Kidder, Robert, 8
Kim Hyunsun, 213
Kirkland, Russell, 28
KMT regime. *See* Kuomintang regime
Knowledge and Opinion about Law (KOL), 144–5
Koizumi Jun'ichirō, 69, 238

KOL. *See* Knowledge and Opinion about Law
Kottiswaran, Prabha, 221
K'ung Ch'iu, 29
K'ung-tzu, 29
Kuomintang (KMT) regime, in Taiwan, 297–8, 300–2
Kwok, Dennis, 270
Kyaw Kyaw, 193

labour law
  law and society scholarship on, 364–7
  in Vietnam, legal mobilization for, 196–9
  rightful resistance, 196–9
LASSnet. *See* Law and Social Sciences Research Network
law and development, as legal concept, law and society as distinct from, 4
Law and Social Sciences Research Network (LASSnet), 8–9
law and society, as legal concept. *See also* China; India; Indonesia; Japan
  black letter law and, 3–4
  colonialism as influence on, 10, 12
  critical legal studies as distinct from, 4
  definition of, 2–6
    empirical research and, 3
  evolution of, 6–9
    traditional legal education, 6
  hierarchies in, 11
    of living law, 11
    of social class, 11
  identity construction in, 12
  inequality in, 11
  law and development as distinct from, 4
  law and social science compared to, 5–6
  legal and political transformations in, 10–11
  methodological approaches to, 2, 9–17
  rights theory and, 11–12
  skepticism in, 4
  theoretical foundations of, 3–4
law and society scholarship
  in China
    ethnographic studies on social media users, 376–83
    Islamic law in, 356–61
  in digital age, 376–83
    ethics in online groups, 377–82
    ethnographic studies on social media users, in China, 376–83
    identity construction and, navigation of, 367–76

  in India
    Constitution of 1947, 361–4
    indigeneity and, 367–71
    legal pluralism and, 367–71
    for rape trials, 371–6
    Supreme Court of India, 362–3
  in Malaysia
    Islamic law in, 354–6
    liberal rights in, 354–6
  methodological approaches to, 350
  in Thailand, legal consciousness in, 350–3
    Chiangmai Provincial Court, 352–3
    pyramid model of litigation, 351–2
  in Vietnam, labour law in, 364–7
law of sacred centers, 35–43
  household as sacred center, 36–8
  temples as sacred center, 37–8
lawyers
  *bengoshi*, in Japan, 237–41
  in China, reappearance of, 246
  in Indonesia, native lawyers and, 229
  in Myanmar, foreign corporate lawyers and, 242–5
  in Taiwan, 258–60
  in Vietnam, cause lawyers and, 254–5
Lawyers' Movement, in Pakistan, 262–7
  active resistance phase, 265
  confrontation phase, 264–5
  emergency measures, 265
  initial mobilization, 264
  pivot and reorientation phase, 266
  retreat and revival phase, 266–7
Lebanon, communal clashes in, 23–64
Lee, Martin, 270
Lee Hsien Loong, 62
"leftover women," in China, 155
legal coercion, 77
legal consciousness. *See also qing*
  development of, in China, 139–41, 153–61
    through acquisition of strategic knowledge, 216–18
    informed disenchantment and, 216–20
    post-dispute activism and, 219–20
    through social support networks, 218–19
  globalization as influence on, 152–81
  hegemony school of, 140–1
  identity school of, 140
  Islamic law and, in Malaysia, 172
    as legal code, 173–5
    as legal method, 173–5
    plurality of, 174

# Index

shari'a and, *fiqh* compared to, 171–5
Shari'a Criminal Offenses Act, 172–3
for women's rights, 169–76
in Japan, 142–7
  dynamic state of, 147
  Kawashima on, 142–4, 146
  Rokumoto on, 144–5
  Knowledge and Opinion about Law and, 144–5
mobilization school of, 141
in Myanmar, 242–5
relational, 176–81
research scope of, 140
sociology of law in, 142–7
in Taiwan, 177–81
  culture concepts in, 179–80
  emotional element of legal consciousness, 179–80
  identity and, 180
  interpretation of family conflict, 178–9
in Thailand, 152–81
  Chiangmai Provincial Court and, 147–9
  ideoscapes and, 150
  injury narratives, 148–52
  law and society scholarship on, 350–3
  mediascapes and, 150
  under People's Constitution of 1977, 151
  remediation systems and, 151
for third gender category, in Pakistan, 162–9
  benefits and costs of, 166–7
  family influences on, 163–4
  Khawaja Sira community, 162–9
  religious benefits of, 164–5
legal mobilization
  conceptual approach to, 183–5
  definition of, 183
  effects of, 208–24
  myth of rights, 208–9
  for gay collective action, in Singapore, 199–201
  in India
    Adivasis activists in, 210–12
    for constitutional rights litigation, 220–4
    for indigeneity, 210–12
    for legal pluralism, 210–12
  for labour law, in Vietnam, 196–9
    rightful resistance, 196–9
  legal pluralism and, 184–5
    in India, 210–12
  of LGBT activism, in Myanmar, 192–6
    as human rights issue, 193–6
    negative feeling rules and, 195–6
  litigation dilemmas and, in Philippines, 205–8
    SELDA (NGO), 206–8
  in Nepal, for women's rights, 186–92
    for citizenship, 189–92
    at local level, 189–92
    Sangam (NGO), 189–92
    support structure for legal mobilization, 186
    for widows' rights, 186–9
    Women for Human Rights, 186–9
  through performance artivism
    in China, 201–5
    for feminist activism, 201–3
    in online contexts, 203–5
  rights mobilization and, 184
  scope of, 185
  tactics for, 185–201
    for gay collective action, in Singapore, 199–201
    for labour law, in Vietnam, 196–9
    of LGBT activism, in Myanmar, 192–6
    performance artivism, 201–5
  vernacularization of human rights and, in South Korea, 212–15
    criminalization of sex workers, 212–15
    reinforcement of gender roles, 214–15
    victimhood and, of prostitution, 212–14
legal pluralism
  Adat School and, 77, 80
  in Buddhism, 83
  in China, 92–101
    governance structures for, 93–4
    informal law and, 98–101
  during colonial era, 78–80
    in Africa, 80
    customary law and, 80–1
    modern law and, 78
    primitive law and, 78
  complexity of, 78–9, 81–2
  conceptual approach to, 74–7
  evolution of, 77
  legal political conception, 76
  definition of, 74–5
  descriptive view of, 75
  early history of, 78–9
    during colonial era, 78–80

legal pluralism (cont.)
  factual, 82
  as global doctrine, 83-7
  in Hinduism, 83
  in Islam, 83
  local knowledge and, 83-7
  in Malaysia, 85-6
  Manchester School and, 80
  negotiating forums and, 109-11
  normative, 81-2
  origins of, 78-82
  in People's Republic of China, 93-4
  during postcolonial era, 79-80
  prescriptive view of, 75
  Sartori on, 75-6
  in Singapore, 85-6
  social theory and, 78-82
  in Southeast Asian legal systems, 75, 83-7
    globalisation-law, 86
    Islamic law, 85
    native law and, 84-5
  as state policy, 82-3
  in Thailand Constitution, 86
  in Timor-Leste, 87-92
    state-based system of, 91-2
legal procedure. See *vyavahāra*
legal professions. See also *specific countries*
  administrative state and, relationship with, 228
  in China
    Anti-Rightist Campaign and, 246
    judges, 248-9
    justice bureaus, 248
    lawyers in, reappearance of, 246
    legal services markets, 246-9
  conceptual approach to, 227-8
  in Hong Kong, cause lawyering, 267-71
    Hong Kong Bill of Rights Ordinance, 267-8
  in Indonesia, 228-32
    colonial influences on, 229-31
    ethnic Chinese in, 231-2
    native lawyers, 229
    the Netherlands and, 229-31
    social status and, in Java, 230-1
  in Japan, control of, 237-41
    *bengoshi*, 237-41
    corporations in, 239-40
    National Legal Examination, 237-8, 241
    reform movement for, 239-40
  in Myanmar, 242-5
    foreign corporate lawyers in, 242-5
    globalization as influence on, 244-5
    legal consciousness and, 242-5
  in Pakistan, as Lawyers' Movement, 262-7
    active resistance phase, 265
    confrontation phase, 264-5
    emergency measures, 265
    initial mobilization, 264
    pivot and reorientation phase, 266
    retreat and revival phase, 266-7
  in Taiwan, 258-62
    ACL Network, 259-60
    judges, 260-1
    Judicial Reform Foundation, 259-60
    lawyers, 258-60
    Prosecutor Reform Association, 261
  in Vietnam
    cause lawyers, 254-5
    juridification of cause advocacy, 253-7
    legal case study, 255-7
    legal system reform, 254-5
legal services markets, in China, 246-9
legal studies. See critical legal studies; sociolegal studies
Leung, Jocelyn, 268
Lev, Daniel S., 7
Li Jinxing, 205
Li Yan, 202-3
Li Zhuang, 203-5
Liang Qichao, 48
*lianggu* practice, in China, 153
  *qing* and, 155-8
Ling Li, 97
litigation, dispute resolution processes and, 120-9
Litigation Behaviour Survey, 146
Liu, Qian, 161-2
Liu, Sida, 245
living law, 11, 142
Long March, 266-7
Lu, Annette, 302
Lu Tai-lang, 261

Maintenance of the Religious Harmony Act, Singapore, 60-2
  creation of, 61-2
Malacca, maritime law in, 84-5
Malaysia
  Adat School in, 51, 84-5
  Anglo-Muslim law in, 51
  *fiqh* in, 52

# Index

Islamic law in, 51–9
  law and society scholarship on, 354–6
  secularism in, 57–9
  shari'a law and, 56
  under state law, 57–9
law and society scholarship in
  Islamic law in, 354–6
  liberal rights in, 354–6
  legal pluralism in, 85–6
  secularism in, 51–9
  state power in, 51–9
  regulation of religion and, 51–2
Malik, Munir, 265
Maliki school, of Islamic law, 52–3
Malinowski, Bronislaw, 80
Manchester School, for legal pluralism, 80
Maoism, 50
Marcos, Ferdinand, 206–8
Marriage Law, PRC (1950), 121–2, 126
Marxism, 49
Mather, Lynn, 3
*maulavi* (Muslim religious teacher/healer), 102–3, 105–6, 110–11
McCann, Michael, 223
mediation boards, in Sri Lanka, 130–5
Mediation Boards Act No. 72, Sri Lanka (1988), 132
Mediation Law, PRC (2010), 96–7
mediators, in dispute-based law, 118–19
Merry, Sally Engle, 192–3
mindfulness. *See sati*
mobilization school, of legal consciousness, 141
modern law
  colonialism and, 78
  legal pluralism and, 78
  project of modernity, 43
  secularism and, 43–4
Mohammad, Mahathir, 57
monasticism
  in Buddhism, 26–7
    *saṅgha* and, 26
  *Vinayas* and, 27–8
Moore, Sally Falk, 100, 115–16
Mori, Yoshiro, 238
Morocco
  Islamic law in, 170–1
  women's rights in, 170–1
Moustafa, Tamir, 98–9
Müller, Dominik M., 59–60
Murayama, Masayuki, 146

Murayama Tomiichi, 71
Musharraf, Pervez, 263–4. *See also* Lawyers' Movement
Muslim mandarins, 92–3
  in PRC, 95–8
Muslim religious teacher/healer. *See maulavi*
Myanmar
  legal professions in, 242–5
    foreign corporate lawyers in, 242–5
    globalization as influence on, 244–5
    legal consciousness and, 242–5
  LGBT activism in, 192–6
    as human rights issue, 193–6
    negative feeling rules and, 195–6
myth of reluctant litigant, in Japan, 142
myth of rights, 208–9

Nader, Laura, 115–16
Narcotic Drug and Psychotropic Substances Law, Vietnam (1993), 341–3
National Legal Examination (NLE), 237–8, 241
native law
  legal pluralism and, 84–5
  in Southeast Asian legal systems, 84–5
negligence, in Buddhism, 41–3
  karma and, 41–2
negotiating forums, in Rajasthan, India, 109–11
Nehru, Motilal, 236–7
Nehru, Rameshwari, 221
neo-Kantianism, 49
Nepal, legal mobilization in, for women's rights, 186–92
  for citizenship rights, 189–92
  at local level, 189–92
  Sangam (NGO), 189–92
  support structure for, 186
  for widows' rights, 186–9
  Women for Human Rights, 186–9
the Netherlands, Indonesian law and society influenced by, 7
Nihon Bunka Kaigi, 145
Ng, Margaret, 268
NLE. *See* National Legal Examination
non-action/non-doing. *See wu-wei*
normative legal pluralism, 81–2
Northern Ireland, communal clashes in, 23–64

Obuchi, Keizo, 238
Oki, Masao, 146
one-child policy, in China, 156–7
Ozaki, Ichiro, 145

Pakistan
  Lawyers' Movement in, 262–7
    active resistance phase, 265
    confrontation phase, 264–5
    emergency measures, 265
    initial mobilization, 264
    pivot and reorientation phase, 266
    retreat and revival phase, 266–7
  Long March, 266–7
  rights consciousness in, for third gender category, 162–9
    benefits and costs of, 166–7
    family influences on, 163–4
    Khawaja Sira community, 162–9
    religious benefits of, 164–5
*panchayats* (dispute resolution forum), 45–6
  in Rajasthan, India, 106–11
    caste *panchayats*, 106–8
penances. See prāyaścitta
People's Constitution of 1977 (Thailand), 151
People's Republic of China (PRC)
  Civil Procedure Law, 96–7
  crime and punishment concept in
    capital punishment in, 319–23
    criminal justice system in, 323–9
    ideological reform, 324
    philosophical foundations for, 328–9
    secrecy about death penalty, 322–3
    Supreme People's Court, 319–21
    traditional notions of injustice, 326
  dispute resolution processes in
    by basic-level legal workers, 122
    for child custody, 122–5
    for divorce, 121–9
    for domestic violence, 126–9
    for gender inequality, 121–9
    initiation stage, 126–9
    manipulative interpretation of state law, 125–6
    under Marriage Law, 121–2, 126
    normalization of abuse in, 126–8
    for spousal abuse, 126–9
  Hui customary law, 94
    in autonomous regions, 94
  informalization of adjudication in, 95–101
    Chinese Communist Party Oversight of, 97–8
  Islamic law in, 93–4
    Muslim mandarins, 95–8
  legal pluralism in, 93–4

Marriage Law in, 121–2, 126
  Mediation Law, 96–7
People's Republic of Kampuchea (Cambodia), 304–6
  judicial corruption, 305–6
performance artivism
  in China, 201–5
  for feminist activism, 201–3
  in online contexts, 203–5
*phi tai hong* (ghosts), 40
the Philippines
  communal clashes in, 23–64
  legal mobilization in, for litigation dilemmas, 205–8
    SELDA, 206–8
  war on drugs in, 315–19
    drug use rates, 317–19
    homicide rates, 317
    state killings and, 315–16
Piric, Fernanda, 34
pluralism. See also legal pluralism; religious pluralism
  Islamic law and, 54–5
police forces, in Japan, 311–15
Pospisil, Leopold, 77
postcolonialism, legal pluralism and, 79–80
Pound, Roscoe, 7, 142
PRA. See Prosecutor Reform Association
Prasad, Nita Verma, 221
*Prātimoksa*, 28
prāyaścitta (penances), 22–3
prescriptive view, of legal pluralism, 75
primitive law
  colonialism and, 78
  legal pluralism, 78
Prosecutor Reform Association (PRA), 261
Pun, Hectar, 268, 270
Punishment and the Protection Act, South Korea (2004), 212–13
punishment dynamic, in crime and punishment context, 310–23
punishments. See daṇḍa
Pyae Soe, 193–5

*qing* (sense of humanity), in China, 153–61
  alliance with state law, 159–61
  as embrace of state law, 159–60
  weakness of state law, 160–1
  lianggu practice and, 153, 155–8

## Index

opposition to state law, 155–9
  through avoidance of state law, 155–6
  lianggu practice and, 155–7
  as mitigation for undesirable legal results, 156–7
  resistance to state law, 157–8
scope of, 154
state law and
  in alliance with *qing*, 159–61
  dismissal of, 158–9
  interactions between, 154–5
  one-child policy, 156–7
  in opposition to *qing*, 155–9
  resistance to, 157–8
Qur'an, 31–4. *See also* shari'a
  Islamic law in, 54–5

Rahardjo, Satjipto, 7
Rajasthan, India, legal pluralism in, 102–11
  for conflict resolution, 103–4
  *maulavi* in, 102–3, 105–6, 110–11
  negotiating forums in, 109–11
  *panchayats* in, 106–11
  caste, 106–8
  somatization of conflict, 105
  state courts in, 109
Ramseyer, J. Mark, 146
rape trials, in India, 343–5
  scholarship on, 371–6
rationalism, 49–50
relational legal consciousness, 176–81
religion, religious tradition and
  conceptual approach to, 19–20
  modernization of, 59–60
religious harmony, in Singapore, 60–4
  under Maintenance of the Religious Harmony Act, 60–2
religious law
  in Singapore, 62–4
  in Sri Lanka, religious litigation in, 64–9
  Buddhism and, 68–9
  under supreme law, 65
religious pluralism, in Singapore, 60–4
remediation mechanisms, in Thailand, 151
repressive law, 323
Research Committee on Sociology of Law, 6
restorative justice, in South Korea, 329–34
  Bucheon Branch Court, 331–2
  under Criminal Procedure Act, 330
  justice agencies, 330
  victim protection, 330

Reynolds, Frank, 25
rightful resistance, 196–9
rights consciousness
  entitlements and, 161–2
  for third gender category, in Pakistan, 162–9
  benefits and costs of, 166–7
  family influences on, 163–4
  Khawaja Sira community, 162–9
  religious benefits of, 164–5
rights theory, law and society and, 11–12
Roff, William, 56
Rokumoto, Kahei, 144–6
Rudolph, Lloyd, 8
Rudolph, Susanne Hoeber, 8
rural identities, 12

Sangam (NGO), 189–92
*sangha*
  Buddha in, 24–5
  in Buddhism, 26
Santos, Boaventura de Sousa, 100
Sartori, Paolo, 75–6
Sasana, in Sri Lanka, 64–9
*sati* (mindfulness), 41
scientism, 49–50
secularism
  in China, 47–51
  as anti-clericalism, 48–9
  rationalism and, 49–50
  scientism and, 49–50
  "smash temples, build schools," 48
  in India, 47–51
  Islamic law and, 57–9
  modern law and, 43–4
  stability of, 43–4
Seidel, Anna, 30
SELDA (NGO), 206–8
sense of humanity. *See qing*
sex workers, criminalization of, 212–15
Shafi'i school, of Islamic law, 52–3
Shapiro, Martin, 290
Sharafi, Mitra, 221
shari'a
  courts, women's treatment in, 281–2
  definition of, 32
  *fiqh* and, 33
    definition of, 32
    implementation of, 32–3

shari'a (cont.)
    as Islamic law, 31–4, 53–4
        as legal rules, 33–4
        in Malaysia, 56
        sources for, 32
    legal consciousness and, in Malaysia, 171–5
    non-legal elements of, 32
    as principal values, 33–4
Shari'a Criminal Offenses Act, 172–3
Shintoism, 69–72
    Yasukuni shrine, 69–72
shrine communities, in Japan, 77
Singapore
    legal mobilization in, for gay collective action, 199–201
    legal pluralism in, 85–6
    Maintenance of the Religious Harmony Act, 60–2
        creation of, 61–2
    religious harmony in, 60–4
        under Maintenance of the Religious Harmony Act, 60–2
    religious law in, 62–4
    religious pluralism in, 60–4
Singhvi, Abhishek Manu, 235
*Skandhaka*, 28
skepticism, in law and society, 4
"smash temples, build schools," 48
social Darwinism, 49
social hierarchies, 11
social theory, legal pluralism and, 78–82
sociolegal studies, 5–6
sociology of law, 5–6
    in legal consciousness, 142–7
somatization of conflict, 105
South Korea
    legal mobilization in, 212–15
    Punishment and the Protection Act, 212–13
    restorative justice in, 329–34
        Bucheon Branch Court, 331–2
        under Criminal Procedure Act, 330
        justice agencies, 330
        victim protection, 330
    vernacularization of human rights in, 212–15
        criminalization of sex workers, 212–15
        reinforcement of gender roles, 214–15
        victimhood and, of prostitution, 212–14

Southeast Asian legal systems. *See also specific countries*
    legal pluralism in, 75, 83–7
    globalisation-law, 86
    Islamic law, 85
    native law and, 84–5
SPC. *See* Supreme People's Court
spirits. *See* guardian spirits
spousal abuse, in People's Republic of China, 126–9
Sri Lanka
    Buddhist Constitutionalism in, 64–9
        protections for Buddhism under, 65–8
        under supreme law, 65
    Christian organizations in, 67–8
    communal clashes in, 23–64, 68–9
    religious litigation in, 64–9
        Buddhism and, 68–9
        under supreme law, 65
    Sasana in, 64–9
state courts, in Rajasthan, India, 109
state monopoly on religious law, 56–7
structural interpenetration, 100
Suehiro, Izutaro, 7, 142
Sunna, Islamic law in, 54–5
Suppression of Immoral Traffic in Women and Girls Act of 1956, India, 220
Supreme People's Court (SPC), in PRC, 319–21
*Sūtravibhanga*, 28
Swift, Robert, 206
Syariah Criminal Offenses Act, 55–6
Syariah Criminal Procedure Act, 55–6

Tahir, Juma, 98, 100
Taiwan
    courts in, judicialization of politics in, 297–303
        under Act Governing the Recovery of Damage of Individual Rights, 301–2
        Constitutional Court, 297–303
        expansion of judicial power, 298–9
        during Kuomintang regime, 297–8, 300–2
        lawmaking by, 303
        structural division of, 298
        during transition to democracy, 300
    legal consciousness in, 177–81
        culture concepts in, 179–80
        emotional element of, 179–80
        emotional element of legal consciousness, 179–80

identity and, 180
interpretation of family conflict, 178–9
legal professions in, 258–62
  ACL Network, 259–60
  judges, 260–1
  Judicial Reform Foundation, 259–60
  lawyers, 258–60
  Prosecutor Reform Association, 261
zìjǐrén in, 178–81
Taixu, 48
Tamanaha, Brian, 93
Tamney, Joseph B., 61
Tanase, Takeo, 145–6
*Tao te ching*, 30–1
Taoism
  Celestial Masters and, 31
  classical, 29–31
  Confucianism and, 28–9
  legal tradition and, 28–31
  as religious movement, 31
  T'ien-shih movement, 31
  sources of, 30
Taussig, Michael, 343–4
temples as sacred center, 37–8
Thai Law of the Three Seals, 84–5
Thailand
  Buddhism in, 35–43, 152
    household as sacred center, 36–8
    temples as sacred center, 37–8
  Chiangmai Provincial Court, 147–9, 352–3
  courts in, 283–8
    judges' role in, 283–8
    *Khru juling* case, 286–7
    trials in, increase in, 285
  Islamic law in, women's rights under, 169–76
  law and society scholarship in, legal consciousness in, 350–3
    Chiangmai Provincial Court, 352–3
    pyramid model of litigation, 351–2
  legal consciousness in, 152–81
    Chiangmai Provincial Court and, 147–9
    ideoscapes and, 150
    injury narratives, 148–52
    mediascapes and, 150
    under People's Constitution of 1977, 151
    remediation systems and, 151
  legal pluralism in, in Constitution, 86
Thapa, Lily, 186–9
Thero, Daranagama Kusaladhamma, 66–7

third gender category, in Pakistan, legal consciousness for, 162–9
  benefits and costs of, 166–7
  family influences on, 163–4
  Khawaja Sira community, 162–9
  religious benefits of, 164–5
Third World Approaches to International Law (TWAIL), 209
Thurnwald, Richard, 80
*T'ien* (Confucian text), 29
T'ien-shih movement, 31
Timor-Leste
  democratic culture in, establishment in, 88–92
  legal pluralism in, 90–2
  state-based system of, 91–2
  traditional social systems in, 87–8
  witch killings in, 87–92
    as customary punishment, 89–90
    early reports on, 88–9
Tin Hla, 193
Tu, Nguyên Phuong, 196–9
Tun Tun, 193–4, 196
Tung Chung-shu, 32
TWAIL. *See* Third World Approaches to International Law

Ubink, Janine, 76–7
Upham, Frank, 146
urban identities, 12
*usul al-fiqh* (Islamic legal theory), 52–3, 58–9

Vidler, Michael, 268–9
Vietnam
  criminal sentencing in, in Vietnamese courts, 334–6
  judicial corruption in, 337–43
    lab results issues, 342
    under Narcotic Drug and Psychotropic Substances Law, 341–3
    for narcotics cases, 341–2
  law and society scholarship in, for labour law, 364–7
  legal mobilization for labour law in, 196–9
  rightful resistance, 196–9
  legal professions in
    cause lawyers, 254–5
    juridification of cause advocacy, 253–7
    legal case study, 255–7
    legal system reform, 254–5
Villagers' Buddhism, 35, 39

Vinayas
  in Buddhist legal tradition,
    27–8
  as law, 27–8
  monastic rules in, 27–8
  Prātimoksa, 28
  preservation of, 27
  Skandhaka, 28
  structure of, 28
  Sūtravibhanga, 28
Vinayas (Buddhist law codes), 24–5
van Vollenhoven, Cornelis, 7
vyavahāra (legal procedure), 22–3

Wada, Yoshitaka, 145
Wallschaeger, Christian, 146
Weber, Max, 29
  on legal coercion, 77
wheel-turning kings. See cakravartin kings
WHR. See Women for Human Rights
widows' rights, in Nepal, 186–9
winyan, in Buddhism, 39
witch killings, in Timor-Leste,
    87–92
  as customary punishment,
    89–90
  early reports on, 88–9
women. See also gender inequality; gender roles; specific countries
  cultural capital for, in Chinese courts,
    295–6
  in India
    in legal professions, 236, 249–53
  under Suppression of Immoral Traffic in Women and Girls Act of 1956, 220
  as judges
    in China, 293–6
    feminization of courts, global influences on, 293–6
  in Malaysia, under Islamic law, 169–76
  in Nepal, legal mobilization for rights of,
    186–92
    for citizenship rights, 189–92
    at local level, 189–92
    Sangam (NGO), 189–92
    support structure for, 186
    for widows' rights, 186–9
    Women for Human Rights, 186–9
  in shari'a courts, 281–2
Women for Human Rights (WHR),
  186–9
Wright, Warren, 90
wu-wei (non-action/non-doing), 29

Xi Jinping, 99, 326–7, 329

Yang Jinzhu, 204–5
Yasukuni shrine, 69–72
Yu Mei-nu, 259–60

Zardari, Asif Ali, 266
Zhang Binglin, 48
Zhou, Xueguang, 289–90
Zhu, Suli, 8
zìjĭrén (belonging and acceptance as proper child/parent), 178–81